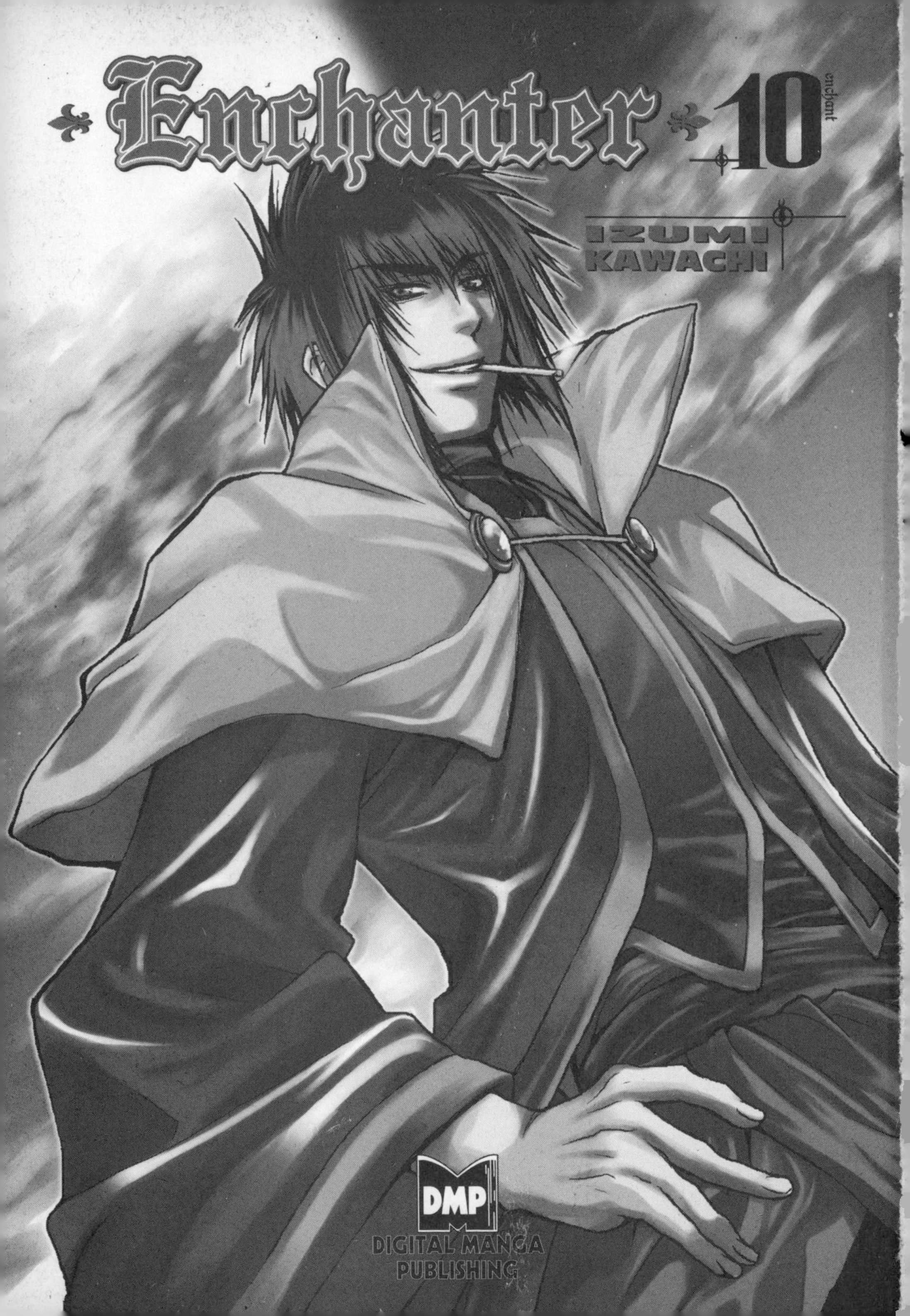
Enchanter
10
enchant
IZUMI
KAWACHI
DMP
DIGITAL MANGA
PUBLISHING

Enchanter 10

CONTENTS

Translation	Sachiko Sato
Lettering	IHL
Graphic Design	Fred Lui
Editing	Stephanie Donnelly
Editor in Chief	Fred Lui
Publisher	Hikaru Sasahara

English Edition Published by
DIGITAL MANGA PUBLISHING
A division of DIGITAL MANGA, Inc.
1487 W 178th Street, Suite 300
Gardena, CA 90248

www.dmpbooks.com

First Edition: February 2009
ISBN-10: 1-56970-857-6
ISBN-13: 978-1-56970-857-6

1 3 5 7 9 10 8 6 4 2

Printed in Canada

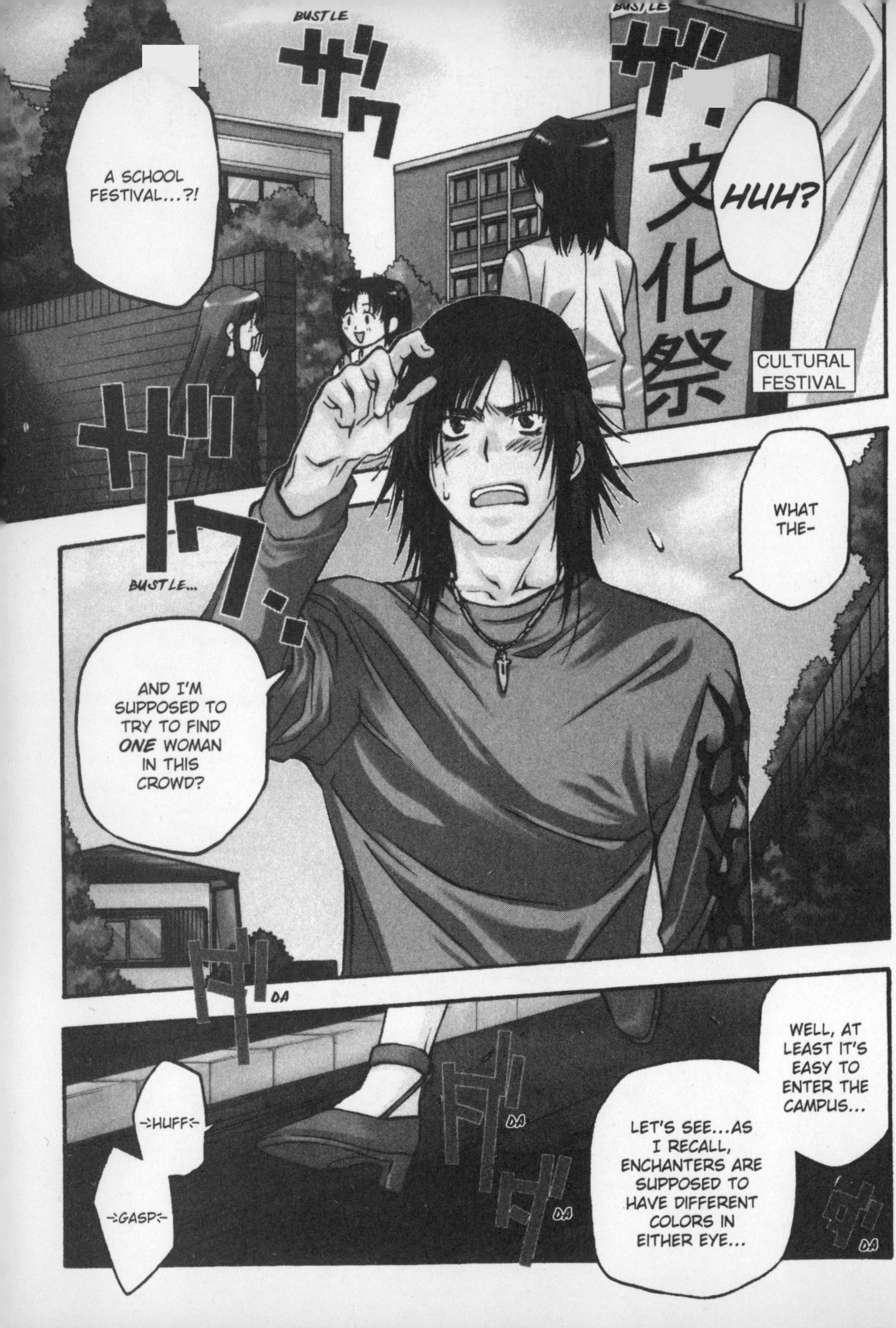
BUSTLE
HUH?
文化祭
CULTURAL FESTIVAL
BUSTLE
A SCHOOL FESTIVAL...?!
WHAT THE-
BUSTLE...
AND I'M SUPPOSED TO TRY TO FIND *ONE* WOMAN IN THIS CROWD?
WELL, AT LEAST IT'S EASY TO ENTER THE CAMPUS...
LET'S SEE...AS I RECALL, ENCHANTERS ARE SUPPOSED TO HAVE DIFFERENT COLORS IN EITHER EYE...
DA
DA
DA
DA
-HUFF-
-GASP-

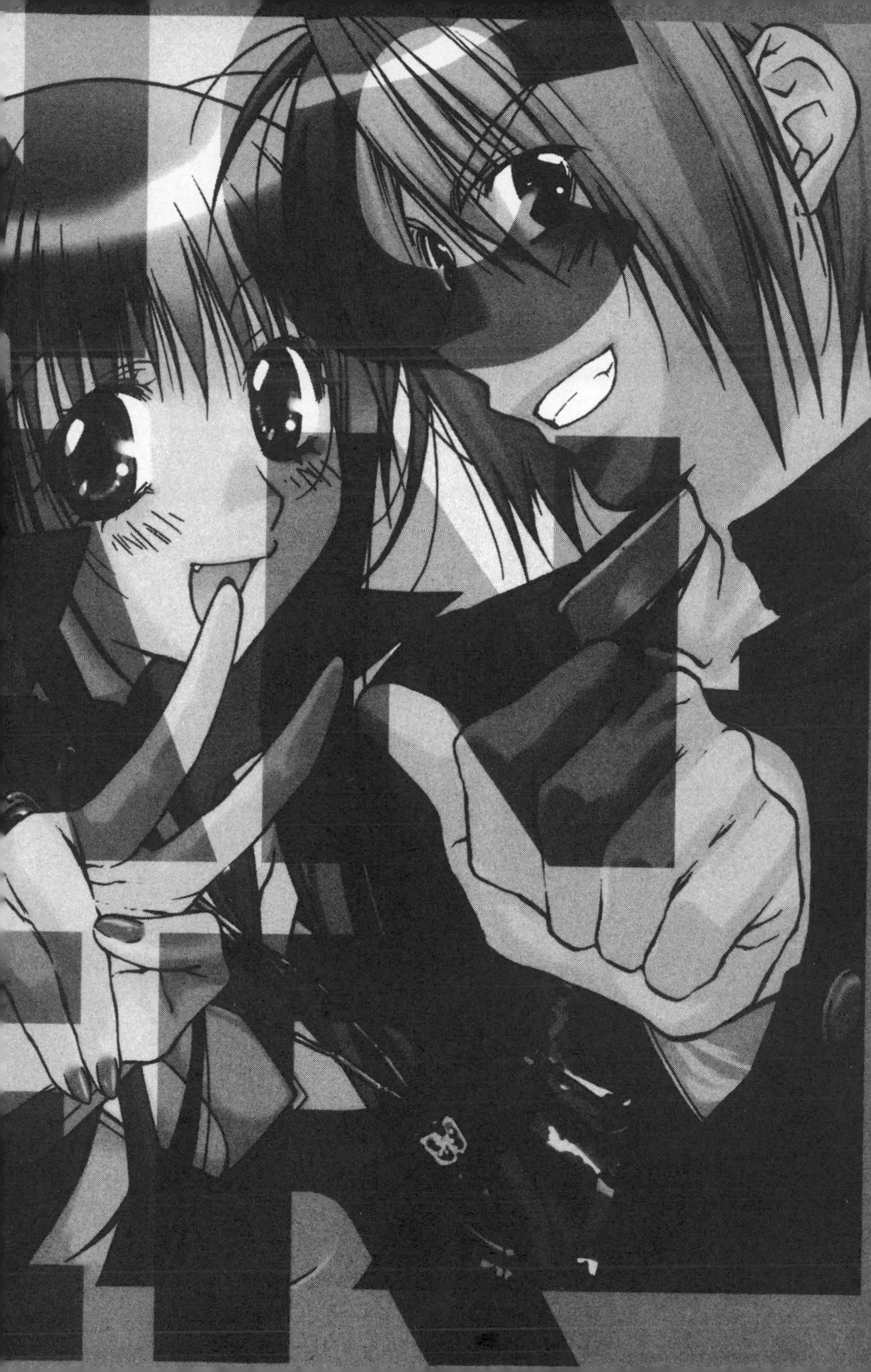

エンチャント
enchant. 37

キャット アンド フィッシュ
Cat and Fish

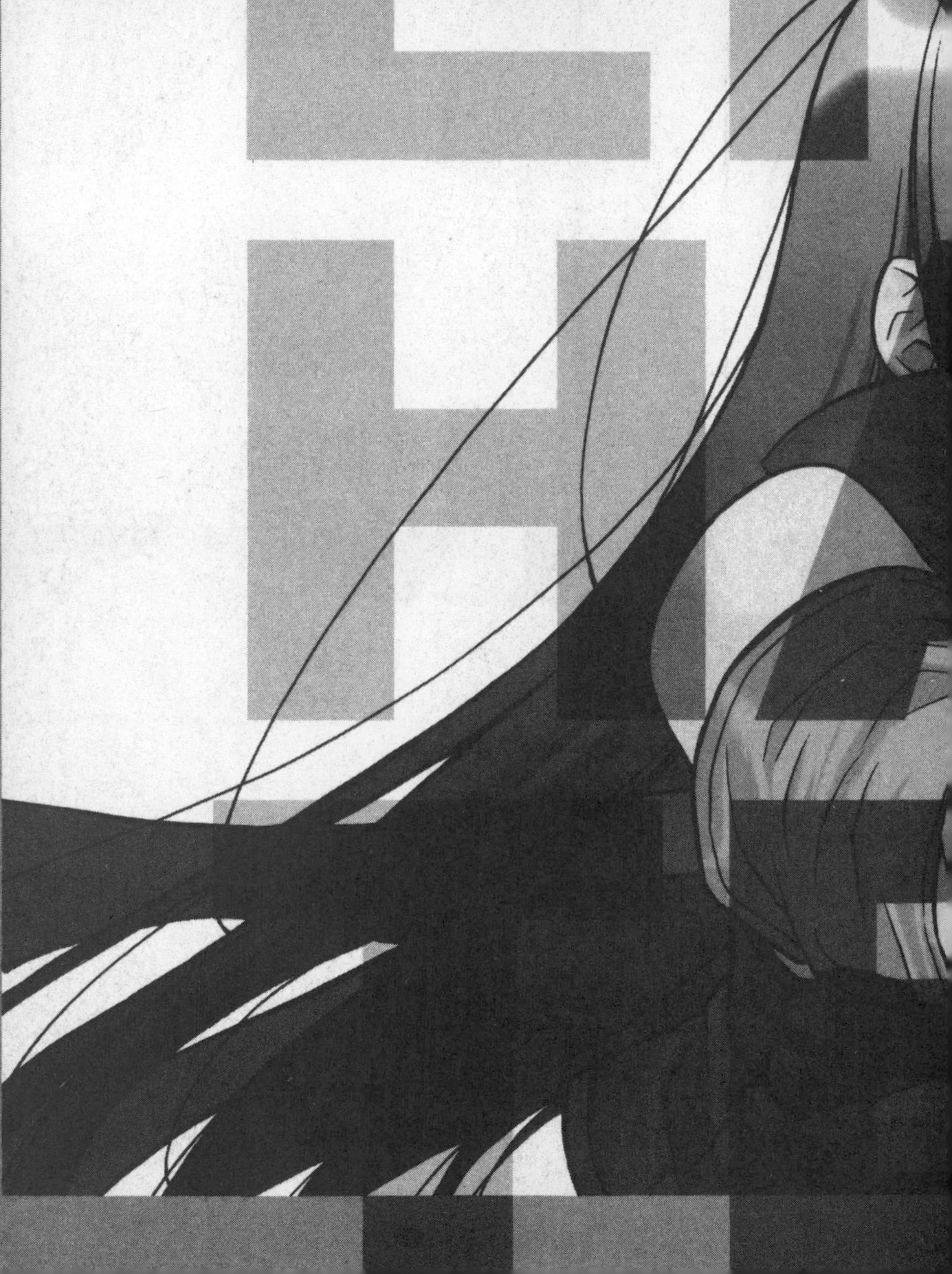

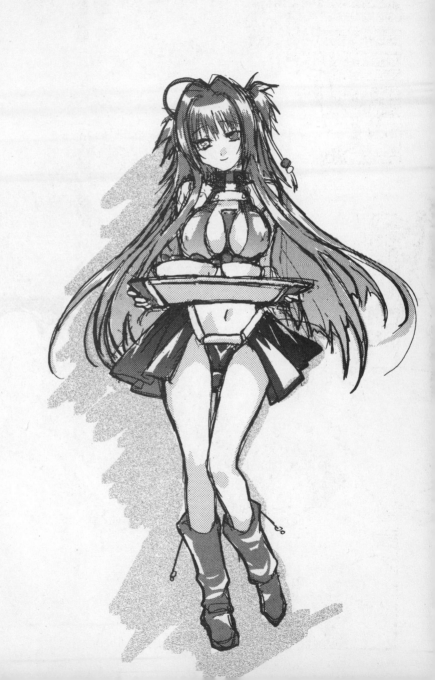

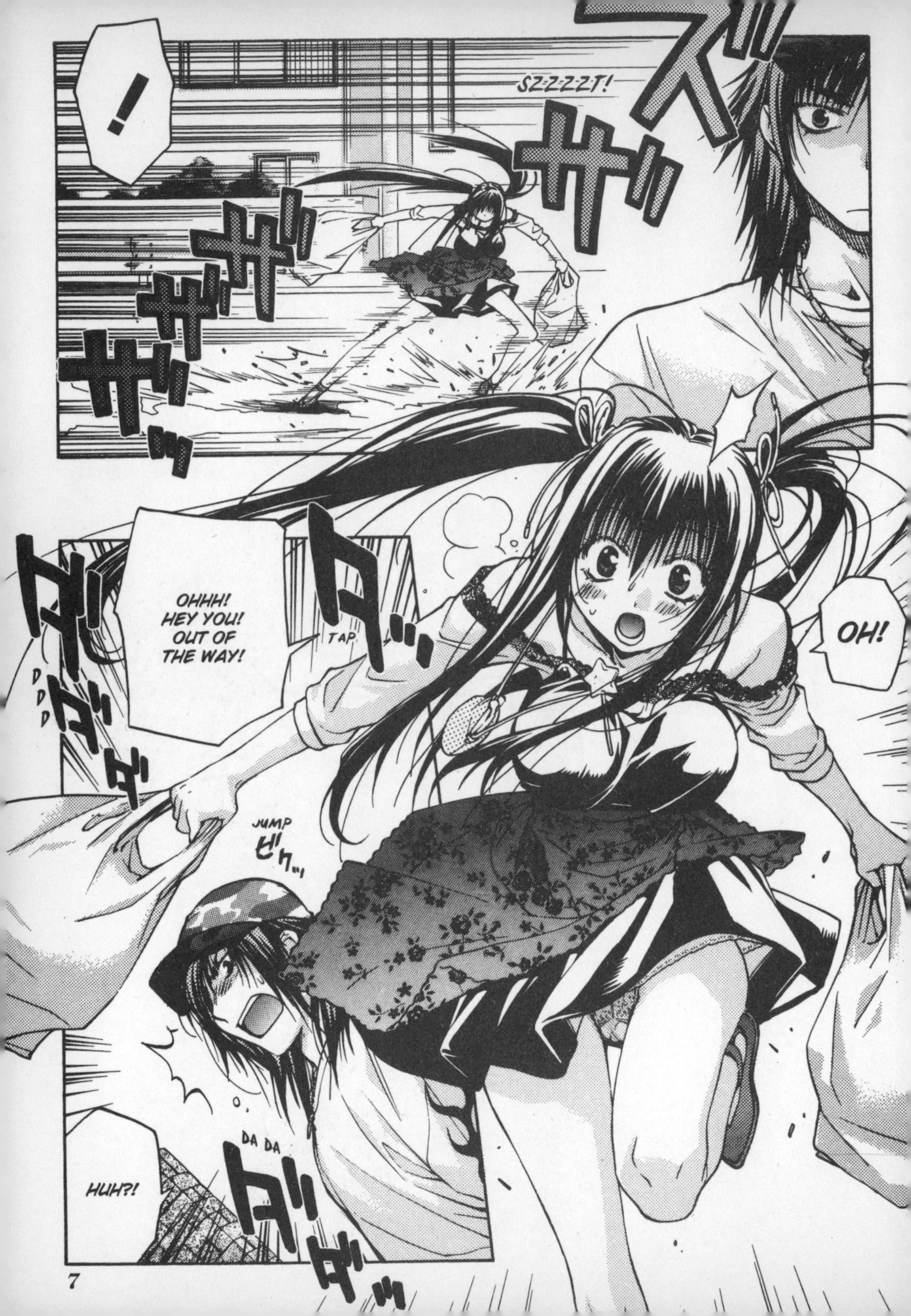
SZ-Z-Z-Z-T!
!
OH!
TAP
OHHH! HEY YOU! OUT OF THE WAY!
D D D
JUMP
DA DA
HUH?!

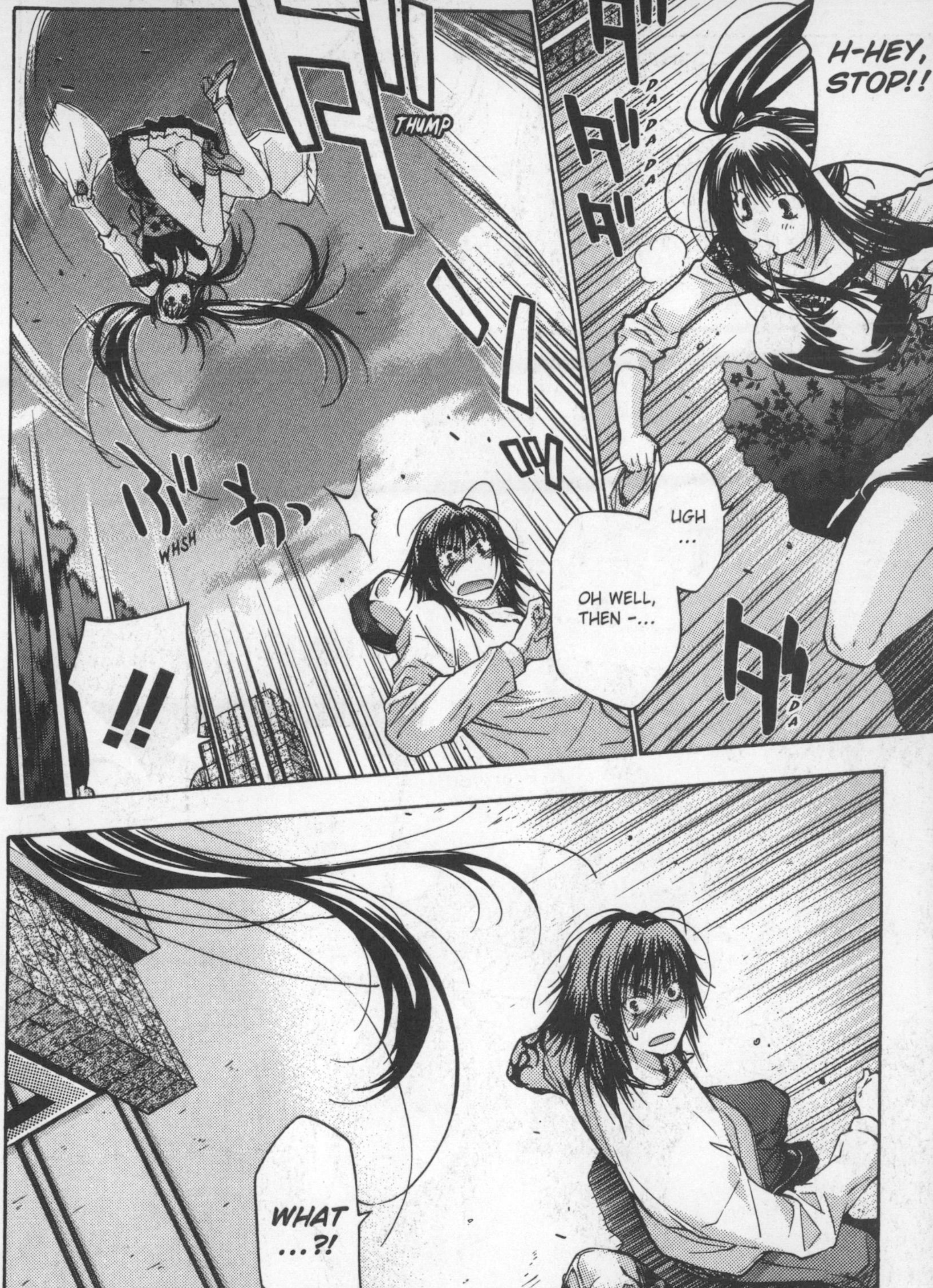
H-HEY, STOP!!
DA DA DA DA
UGH ...
OH WELL, THEN -...
DA
THUMP
WHSH
!!
WHAT ...?!

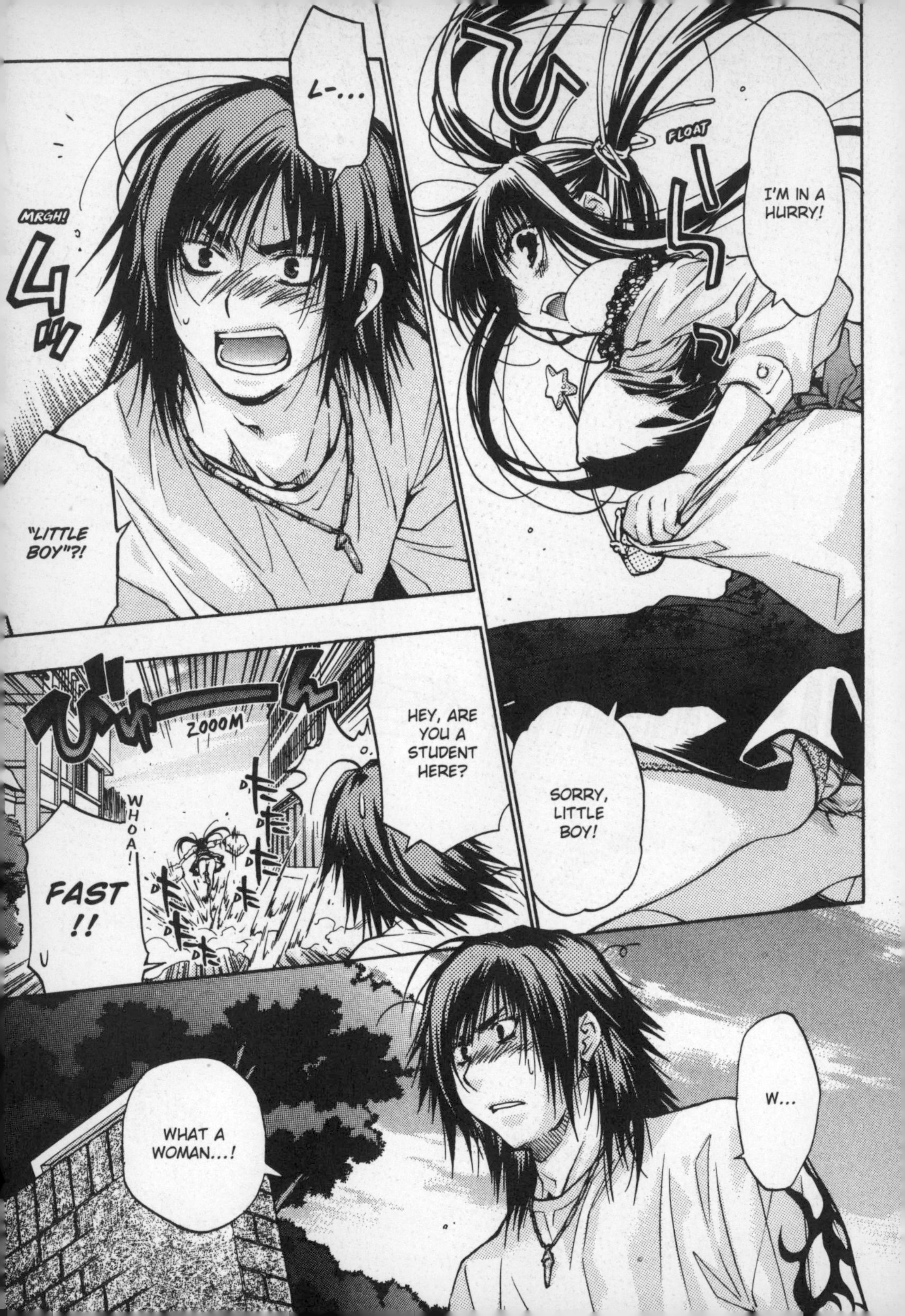
FLOAT
I'M IN A HURRY!
ム-...
MRGH!
"LITTLE BOY"?!
SORRY, LITTLE BOY!
HEY, ARE YOU A STUDENT HERE?
ZOOOM
WHOA!
FAST !!
W...
WHAT A WOMAN...!

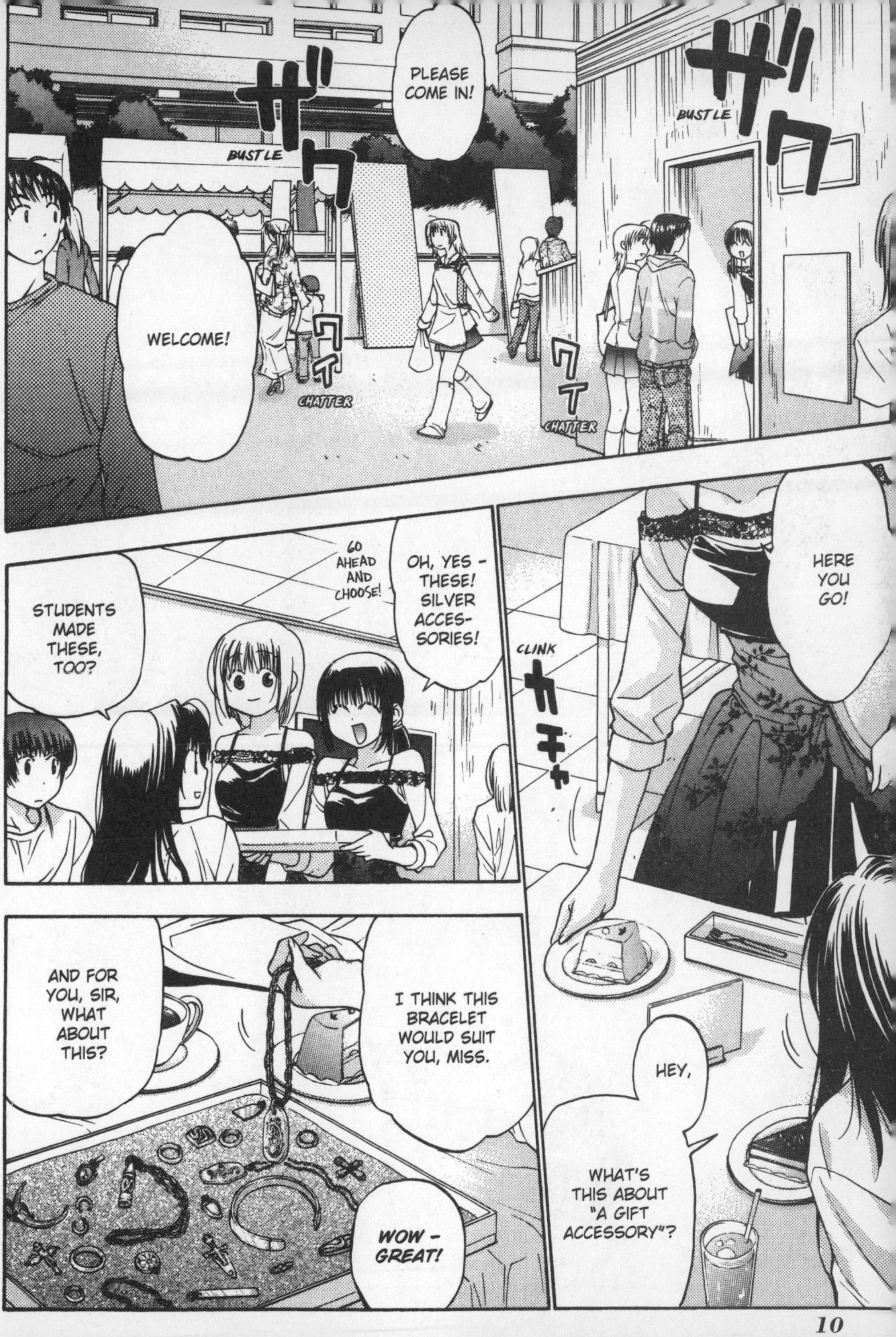
ザク
BUSTLE
PLEASE COME IN!
ザク
BUSTLE
WELCOME!
ワイ
CHATTER
ワイ
CHATTER
HERE YOU GO!
CLINK
カチャ
HEY,
WHAT'S THIS ABOUT "A GIFT ACCESSORY"?
OH, YES - THESE! SILVER ACCES-SORIES!
GO AHEAD AND CHOOSE!
STUDENTS MADE THESE, TOO?
I THINK THIS BRACELET WOULD SUIT YOU, MISS.
AND FOR YOU, SIR, WHAT ABOUT THIS?
WOW - GREAT!

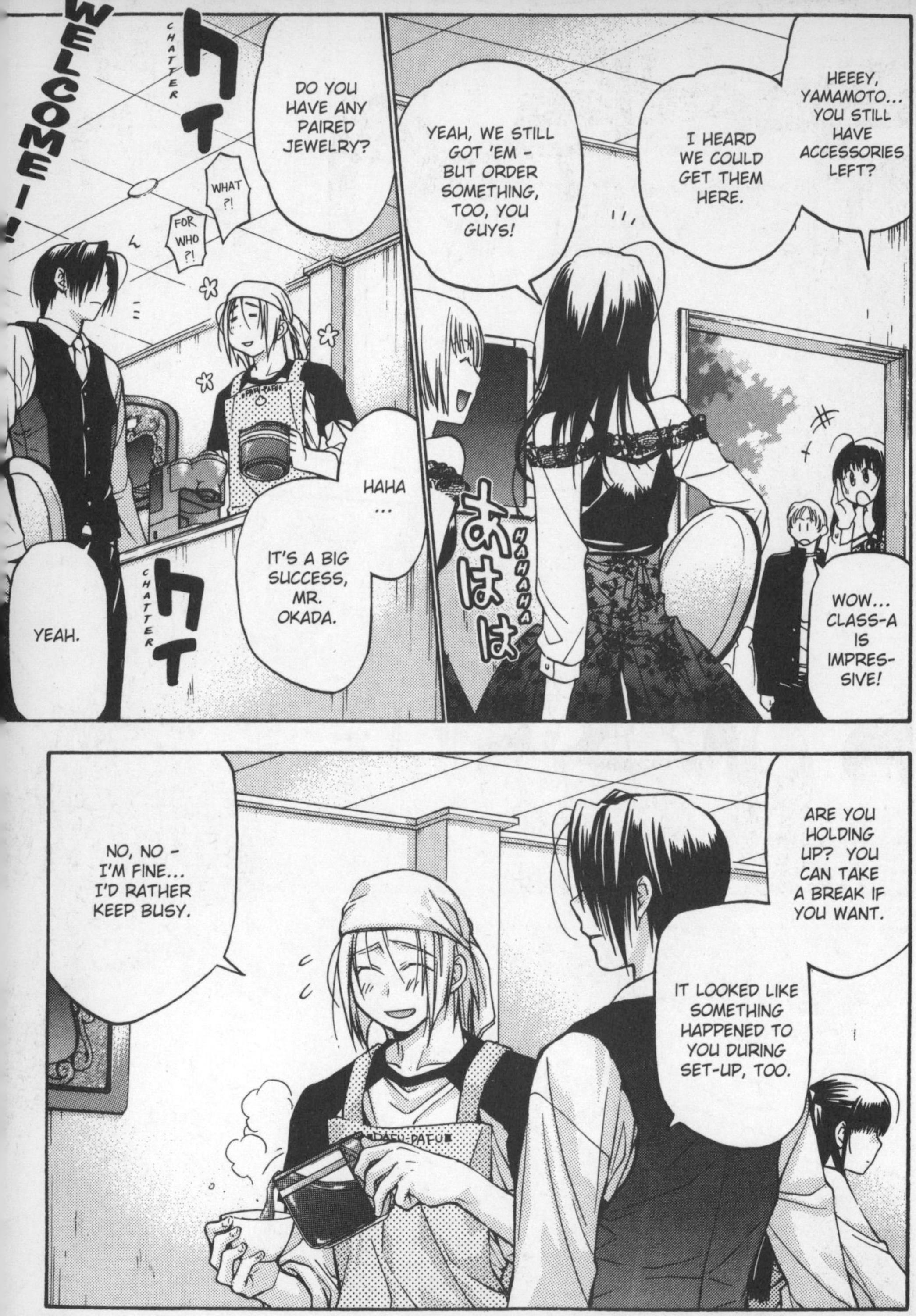
HEEEY, YAMAMOTO... YOU STILL HAVE ACCESSORIES LEFT?
I HEARD WE COULD GET THEM HERE.
YEAH, WE STILL GOT 'EM - BUT ORDER SOMETHING, TOO, YOU GUYS!
WOW... CLASS-A IS IMPRESSIVE!
あはは
HAHAHA
DO YOU HAVE ANY PAIRED JEWELRY?
CHATTER
WHAT ?!
FOR WHO ?!
WELCOME!!
HAHA ...
IT'S A BIG SUCCESS, MR. OKADA.
CHATTER
YEAH.
ARE YOU HOLDING UP? YOU CAN TAKE A BREAK IF YOU WANT.
IT LOOKED LIKE SOMETHING HAPPENED TO YOU DURING SET-UP, TOO.
NO, NO - I'M FINE... I'D RATHER KEEP BUSY.
PAFU-PAFU

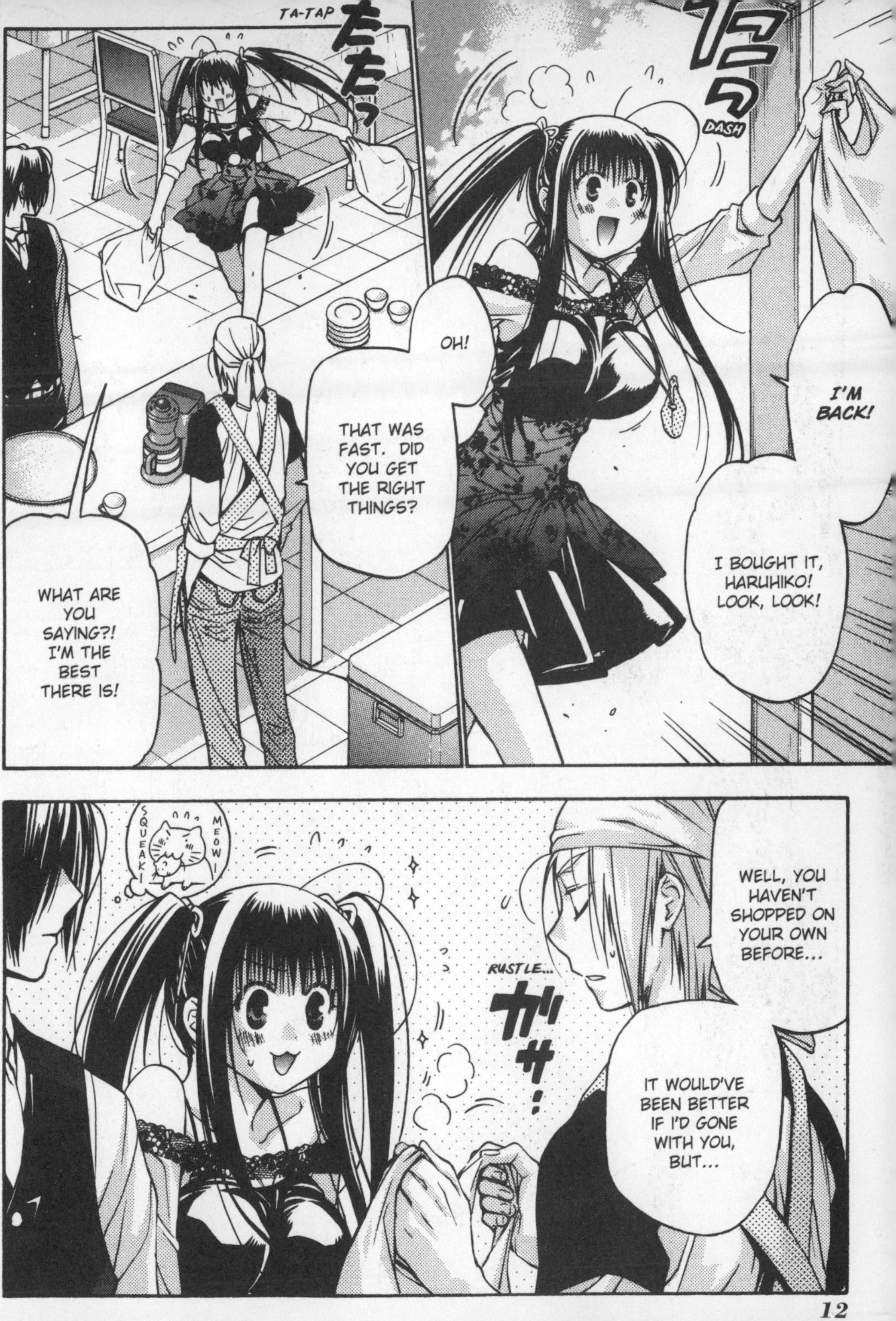
DASH
I'M BACK!
I BOUGHT IT, HARUHIKO! LOOK, LOOK!
TA-TAP
OH!
THAT WAS FAST. DID YOU GET THE RIGHT THINGS?
WHAT ARE YOU SAYING?! I'M THE BEST THERE IS!
WELL, YOU HAVEN'T SHOPPED ON YOUR OWN BEFORE...
IT WOULD'VE BEEN BETTER IF I'D GONE WITH YOU, BUT...
RUSTLE...
MEOW!
SQUEAK!

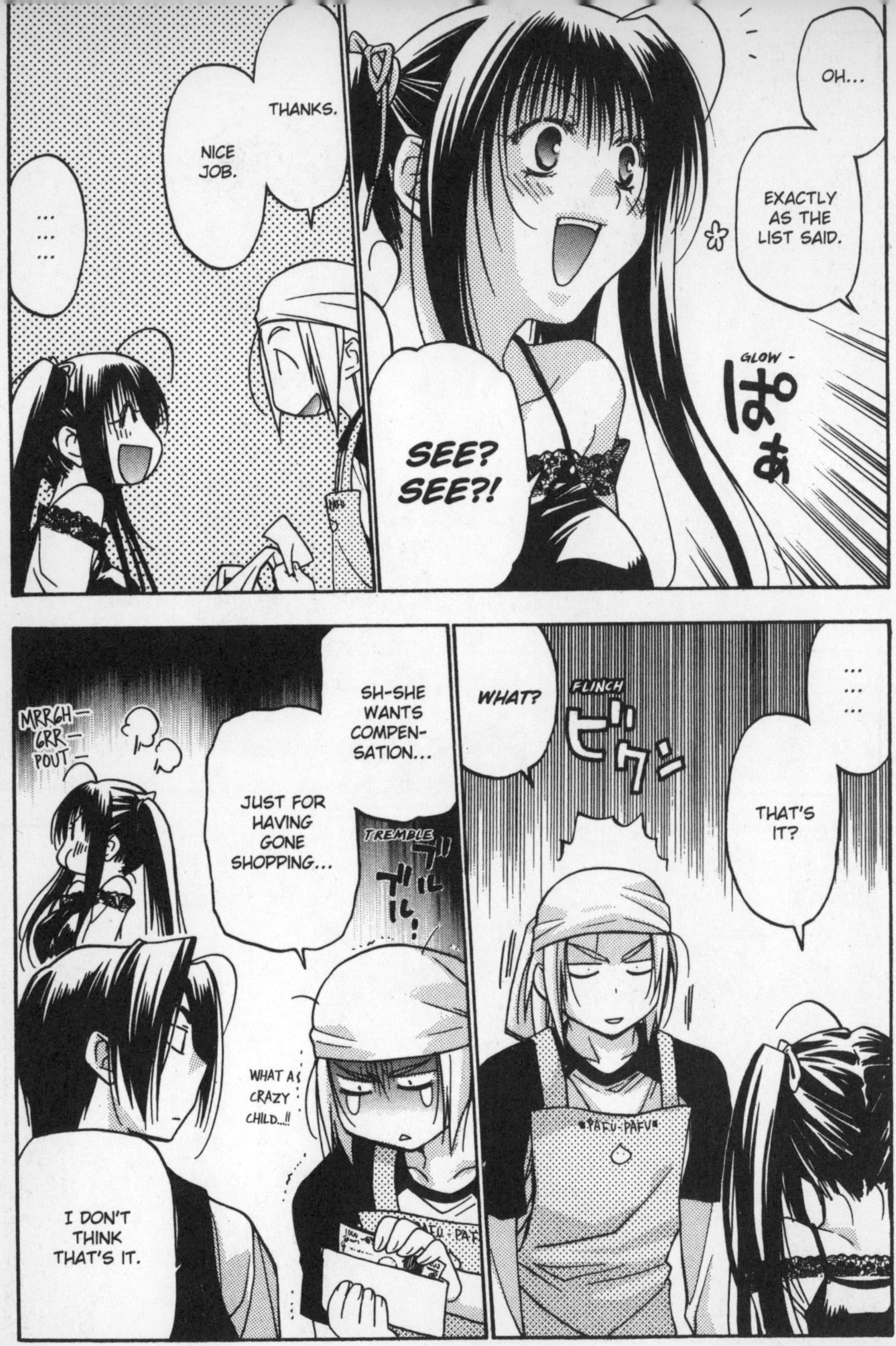
OH...
EXACTLY AS THE LIST SAID.
GLOW -
ぱぁ
SEE? SEE?!
THANKS.
NICE JOB.
... ...
... ...
THAT'S IT?
FLINCH
ビクン
WHAT?
PAFU-PAFU
SH-SHE WANTS COMPEN-SATION...
JUST FOR HAVING GONE SHOPPING...
TREMBLE
ブルブル
MRRGH-
GRR-
POUT
WHAT A CRAZY CHILD...!!
I DON'T THINK THAT'S IT.

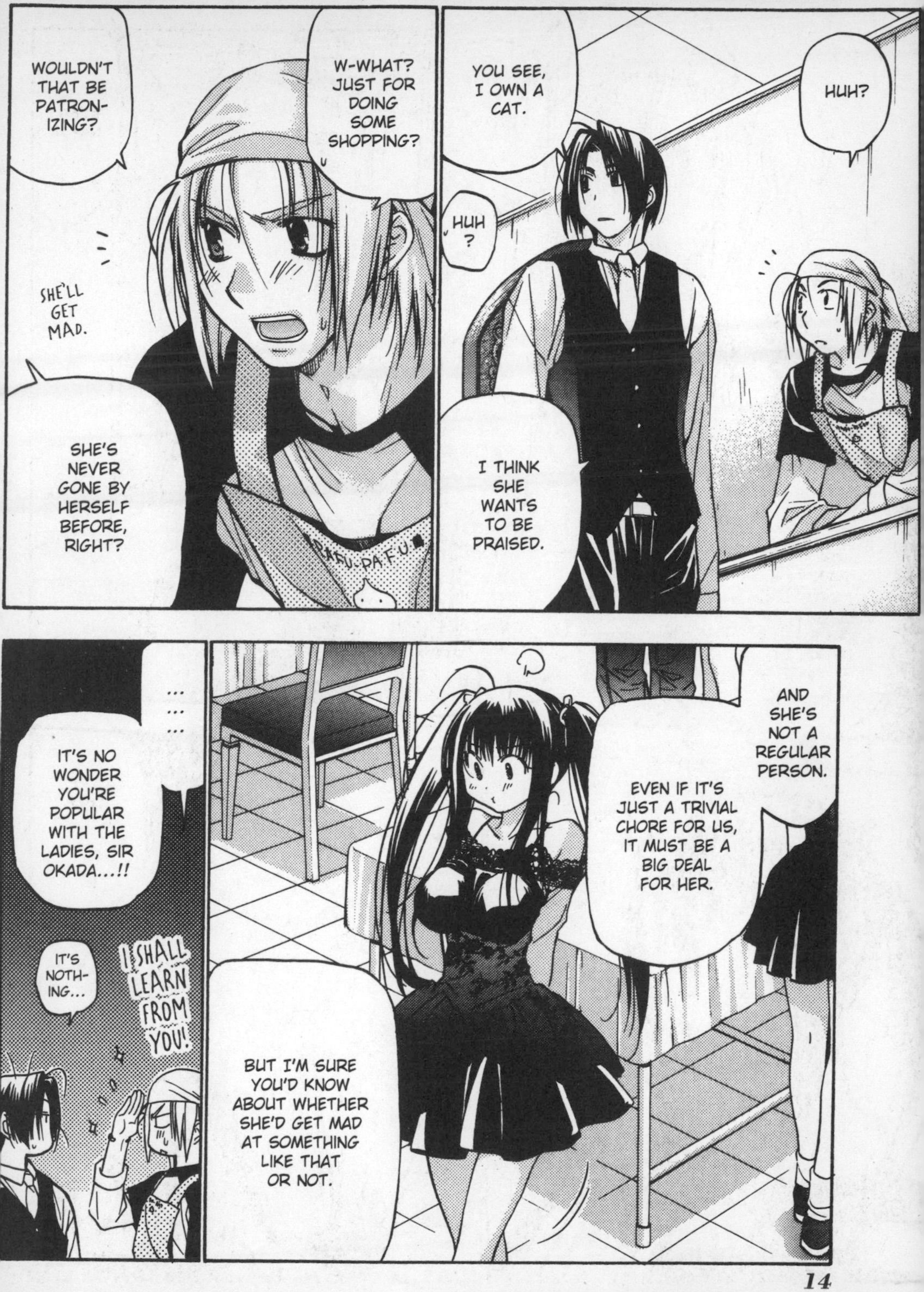
HUH?
YOU SEE, I OWN A CAT.
HUH?
I THINK SHE WANTS TO BE PRAISED.
W-WHAT? JUST FOR DOING SOME SHOPPING?
WOULDN'T THAT BE PATRON-IZING?
SHE'LL GET MAD.
SHE'S NEVER GONE BY HERSELF BEFORE, RIGHT?
AND SHE'S NOT A REGULAR PERSON.
EVEN IF IT'S JUST A TRIVIAL CHORE FOR US, IT MUST BE A BIG DEAL FOR HER.
BUT I'M SURE YOU'D KNOW ABOUT WHETHER SHE'D GET MAD AT SOMETHING LIKE THAT OR NOT.
... ...
IT'S NO WONDER YOU'RE POPULAR WITH THE LADIES, SIR OKADA...!!
I SHALL LEARN FROM YOU!
IT'S NOTH-ING...

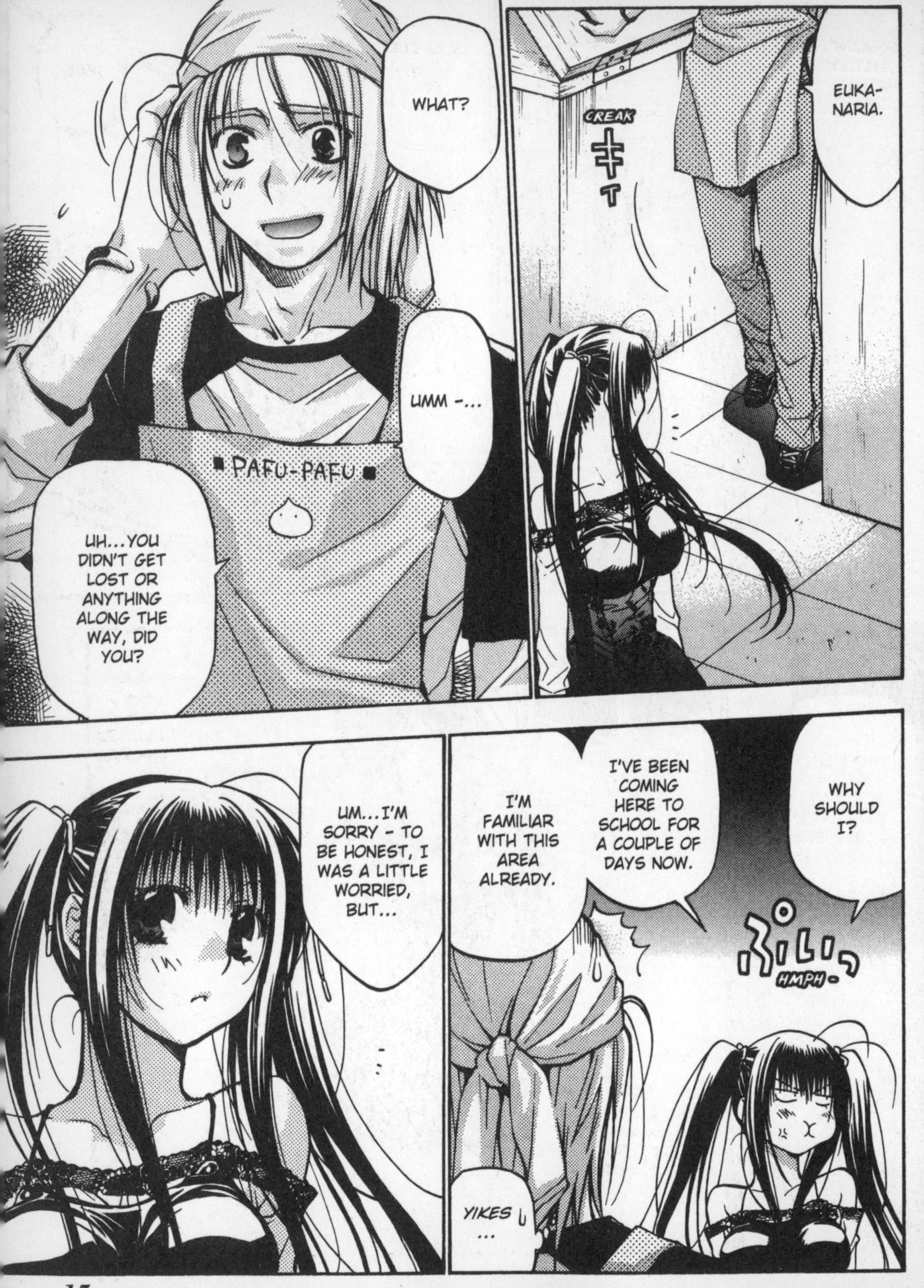
EUKA-NARIA.
CREAK
WHAT?
UMM -...
PAFU-PAFU
UH...YOU DIDN'T GET LOST OR ANYTHING ALONG THE WAY, DID YOU?
WHY SHOULD I?
I'VE BEEN COMING HERE TO SCHOOL FOR A COUPLE OF DAYS NOW.
I'M FAMILIAR WITH THIS AREA ALREADY.
HMPH
YIKES ...
UM...I'M SORRY - TO BE HONEST, I WAS A LITTLE WORRIED, BUT...

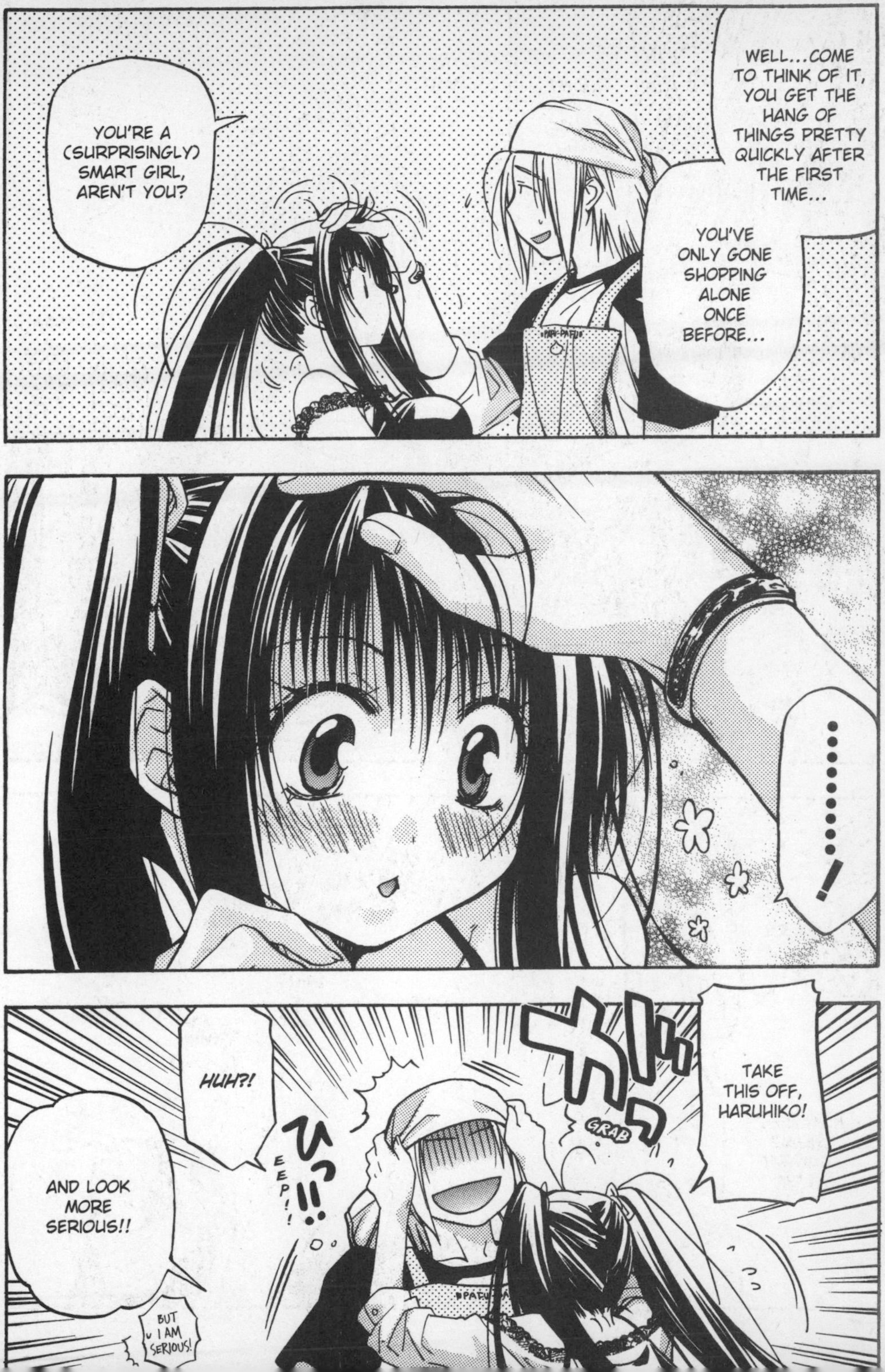
WELL...COME TO THINK OF IT, YOU GET THE HANG OF THINGS PRETTY QUICKLY AFTER THE FIRST TIME...
YOU'VE ONLY GONE SHOPPING ALONE ONCE BEFORE...
YOU'RE A (SURPRISINGLY) SMART GIRL, AREN'T YOU?
......!
TAKE THIS OFF, HARUHIKO!
GRAB
HUH?!
EEP!!
AND LOOK MORE SERIOUS!!
BUT I AM SERIOUS!

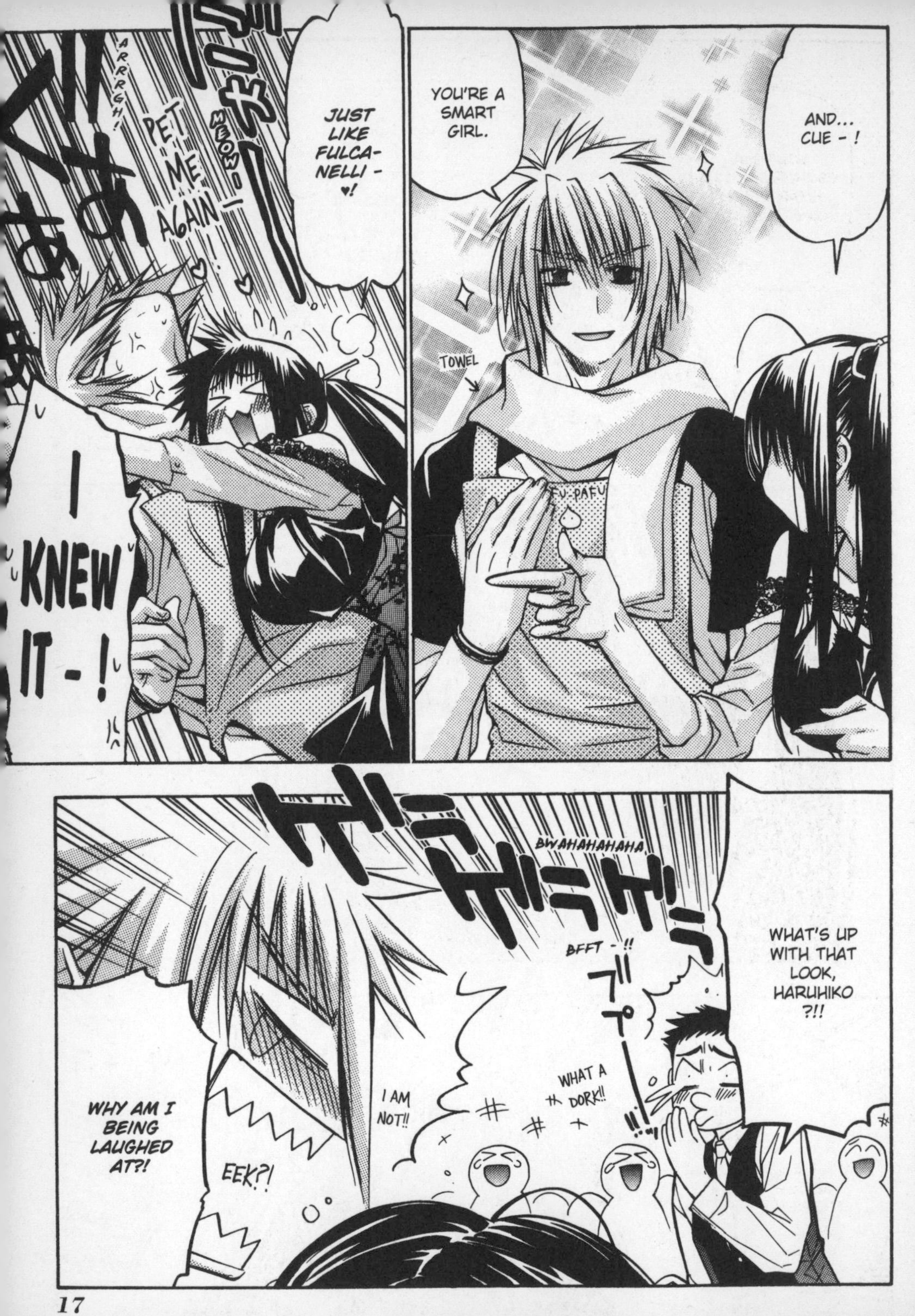
AND... CUE - !
YOU'RE A SMART GIRL.
TOWEL
JUST LIKE FULCA-NELLI - ♥!
MEOW!
PET ME AGAIN—!
ARRRGH!
I KNEW IT - !
WHAT'S UP WITH THAT LOOK, HARUHIKO ?!!
BWAHAHAHAHA
BFFT - !!
WHAT A DORK!!
I AM NOT!!
EEK?!
WHY AM I BEING LAUGHED AT?!

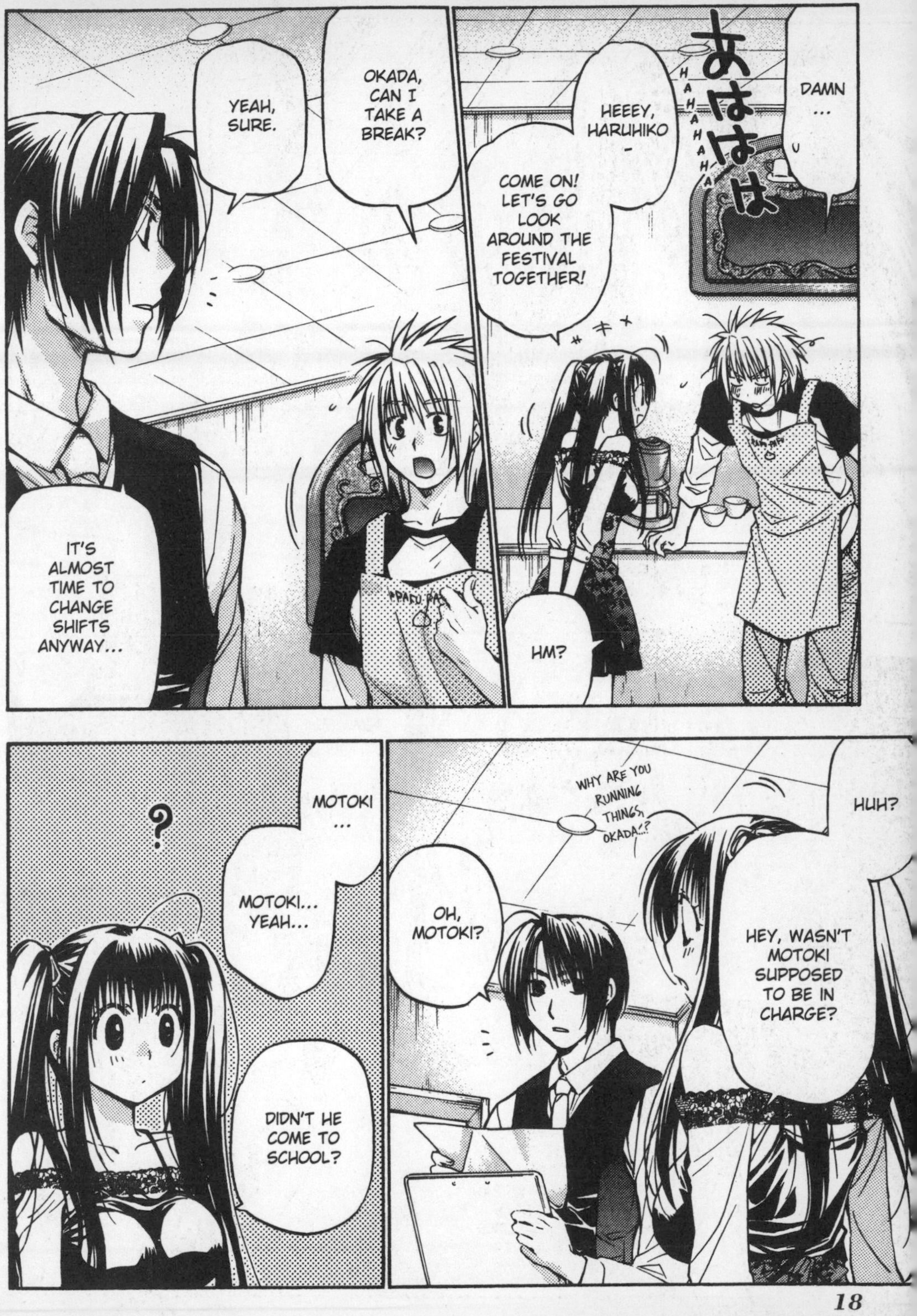
DAMN ...
あははは
HAHAHAHA
HEEEY, HARUHIKO -
COME ON! LET'S GO LOOK AROUND THE FESTIVAL TOGETHER!
HM?
OKADA, CAN I TAKE A BREAK?
YEAH, SURE.
IT'S ALMOST TIME TO CHANGE SHIFTS ANYWAY...
HUH?
WHY ARE YOU RUNNING THINGS, OKADA...?
HEY, WASN'T MOTOKI SUPPOSED TO BE IN CHARGE?
OH, MOTOKI?
MOTOKI ...
MOTOKI... YEAH...
?
DIDN'T HE COME TO SCHOOL?

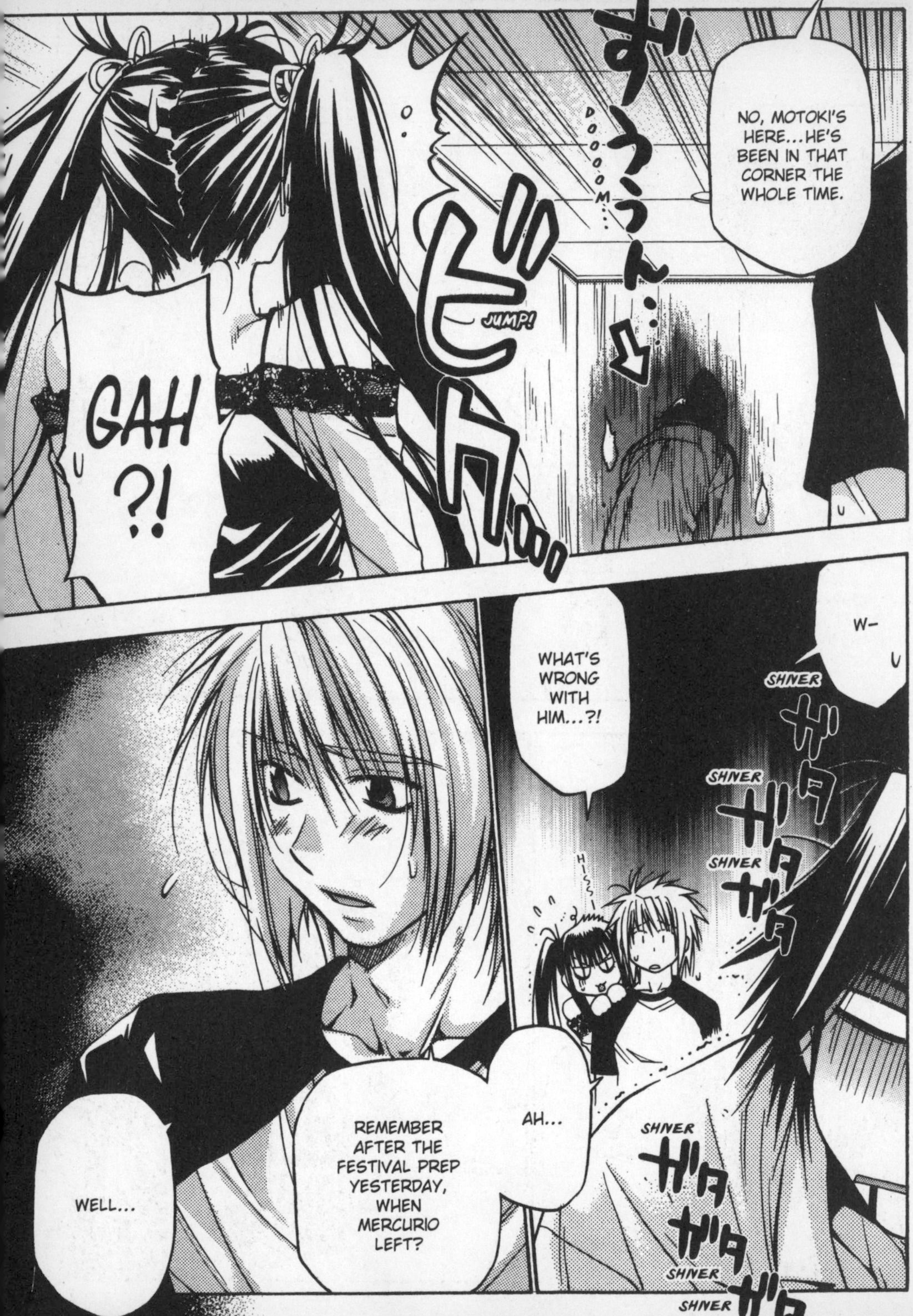
NO, MOTOKI'S HERE...HE'S BEEN IN THAT CORNER THE WHOLE TIME.
DOOOOOM...
JUMP!
GAH ?!
W-
SHIVER
SHIVER
SHIVER
WHAT'S WRONG WITH HIM...?!
HISS
AH...
REMEMBER AFTER THE FESTIVAL PREP YESTERDAY, WHEN MERCURIO LEFT?
WELL...
SHIVER
SHIVER
SHIVER

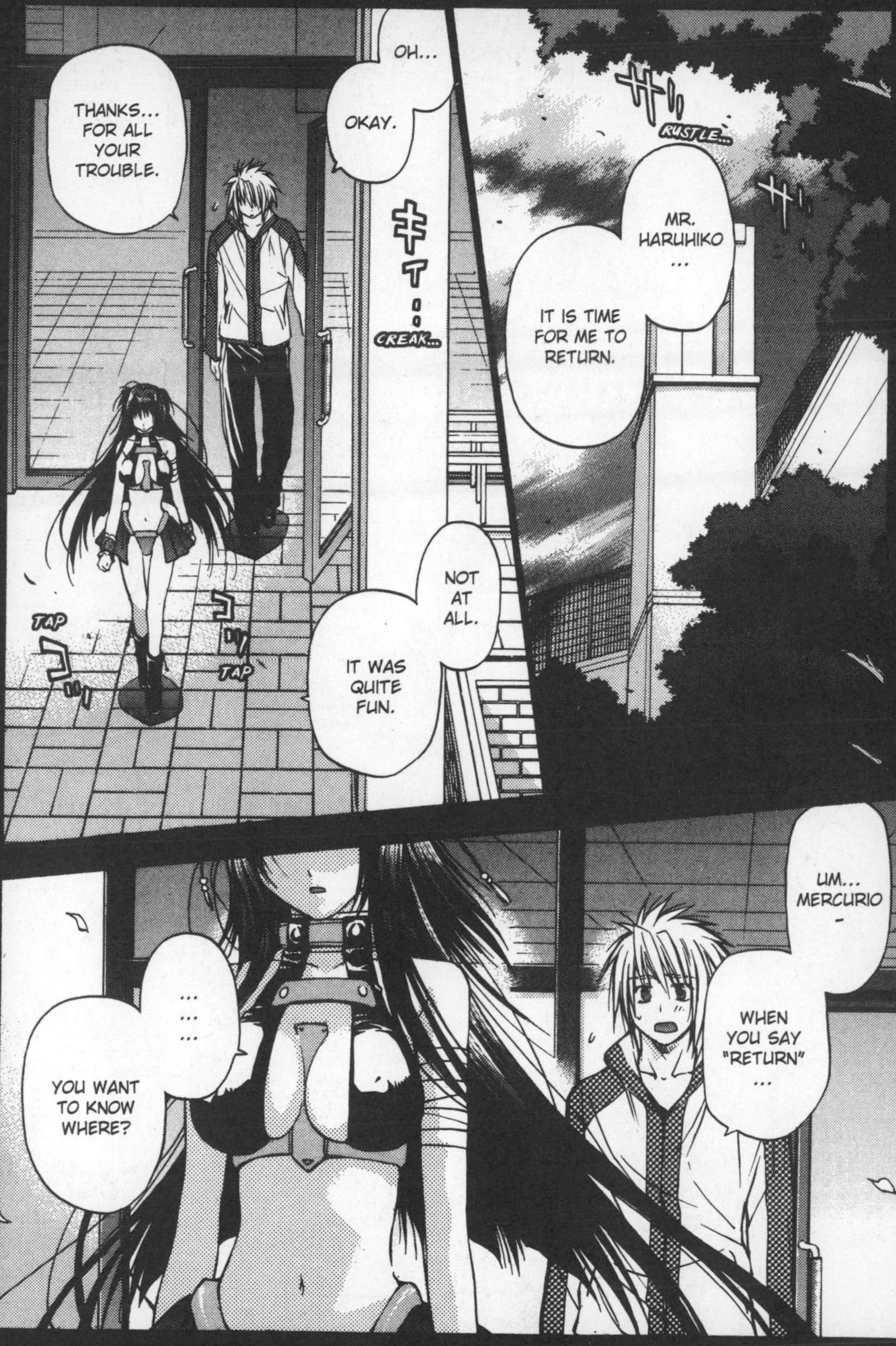
RUSTLE...
MR. HARUHIKO ...
IT IS TIME FOR ME TO RETURN.
OH... OKAY.
CREAK...
THANKS... FOR ALL YOUR TROUBLE.
NOT AT ALL.
IT WAS QUITE FUN.
TAP
TAP
UM... MERCURIO -
WHEN YOU SAY "RETURN" ...
... ...
YOU WANT TO KNOW WHERE?

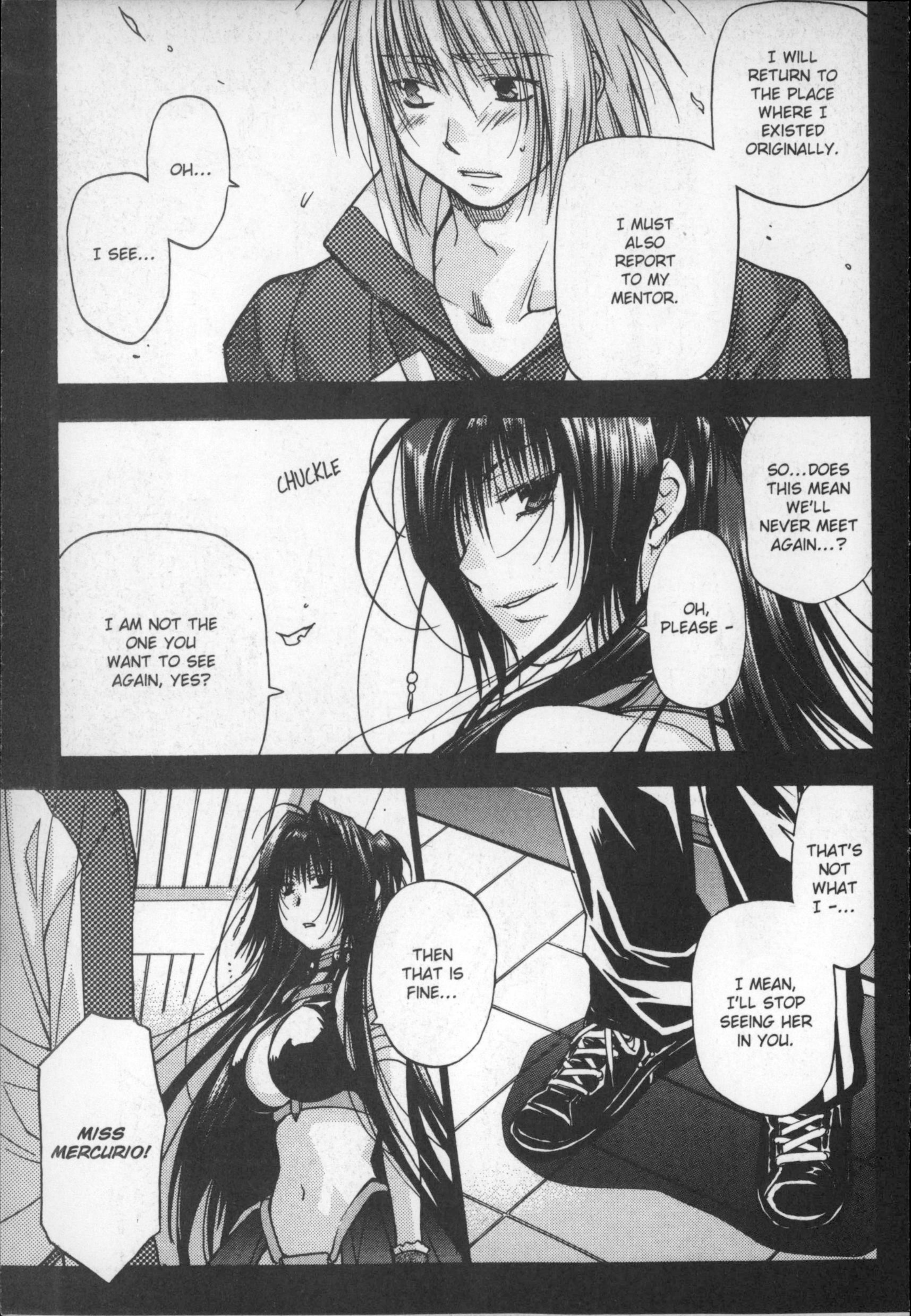
I WILL RETURN TO THE PLACE WHERE I EXISTED ORIGINALLY.
I MUST ALSO REPORT TO MY MENTOR.
OH...
I SEE...
SO...DOES THIS MEAN WE'LL NEVER MEET AGAIN...?
CHUCKLE
OH, PLEASE -
I AM NOT THE ONE YOU WANT TO SEE AGAIN, YES?
THAT'S NOT WHAT I -...
I MEAN, I'LL STOP SEEING HER IN YOU.
THEN THAT IS FINE...
MISS MERCURIO!

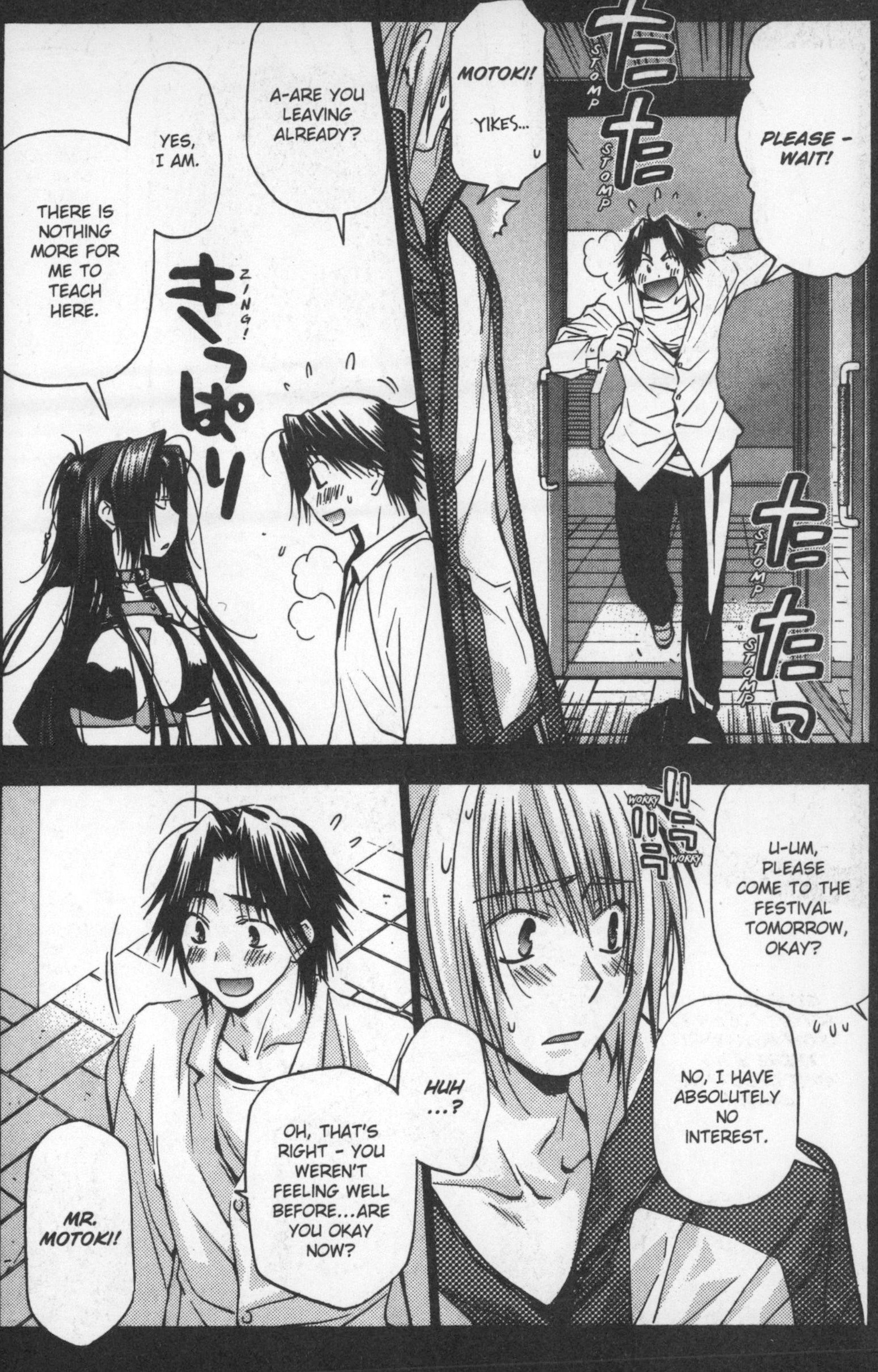
PLEASE - WAIT!
STOMP STOMP
STOMP STOMP
MOTOKI!
YIKES...
A-ARE YOU LEAVING ALREADY?
YES, I AM.
THERE IS NOTHING MORE FOR ME TO TEACH HERE.
ZING!
WORRY WORRY
U-UM, PLEASE COME TO THE FESTIVAL TOMORROW, OKAY?
NO, I HAVE ABSOLUTELY NO INTEREST.
HUH ...?
OH, THAT'S RIGHT - YOU WEREN'T FEELING WELL BEFORE...ARE YOU OKAY NOW?
MR. MOTOKI!

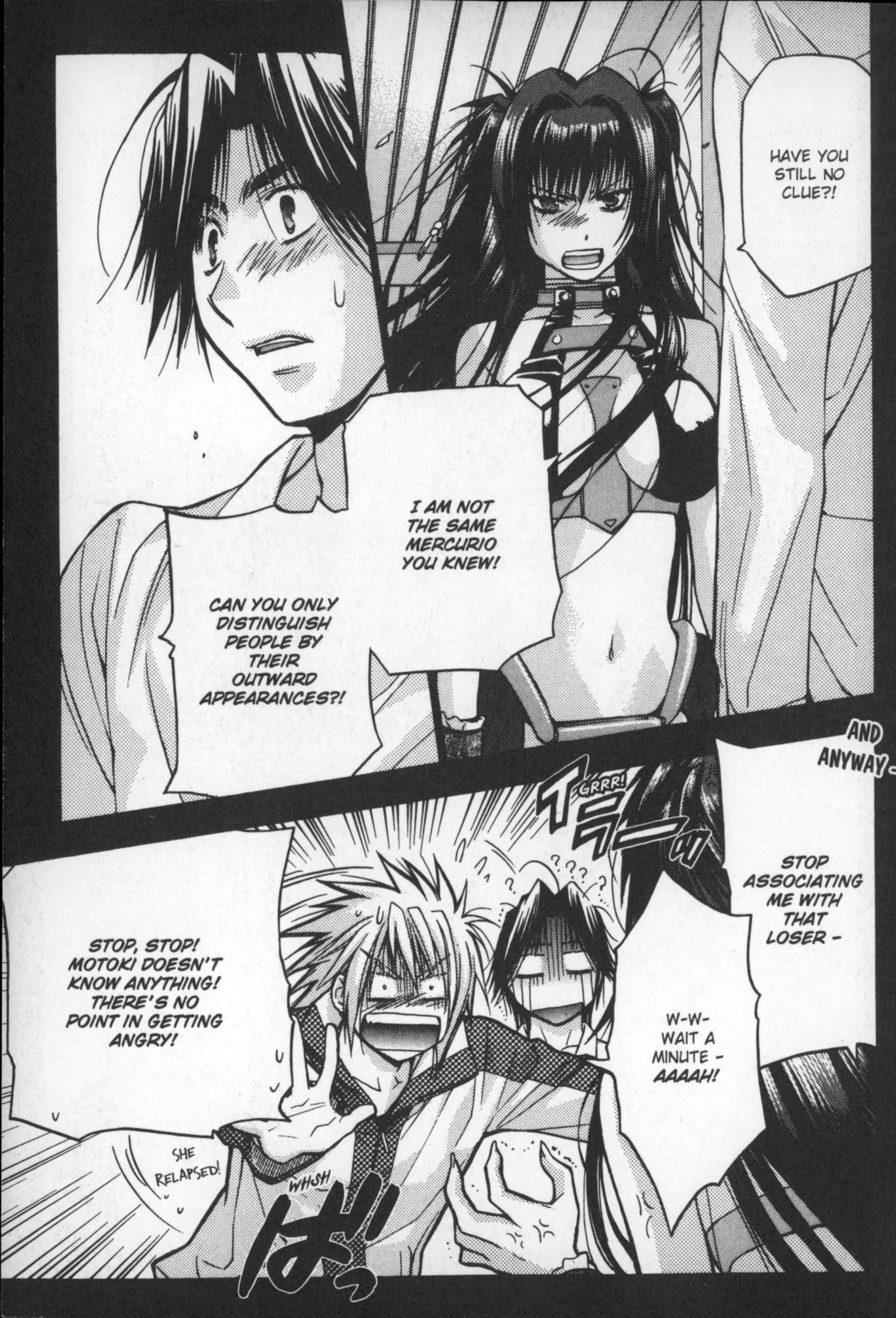
HAVE YOU STILL NO CLUE?!
I AM NOT THE SAME MERCURIO YOU KNEW!
CAN YOU ONLY DISTINGUISH PEOPLE BY THEIR OUTWARD APPEARANCES?!
AND ANYWAY -
GRRR!
STOP ASSOCIATING ME WITH THAT LOSER -
W-W-WAIT A MINUTE - AAAAH!
STOP, STOP! MOTOKI DOESN'T KNOW ANYTHING! THERE'S NO POINT IN GETTING ANGRY!
SHE RELAPSED!
WHSH

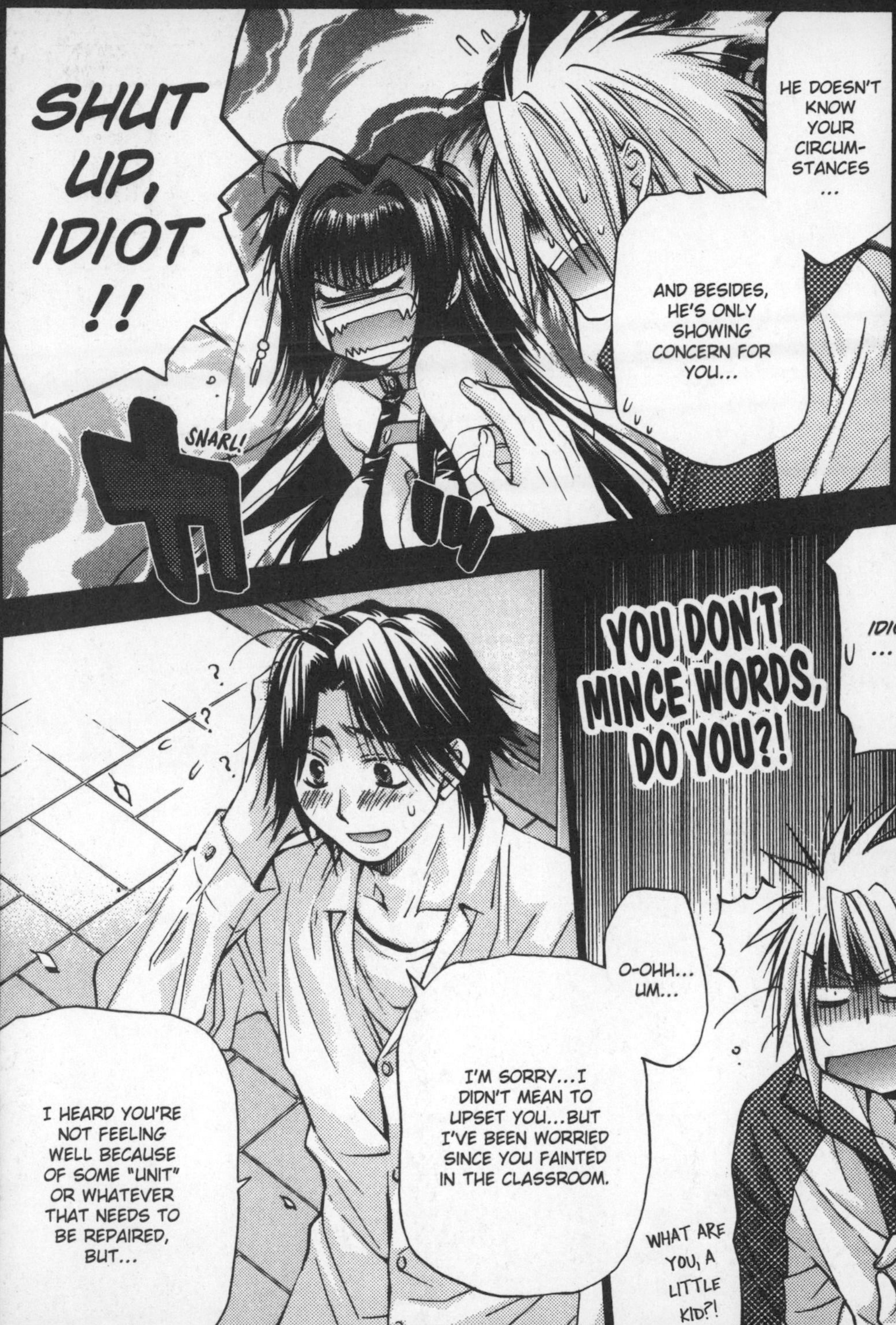

HE DOESN'T KNOW YOUR CIRCUM-STANCES ...
AND BESIDES, HE'S ONLY SHOWING CONCERN FOR YOU...
SHUT UP, IDIOT !!
SNARL!
IDIOT ...?!
YOU DON'T MINCE WORDS, DO YOU?!
O-OHH... UM...
I'M SORRY...I DIDN'T MEAN TO UPSET YOU...BUT I'VE BEEN WORRIED SINCE YOU FAINTED IN THE CLASSROOM.
I HEARD YOU'RE NOT FEELING WELL BECAUSE OF SOME "UNIT" OR WHATEVER THAT NEEDS TO BE REPAIRED, BUT...
WHAT ARE YOU, A LITTLE KID?!

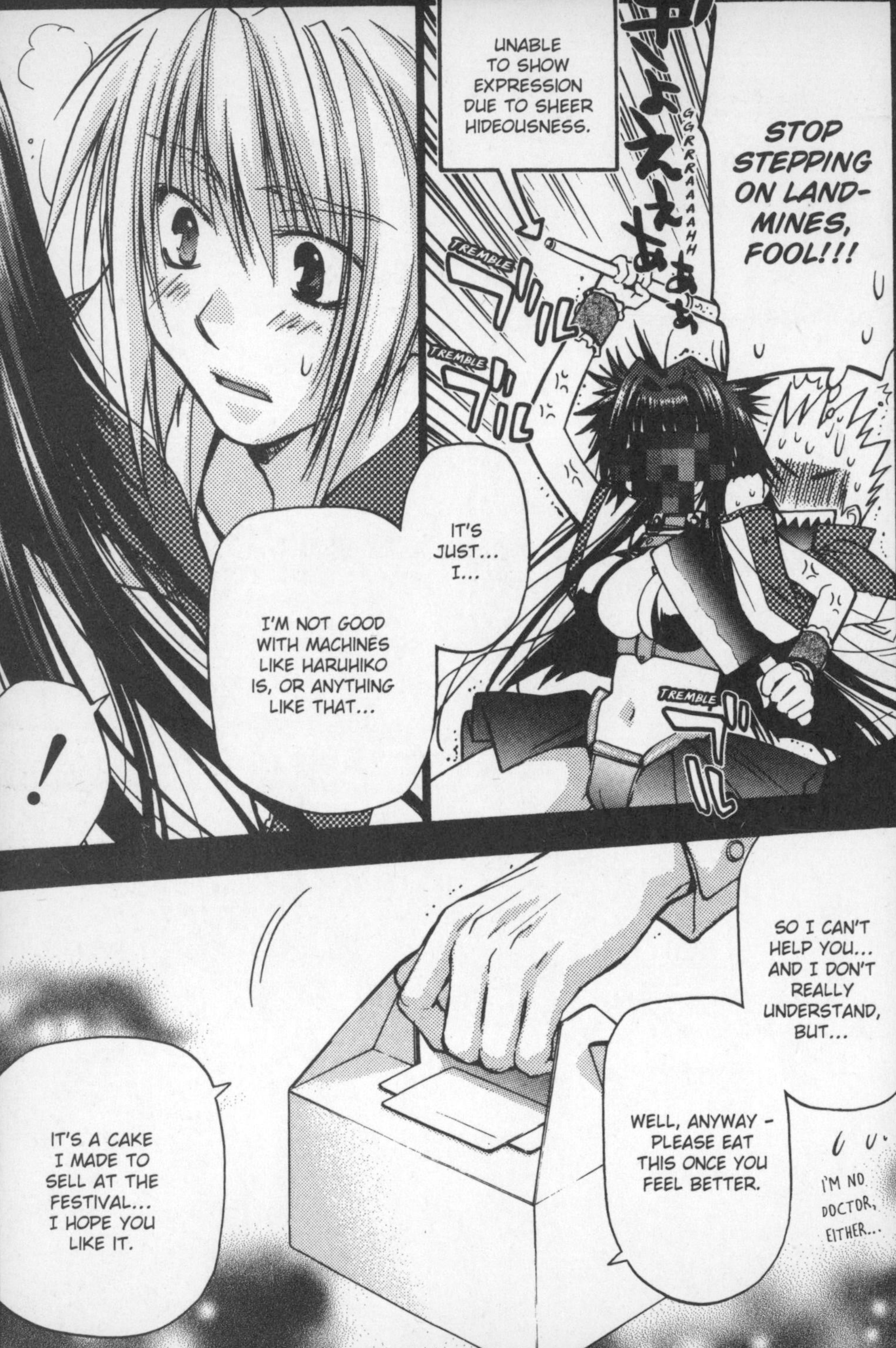
UNABLE TO SHOW EXPRESSION DUE TO SHEER HIDEOUSNESS.
GRRRAAAAHH
STOP STEPPING ON LAND-MINES, FOOL!!!
TREMBLE
TREMBLE
TREMBLE
IT'S JUST... I...
I'M NOT GOOD WITH MACHINES LIKE HARUHIKO IS, OR ANYTHING LIKE THAT...
!
SO I CAN'T HELP YOU... AND I DON'T REALLY UNDERSTAND, BUT...
I'M NO DOCTOR, EITHER...
WELL, ANYWAY - PLEASE EAT THIS ONCE YOU FEEL BETTER.
IT'S A CAKE I MADE TO SELL AT THE FESTIVAL... I HOPE YOU LIKE IT.

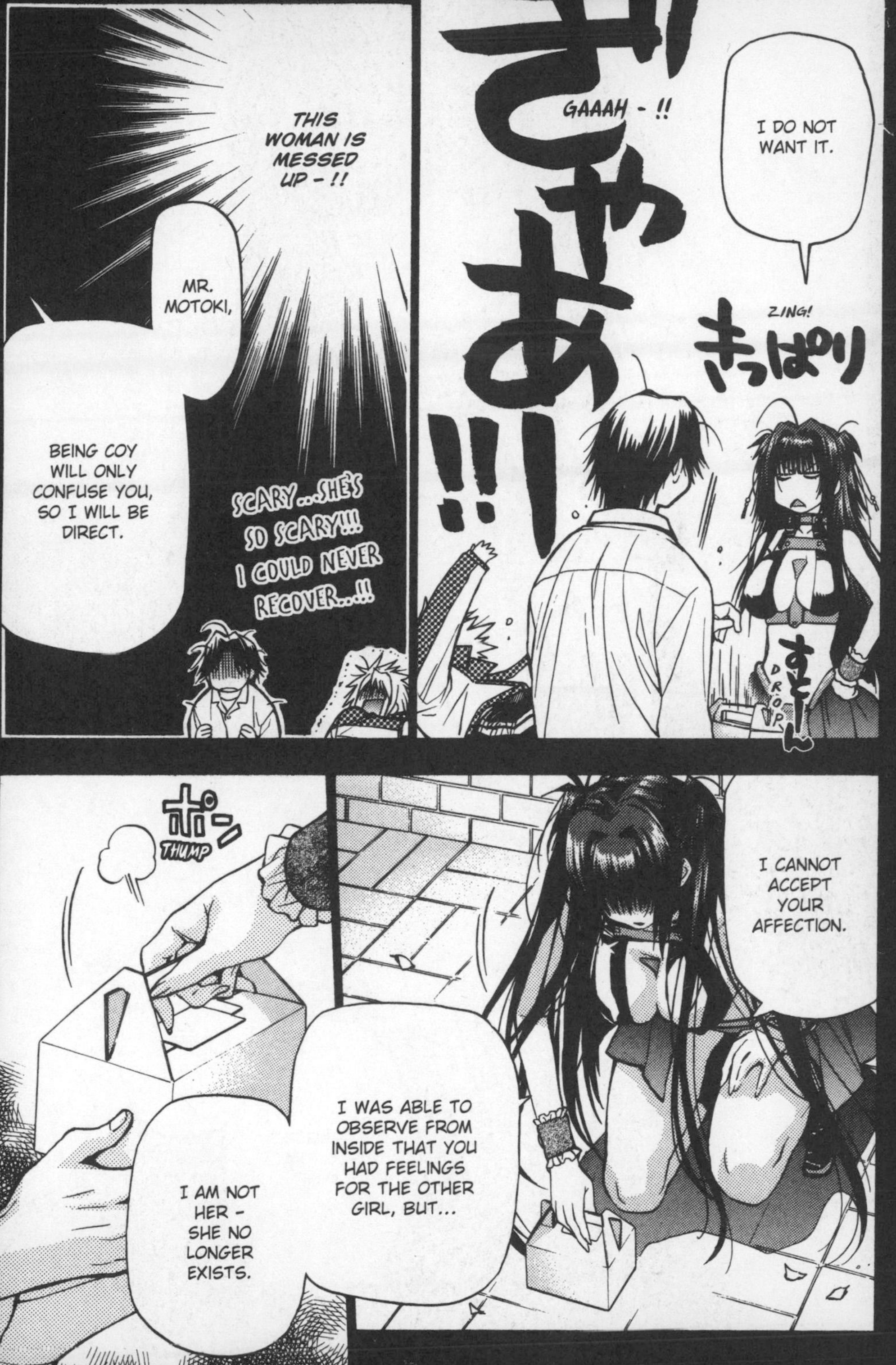
I DO NOT WANT IT.
きっぱり
ZING!
ぎゃあー!!
GAAAH - !!
すとーん
DROP
THIS WOMAN IS MESSED UP - !!
MR. MOTOKI,
BEING COY WILL ONLY CONFUSE YOU, SO I WILL BE DIRECT.
SCARY...SHE'S SO SCARY!!! I COULD NEVER RECOVER...!!
I CANNOT ACCEPT YOUR AFFECTION.
THUMP
I WAS ABLE TO OBSERVE FROM INSIDE THAT YOU HAD FEELINGS FOR THE OTHER GIRL, BUT...
I AM NOT HER - SHE NO LONGER EXISTS.

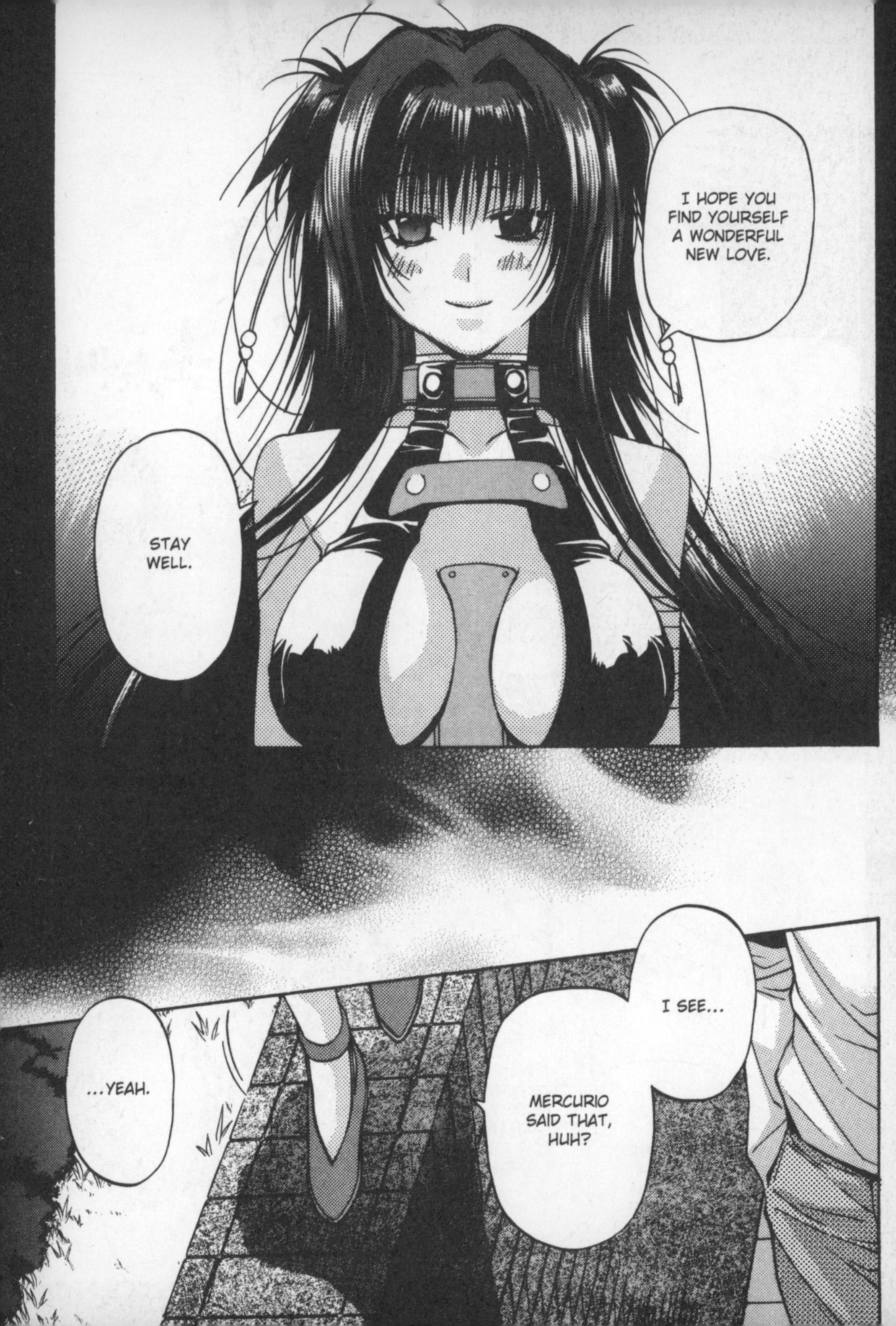
I HOPE YOU FIND YOURSELF A WONDERFUL NEW LOVE.
STAY WELL.
I SEE...
MERCURIO SAID THAT, HUH?
...YEAH.

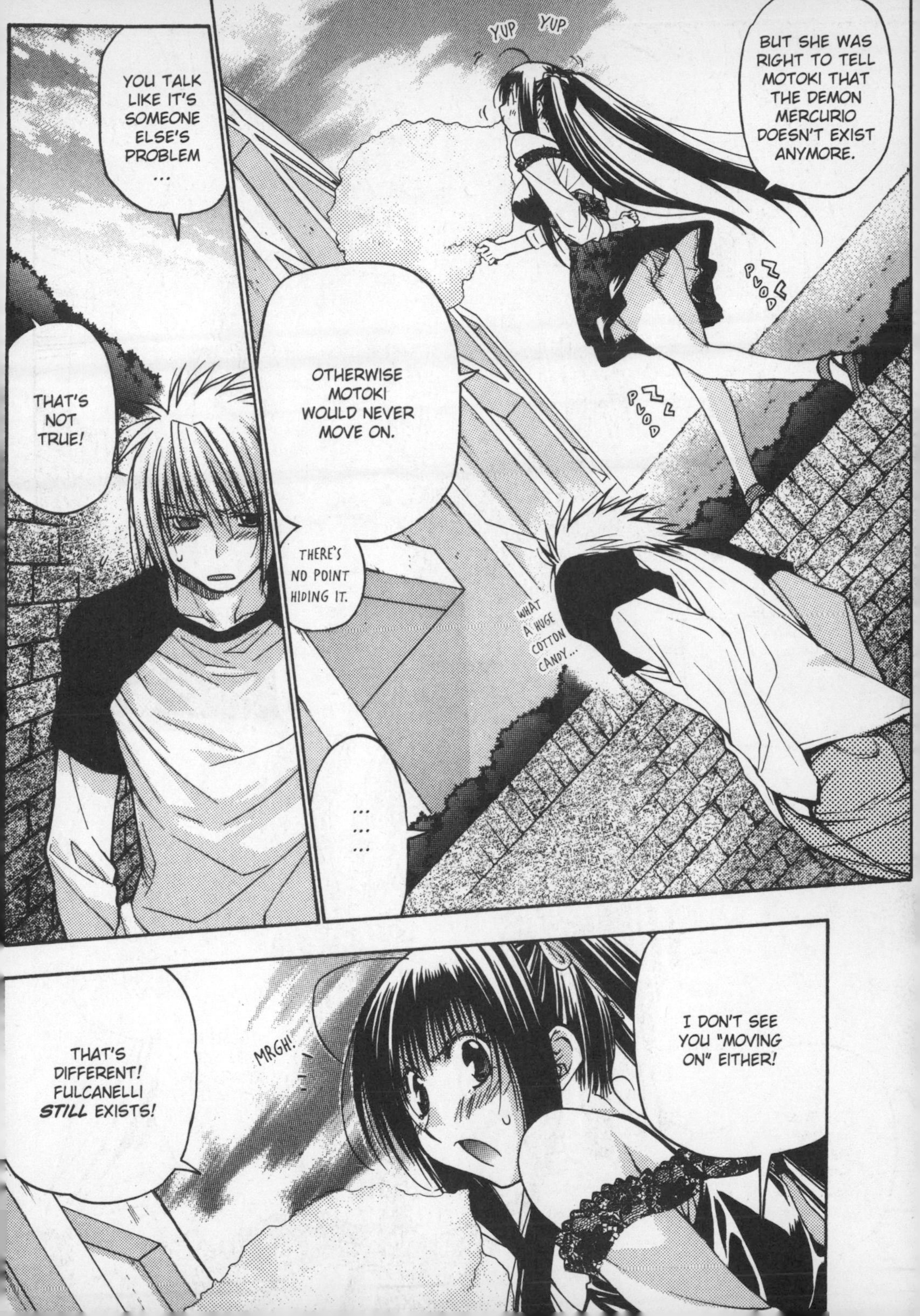
YUP YUP
BUT SHE WAS RIGHT TO TELL MOTOKI THAT THE DEMON MERCURIO DOESN'T EXIST ANYMORE.
PVOD
PVOD
OTHERWISE MOTOKI WOULD NEVER MOVE ON.
THERE'S NO POINT HIDING IT.
WHAT A HUGE COTTON CANDY...
... ...
YOU TALK LIKE IT'S SOMEONE ELSE'S PROBLEM ...
THAT'S NOT TRUE!
I DON'T SEE YOU "MOVING ON" EITHER!
MRGH!
THAT'S DIFFERENT! FULCANELLI ***STILL*** EXISTS!

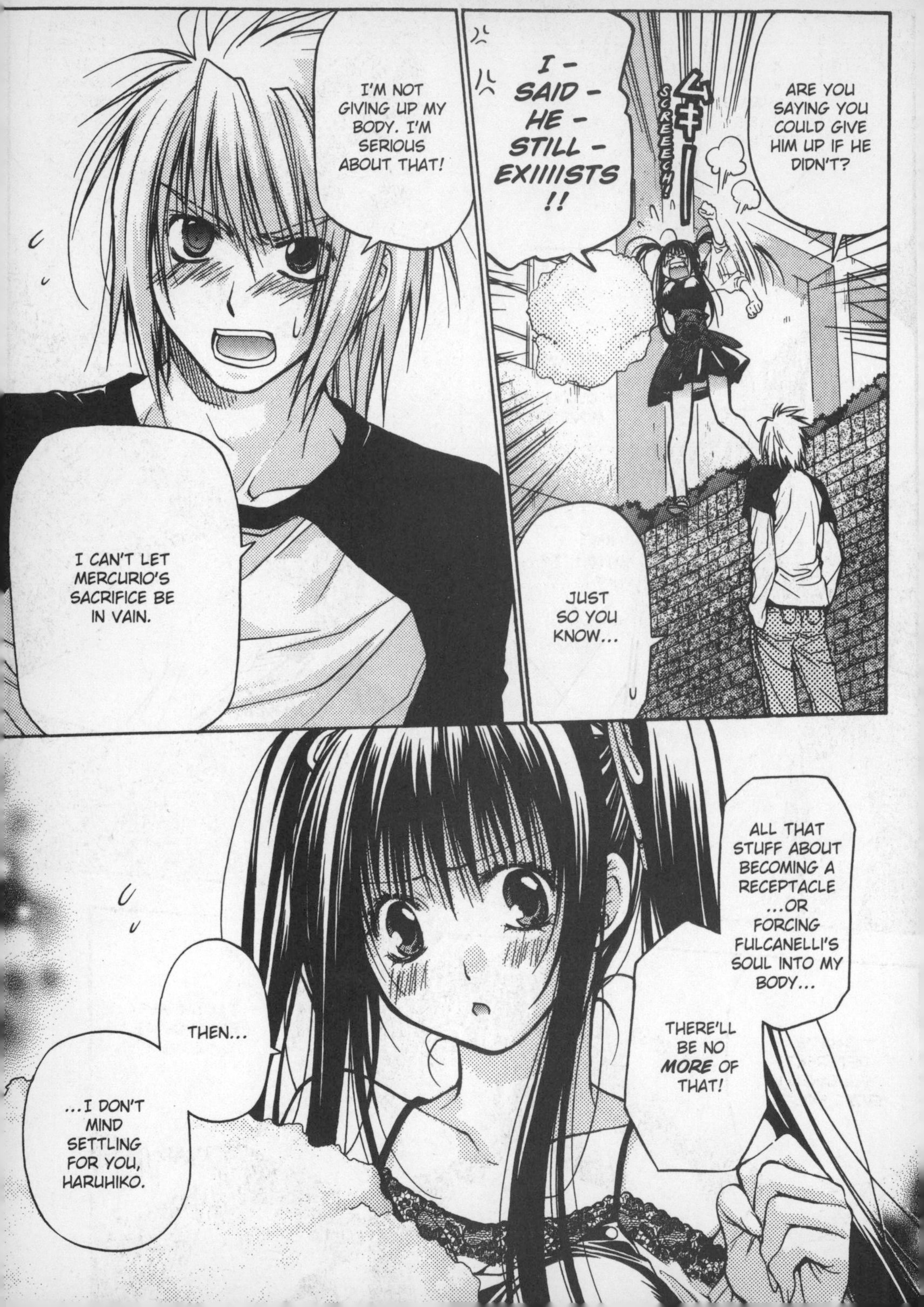
ARE YOU SAYING YOU COULD GIVE HIM UP IF HE DIDN'T?
I - SAID - HE - STILL - EXIIIISTS !!
SCREEECH!
JUST SO YOU KNOW...
I'M NOT GIVING UP MY BODY. I'M SERIOUS ABOUT THAT!
I CAN'T LET MERCURIO'S SACRIFICE BE IN VAIN.
ALL THAT STUFF ABOUT BECOMING A RECEPTACLE ...OR FORCING FULCANELLI'S SOUL INTO MY BODY...
THERE'LL BE NO MORE OF THAT!
THEN...
...I DON'T MIND SETTLING FOR YOU, HARUHIKO.

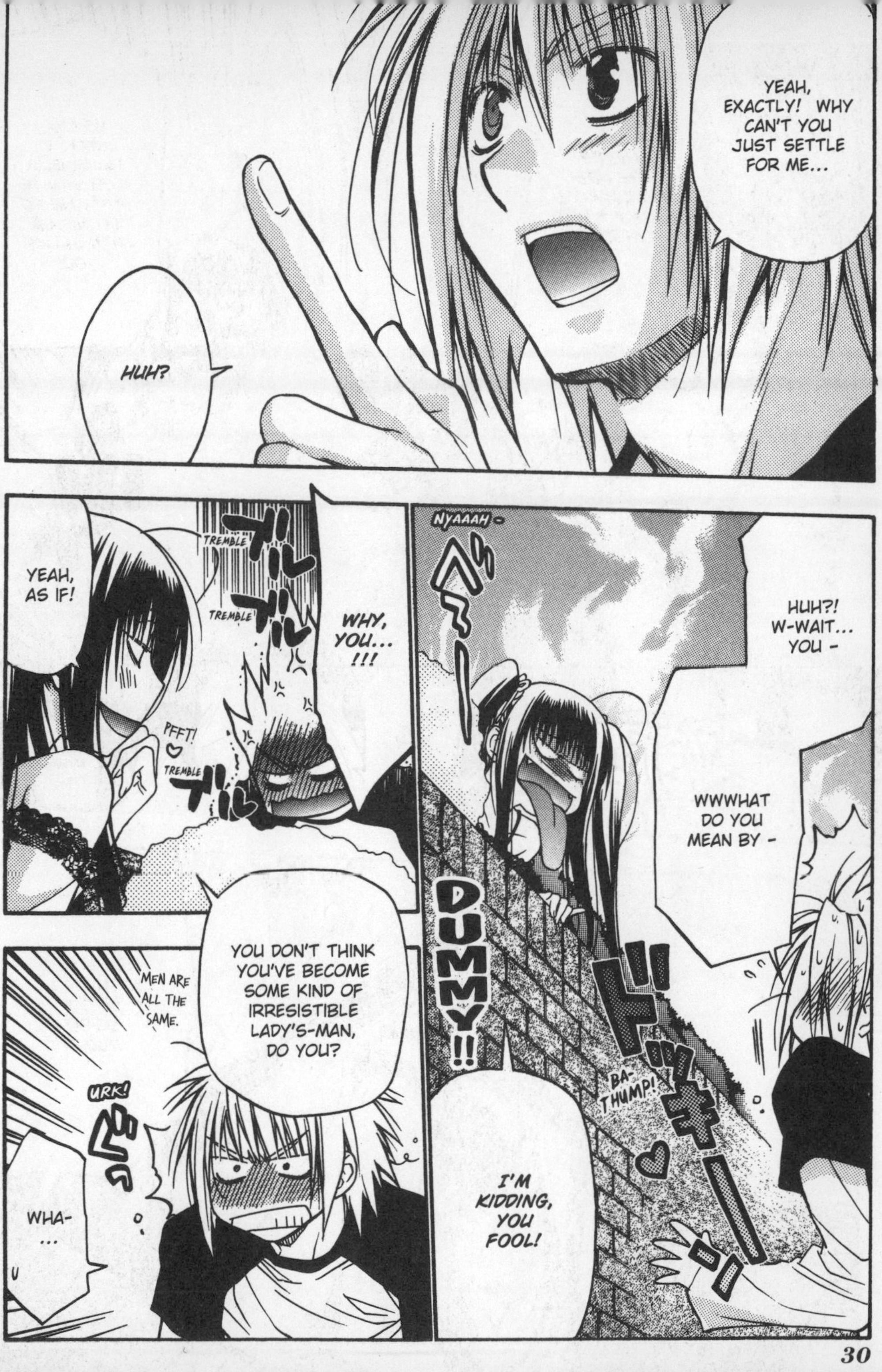
YEAH, EXACTLY! WHY CAN'T YOU JUST SETTLE FOR ME...
HUH?
HUH?! W-WAIT... YOU -
NYAAAH -
WWWHAT DO YOU MEAN BY -
DUMMY!!
BA-THUMP!
I'M KIDDING, YOU FOOL!
WHY, YOU... !!!
TREMBLE
TREMBLE
TREMBLE
YEAH, AS IF!
PFFT! ♥
YOU DON'T THINK YOU'VE BECOME SOME KIND OF IRRESISTIBLE LADY'S-MAN, DO YOU?
MEN ARE ALL THE SAME.
URK!
WHA- ...

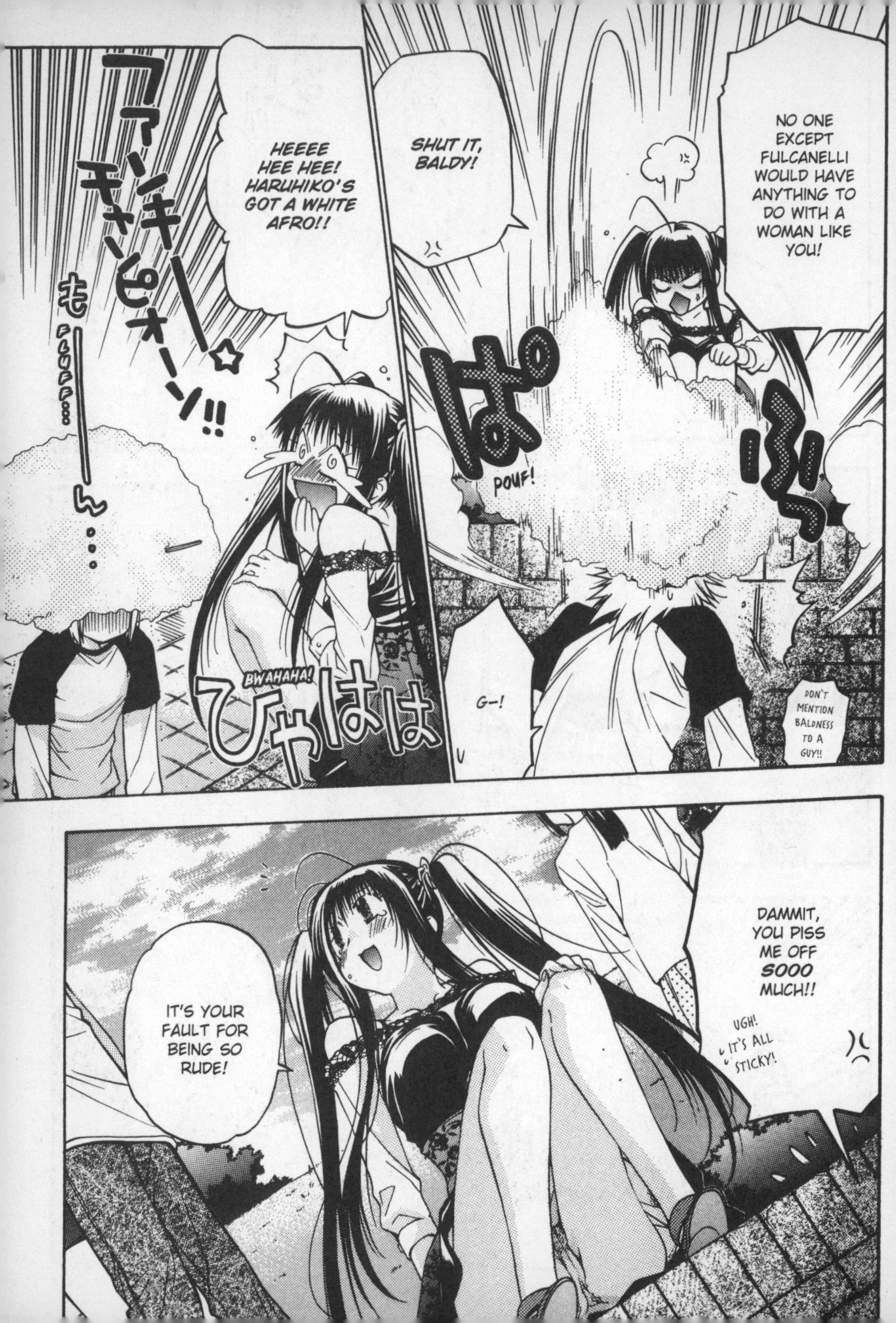
NO ONE EXCEPT FULCANELLI WOULD HAVE ANYTHING TO DO WITH A WOMAN LIKE YOU!
SHUT IT, BALDY!
ぱふ
POUF!
G-!
DON'T MENTION BALDNESS TO A GUY!!
HEEEE HEE HEE! HARUHIKO'S GOT A WHITE AFRO!!
ファンキーチャンピオーン!!☆
もーーーん…
FLUFF!!
ひゃはは
BWAHAHA!
DAMMIT, YOU PISS ME OFF SOOO MUCH!!
UGH! IT'S ALL STICKY!
IT'S YOUR FAULT FOR BEING SO RUDE!

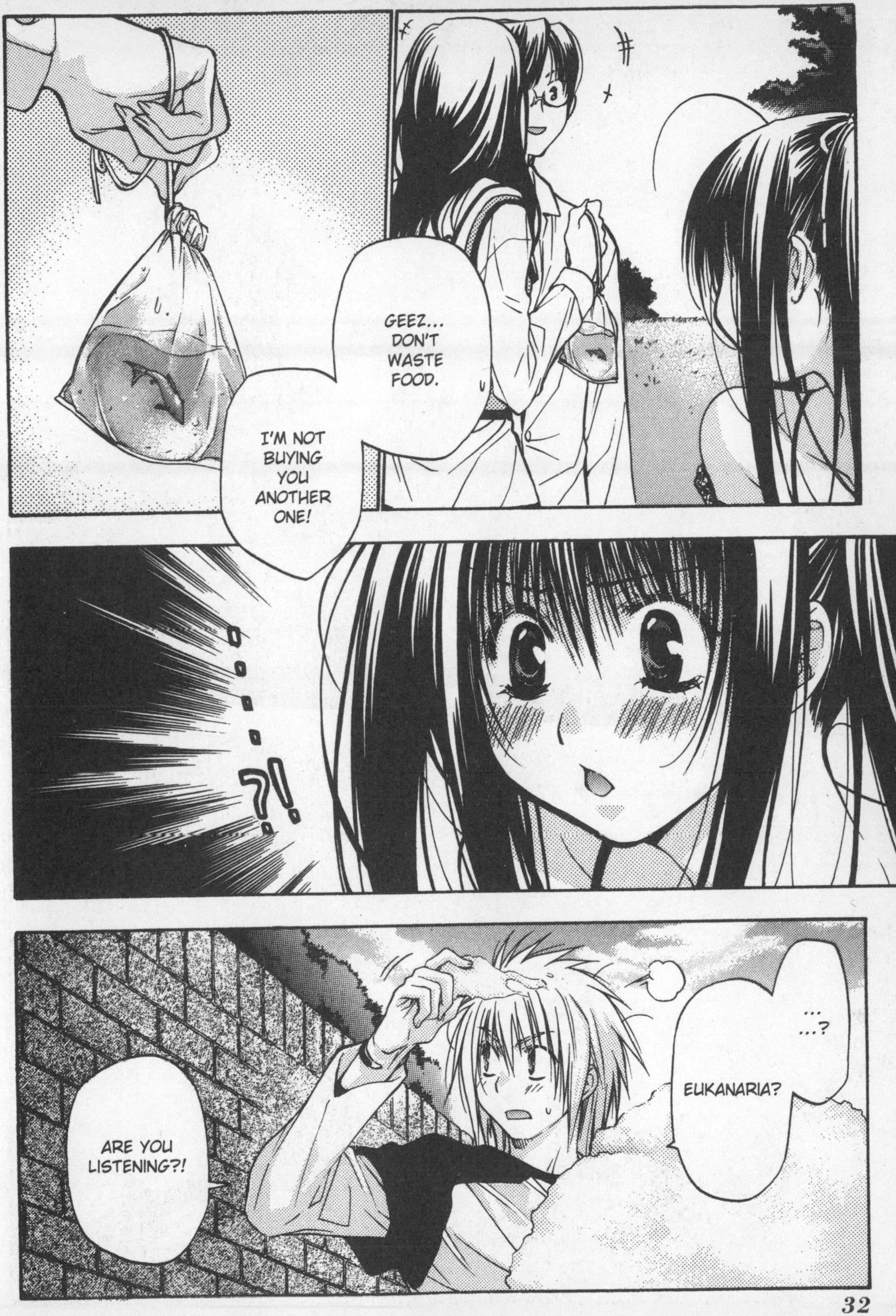
GEEZ... DON'T WASTE FOOD.
I'M NOT BUYING YOU ANOTHER ONE!
......?!
...
...?
EUKANARIA?
ARE YOU LISTENING?!

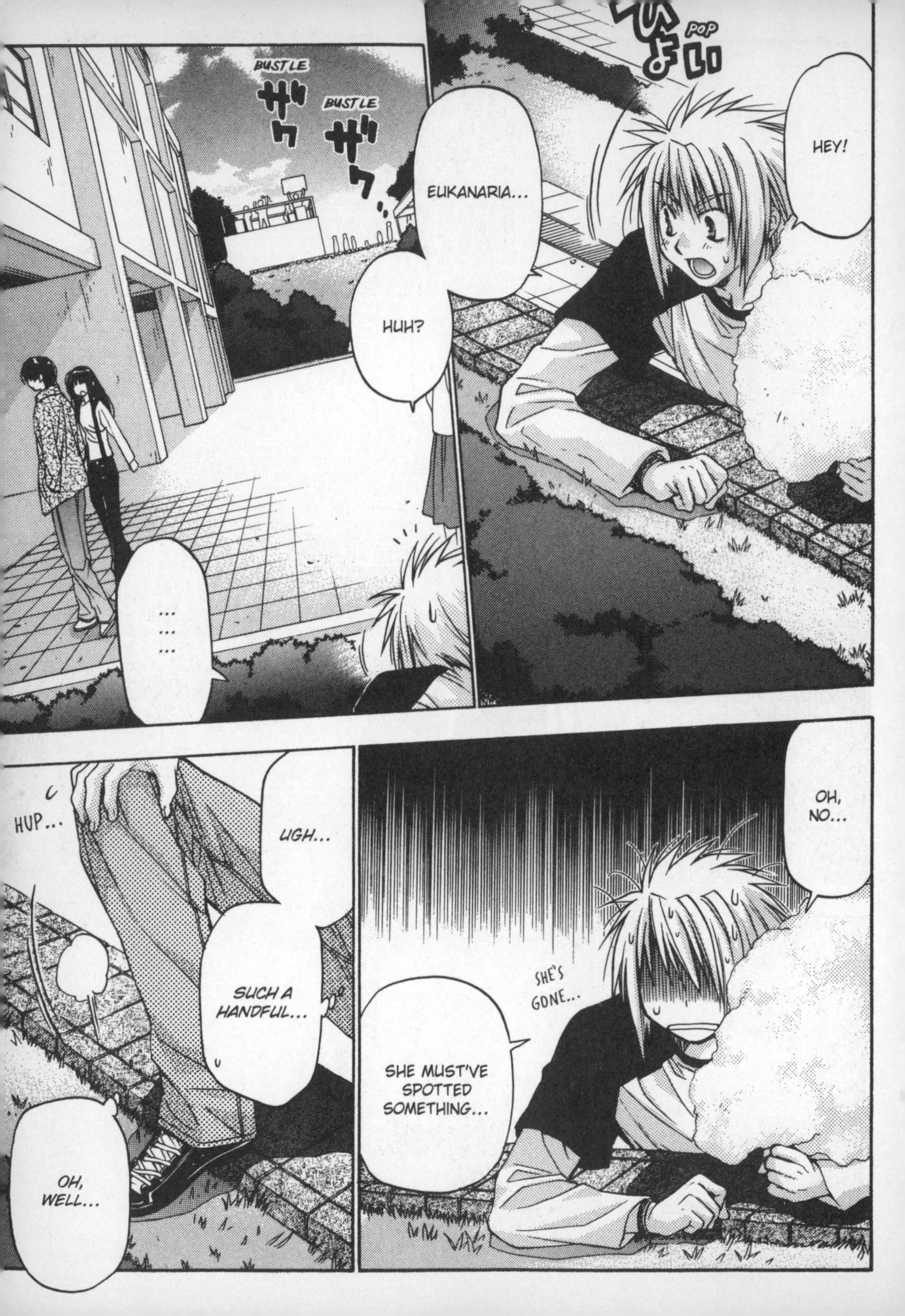
POP
HEY!
BUSTLE
BUSTLE
EUKANARIA...
HUH?
...
...
...
OH, NO...
SHE'S GONE...
SHE MUST'VE SPOTTED SOMETHING...
UGH...
HUP...
SUCH A HANDFUL...
OH, WELL...

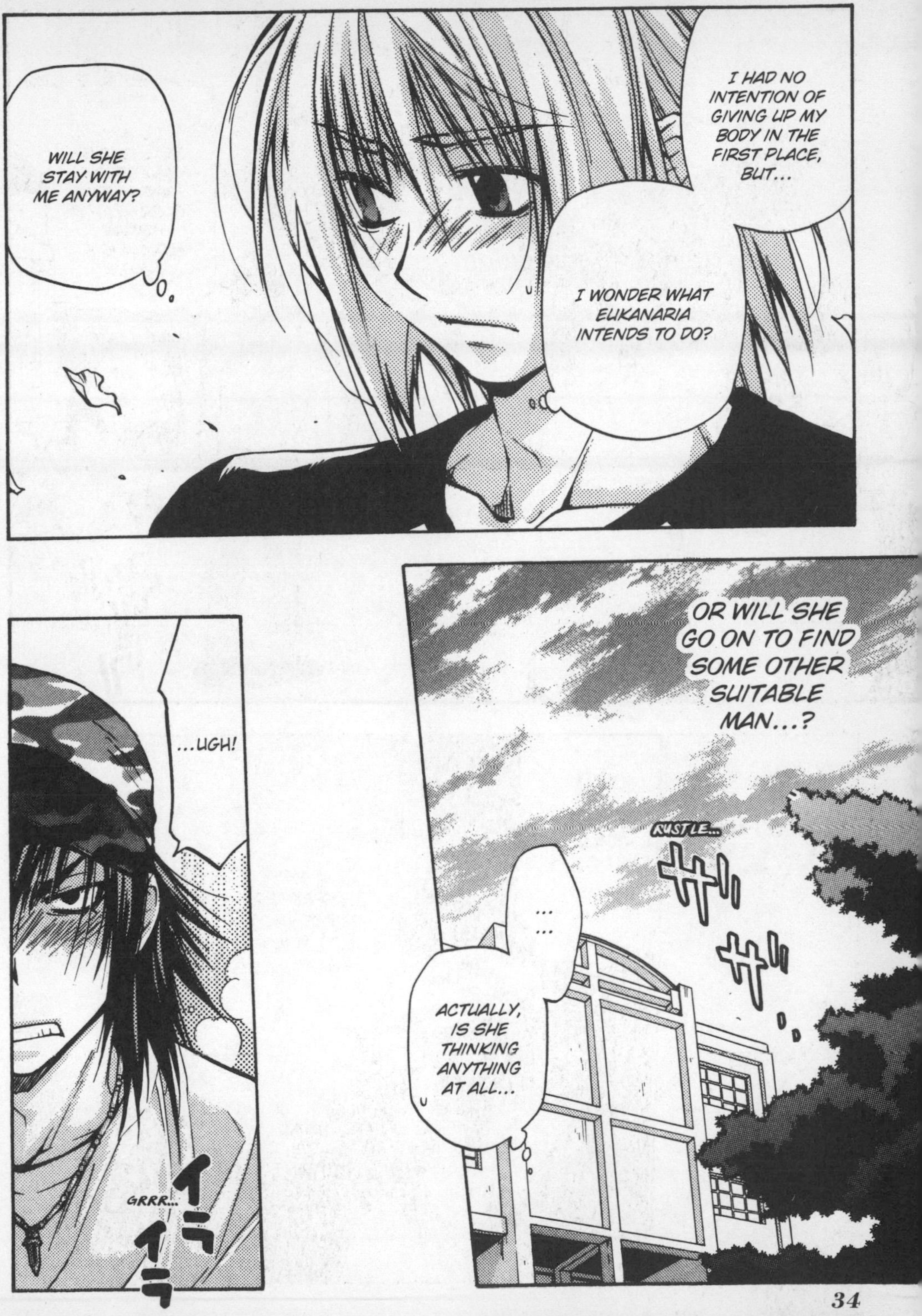
I HAD NO INTENTION OF GIVING UP MY BODY IN THE FIRST PLACE, BUT...
I WONDER WHAT EUKANARIA INTENDS TO DO?
WILL SHE STAY WITH ME ANYWAY?
OR WILL SHE GO ON TO FIND SOME OTHER SUITABLE MAN...?
RUSTLE...
......
ACTUALLY, IS SHE THINKING ANYTHING AT ALL...
...UGH!
GRRR...

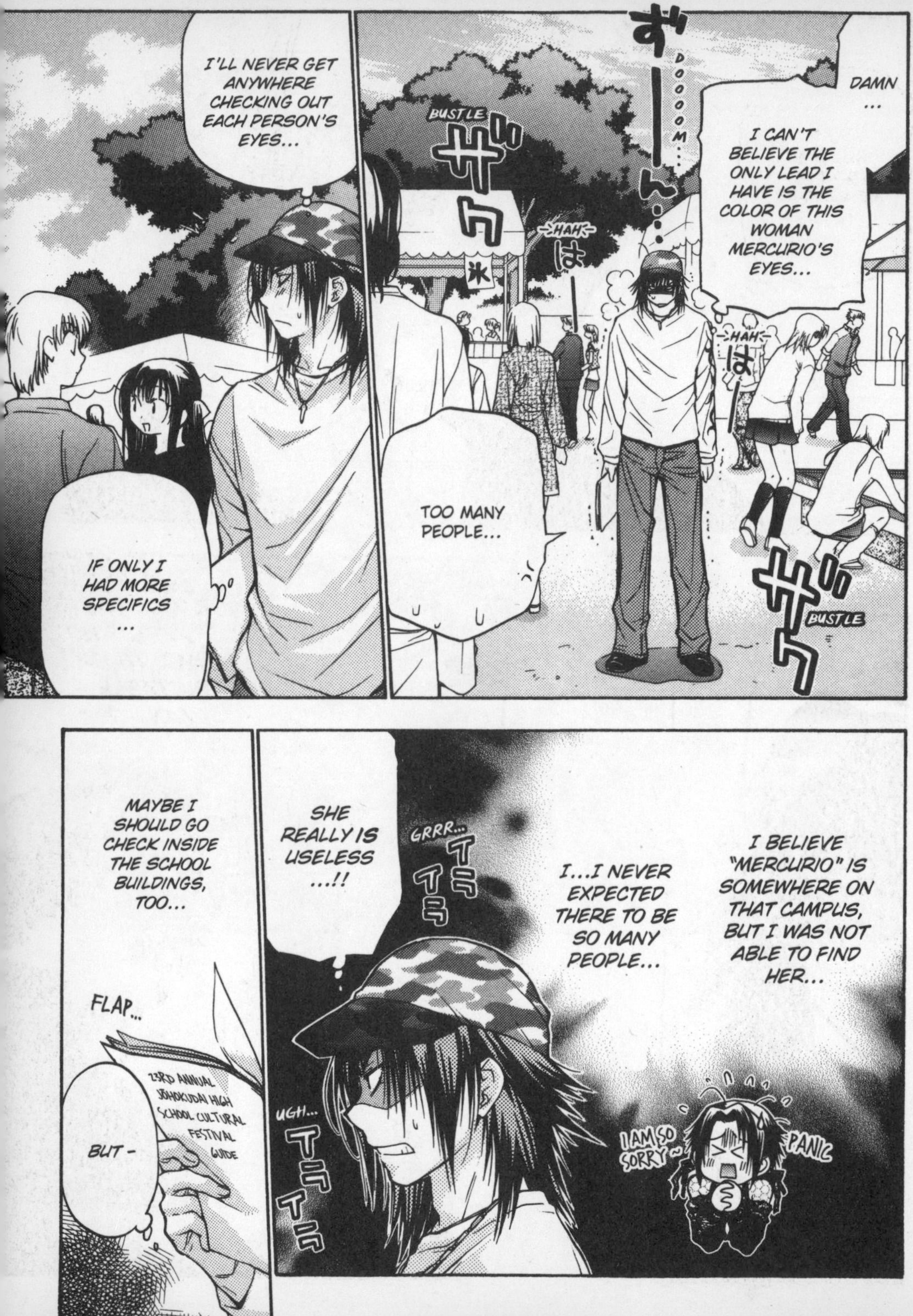
ずーん…
DOOOOOM...
DAMN ...
I CAN'T BELIEVE THE ONLY LEAD I HAVE IS THE COLOR OF THIS WOMAN MERCURIO'S EYES...
BUSTLE
ザワ
HAH
は
TOO MANY PEOPLE...
HAH
は
ザワ
BUSTLE
I'LL NEVER GET ANYWHERE CHECKING OUT EACH PERSON'S EYES...
IF ONLY I HAD MORE SPECIFICS ...
I BELIEVE "MERCURIO" IS SOMEWHERE ON THAT CAMPUS, BUT I WAS NOT ABLE TO FIND HER...
I...I NEVER EXPECTED THERE TO BE SO MANY PEOPLE...
SHE REALLY IS USELESS ...!!
GRRR...
イライラ
PANIC
I AM SO SORRY~
UGH...
イライラ
MAYBE I SHOULD GO CHECK INSIDE THE SCHOOL BUILDINGS, TOO...
FLAP...
23RD ANNUAL JŌHOKUDAI HIGH SCHOOL CULTURAL FESTIVAL GUIDE
BUT -

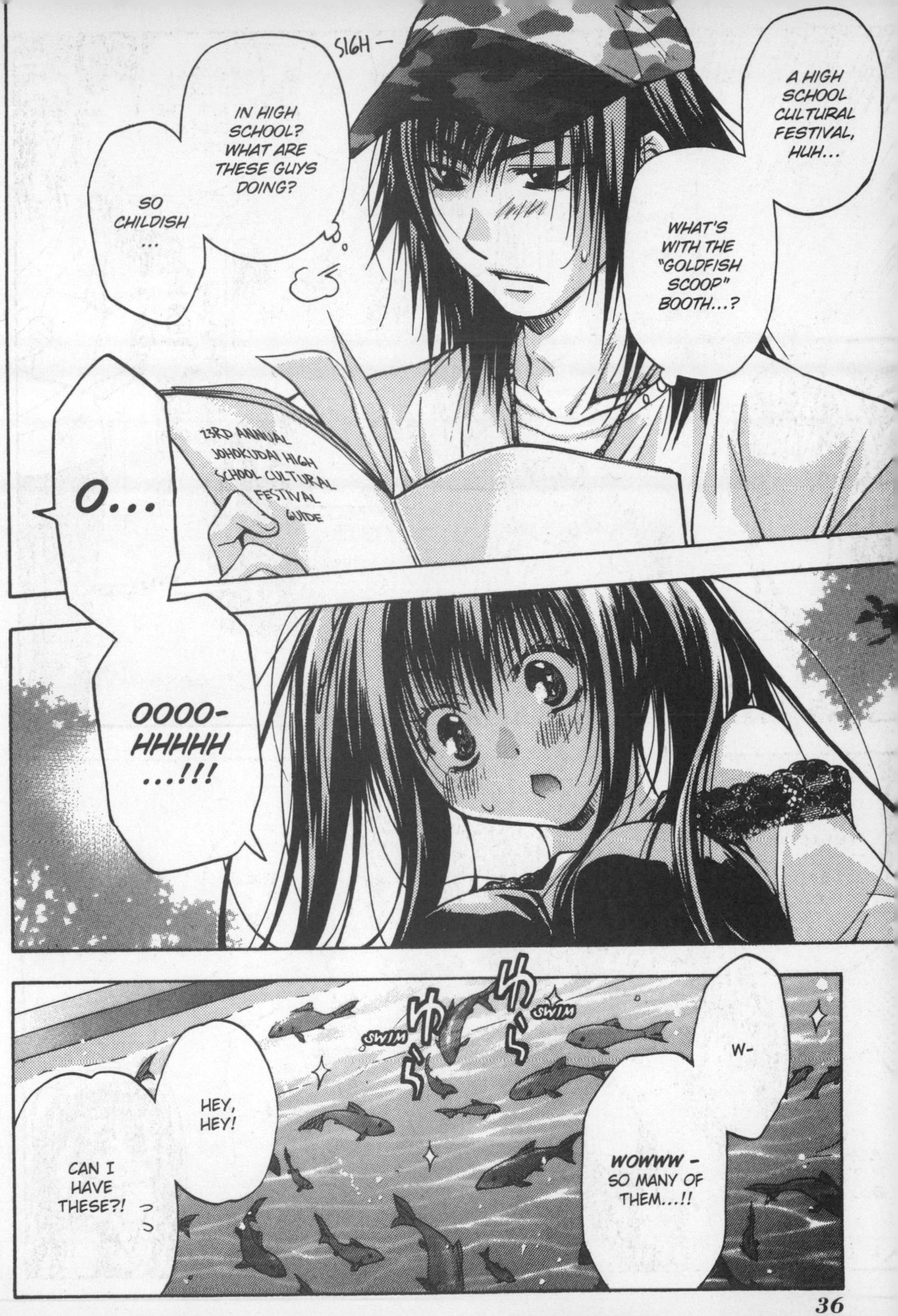

A HIGH SCHOOL CULTURAL FESTIVAL, HUH...
WHAT'S WITH THE "GOLDFISH SCOOP" BOOTH...?
SIGH—
IN HIGH SCHOOL? WHAT ARE THESE GUYS DOING?
SO CHILDISH ...
23RD ANNUAL JOHOKUDAI HIGH SCHOOL CULTURAL FESTIVAL GUIDE
O...
OOOO-HHHHH ...!!!
W-
WOWWW - SO MANY OF THEM...!!
SWIM
SWIM
HEY, HEY!
CAN I HAVE THESE?!

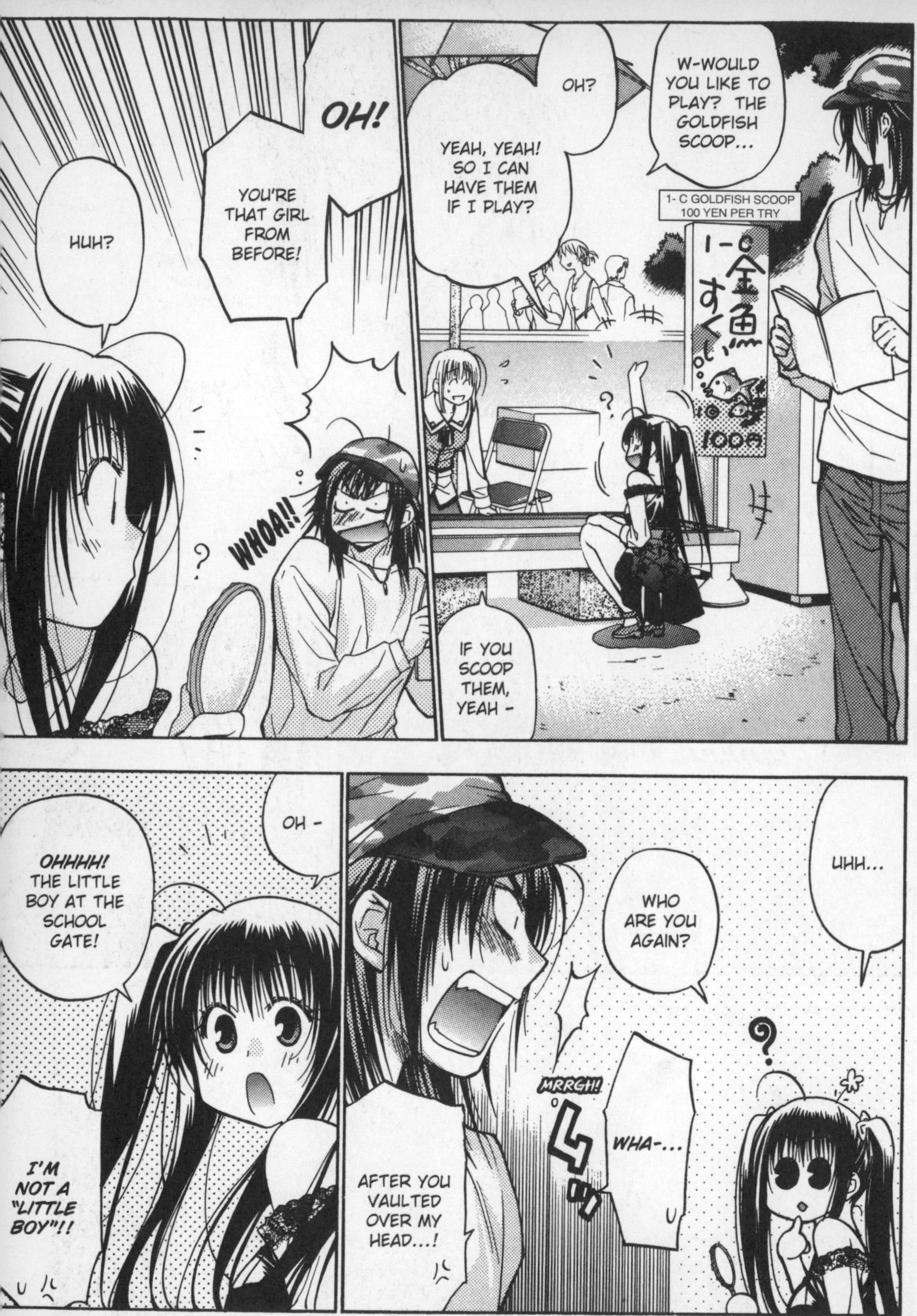
W-WOULD YOU LIKE TO PLAY? THE GOLDFISH SCOOP...
1- C GOLDFISH SCOOP 100 YEN PER TRY
1-C 金魚すくい 100円
OH?
YEAH, YEAH! SO I CAN HAVE THEM IF I PLAY?
IF YOU SCOOP THEM, YEAH -
OH!
YOU'RE THAT GIRL FROM BEFORE!
WHOA!!
HUH?
UHH...
WHO ARE YOU AGAIN?
MRRGH!
WHA-...
AFTER YOU VAULTED OVER MY HEAD...!
OH -
OHHHH! THE LITTLE BOY AT THE SCHOOL GATE!
I'M NOT A "LITTLE BOY"!!

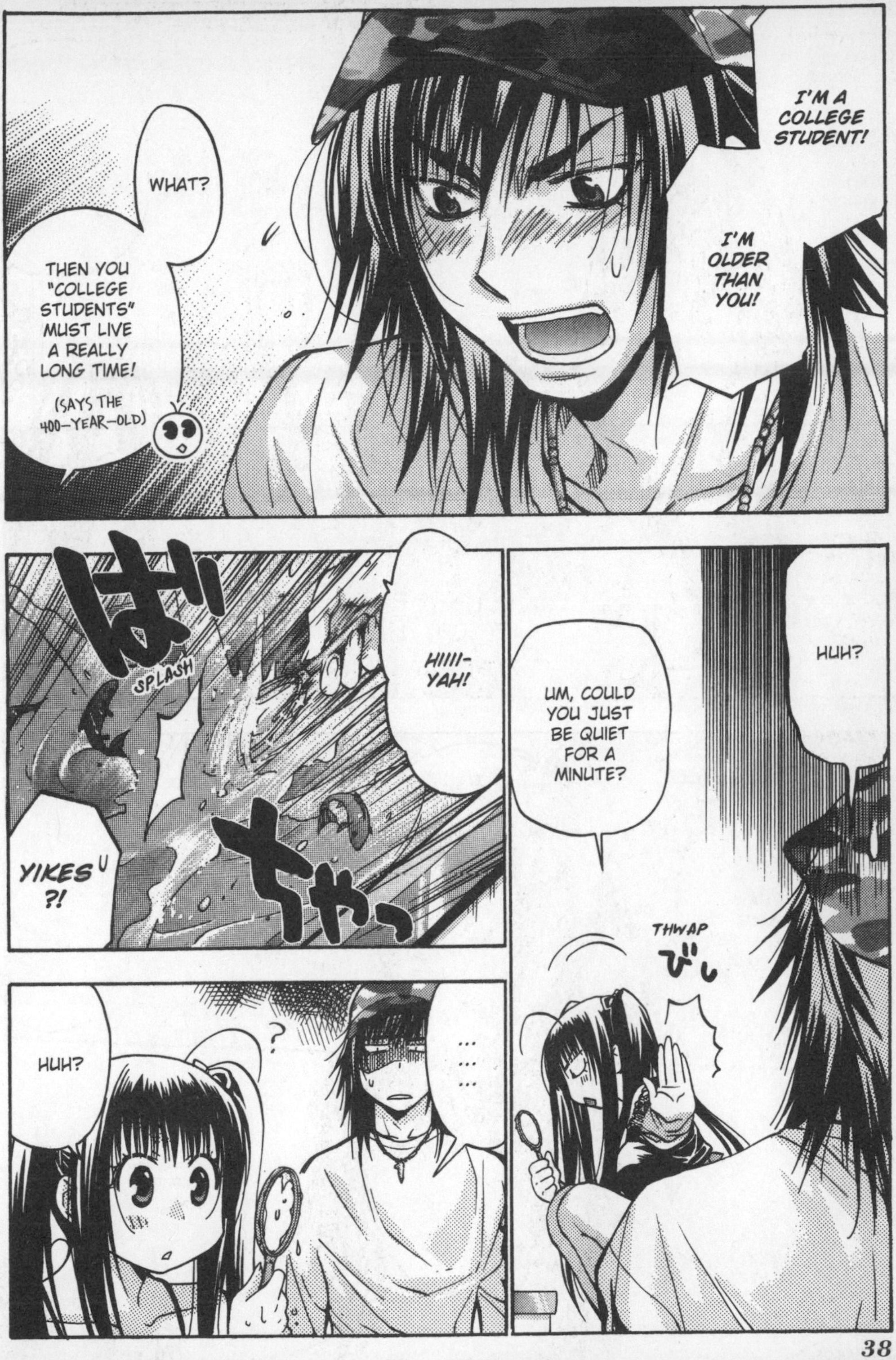
I'M A COLLEGE STUDENT!
I'M OLDER THAN YOU!
WHAT?
THEN YOU "COLLEGE STUDENTS" MUST LIVE A REALLY LONG TIME!
(SAYS THE 400-YEAR-OLD)
HUH?
UM, COULD YOU JUST BE QUIET FOR A MINUTE?
THWAP
びし
HIIII-YAH!
ばしゃっ
SPLASH
YIKES?!
...
...
...
HUH?

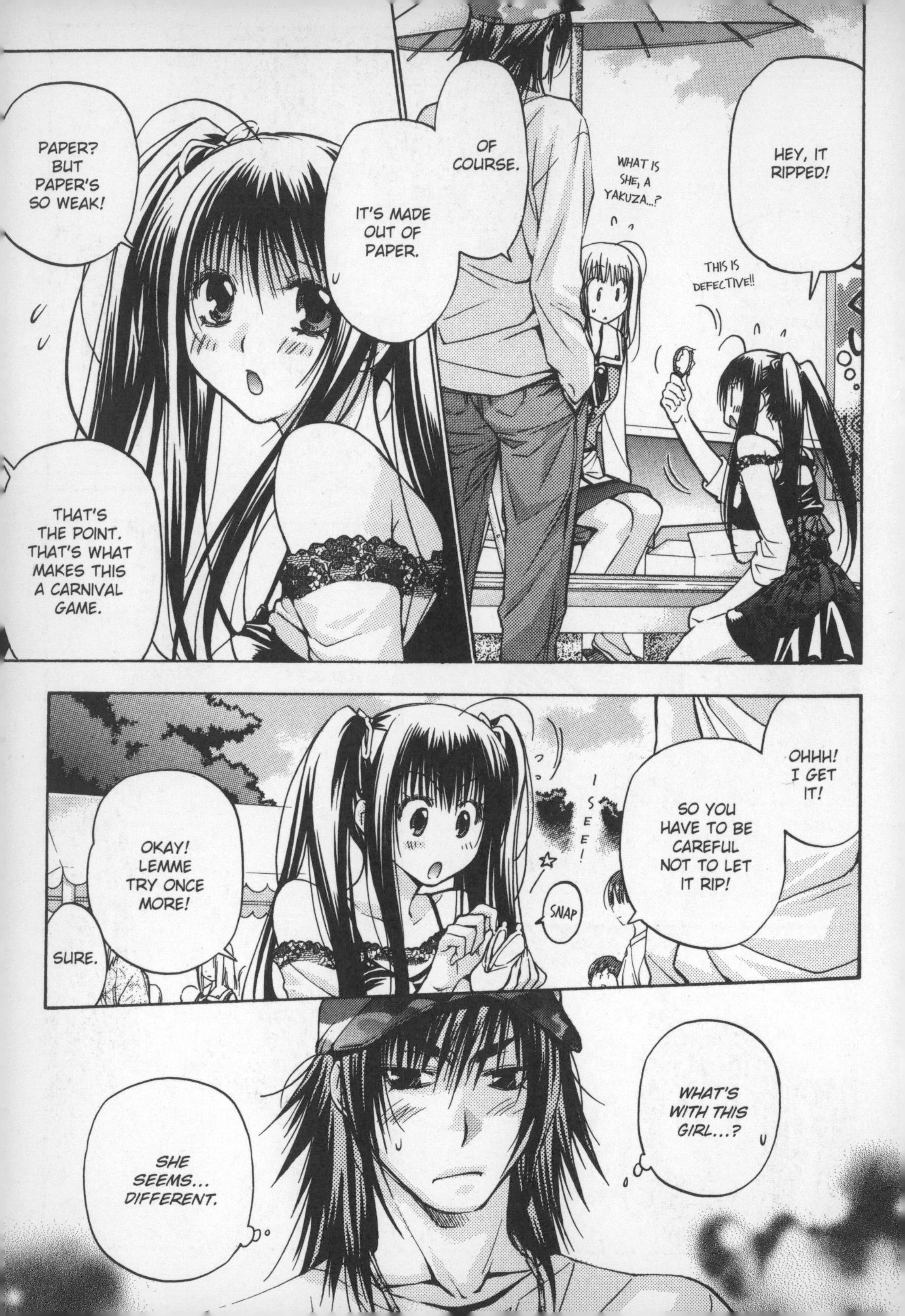
HEY, IT RIPPED!
THIS IS DEFECTIVE!!
WHAT IS SHE, A YAKUZA...?
OF COURSE.
IT'S MADE OUT OF PAPER.
PAPER? BUT PAPER'S SO WEAK!
THAT'S THE POINT. THAT'S WHAT MAKES THIS A CARNIVAL GAME.
OHHH! I GET IT!
SO YOU HAVE TO BE CAREFUL NOT TO LET IT RIP!
I SEE!
SNAP
OKAY! LEMME TRY ONCE MORE!
SURE.
WHAT'S WITH THIS GIRL...?
SHE SEEMS... DIFFERENT.

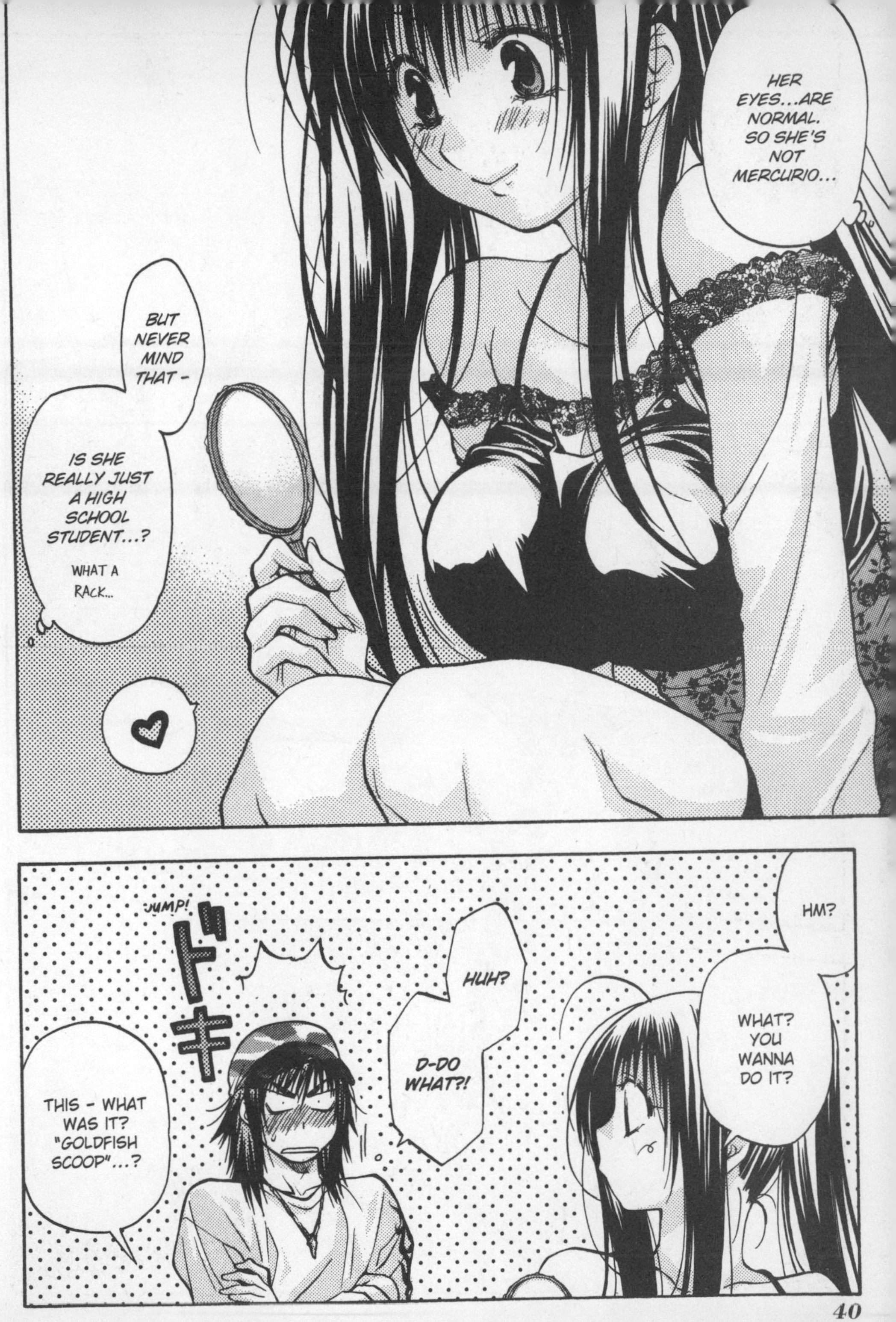
HER EYES...ARE NORMAL. SO SHE'S NOT MERCURIO...
BUT NEVER MIND THAT -
IS SHE REALLY JUST A HIGH SCHOOL STUDENT...?
WHAT A RACK...
♥
THIS - WHAT WAS IT? "GOLDFISH SCOOP"...?
HM?
WHAT? YOU WANNA DO IT?
JUMP!
HUH?
D-DO WHAT?!

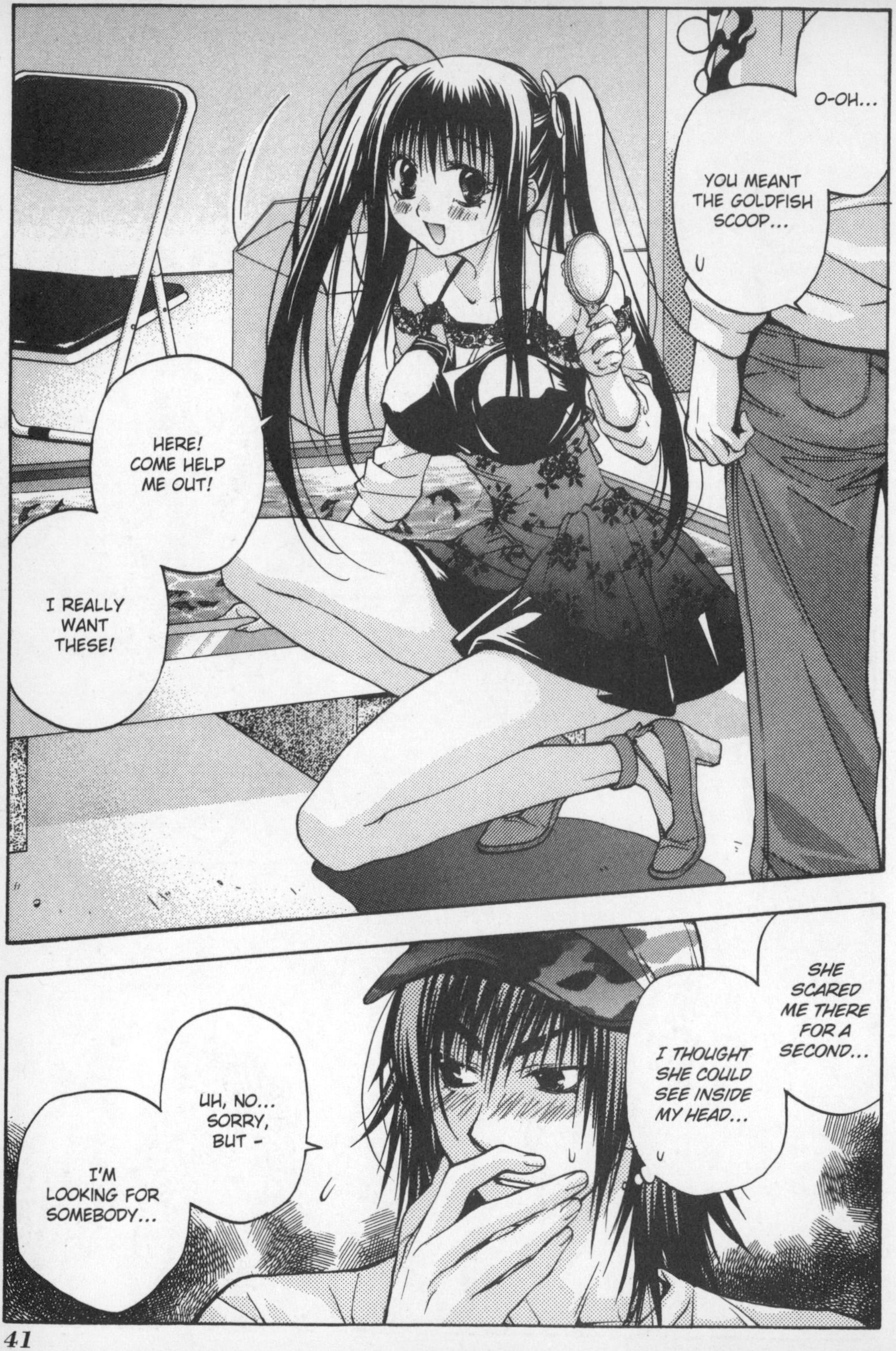
O-OH...
YOU MEANT THE GOLDFISH SCOOP...
HERE! COME HELP ME OUT!
I REALLY WANT THESE!
SHE SCARED ME THERE FOR A SECOND...
I THOUGHT SHE COULD SEE INSIDE MY HEAD...
UH, NO... SORRY, BUT -
I'M LOOKING FOR SOMEBODY...

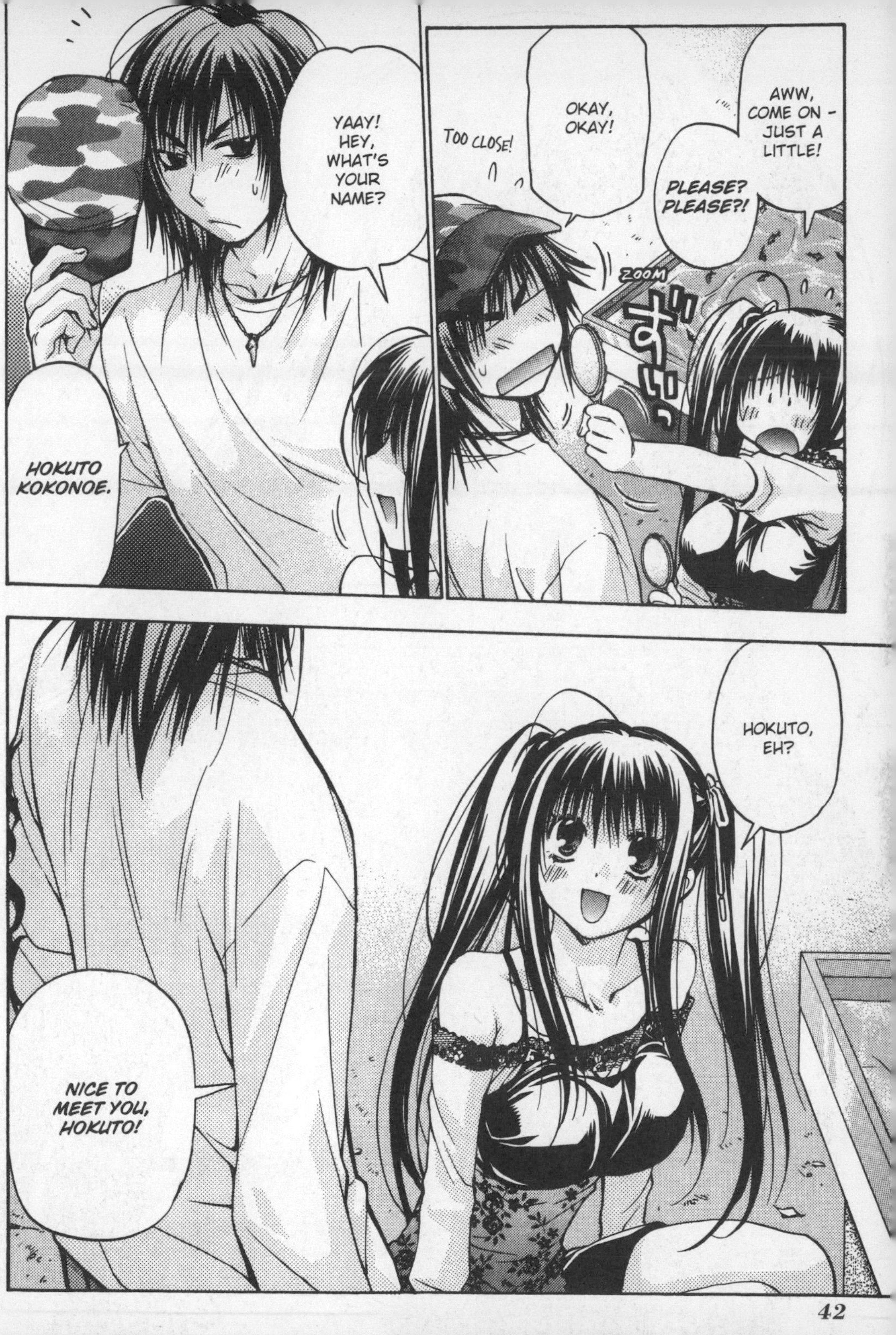
AWW, COME ON - JUST A LITTLE!
OKAY, OKAY!
PLEASE? PLEASE?!
TOO CLOSE!
ZOOM
YAAY! HEY, WHAT'S YOUR NAME?
HOKUTO KOKONOE.
HOKUTO, EH?
NICE TO MEET YOU, HOKUTO!

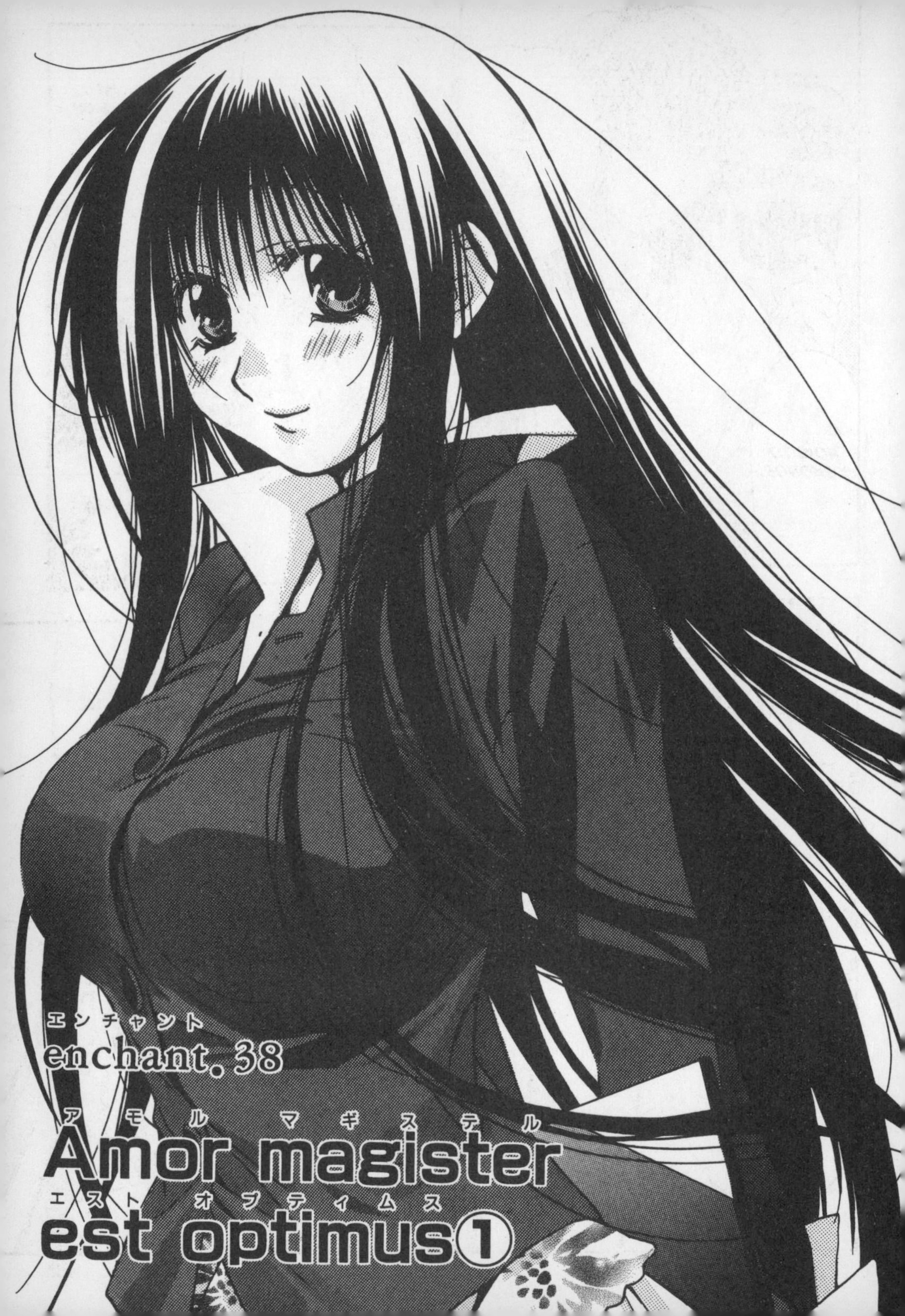
エンチャント
enchant. 38
アモル マギステル
Amor magister
エスト オプティムス
est optimus①

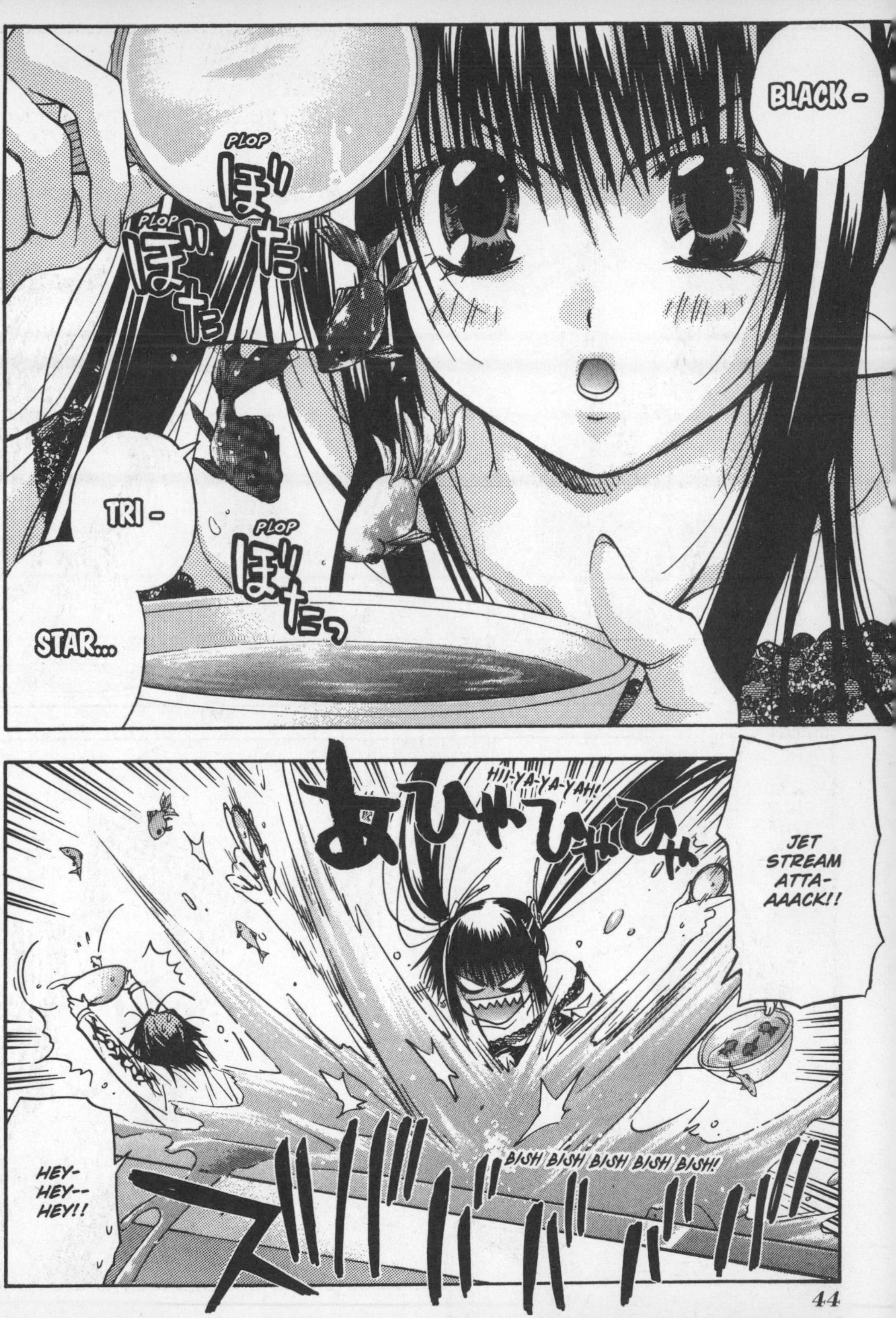

BLACK -
PLOP
ぼたっ
PLOP
ぼたっ
TRI -
PLOP
ぼたっ
STAR...
JET STREAM ATTA-AAACK!!
HII-YA-YA-YAH!
あひゃひゃひゃ
BISH BISH BISH BISH BISH!
ズバババババ
HEY-HEY--HEY!!

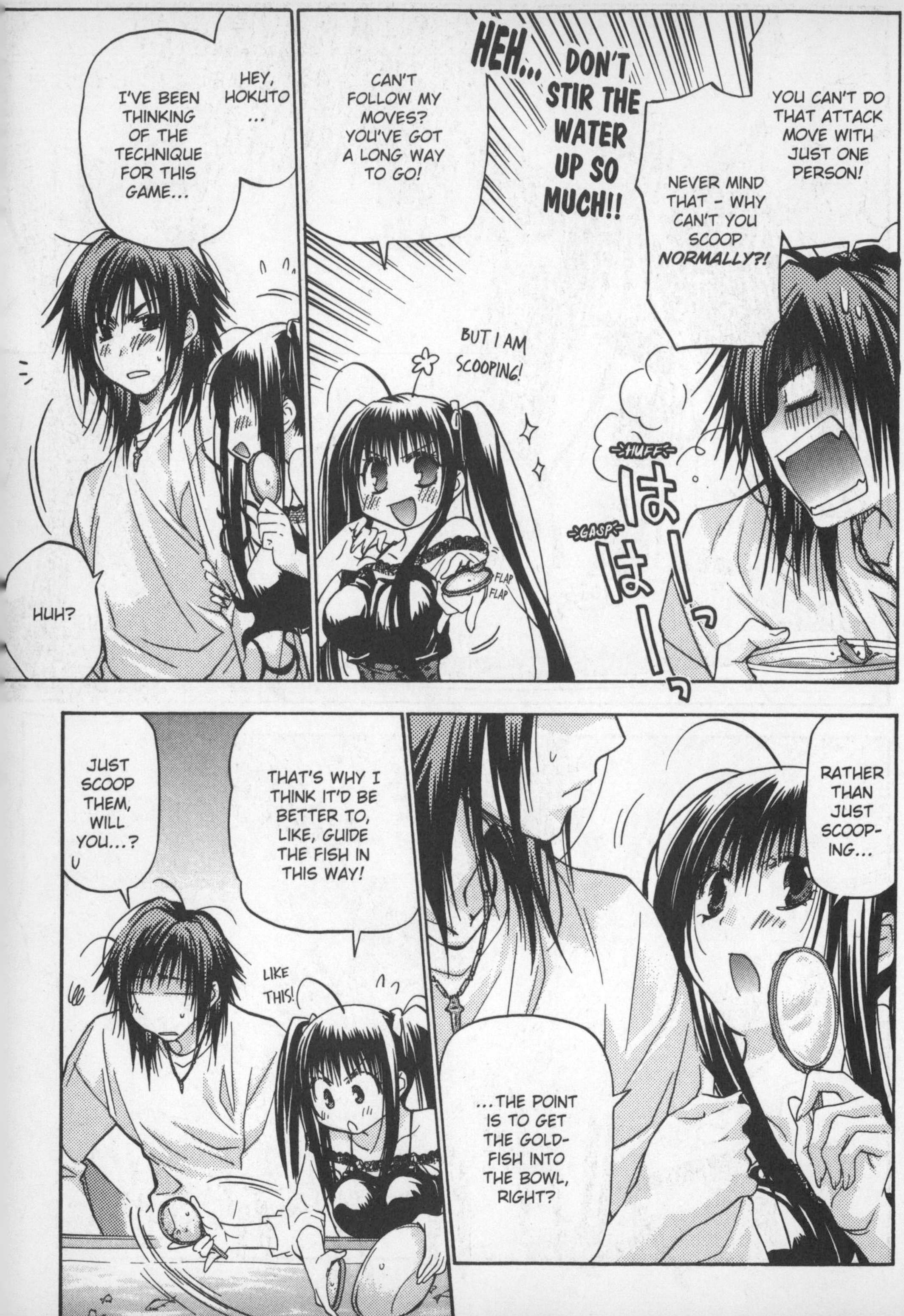
HEH... DON'T STIR THE WATER UP SO MUCH!!
YOU CAN'T DO THAT ATTACK MOVE WITH JUST ONE PERSON!
NEVER MIND THAT - WHY CAN'T YOU SCOOP *NORMALLY?!*
HUFF
はーっ
GASP
はーっ
CAN'T FOLLOW MY MOVES? YOU'VE GOT A LONG WAY TO GO!
BUT I AM SCOOPING!
FLAP FLAP
HEY, HOKUTO...
I'VE BEEN THINKING OF THE TECHNIQUE FOR THIS GAME...
HUH?
RATHER THAN JUST SCOOP-ING...
...THE POINT IS TO GET THE GOLD-FISH INTO THE BOWL, RIGHT?
THAT'S WHY I THINK IT'D BE BETTER TO, LIKE, GUIDE THE FISH IN THIS WAY!
LIKE THIS!
JUST SCOOP THEM, WILL YOU...?

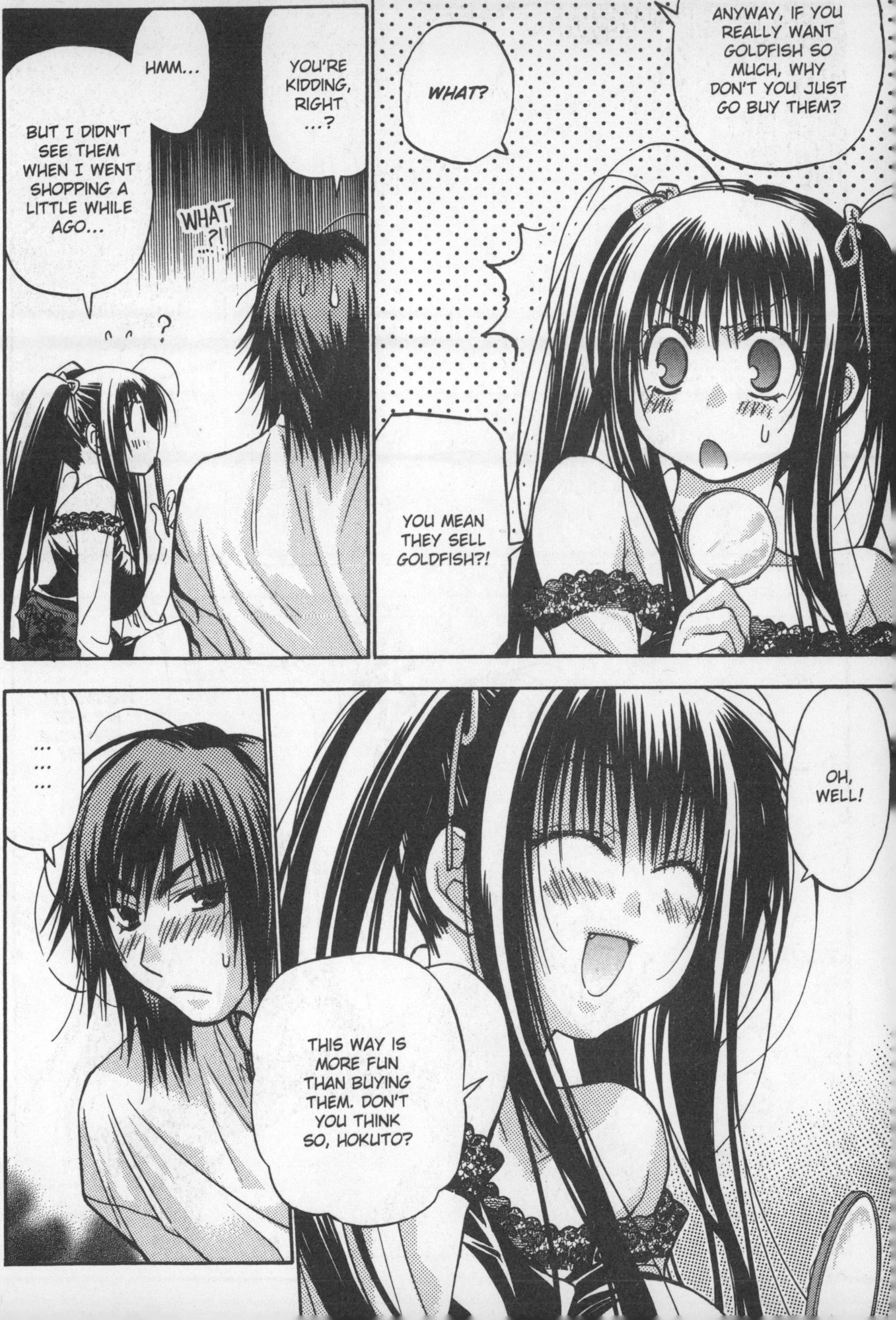
ANYWAY, IF YOU REALLY WANT GOLDFISH SO MUCH, WHY DON'T YOU JUST GO BUY THEM?
WHAT?
YOU MEAN THEY SELL GOLDFISH?!
YOU'RE KIDDING, RIGHT ...?
HMM...
BUT I DIDN'T SEE THEM WHEN I WENT SHOPPING A LITTLE WHILE AGO...
WHAT ?!
...
?
OH, WELL!
THIS WAY IS MORE FUN THAN BUYING THEM. DON'T YOU THINK SO, HOKUTO?
... ...

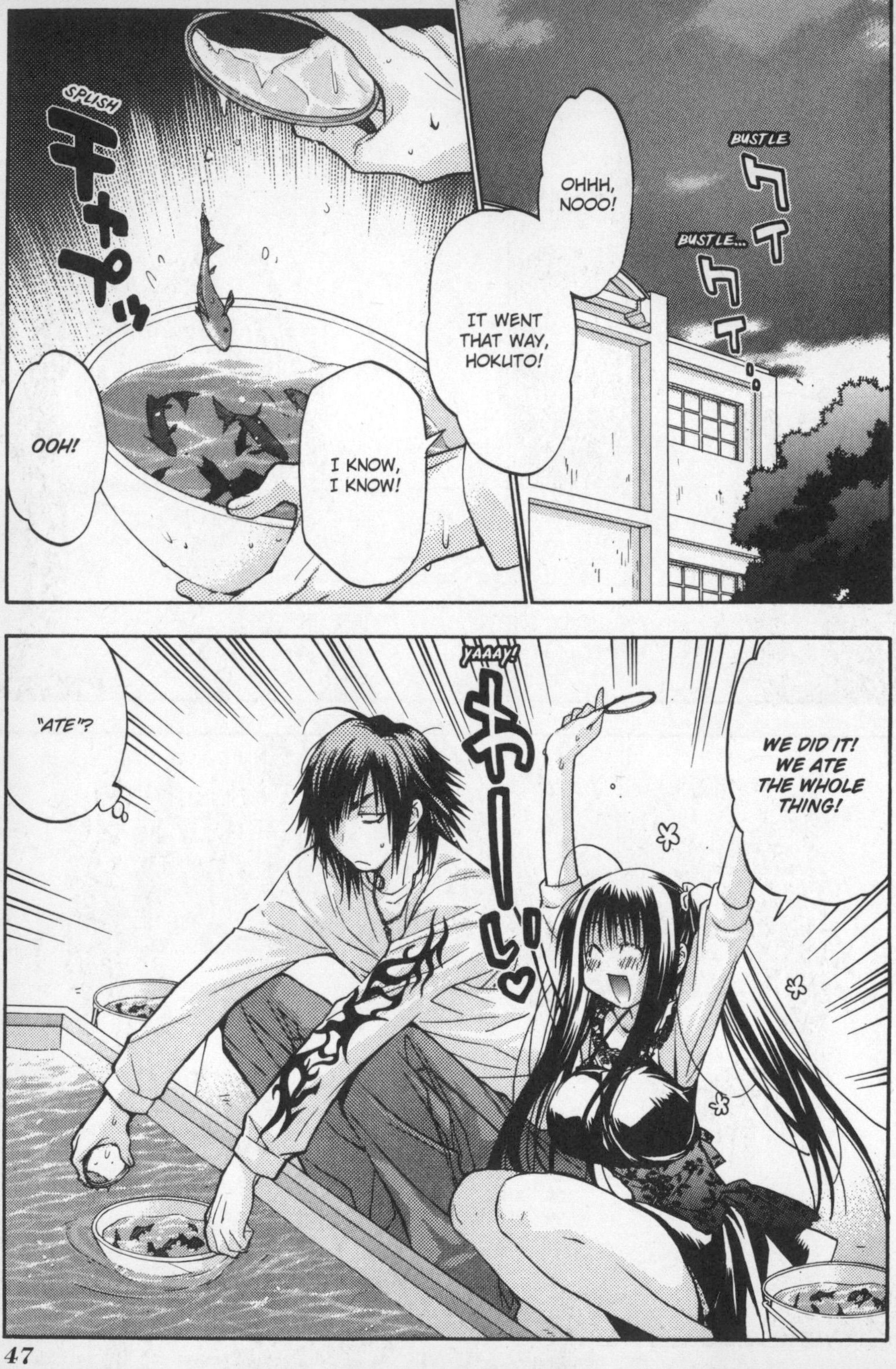
BUSTLE
BUSTLE...
OHHH, NOOO!
IT WENT THAT WAY, HOKUTO!
SPLISH
I KNOW, I KNOW!
OOH!
WE DID IT! WE ATE THE WHOLE THING!
YAAAY!
"ATE"?

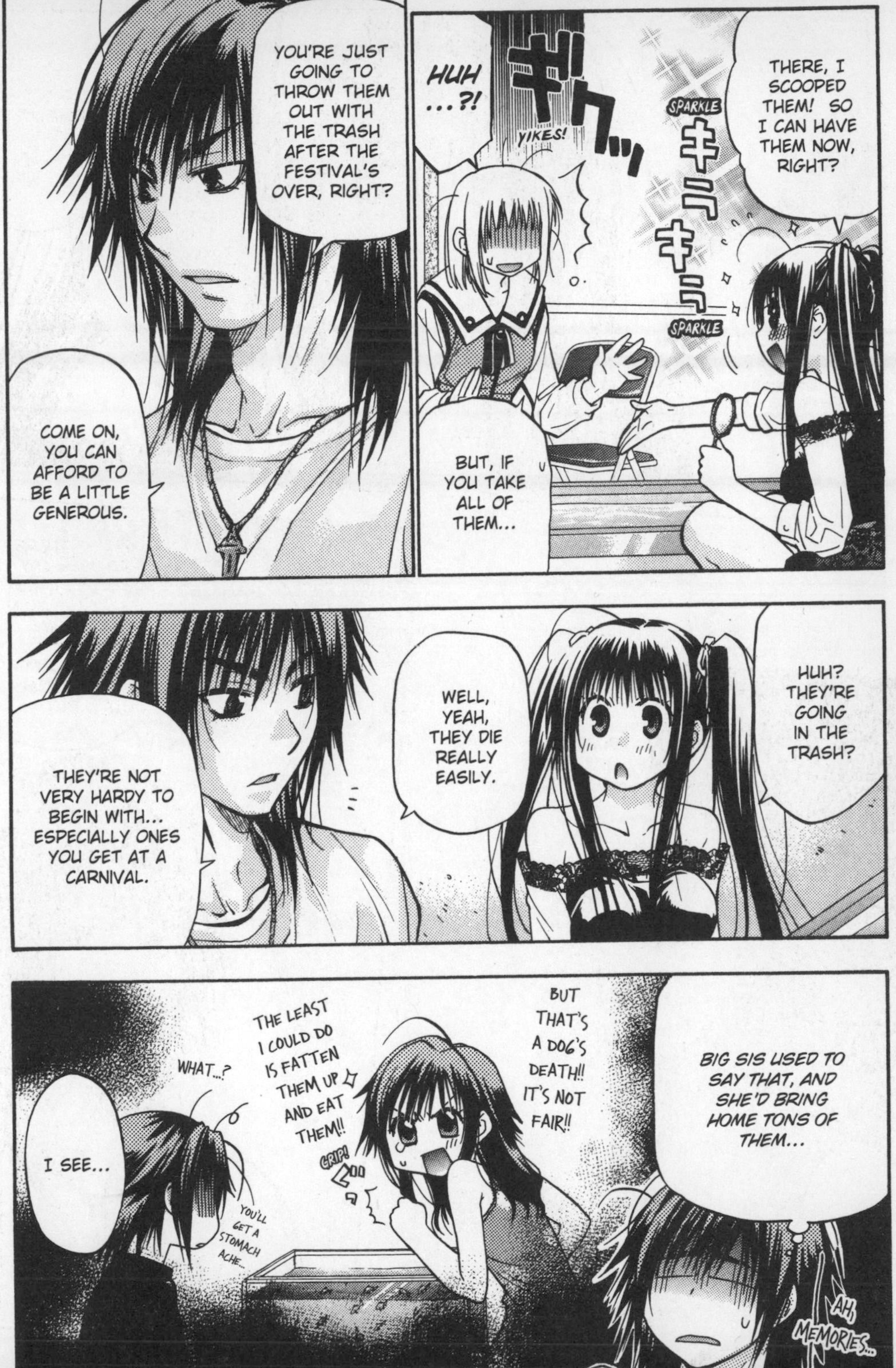
THERE, I SCOOPED THEM! SO I CAN HAVE THEM NOW, RIGHT?
SPARKLE
キラキラ
SPARKLE
HUH ...?!
ギクッ
YIKES!
BUT, IF YOU TAKE ALL OF THEM...
YOU'RE JUST GOING TO THROW THEM OUT WITH THE TRASH AFTER THE FESTIVAL'S OVER, RIGHT?
COME ON, YOU CAN AFFORD TO BE A LITTLE GENEROUS.
HUH? THEY'RE GOING IN THE TRASH?
WELL, YEAH, THEY DIE REALLY EASILY.
THEY'RE NOT VERY HARDY TO BEGIN WITH... ESPECIALLY ONES YOU GET AT A CARNIVAL.
BIG SIS USED TO SAY THAT, AND SHE'D BRING HOME TONS OF THEM...
AH, MEMORIES...
BUT THAT'S A DOG'S DEATH!! IT'S NOT FAIR!!
THE LEAST I COULD DO IS FATTEN THEM UP AND EAT THEM!!
GRIP!
WHAT...?
I SEE...
YOU'LL GET A STOMACH ACHE...

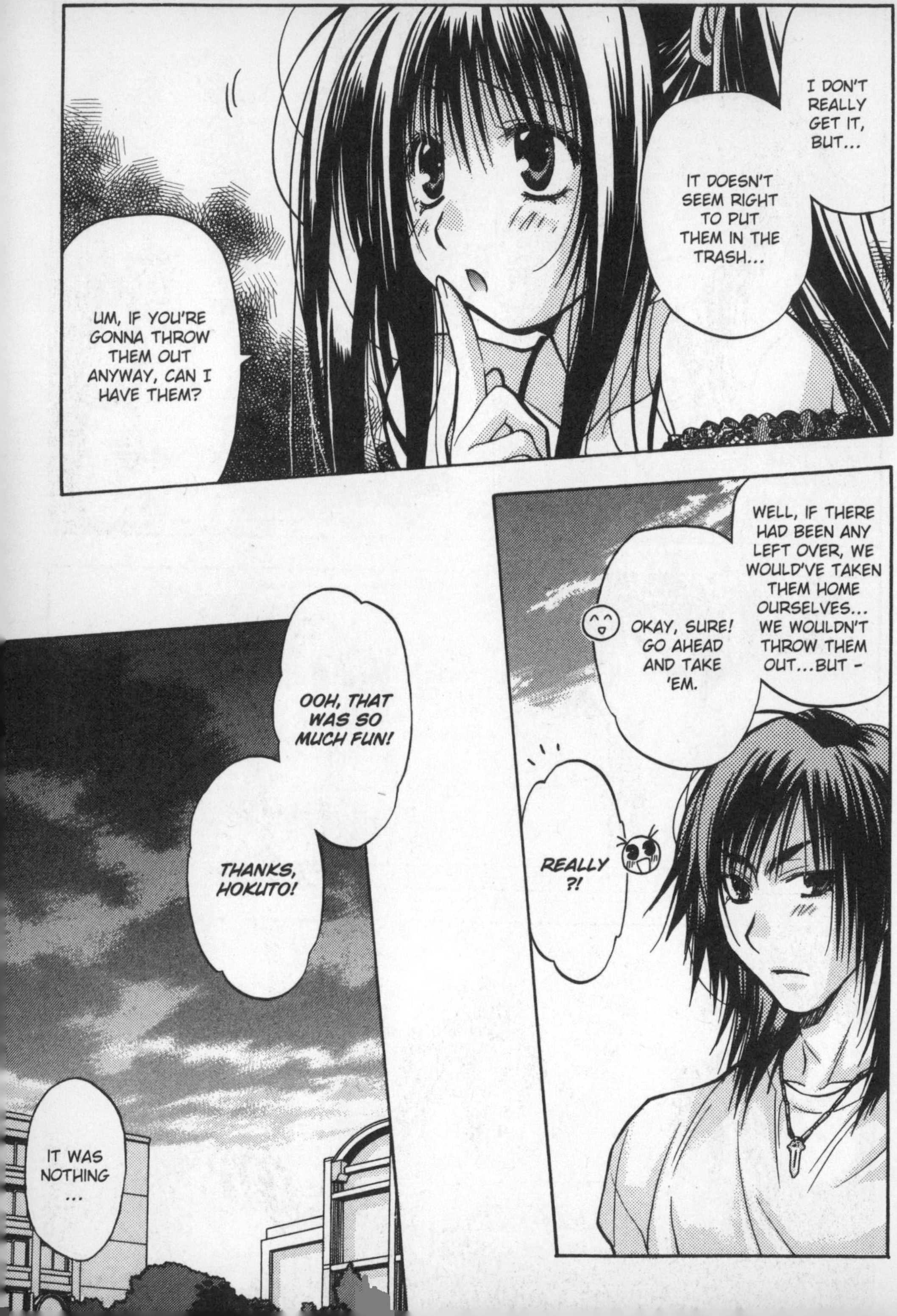
I DON'T REALLY GET IT, BUT...
IT DOESN'T SEEM RIGHT TO PUT THEM IN THE TRASH...
UM, IF YOU'RE GONNA THROW THEM OUT ANYWAY, CAN I HAVE THEM?
WELL, IF THERE HAD BEEN ANY LEFT OVER, WE WOULD'VE TAKEN THEM HOME OURSELVES... WE WOULDN'T THROW THEM OUT...BUT -
OKAY, SURE! GO AHEAD AND TAKE 'EM.
REALLY ?!
OOH, THAT WAS SO MUCH FUN!
THANKS, HOKUTO!
IT WAS NOTHING ...

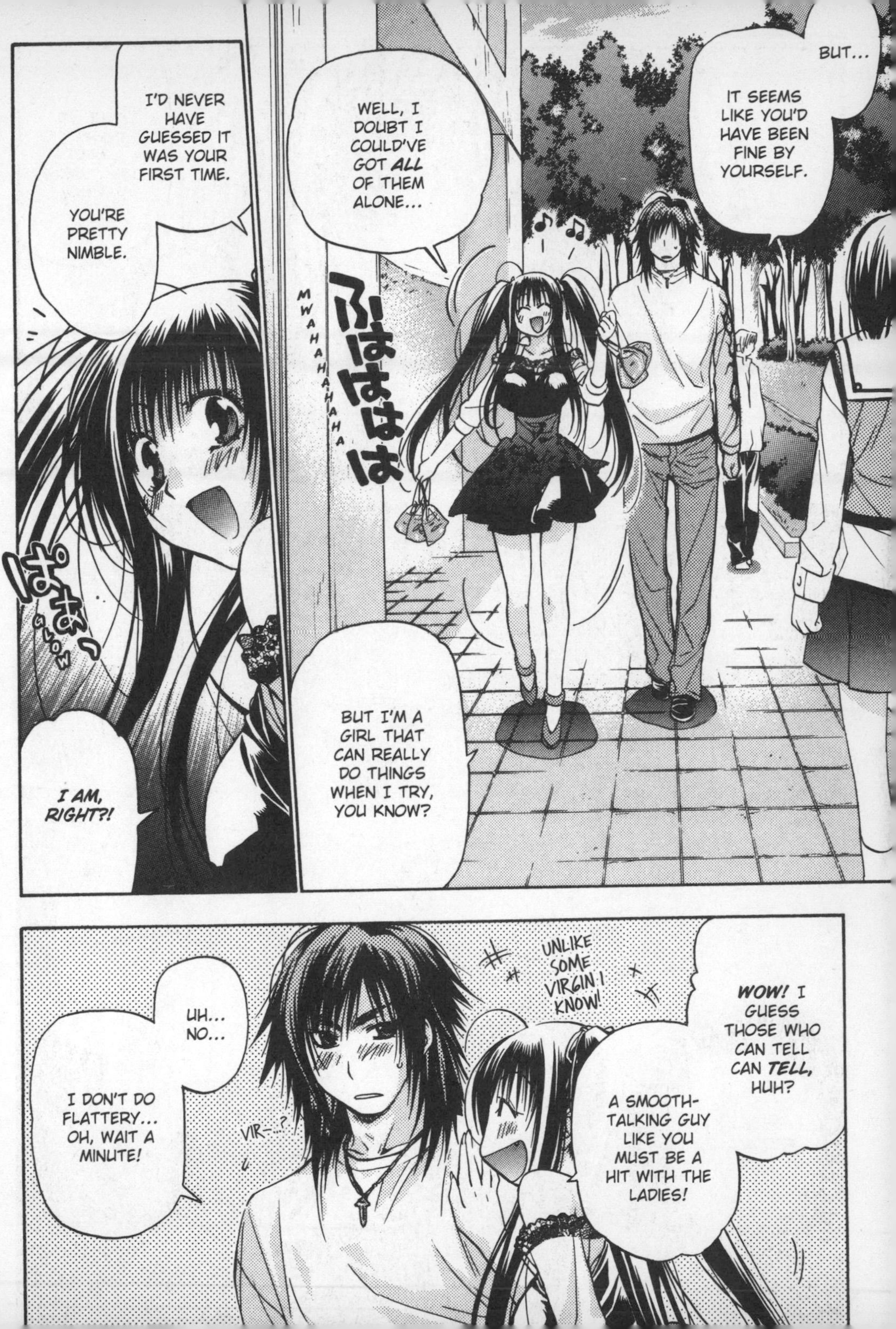
BUT...
IT SEEMS LIKE YOU'D HAVE BEEN FINE BY YOURSELF.
WELL, I DOUBT I COULD'VE GOT ALL OF THEM ALONE...
MWAHAHAHAHA
ふははは は
BUT I'M A GIRL THAT CAN REALLY DO THINGS WHEN I TRY, YOU KNOW?
I'D NEVER HAVE GUESSED IT WAS YOUR FIRST TIME.
YOU'RE PRETTY NIMBLE.
ぱぁっ
GLOW
I AM, RIGHT?!
WOW! I GUESS THOSE WHO CAN TELL CAN TELL, HUH?
UNLIKE SOME VIRGIN I KNOW!
A SMOOTH-TALKING GUY LIKE YOU MUST BE A HIT WITH THE LADIES!
UH... NO...
VIR--?
I DON'T DO FLATTERY... OH, WAIT A MINUTE!

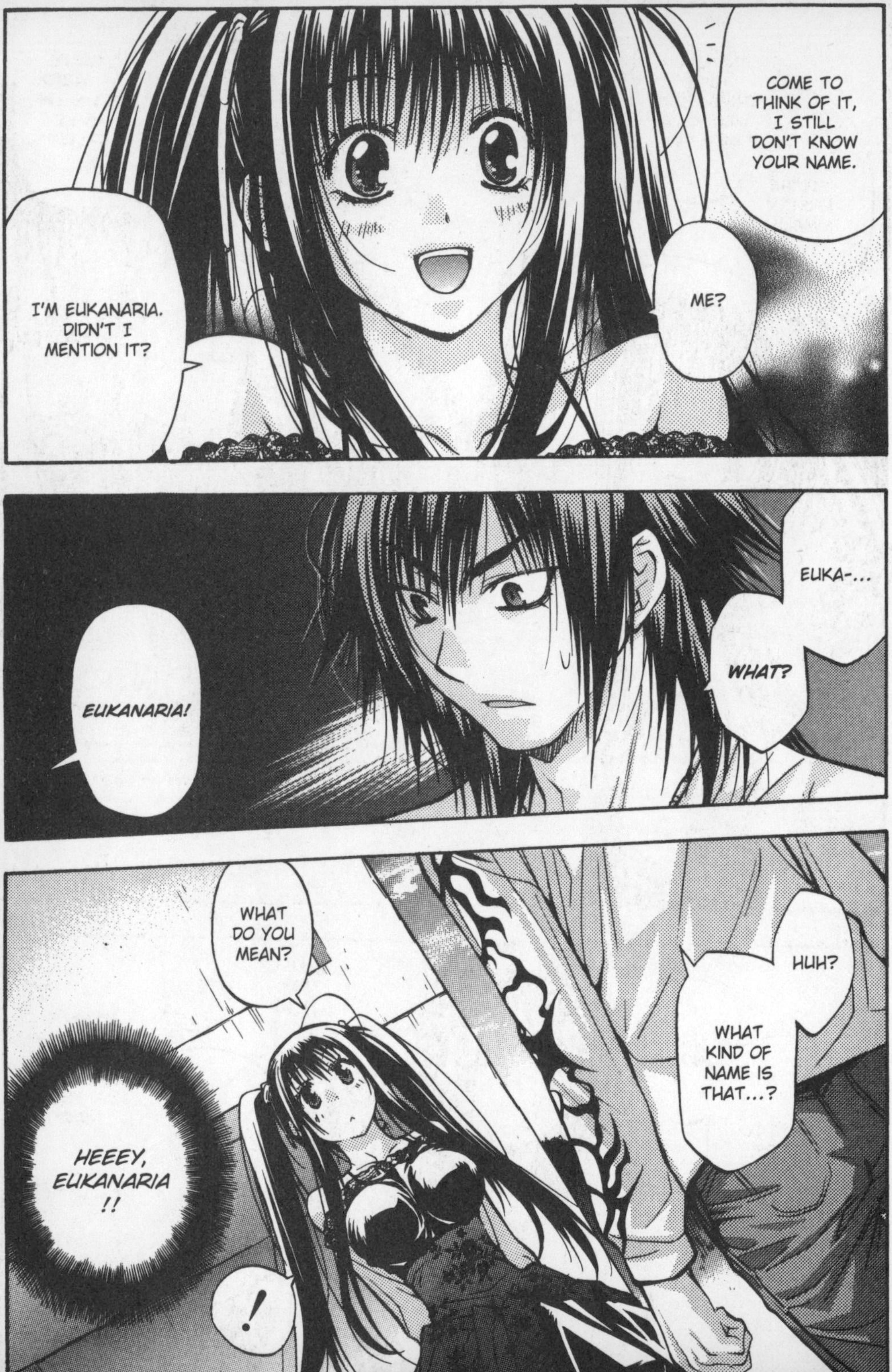
COME TO THINK OF IT, I STILL DON'T KNOW YOUR NAME.
ME?
I'M EUKANARIA. DIDN'T I MENTION IT?
EUKA-...
WHAT?
EUKANARIA!
HUH?
WHAT KIND OF NAME IS THAT...?
WHAT DO YOU MEAN?
HEEEY, EUKANARIA !!
!

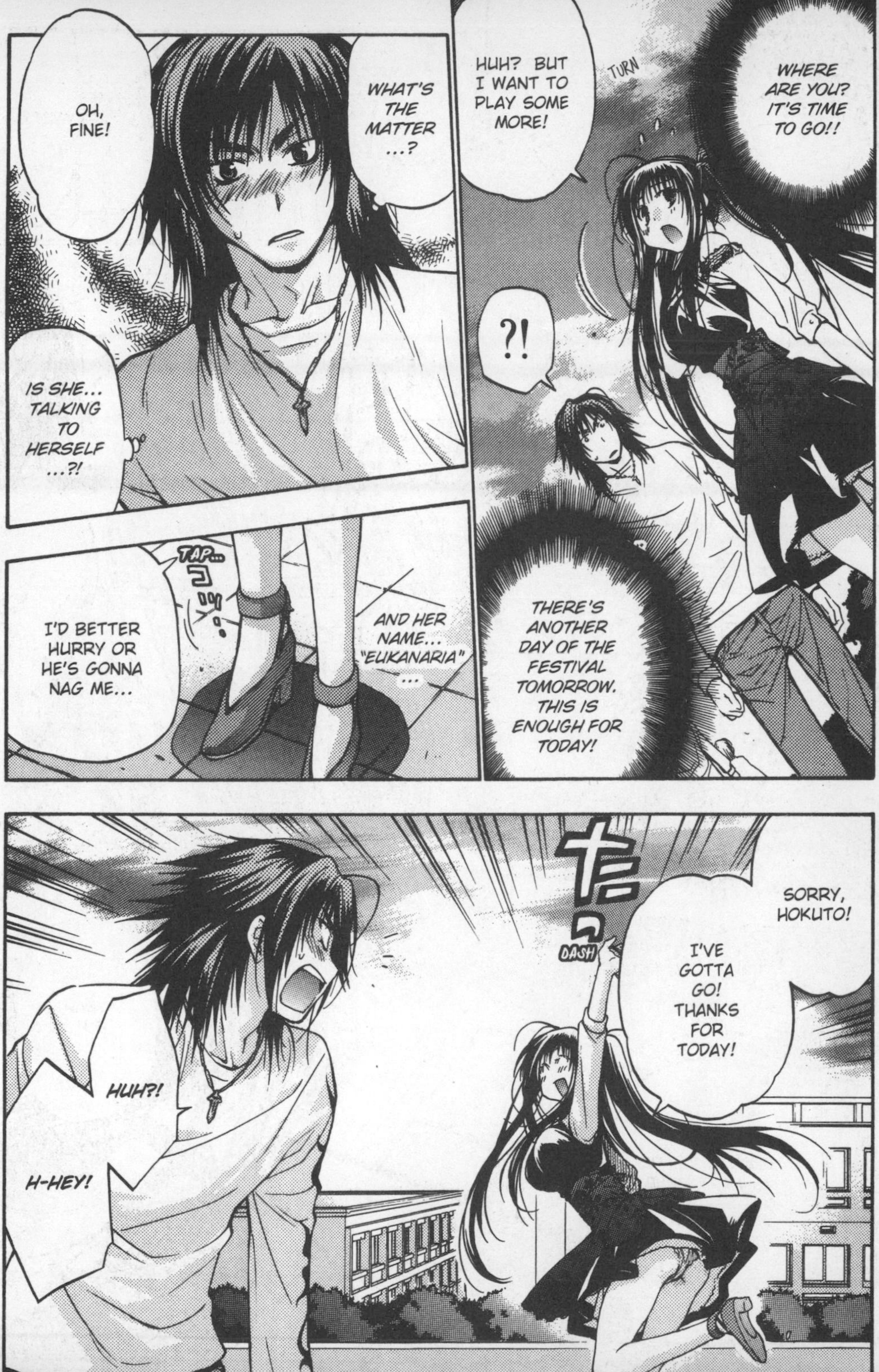
WHERE ARE YOU? IT'S TIME TO GO!!
TURN
HUH? BUT I WANT TO PLAY SOME MORE!
?!
THERE'S ANOTHER DAY OF THE FESTIVAL TOMORROW. THIS IS ENOUGH FOR TODAY!
WHAT'S THE MATTER ...?
OH, FINE!
IS SHE... TALKING TO HERSELF ...?!
AND HER NAME... "EUKANARIA" ...
TAP...
I'D BETTER HURRY OR HE'S GONNA NAG ME...
SORRY, HOKUTO!
I'VE GOTTA GO! THANKS FOR TODAY!
DASH
HUH?!
H-HEY!

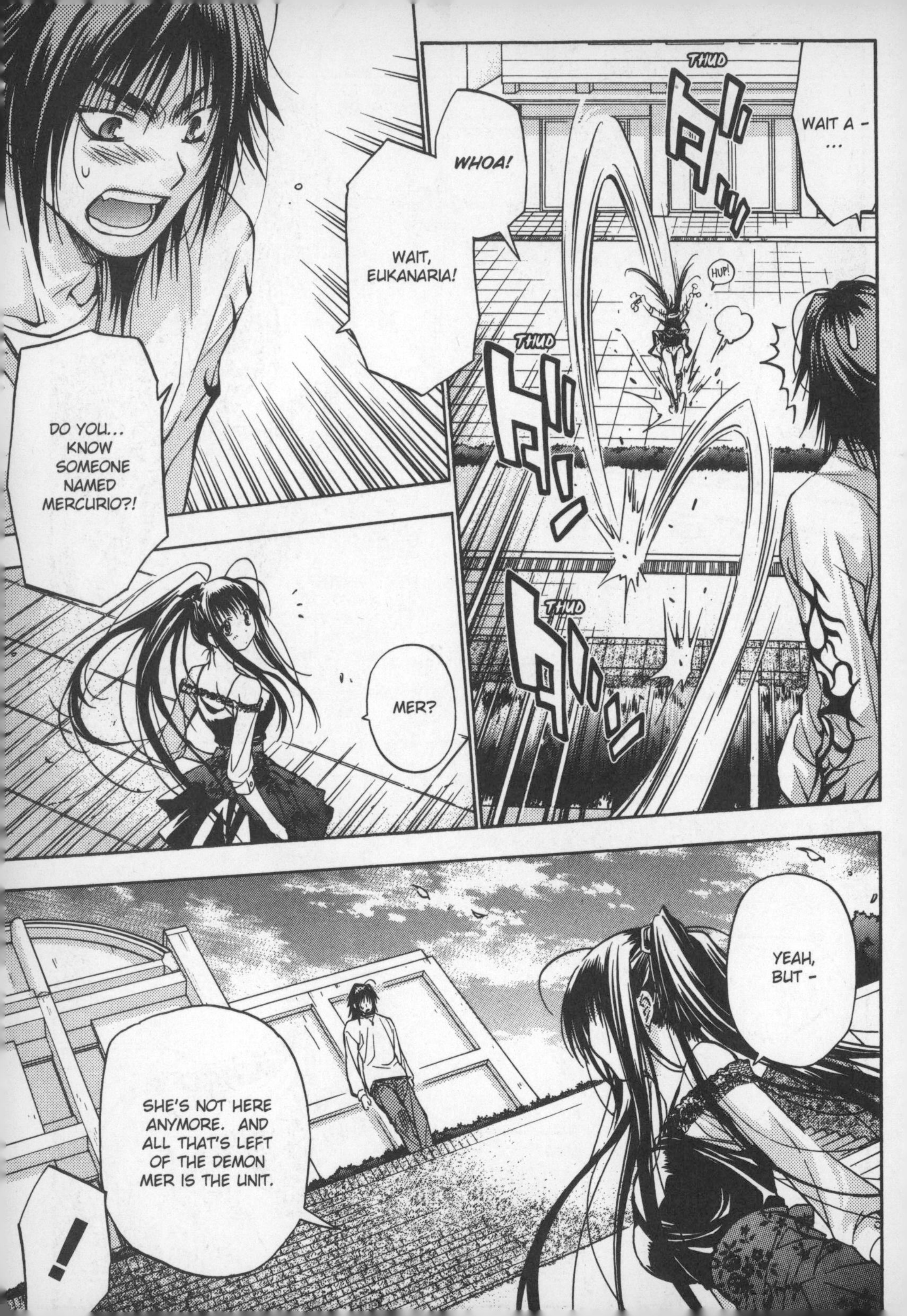
THUD
WAIT A - ...
WHOA!
WAIT, EUKANARIA!
HUP!
THUD
THUD
DO YOU... KNOW SOMEONE NAMED MERCURIO?!
MER?
YEAH, BUT -
SHE'S NOT HERE ANYMORE. AND ALL THAT'S LEFT OF THE DEMON MER IS THE UNIT.
!

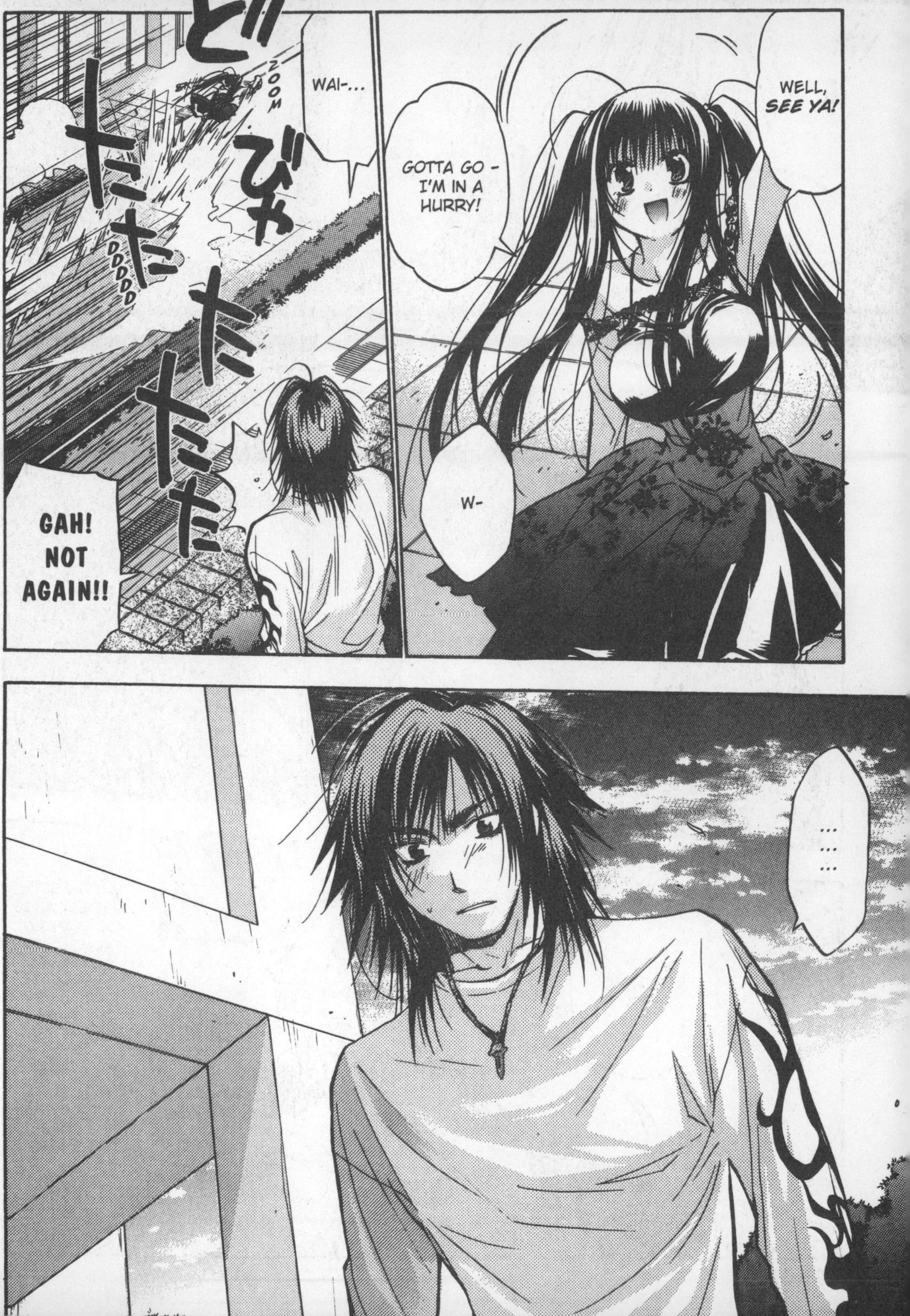
WELL, SEE YA!
GOTTA GO - I'M IN A HURRY!
W-
WAI-...
ZOOM
DDDDD
GAH! NOT AGAIN!!
...
...
...

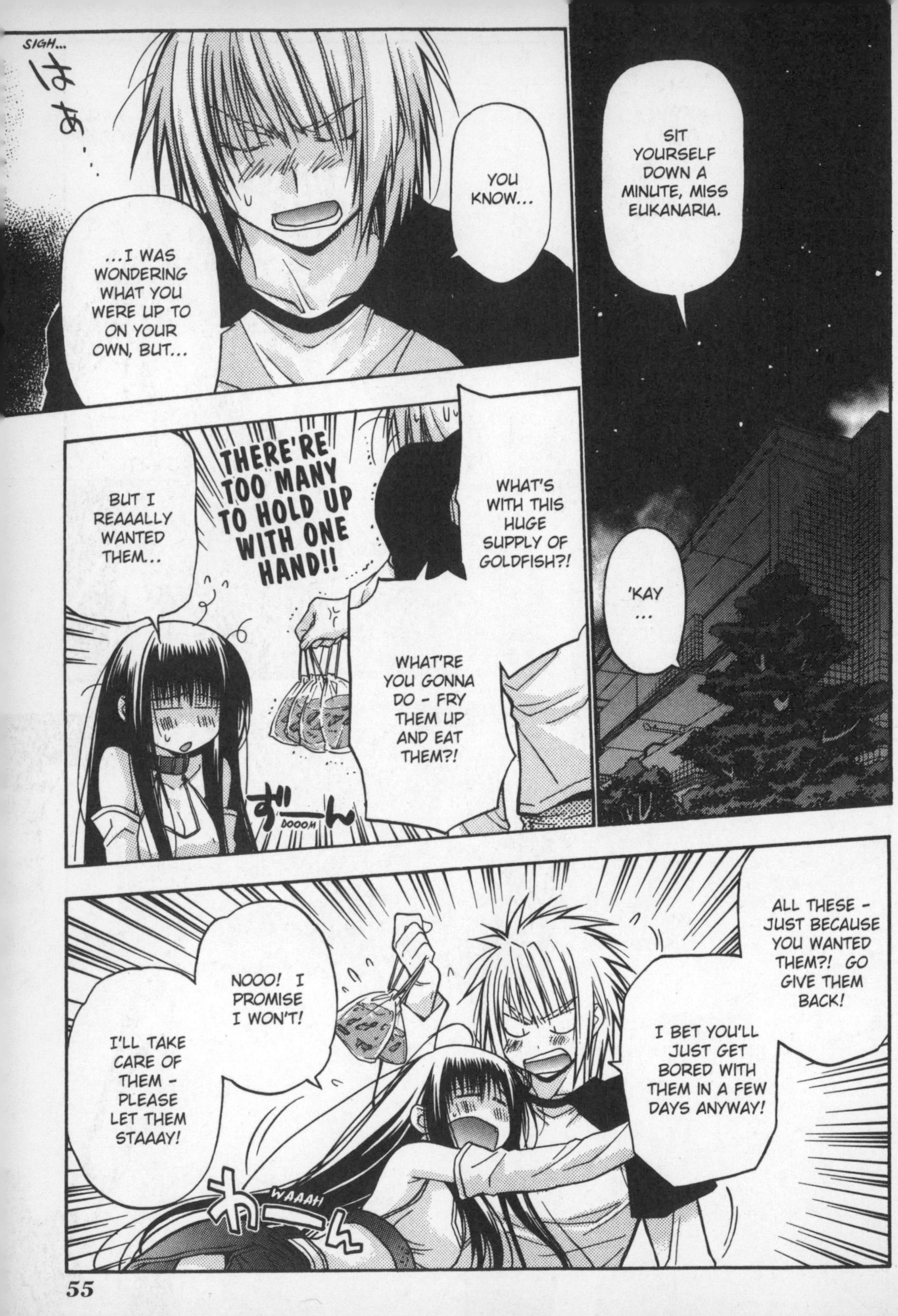
SIT YOURSELF DOWN A MINUTE, MISS EUKANARIA.
'KAY...
SIGH...
はあ...
YOU KNOW...
...I WAS WONDERING WHAT YOU WERE UP TO ON YOUR OWN, BUT...
WHAT'S WITH THIS HUGE SUPPLY OF GOLDFISH?!
WHAT'RE YOU GONNA DO - FRY THEM UP AND EAT THEM?!
THERE'RE TOO MANY TO HOLD UP WITH ONE HAND!!
BUT I REAAALLY WANTED THEM...
ずーん
DOOOM
ALL THESE - JUST BECAUSE YOU WANTED THEM?! GO GIVE THEM BACK!
I BET YOU'LL JUST GET BORED WITH THEM IN A FEW DAYS ANYWAY!
NOOO! I PROMISE I WON'T!
I'LL TAKE CARE OF THEM - PLEASE LET THEM STAAAY!
わーん
WAAAH

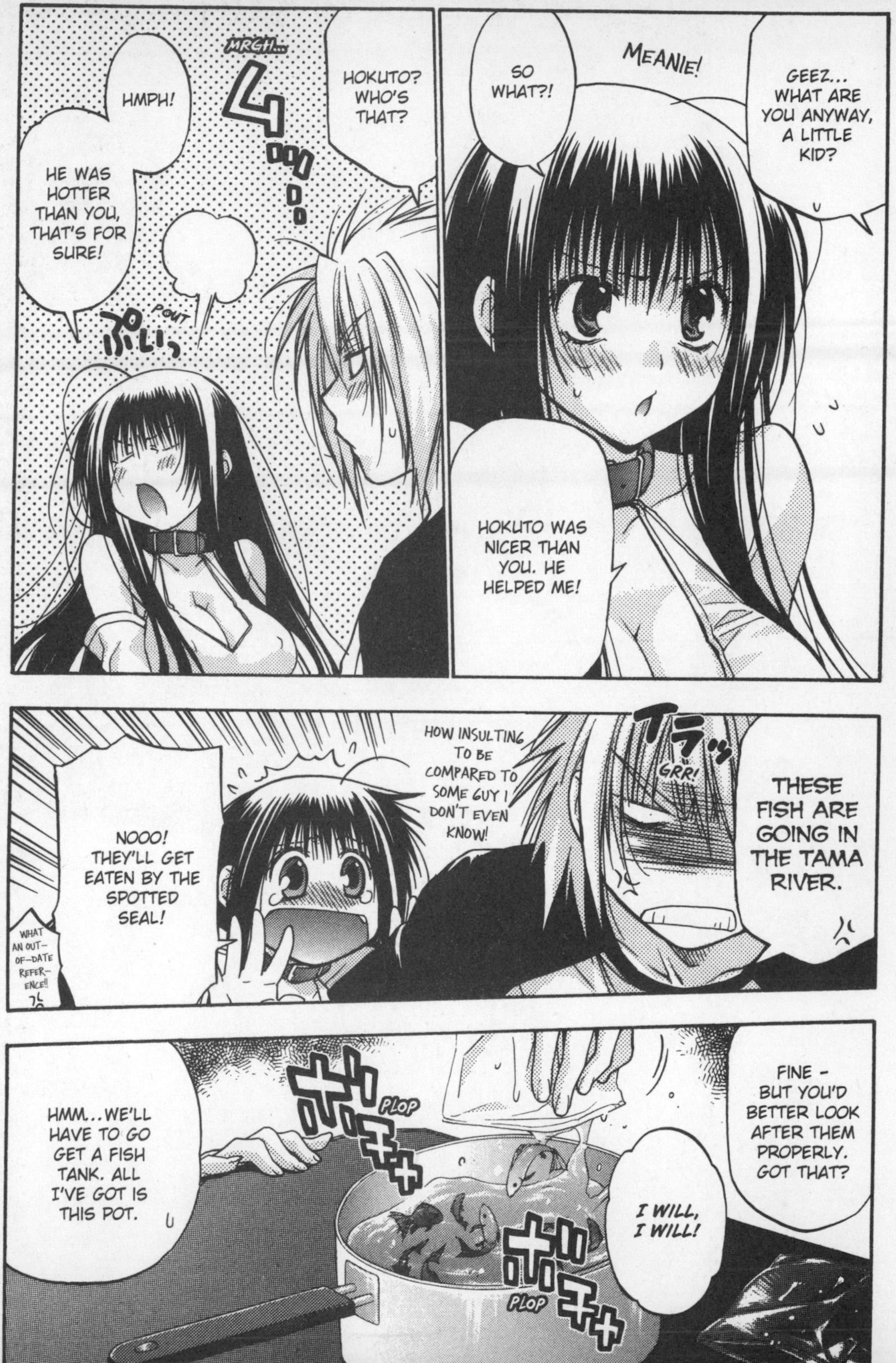
GEEZ... WHAT ARE YOU ANYWAY, A LITTLE KID?
MEANIE!
SO WHAT?!
HOKUTO WAS NICER THAN YOU. HE HELPED ME!
HOKUTO? WHO'S THAT?
MRGH...
HMPH!
HE WAS HOTTER THAN YOU, THAT'S FOR SURE!
POUT
THESE FISH ARE GOING IN THE TAMA RIVER.
GRR!
HOW INSULTING TO BE COMPARED TO SOME GUY I DON'T EVEN KNOW!
NOOO! THEY'LL GET EATEN BY THE SPOTTED SEAL!
WHAT AN OUT-OF-DATE REFERENCE!!
FINE - BUT YOU'D BETTER LOOK AFTER THEM PROPERLY. GOT THAT?
I WILL, I WILL!
PLOP
PLOP
HMM...WE'LL HAVE TO GO GET A FISH TANK. ALL I'VE GOT IS THIS POT.

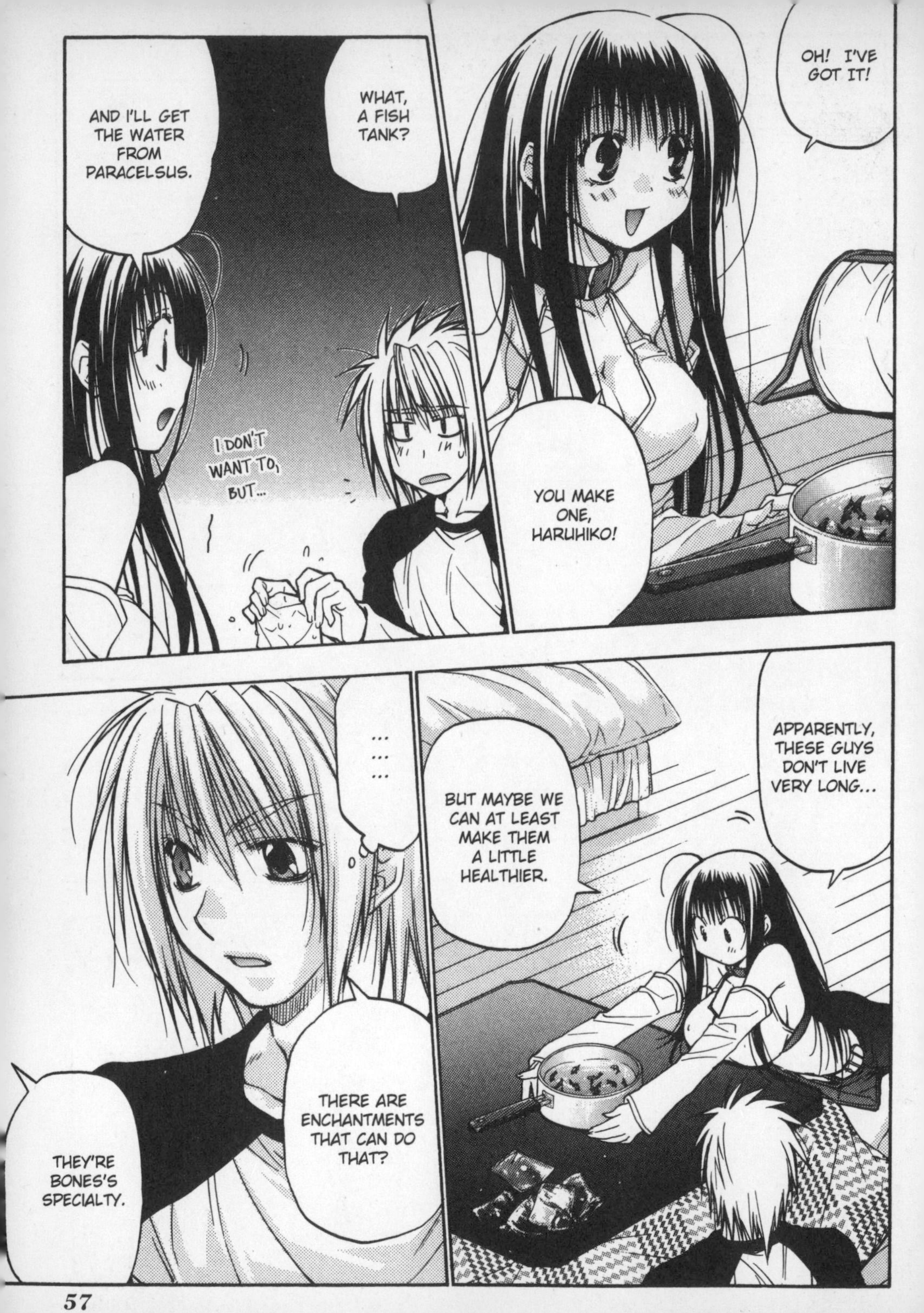
OH! I'VE GOT IT!
YOU MAKE ONE, HARUHIKO!
WHAT, A FISH TANK?
AND I'LL GET THE WATER FROM PARACELSUS.
I DON'T WANT TO, BUT...
APPARENTLY, THESE GUYS DON'T LIVE VERY LONG...
BUT MAYBE WE CAN AT LEAST MAKE THEM A LITTLE HEALTHIER.
... ...
THERE ARE ENCHANTMENTS THAT CAN DO THAT?
THEY'RE BONES'S SPECIALTY.

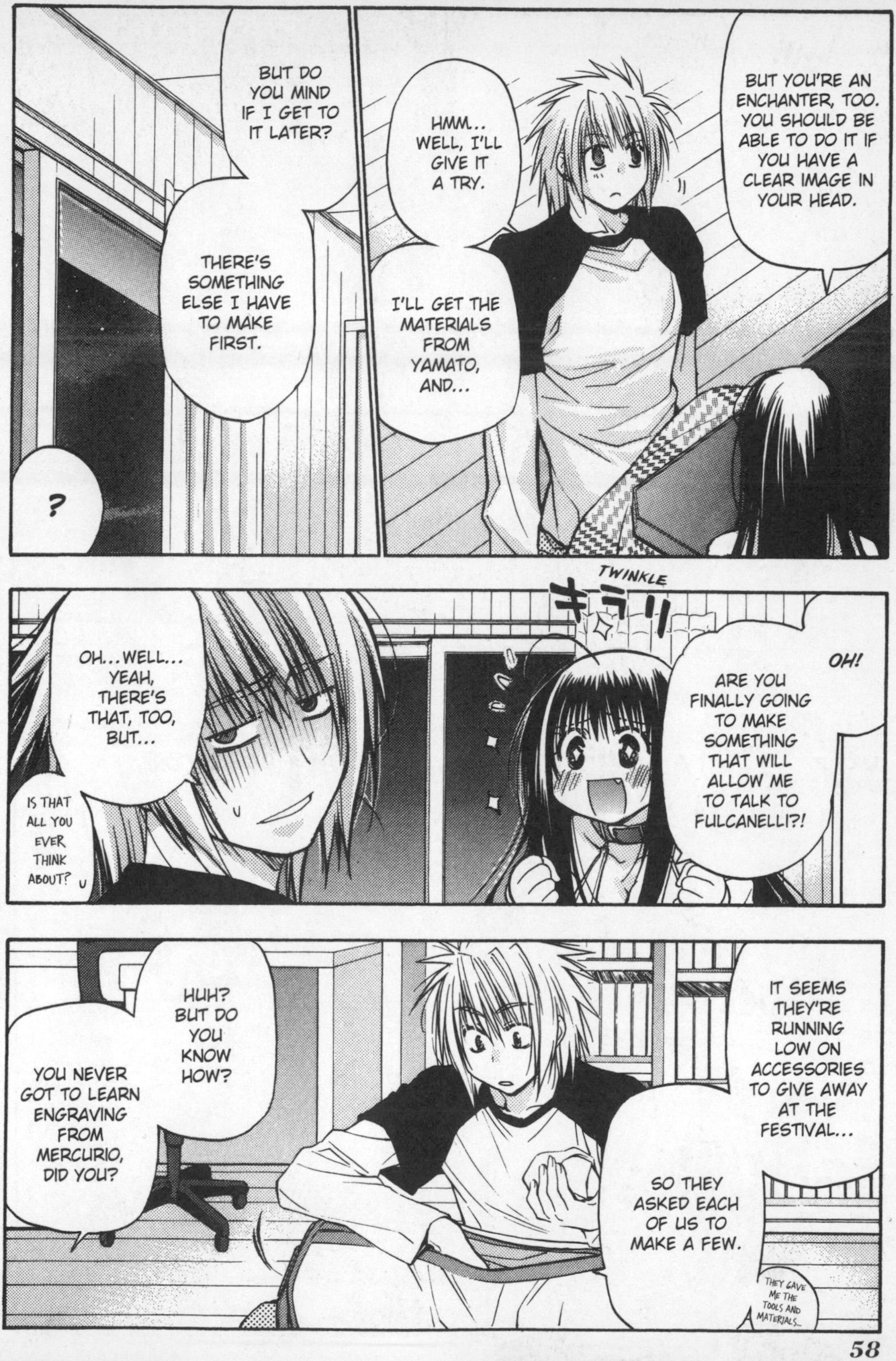
BUT YOU'RE AN ENCHANTER, TOO. YOU SHOULD BE ABLE TO DO IT IF YOU HAVE A CLEAR IMAGE IN YOUR HEAD.
HMM... WELL, I'LL GIVE IT A TRY.
I'LL GET THE MATERIALS FROM YAMATO, AND...
BUT DO YOU MIND IF I GET TO IT LATER?
THERE'S SOMETHING ELSE I HAVE TO MAKE FIRST.
?
TWINKLE
キラリ
OH!
ARE YOU FINALLY GOING TO MAKE SOMETHING THAT WILL ALLOW ME TO TALK TO FULCANELLI?!
OH...WELL... YEAH, THERE'S THAT, TOO, BUT...
IS THAT ALL YOU EVER THINK ABOUT?
IT SEEMS THEY'RE RUNNING LOW ON ACCESSORIES TO GIVE AWAY AT THE FESTIVAL...
SO THEY ASKED EACH OF US TO MAKE A FEW.
THEY GAVE ME THE TOOLS AND MATERIALS...
HUH? BUT DO YOU KNOW HOW?
YOU NEVER GOT TO LEARN ENGRAVING FROM MERCURIO, DID YOU?

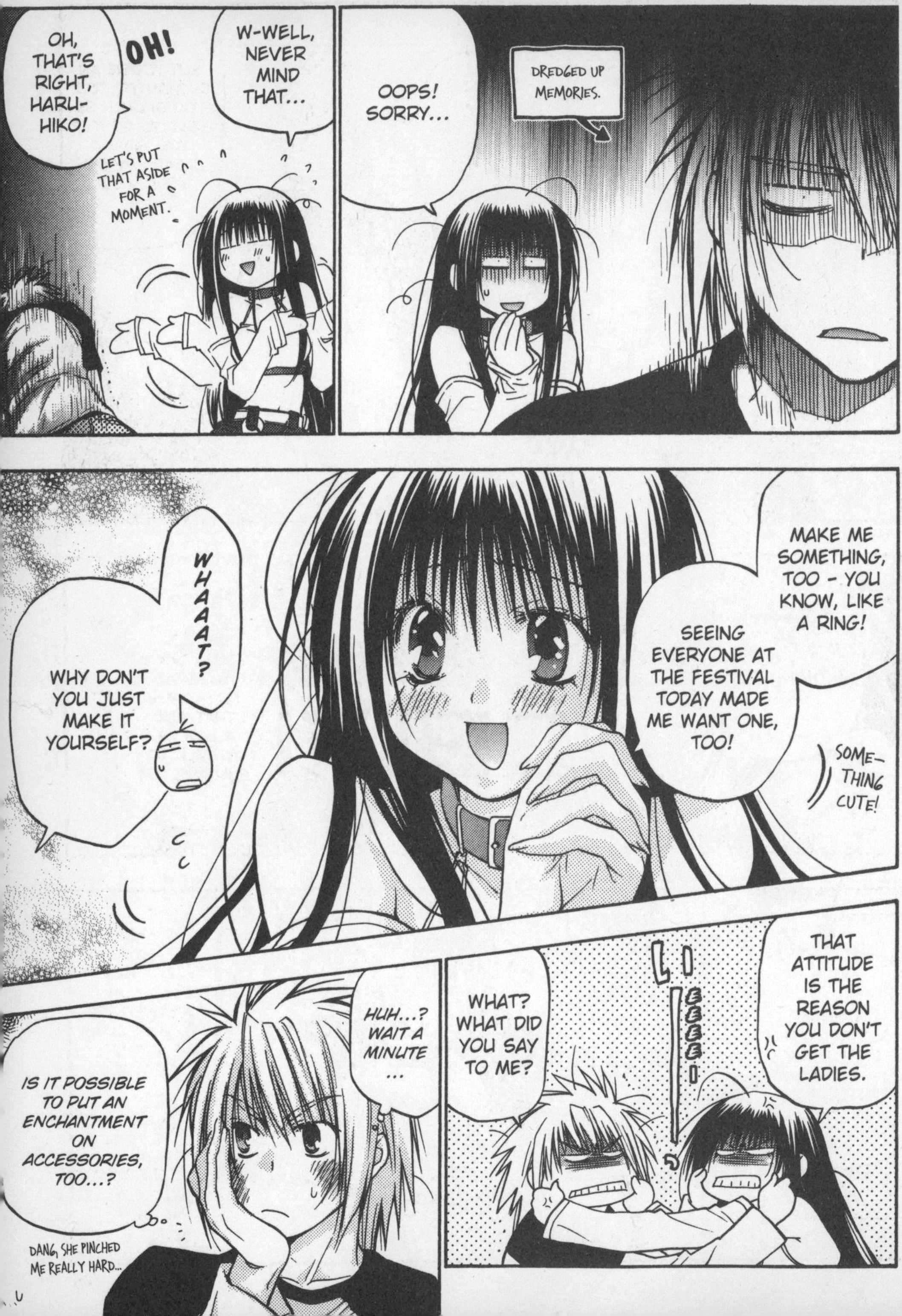
DREDGED UP MEMORIES.
OOPS! SORRY...
W-WELL, NEVER MIND THAT...
OH!
OH, THAT'S RIGHT, HARUHIKO!
LET'S PUT THAT ASIDE FOR A MOMENT.
MAKE ME SOMETHING, TOO - YOU KNOW, LIKE A RING!
SEEING EVERYONE AT THE FESTIVAL TODAY MADE ME WANT ONE, TOO!
SOMETHING CUTE!
WHAAAAT?
WHY DON'T YOU JUST MAKE IT YOURSELF?
THAT ATTITUDE IS THE REASON YOU DON'T GET THE LADIES.
EEEEE
WHAT? WHAT DID YOU SAY TO ME?
HUH...? WAIT A MINUTE...
IS IT POSSIBLE TO PUT AN ENCHANTMENT ON ACCESSORIES, TOO...?
DANG, SHE PINCHED ME REALLY HARD...

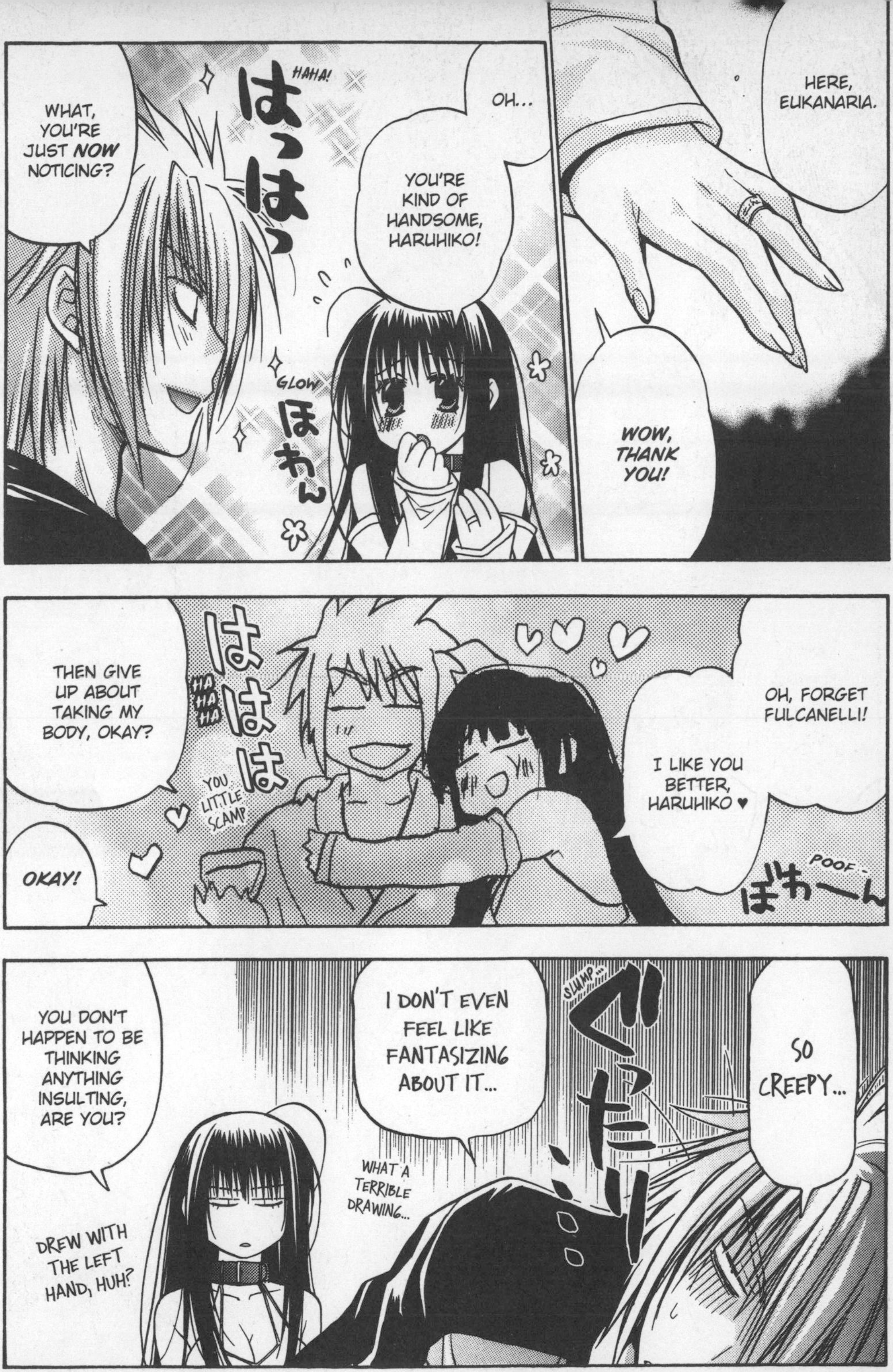
HERE, EUKANARIA.
WOW, THANK YOU!
OH...
YOU'RE KIND OF HANDSOME, HARUHIKO!
HAHA!
はっはっ
WHAT, YOU'RE JUST NOW NOTICING?
GLOW
ほやん
OH, FORGET FULCANELLI!
I LIKE YOU BETTER, HARUHIKO ♥
POOF
ぼわ〜ん
THEN GIVE UP ABOUT TAKING MY BODY, OKAY?
HA HA HA
ははは
YOU LITTLE SCAMP
OKAY!
SO CREEPY...
SLUMP...
ぐったり
I DON'T EVEN FEEL LIKE FANTASIZING ABOUT IT...
WHAT A TERRIBLE DRAWING...
YOU DON'T HAPPEN TO BE THINKING ANYTHING INSULTING, ARE YOU?
DREW WITH THE LEFT HAND, HUH?

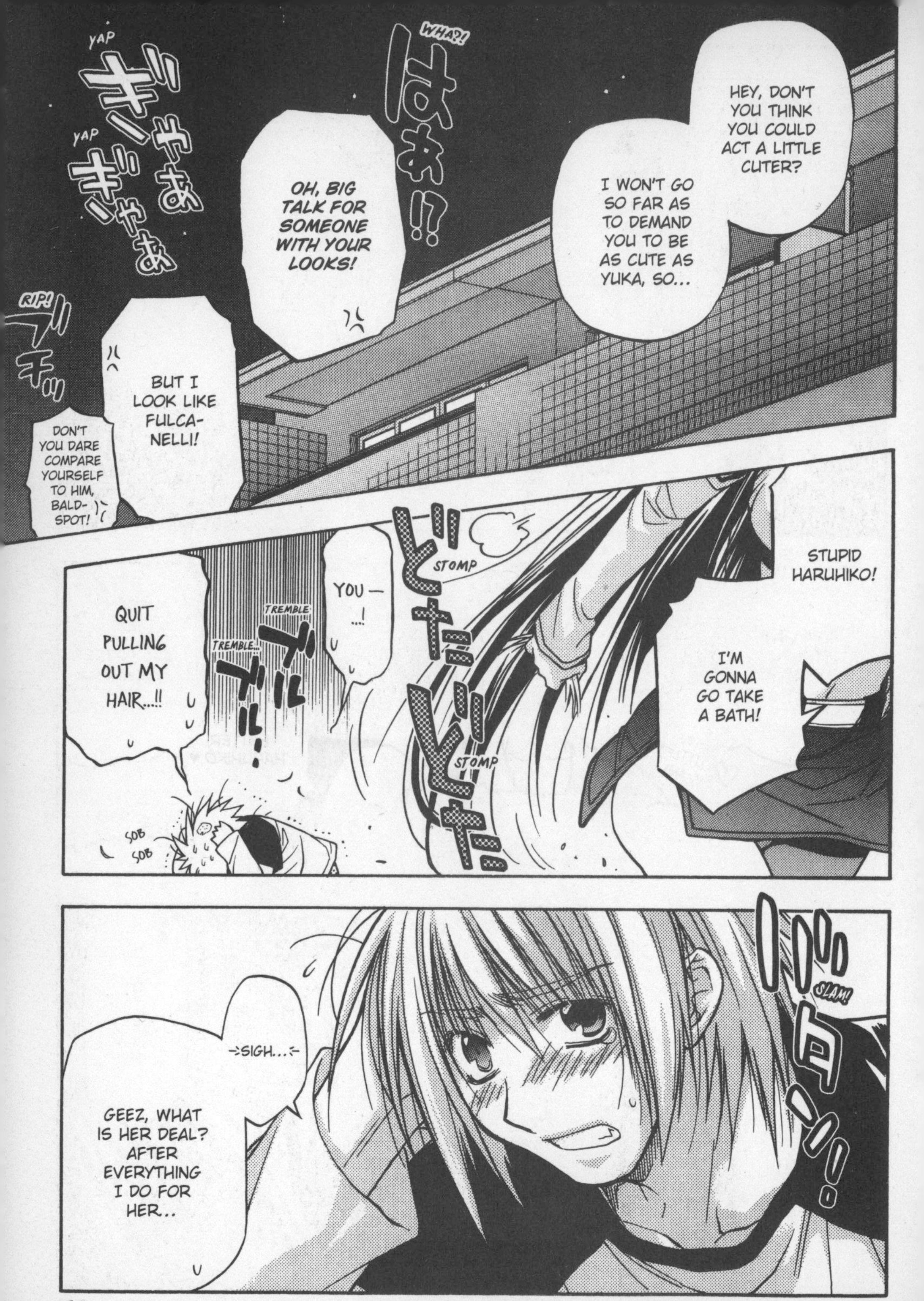
HEY, DON'T YOU THINK YOU COULD ACT A LITTLE CUTER?
I WON'T GO SO FAR AS TO DEMAND YOU TO BE AS CUTE AS YUKA, SO...
WHA?!
OH, BIG TALK FOR SOMEONE WITH YOUR LOOKS!
YAP
YAP
RIP!
BUT I LOOK LIKE FULCA-NELLI!
DON'T YOU DARE COMPARE YOURSELF TO HIM, BALD-SPOT!
STUPID HARUHIKO!
I'M GONNA GO TAKE A BATH!
STOMP
STOMP
YOU— ...!
TREMBLE
TREMBLE...
QUIT PULLING OUT MY HAIR...!!
SOB
SOB
SLAM!
SIGH...
GEEZ, WHAT IS HER DEAL? AFTER EVERYTHING I DO FOR HER...

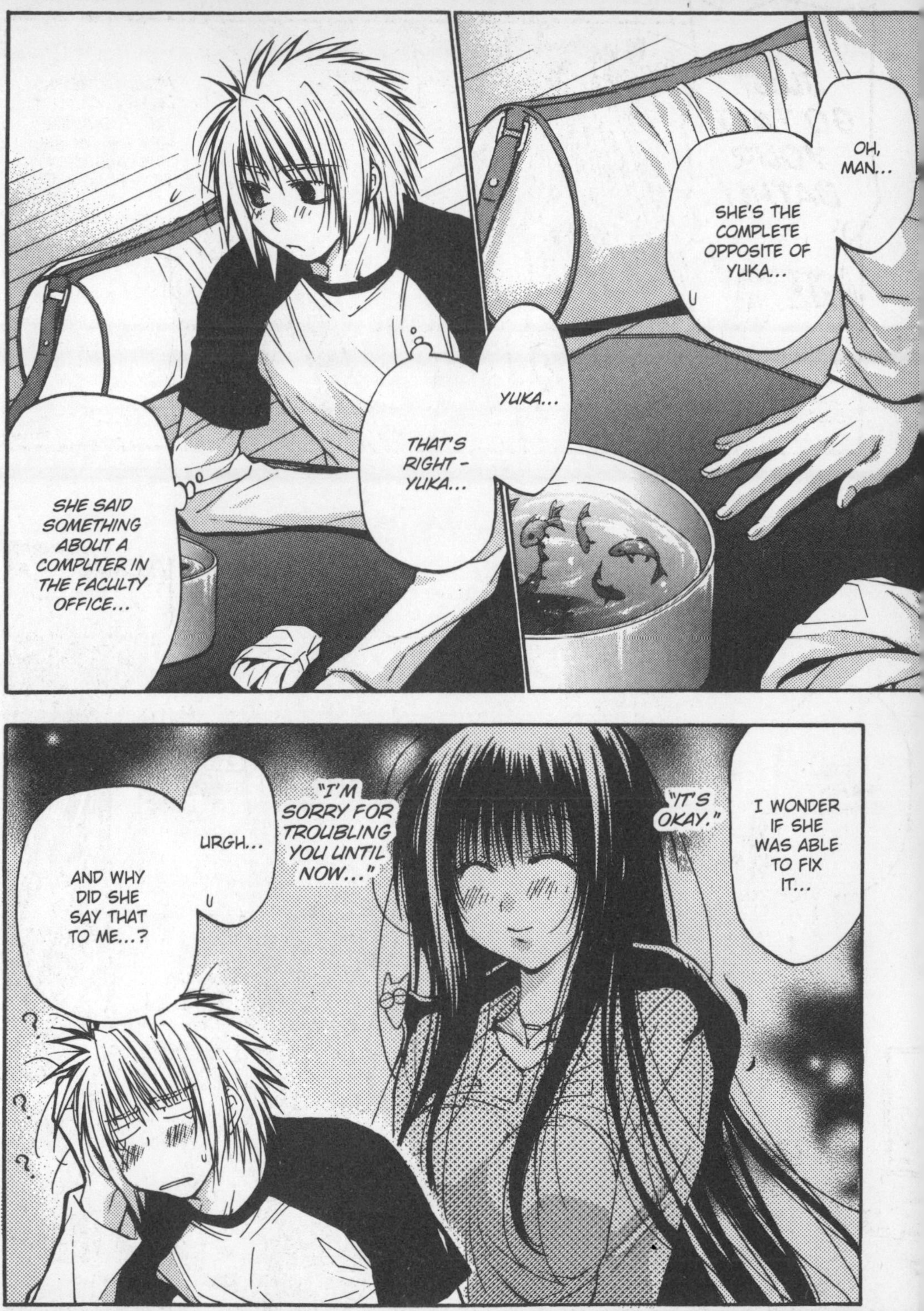
OH, MAN...
SHE'S THE COMPLETE OPPOSITE OF YUKA...
YUKA...
THAT'S RIGHT - YUKA...
SHE SAID SOMETHING ABOUT A COMPUTER IN THE FACULTY OFFICE...
I WONDER IF SHE WAS ABLE TO FIX IT...
"IT'S OKAY."
"I'M SORRY FOR TROUBLING YOU UNTIL NOW..."
URGH...
AND WHY DID SHE SAY THAT TO ME...?

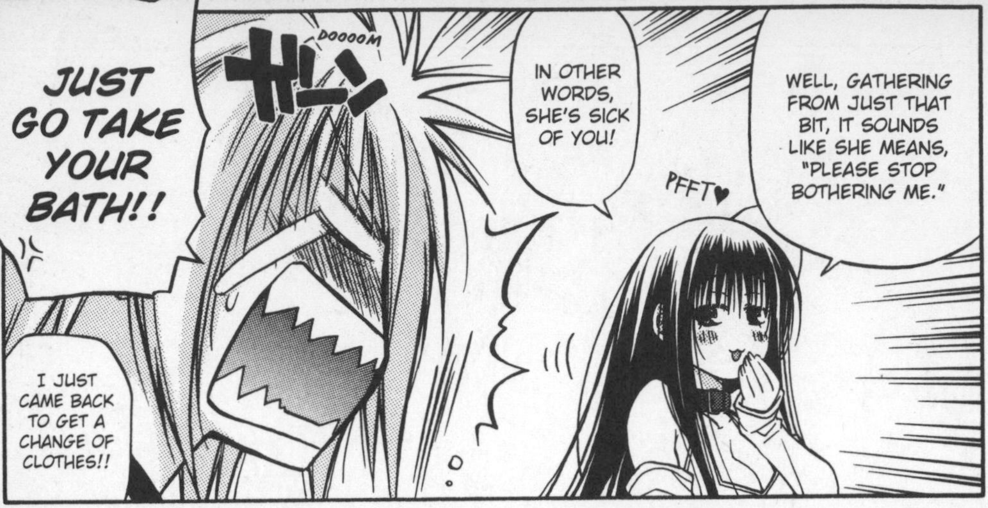
WELL, GATHERING FROM JUST THAT BIT, IT SOUNDS LIKE SHE MEANS, "PLEASE STOP BOTHERING ME."
PFFT♥
IN OTHER WORDS, SHE'S SICK OF YOU!
DOOOOM
JUST GO TAKE YOUR BATH!!
I JUST CAME BACK TO GET A CHANGE OF CLOTHES!!

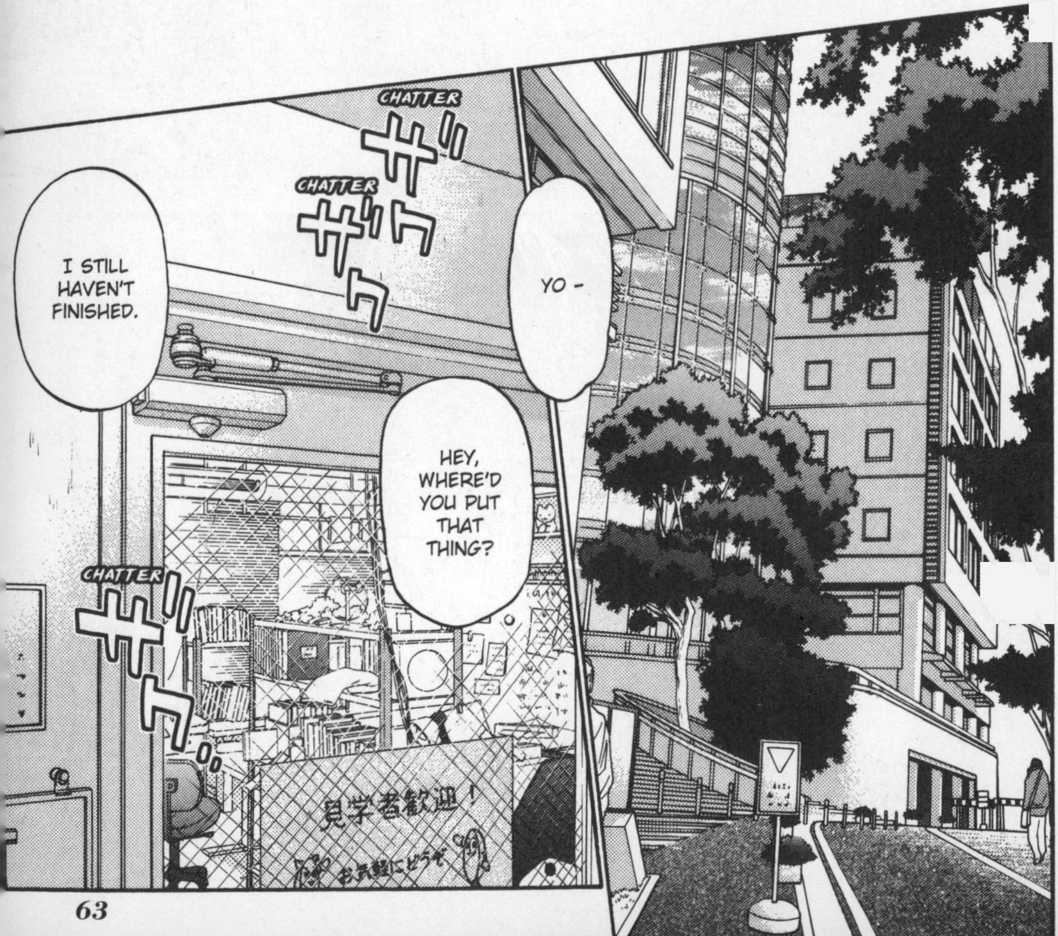
YO -
CHATTER
CHATTER
HEY, WHERE'D YOU PUT THAT THING?
I STILL HAVEN'T FINISHED.
CHATTER
見学者歓迎！
お気軽にどうぞ

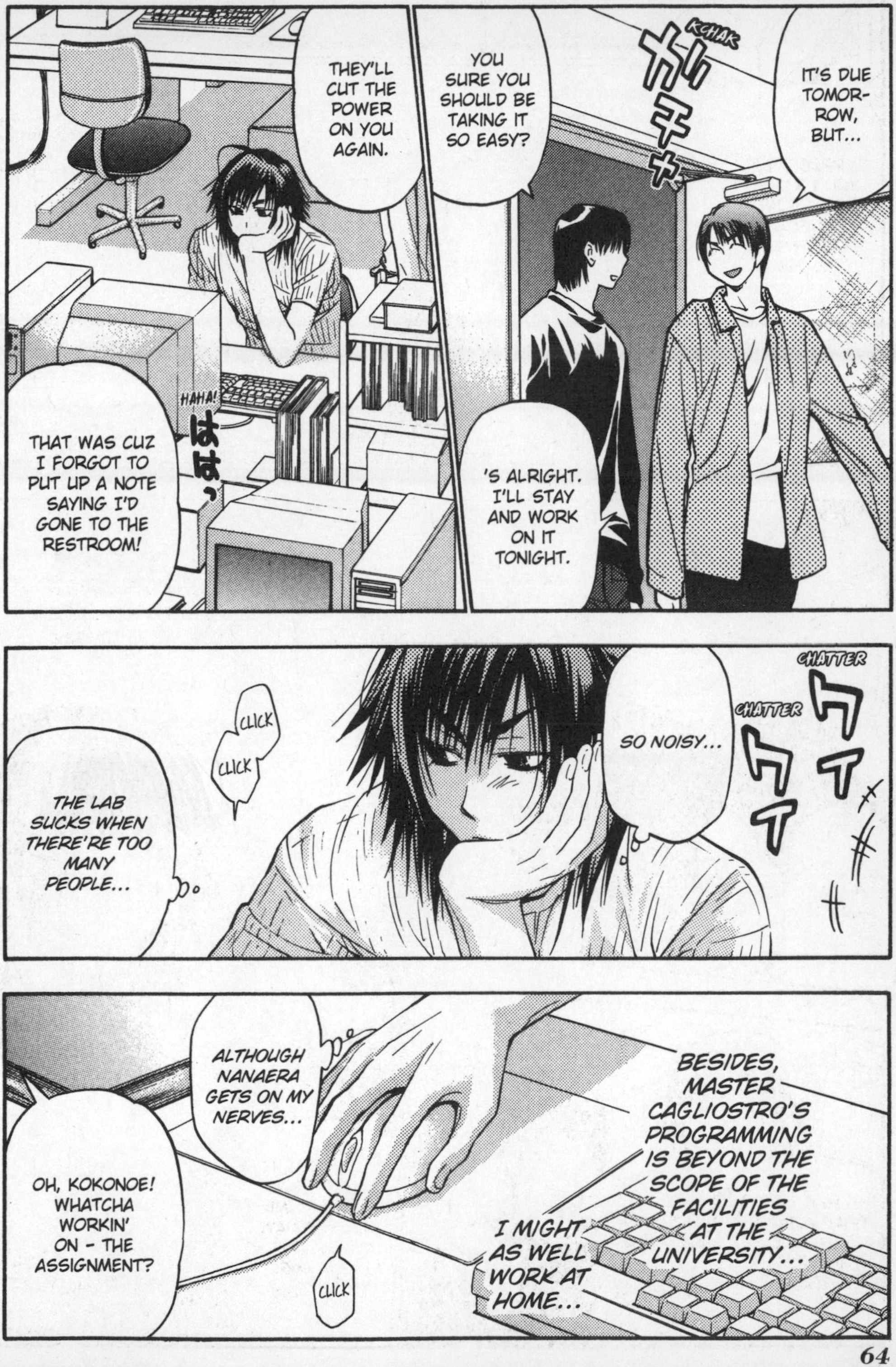
IT'S DUE TOMORROW, BUT...
KCHAK
YOU SURE YOU SHOULD BE TAKING IT SO EASY?
THEY'LL CUT THE POWER ON YOU AGAIN.
'S ALRIGHT. I'LL STAY AND WORK ON IT TONIGHT.
HAHA!
THAT WAS CUZ I FORGOT TO PUT UP A NOTE SAYING I'D GONE TO THE RESTROOM!
CHATTER
CHATTER
SO NOISY...
CLICK
CLICK
THE LAB SUCKS WHEN THERE'RE TOO MANY PEOPLE...
BESIDES, MASTER CAGLIOSTRO'S PROGRAMMING IS BEYOND THE SCOPE OF THE FACILITIES AT THE UNIVERSITY...
I MIGHT AS WELL WORK AT HOME...
ALTHOUGH NANAERA GETS ON MY NERVES...
CLICK
OH, KOKONOE! WHATCHA WORKIN' ON - THE ASSIGNMENT?

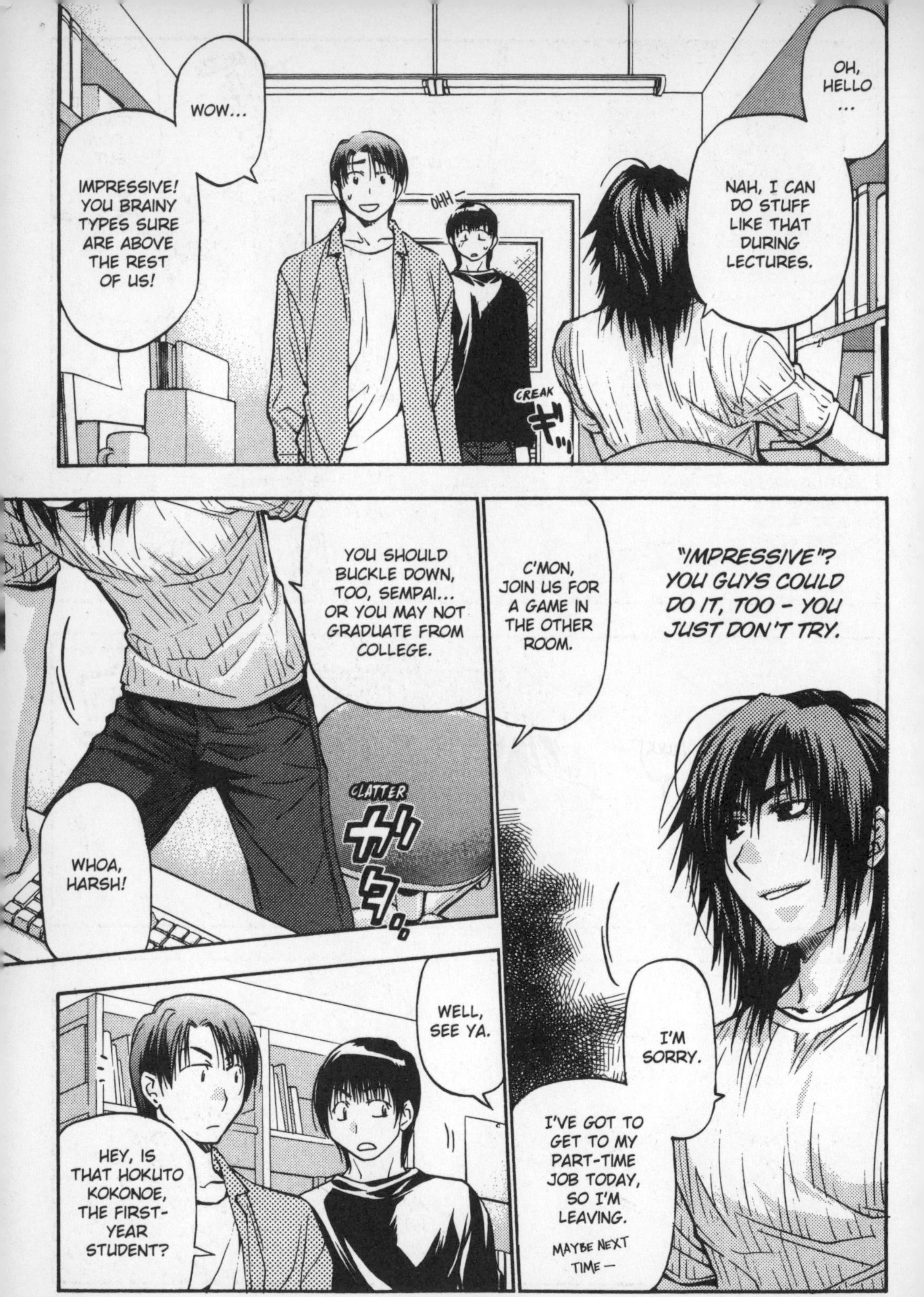
OH, HELLO ...
WOW...
IMPRESSIVE! YOU BRAINY TYPES SURE ARE ABOVE THE REST OF US!
NAH, I CAN DO STUFF LIKE THAT DURING LECTURES.
OHH—
CREAK
"IMPRESSIVE"? YOU GUYS COULD DO IT, TOO - YOU JUST DON'T TRY.
C'MON, JOIN US FOR A GAME IN THE OTHER ROOM.
I'M SORRY.
I'VE GOT TO GET TO MY PART-TIME JOB TODAY, SO I'M LEAVING.
MAYBE NEXT TIME—
YOU SHOULD BUCKLE DOWN, TOO, SEMPAI... OR YOU MAY NOT GRADUATE FROM COLLEGE.
CLATTER
WHOA, HARSH!
WELL, SEE YA.
HEY, IS THAT HOKUTO KOKONOE, THE FIRST-YEAR STUDENT?

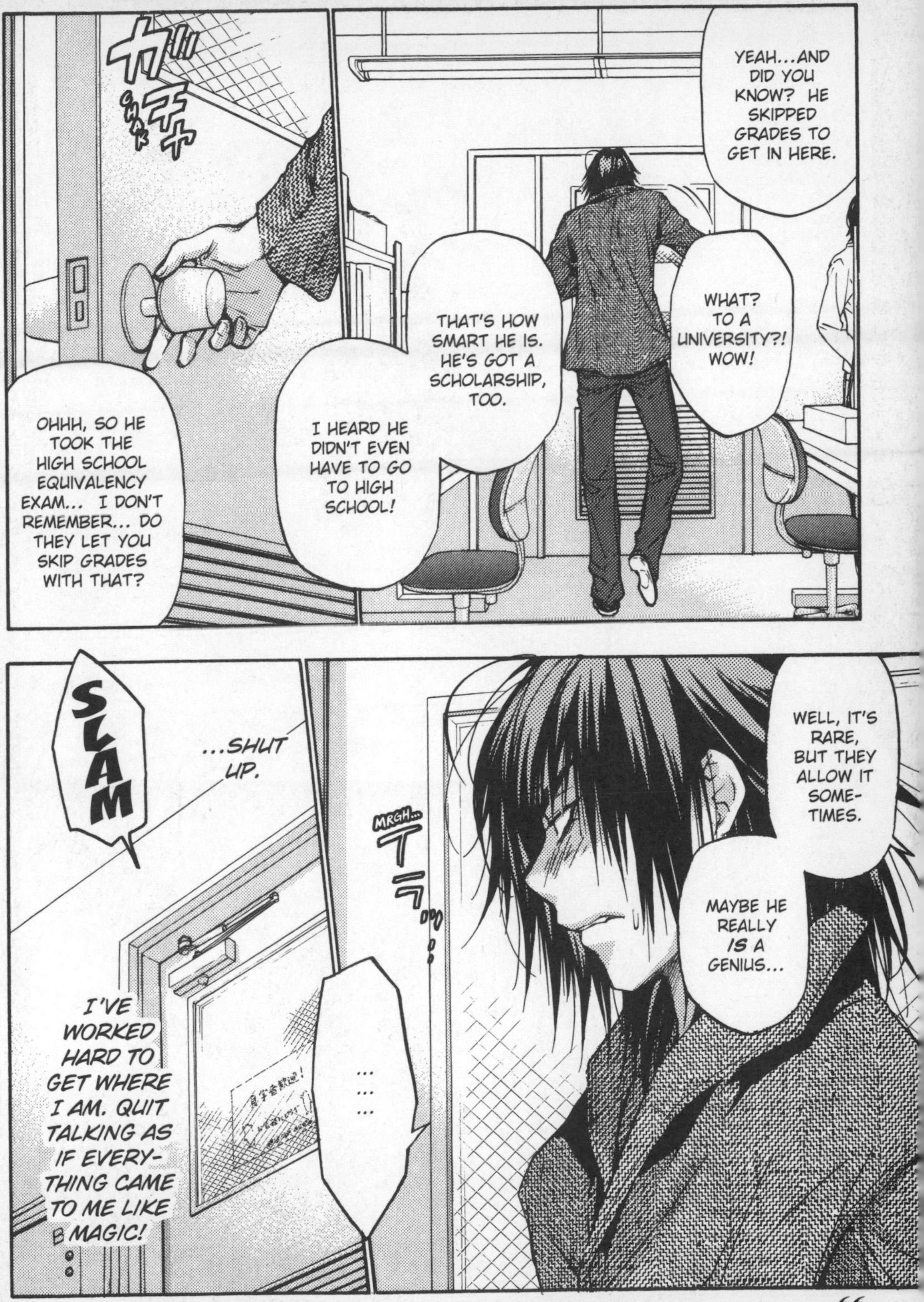
YEAH...AND DID YOU KNOW? HE SKIPPED GRADES TO GET IN HERE.
WHAT? TO A UNIVERSITY?! WOW!
THAT'S HOW SMART HE IS. HE'S GOT A SCHOLARSHIP, TOO.
I HEARD HE DIDN'T EVEN HAVE TO GO TO HIGH SCHOOL!
OHHH, SO HE TOOK THE HIGH SCHOOL EQUIVALENCY EXAM... I DON'T REMEMBER... DO THEY LET YOU SKIP GRADES WITH THAT?
WELL, IT'S RARE, BUT THEY ALLOW IT SOME-TIMES.
MAYBE HE REALLY IS A GENIUS...
MRGH...
......
...SHUT UP.
SLAM
I'VE WORKED HARD TO GET WHERE I AM. QUIT TALKING AS IF EVERY-THING CAME TO ME LIKE MAGIC!

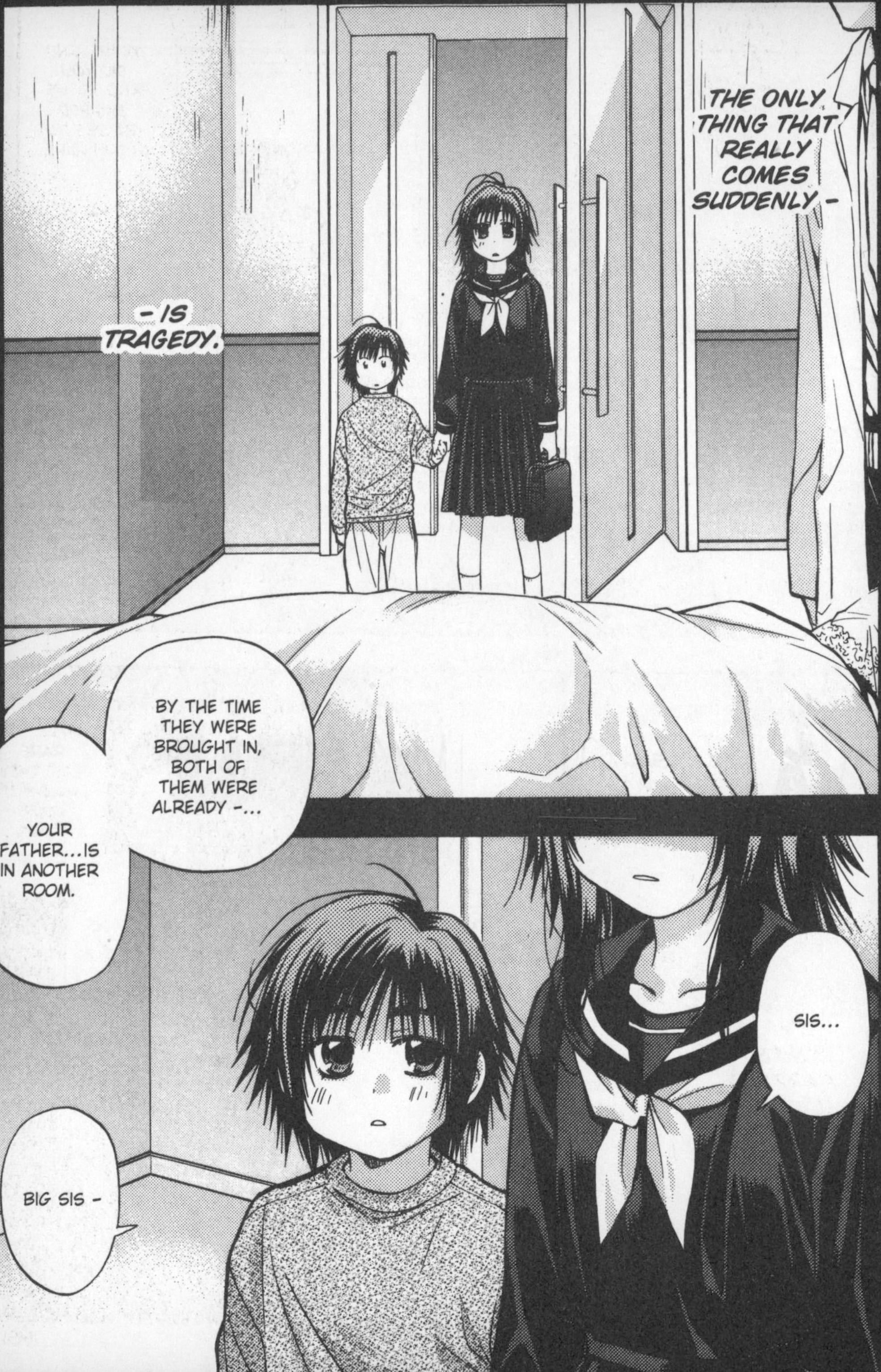
THE ONLY THING THAT REALLY COMES SUDDENLY -
- IS TRAGEDY.
BY THE TIME THEY WERE BROUGHT IN, BOTH OF THEM WERE ALREADY -...
YOUR FATHER...IS IN ANOTHER ROOM.
SIS...
BIG SIS -

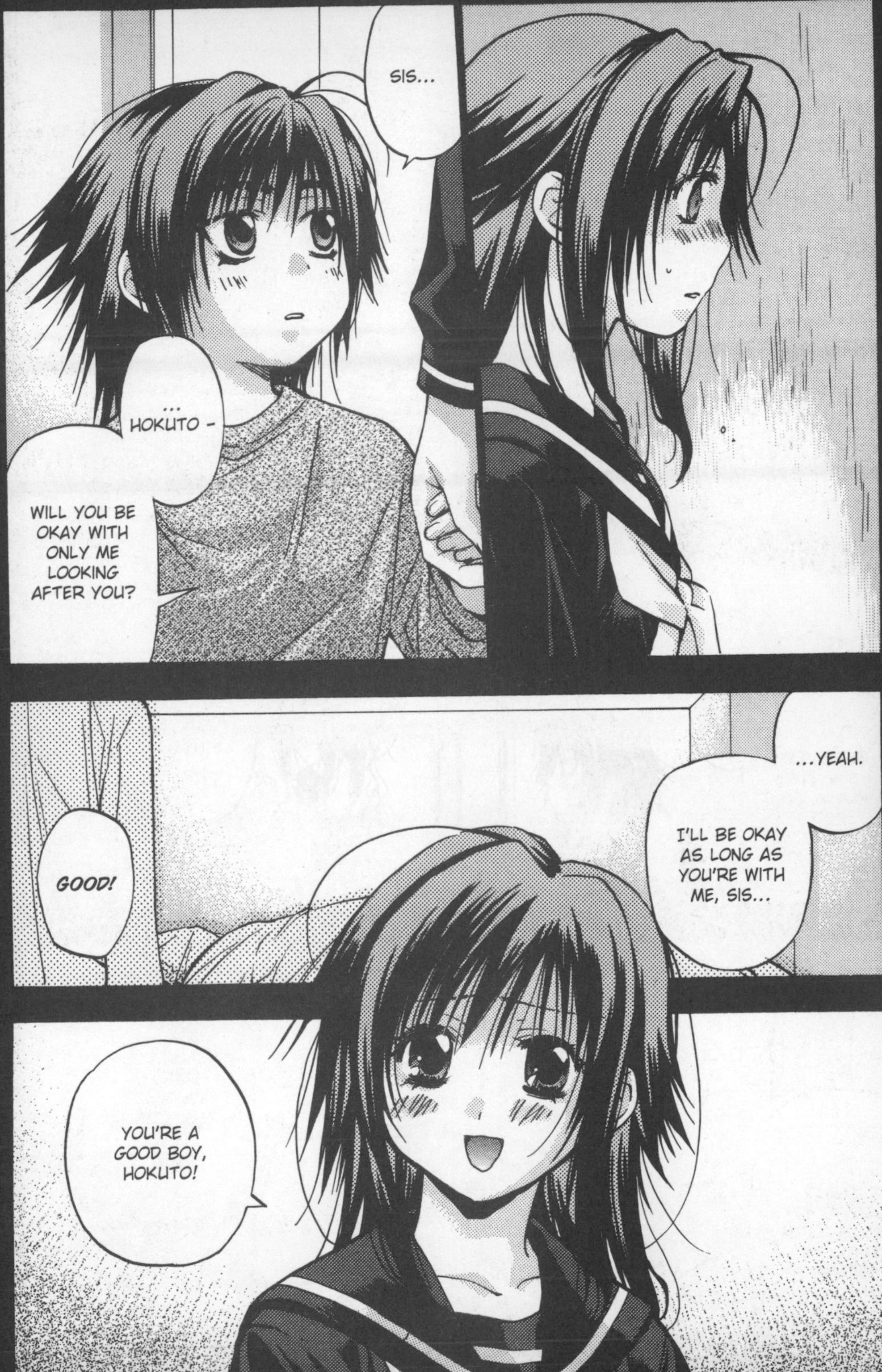
SIS...
... HOKUTO -
WILL YOU BE OKAY WITH ONLY ME LOOKING AFTER YOU?
...YEAH.
I'LL BE OKAY AS LONG AS YOU'RE WITH ME, SIS...
GOOD!
YOU'RE A GOOD BOY, HOKUTO!

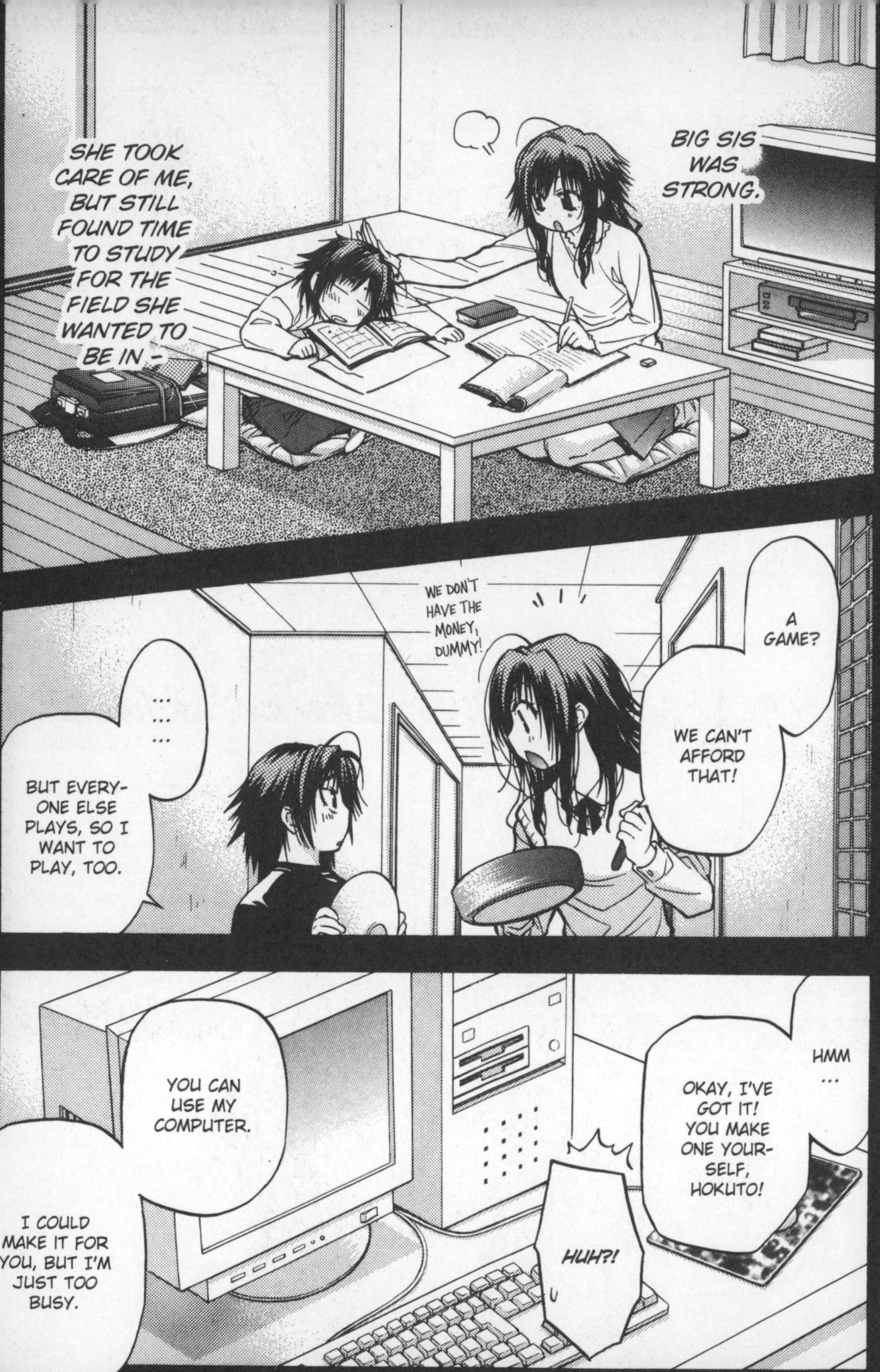
BIG SIS WAS STRONG.
SHE TOOK CARE OF ME, BUT STILL FOUND TIME TO STUDY FOR THE FIELD SHE WANTED TO BE IN –
A GAME?
WE CAN'T AFFORD THAT!
WE DON'T HAVE THE MONEY, DUMMY!
... ...
BUT EVERY-ONE ELSE PLAYS, SO I WANT TO PLAY, TOO.
HMM ...
OKAY, I'VE GOT IT! YOU MAKE ONE YOUR-SELF, HOKUTO!
HUH?!
YOU CAN USE MY COMPUTER.
I COULD MAKE IT FOR YOU, BUT I'M JUST TOO BUSY.

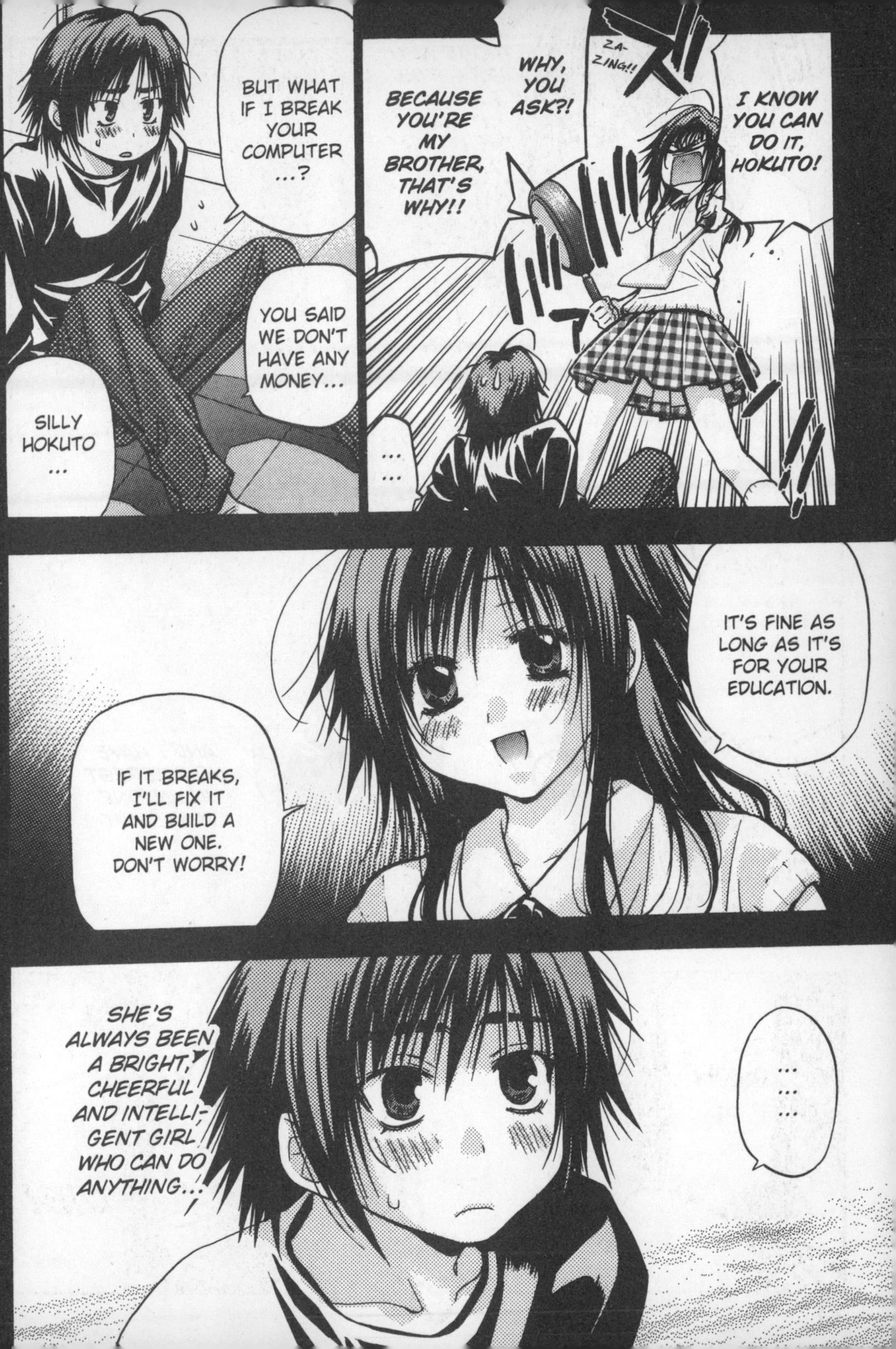

I KNOW YOU CAN DO IT, HOKUTO!
ZA-ZING!!
WHY, YOU ASK?!
BECAUSE YOU'RE MY BROTHER, THAT'S WHY!!
......
BUT WHAT IF I BREAK YOUR COMPUTER ...?
YOU SAID WE DON'T HAVE ANY MONEY...
SILLY HOKUTO ...
IT'S FINE AS LONG AS IT'S FOR YOUR EDUCATION.
IF IT BREAKS, I'LL FIX IT AND BUILD A NEW ONE. DON'T WORRY!
....
SHE'S ALWAYS BEEN A BRIGHT, CHEERFUL AND INTELLI-GENT GIRL WHO CAN DO ANYTHING...

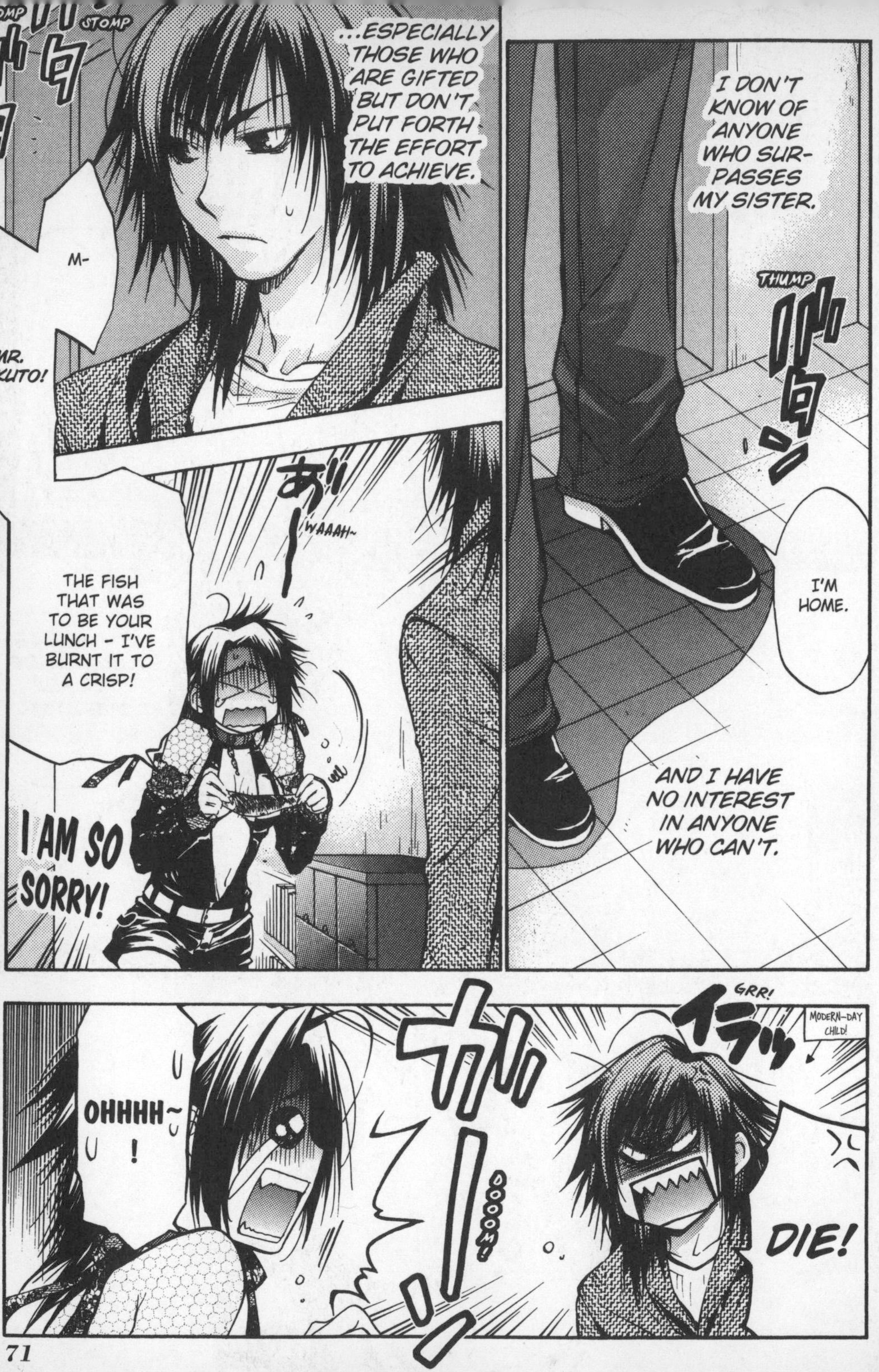
I DON'T KNOW OF ANYONE WHO SUR- PASSES MY SISTER.
THUMP
I'M HOME.
AND I HAVE NO INTEREST IN ANYONE WHO CAN'T.
...ESPECIALLY THOSE WHO ARE GIFTED BUT DON'T PUT FORTH THE EFFORT TO ACHIEVE.
STOMP
STOMP
M-
MR. HOKUTO!
WAAAH~
THE FISH THAT WAS TO BE YOUR LUNCH - I'VE BURNT IT TO A CRISP!
I AM SO SORRY!
GRR!
MODERN-DAY CHILD!
DIE!
DOOOOM!
OHHHH~!

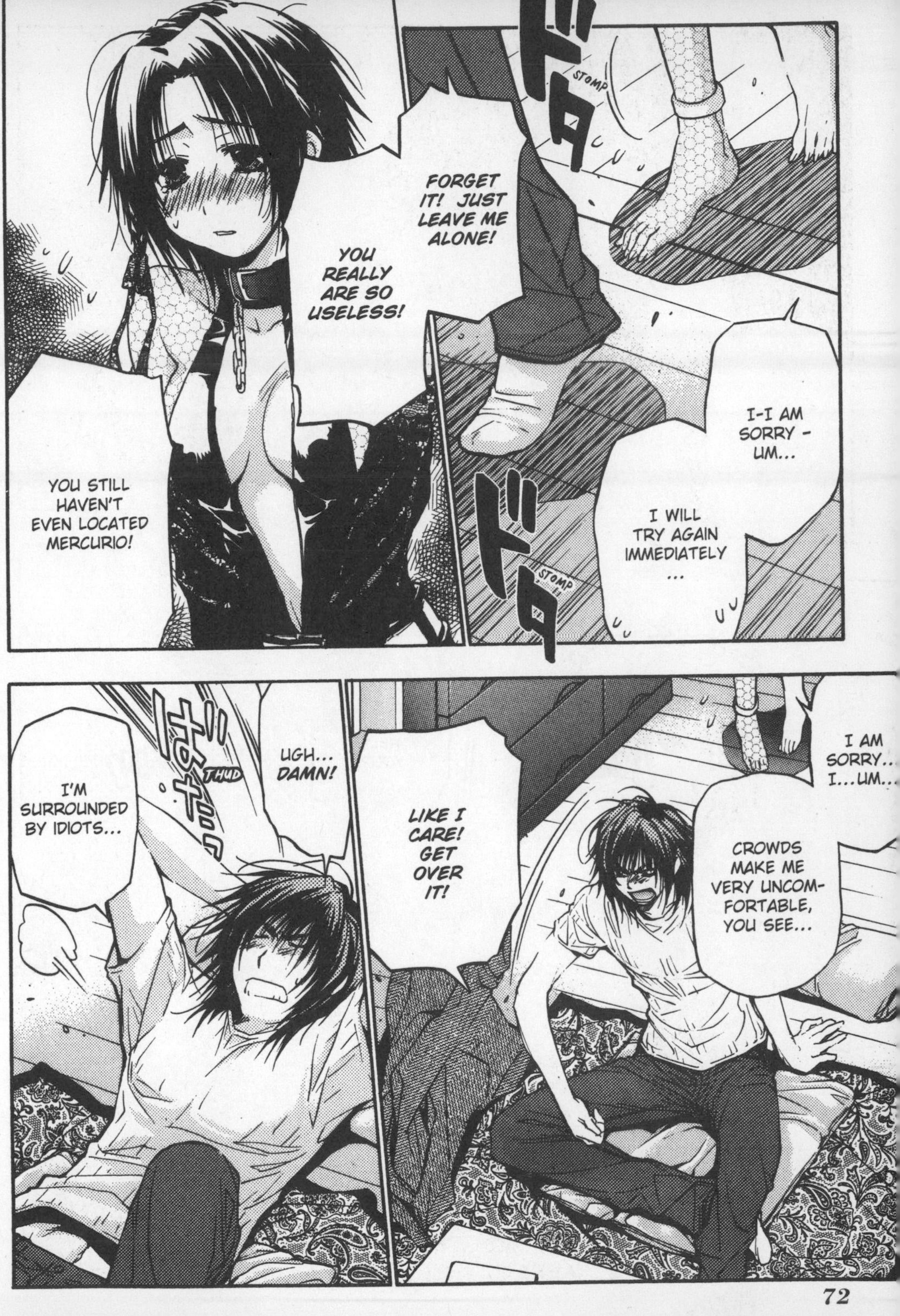
STOMP
FORGET IT! JUST LEAVE ME ALONE!
I-I AM SORRY - UM...
I WILL TRY AGAIN IMMEDIATELY ...
STOMP
YOU REALLY ARE SO USELESS!
YOU STILL HAVEN'T EVEN LOCATED MERCURIO!
I AM SORRY... I...UM...
CROWDS MAKE ME VERY UNCOM-FORTABLE, YOU SEE...
LIKE I CARE! GET OVER IT!
UGH... DAMN!
THUD
I'M SURROUNDED BY IDIOTS...

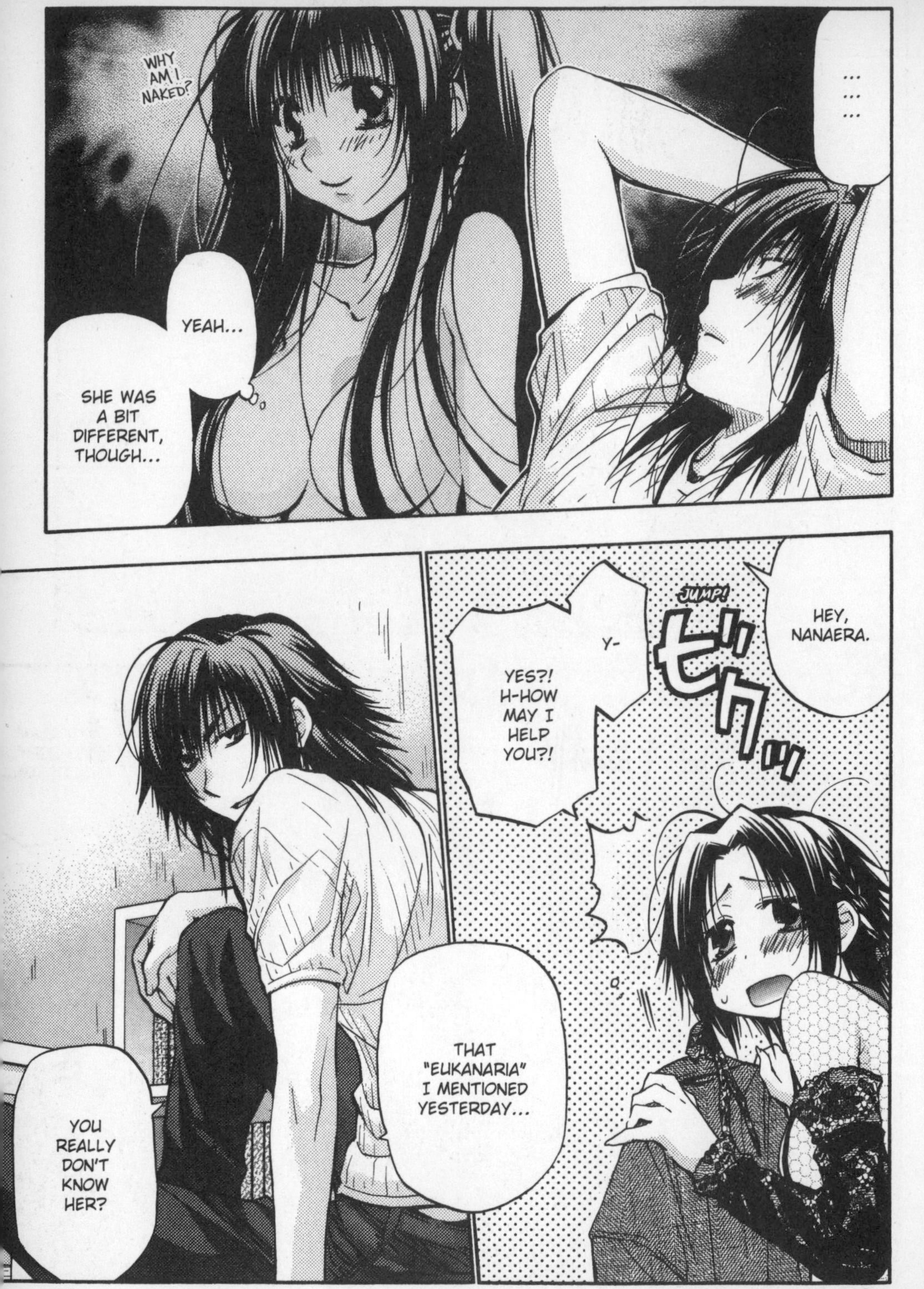
... ...
WHY AM I NAKED?
YEAH...
SHE WAS A BIT DIFFERENT, THOUGH...
HEY, NANAERA.
JUMP!
ビクッ
Y-
YES?! H-HOW MAY I HELP YOU?!
THAT "EUKANARIA" I MENTIONED YESTERDAY...
YOU REALLY DON'T KNOW HER?

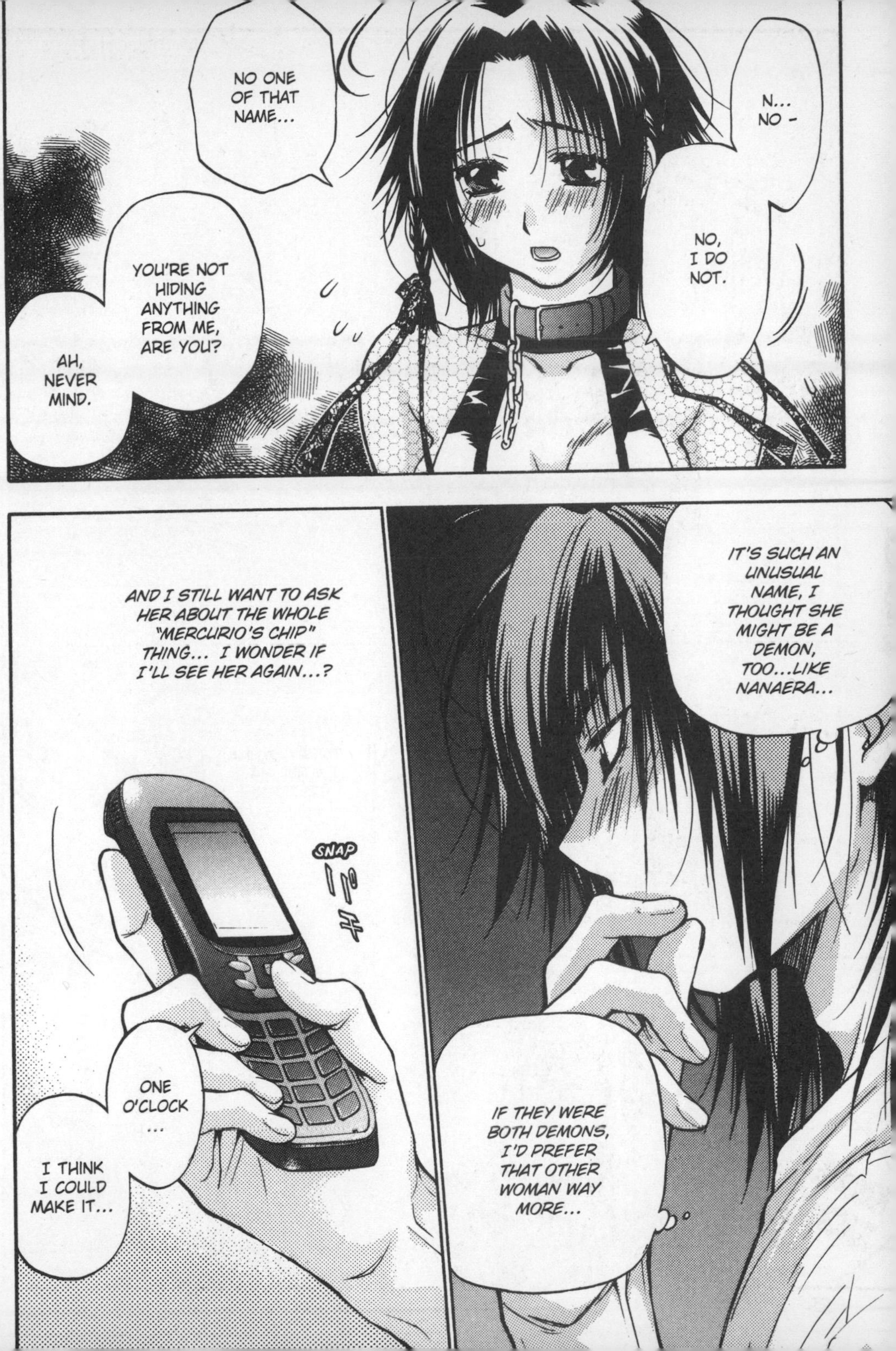
N... NO -
NO ONE OF THAT NAME...
NO, I DO NOT.
YOU'RE NOT HIDING ANYTHING FROM ME, ARE YOU?
AH, NEVER MIND.
IT'S SUCH AN UNUSUAL NAME, I THOUGHT SHE MIGHT BE A DEMON, TOO...LIKE NANAERA...
IF THEY WERE BOTH DEMONS, I'D PREFER THAT OTHER WOMAN WAY MORE...
AND I STILL WANT TO ASK HER ABOUT THE WHOLE "MERCURIO'S CHIP" THING... I WONDER IF I'LL SEE HER AGAIN...?
SNAP
ONE O'CLOCK ...
I THINK I COULD MAKE IT...

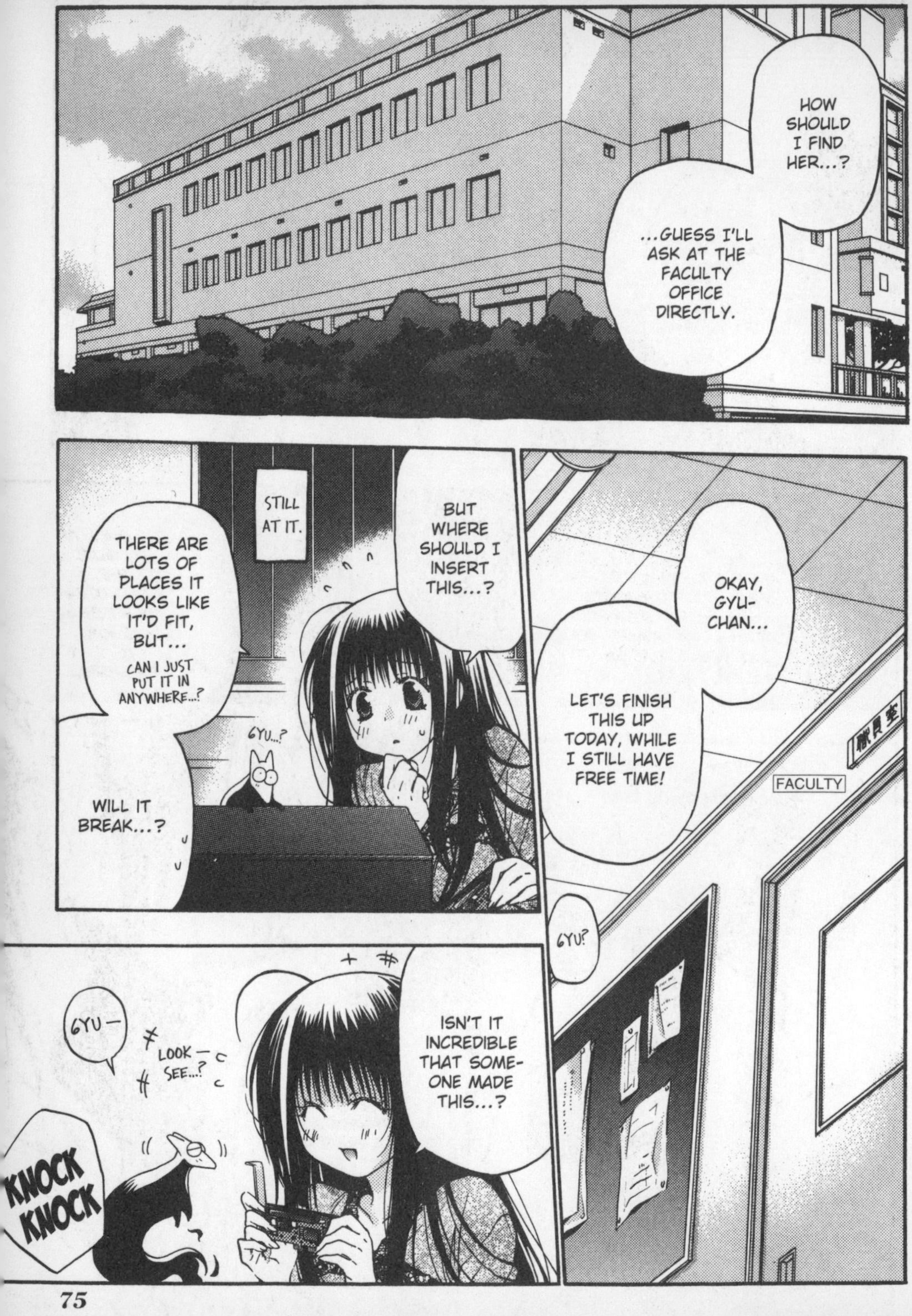
HOW SHOULD I FIND HER...?
...GUESS I'LL ASK AT THE FACULTY OFFICE DIRECTLY.
OKAY, GYU-CHAN...
LET'S FINISH THIS UP TODAY, WHILE I STILL HAVE FREE TIME!
職員室
FACULTY
GYU?
STILL AT IT.
BUT WHERE SHOULD I INSERT THIS...?
THERE ARE LOTS OF PLACES IT LOOKS LIKE IT'D FIT, BUT...
CAN I JUST PUT IT IN ANYWHERE...?
GYU...?
WILL IT BREAK...?
ISN'T IT INCREDIBLE THAT SOMEONE MADE THIS...?
GYU—
LOOK— SEE...?
KNOCK KNOCK

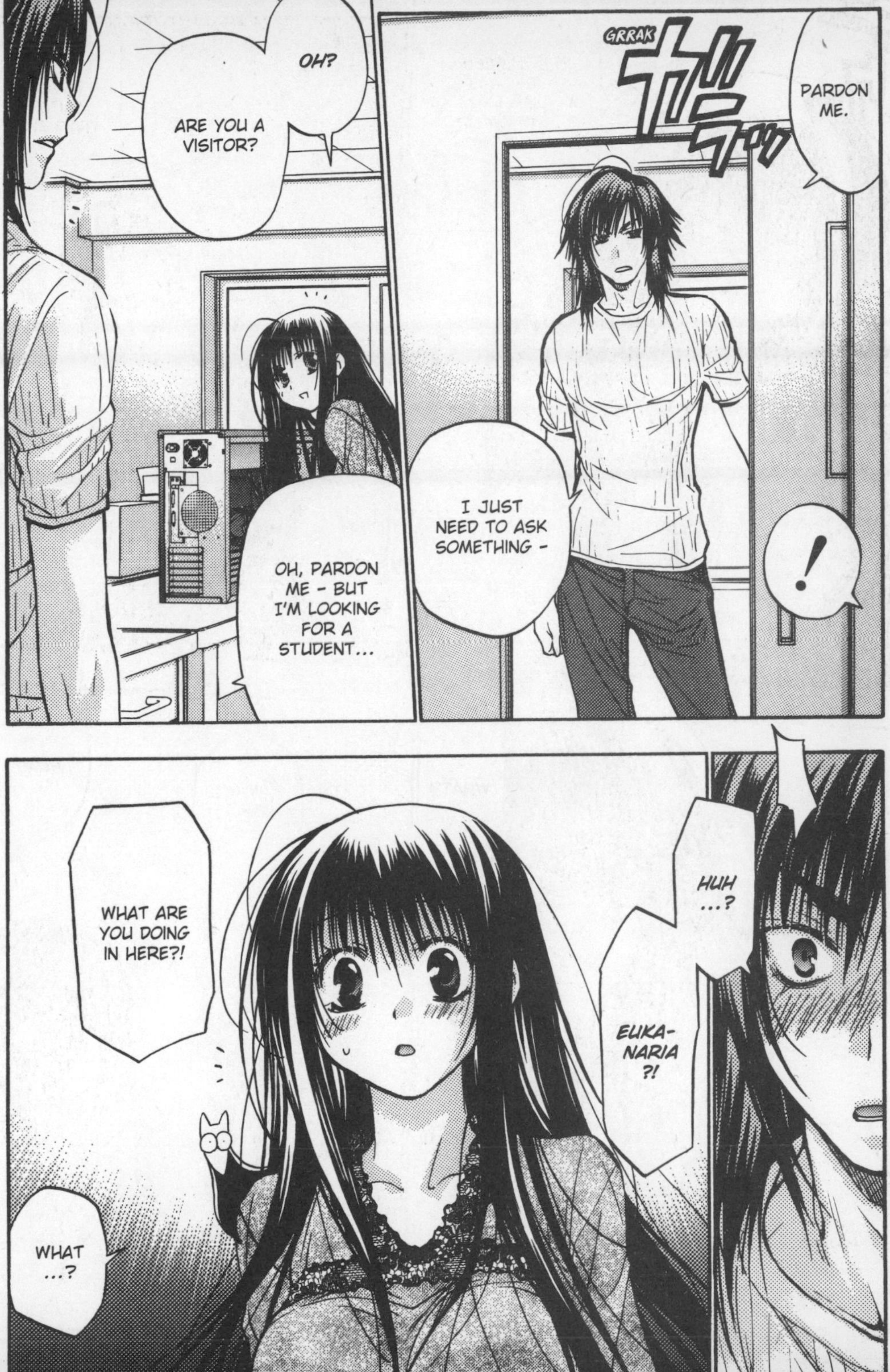
GRRAK
PARDON ME.
I JUST NEED TO ASK SOMETHING -
!
OH?
ARE YOU A VISITOR?
OH, PARDON ME - BUT I'M LOOKING FOR A STUDENT...
HUH ...?
EUKA-NARIA ?!
WHAT ARE YOU DOING IN HERE?!
WHAT ...?

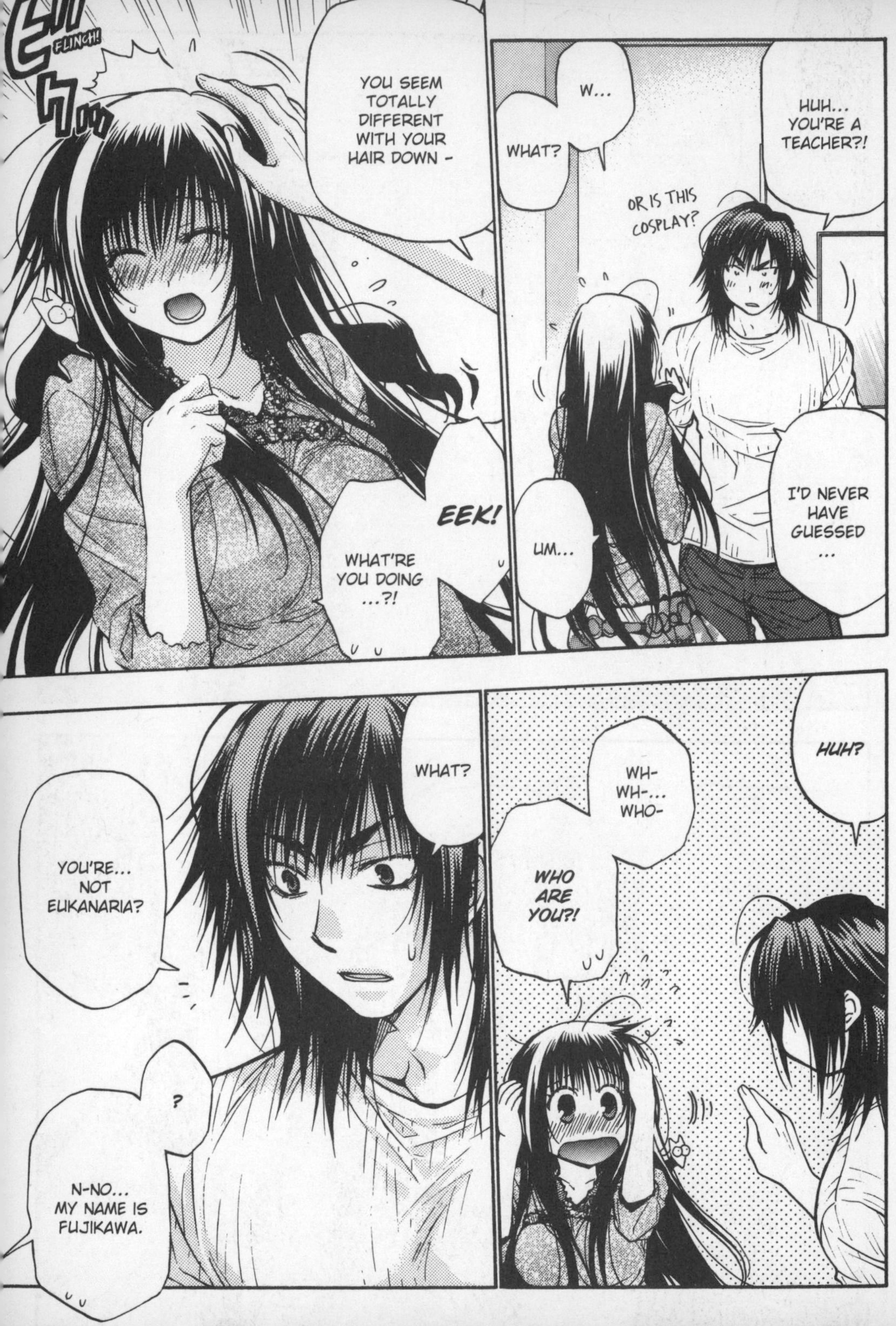
HUH... YOU'RE A TEACHER?!
OR IS THIS COSPLAY?
W... WHAT?
I'D NEVER HAVE GUESSED ...
UM...
YOU SEEM TOTALLY DIFFERENT WITH YOUR HAIR DOWN -
FLINCH!
EEK!
WHAT'RE YOU DOING ...?!
HUH?
WH- WH-... WHO-
WHO ARE YOU?!
WHAT?
YOU'RE... NOT EUKANARIA?
?
N-NO... MY NAME IS FUJIKAWA.

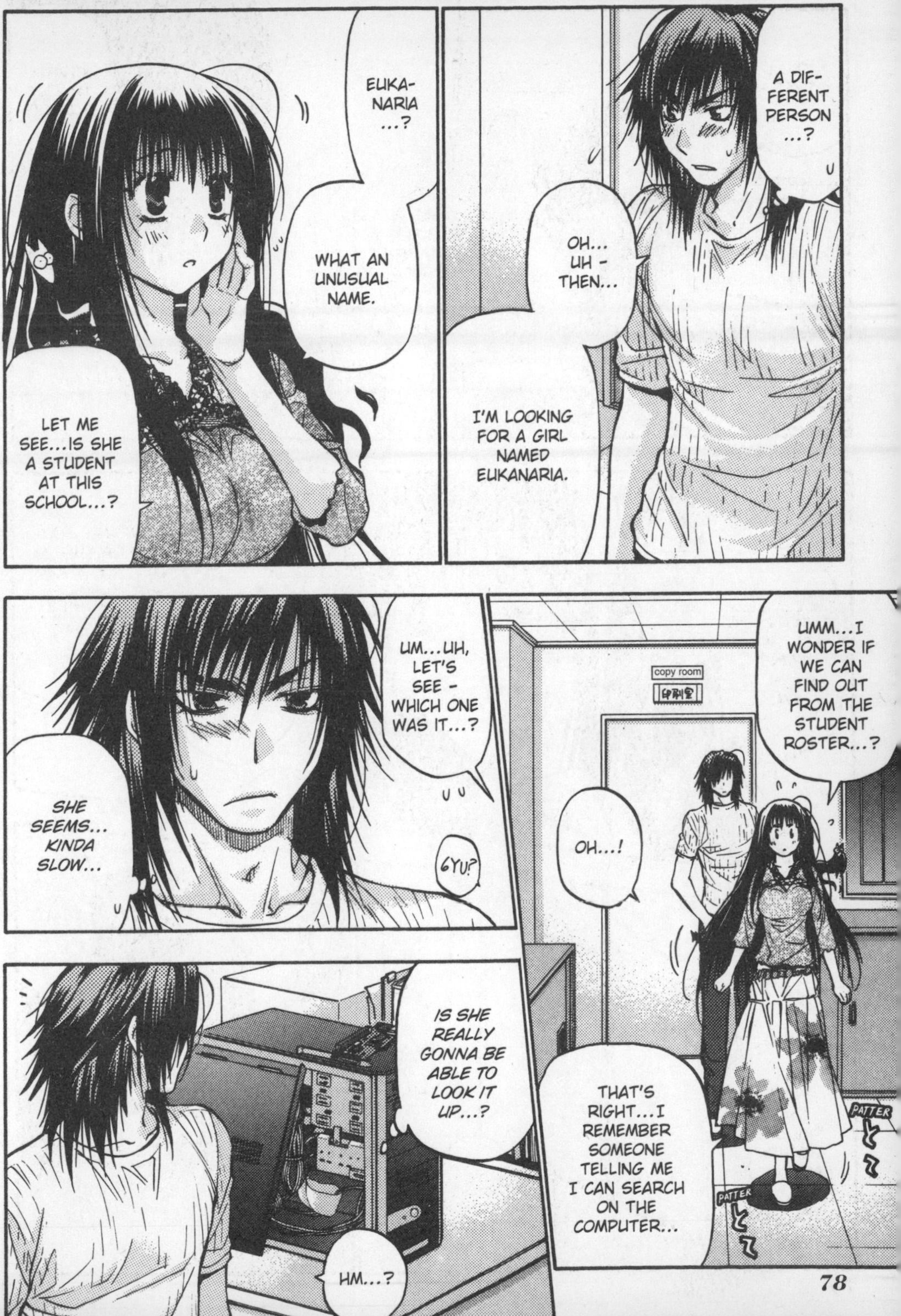
A DIF-FERENT PERSON ...?
OH... UH - THEN...
I'M LOOKING FOR A GIRL NAMED EUKANARIA.
EUKA-NARIA ...?
WHAT AN UNUSUAL NAME.
LET ME SEE...IS SHE A STUDENT AT THIS SCHOOL...?
UMM...I WONDER IF WE CAN FIND OUT FROM THE STUDENT ROSTER...?
copy room
印刷室
OH...!
THAT'S RIGHT...I REMEMBER SOMEONE TELLING ME I CAN SEARCH ON THE COMPUTER...
PATTER
PATTER
UM...UH, LET'S SEE - WHICH ONE WAS IT...?
SHE SEEMS... KINDA SLOW...
6YU?
IS SHE REALLY GONNA BE ABLE TO LOOK IT UP...?
HM...?

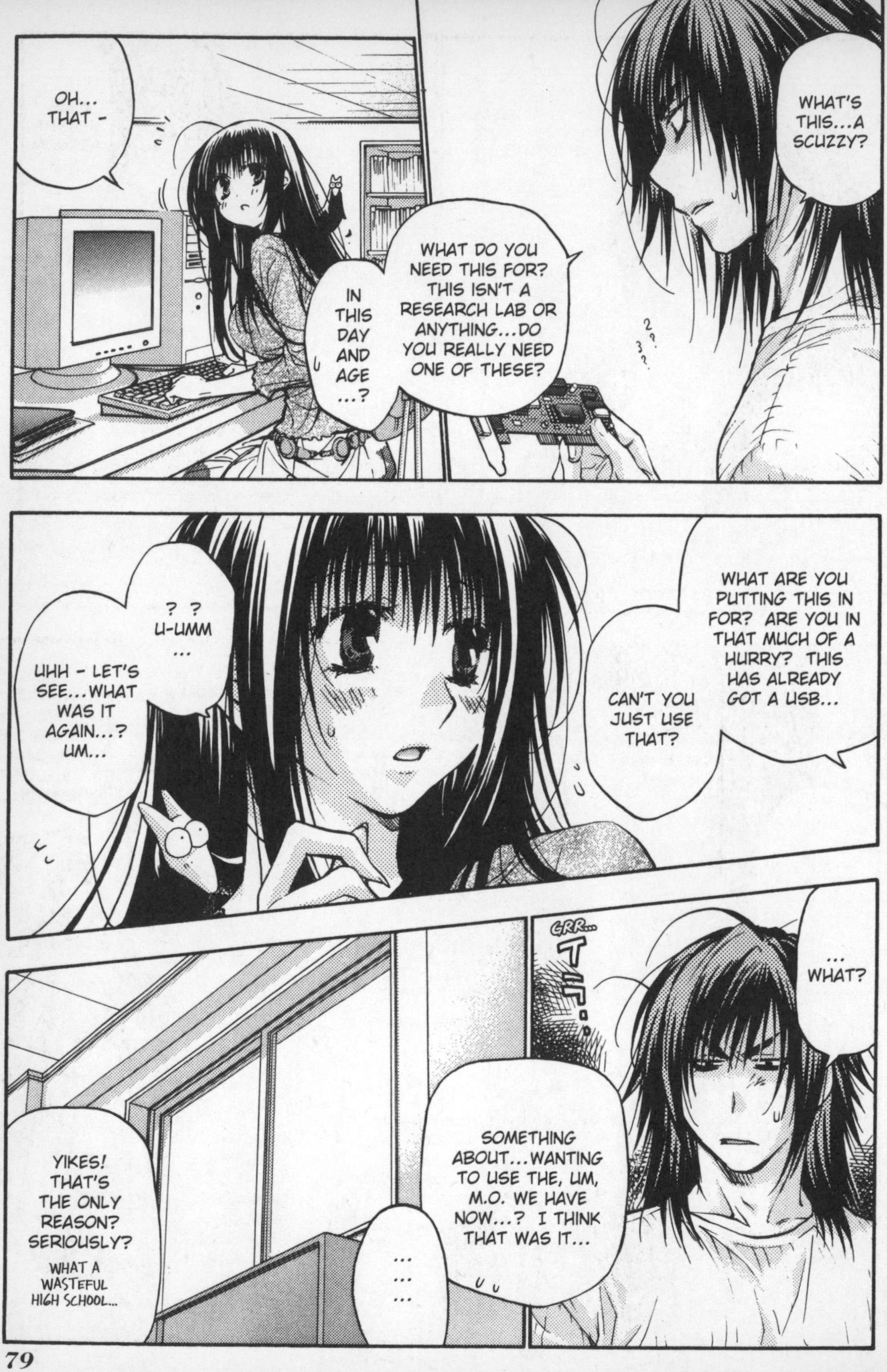
WHAT'S THIS...A SCUZZY?
WHAT DO YOU NEED THIS FOR? THIS ISN'T A RESEARCH LAB OR ANYTHING...DO YOU REALLY NEED ONE OF THESE?
IN THIS DAY AND AGE ...?
OH... THAT -
WHAT ARE YOU PUTTING THIS IN FOR? ARE YOU IN THAT MUCH OF A HURRY? THIS HAS ALREADY GOT A USB...
CAN'T YOU JUST USE THAT?
? ? U-UMM ...
UHH - LET'S SEE...WHAT WAS IT AGAIN...? UM...
... WHAT?
GRR...
SOMETHING ABOUT...WANTING TO USE THE, UM, M.O. WE HAVE NOW...? I THINK THAT WAS IT...
... ...
YIKES! THAT'S THE ONLY REASON? SERIOUSLY?
WHAT A WASTEFUL HIGH SCHOOL...

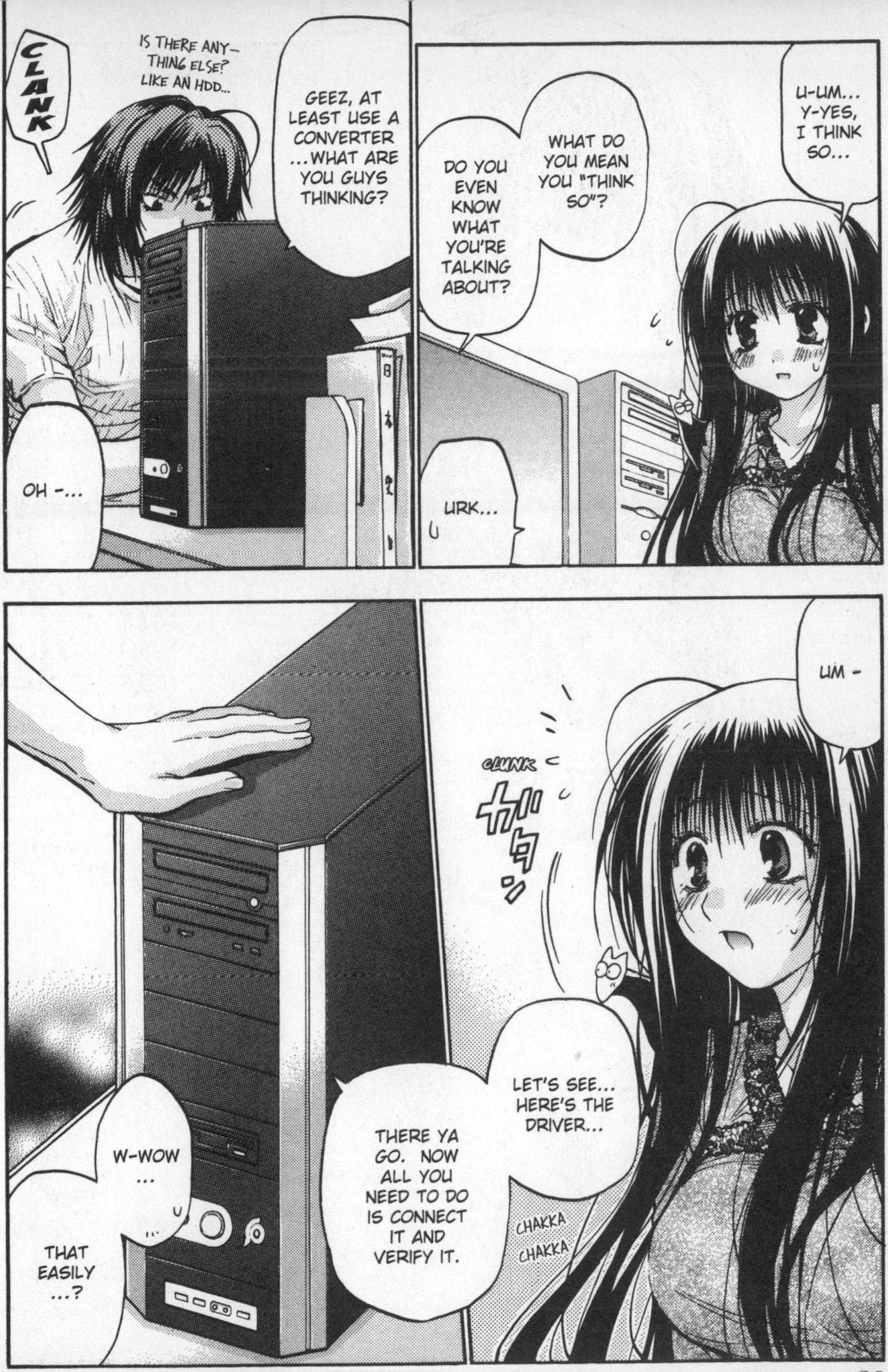
U-UM... Y-YES, I THINK SO...
WHAT DO YOU MEAN YOU "THINK SO"?
DO YOU EVEN KNOW WHAT YOU'RE TALKING ABOUT?
URK...
GEEZ, AT LEAST USE A CONVERTER ...WHAT ARE YOU GUYS THINKING?
IS THERE ANY-THING ELSE? LIKE AN HDD...
CLANK
OH -...
UM -
CLUNK
ガタッ
LET'S SEE... HERE'S THE DRIVER...
THERE YA GO. NOW ALL YOU NEED TO DO IS CONNECT IT AND VERIFY IT.
CHAKKA CHAKKA
W-WOW ...
... THAT EASILY ...?

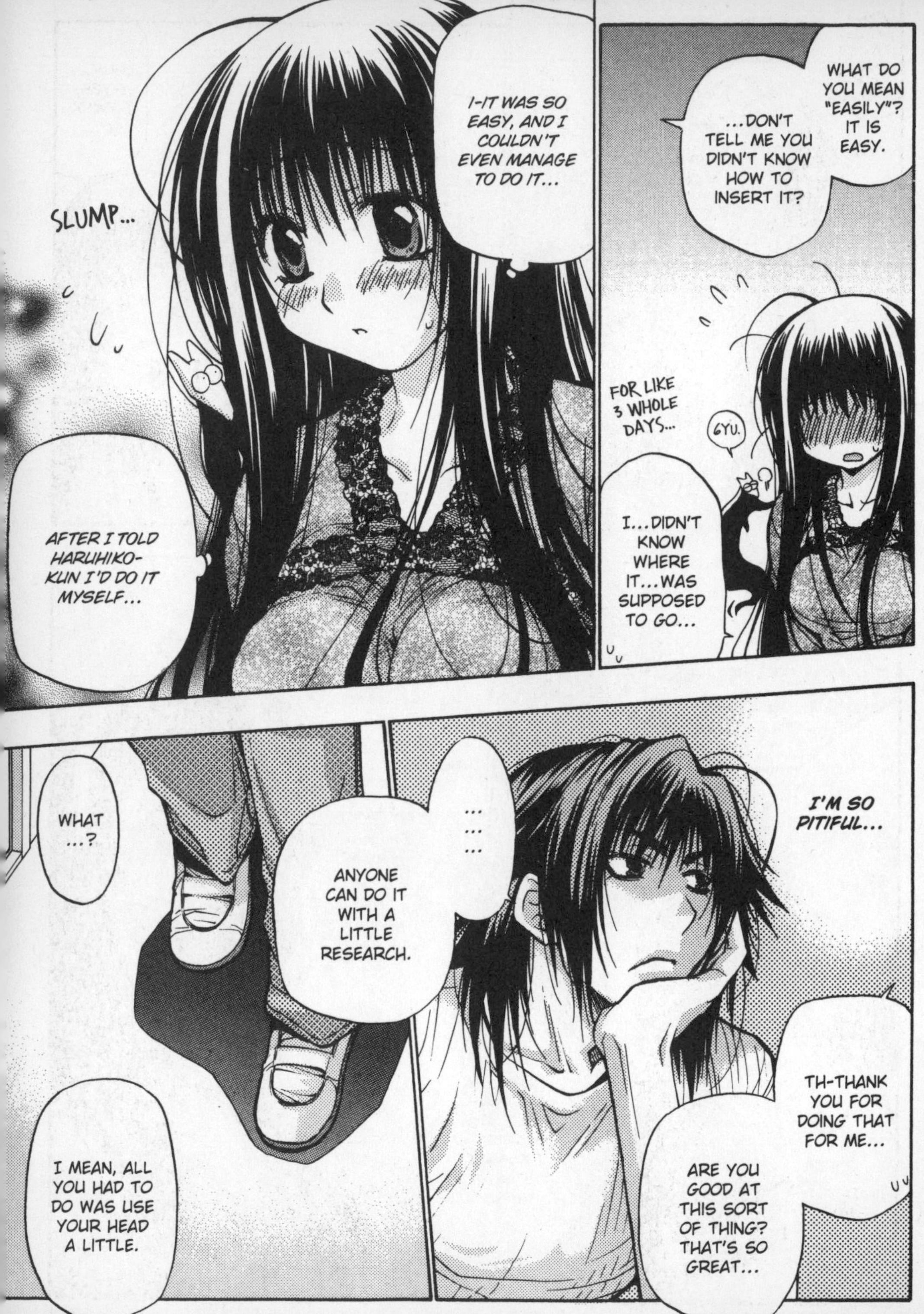
WHAT DO YOU MEAN "EASILY"? IT IS EASY.
...DON'T TELL ME YOU DIDN'T KNOW HOW TO INSERT IT?
FOR LIKE 3 WHOLE DAYS...
GYU.
I...DIDN'T KNOW WHERE IT...WAS SUPPOSED TO GO...
I-IT WAS SO EASY, AND I COULDN'T EVEN MANAGE TO DO IT...
SLUMP...
AFTER I TOLD HARUHIKO-KUN I'D DO IT MYSELF...
I'M SO PITIFUL...
TH-THANK YOU FOR DOING THAT FOR ME...
ARE YOU GOOD AT THIS SORT OF THING? THAT'S SO GREAT...
... ...
ANYONE CAN DO IT WITH A LITTLE RESEARCH.
WHAT ...?
I MEAN, ALL YOU HAD TO DO WAS USE YOUR HEAD A LITTLE.

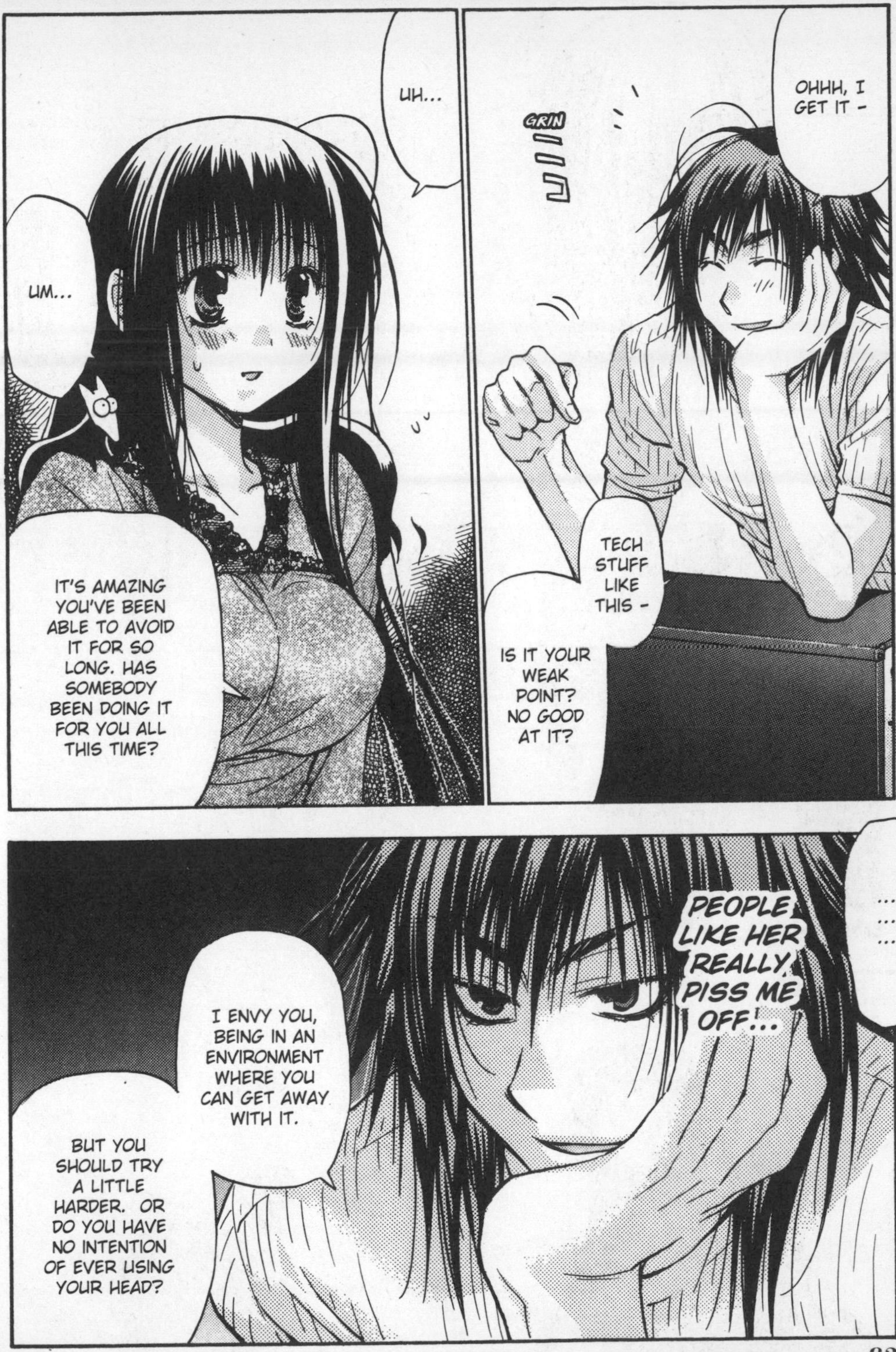
OHHH, I GET IT -
GRIN
TECH STUFF LIKE THIS -
IS IT YOUR WEAK POINT? NO GOOD AT IT?
UH...
UM...
IT'S AMAZING YOU'VE BEEN ABLE TO AVOID IT FOR SO LONG. HAS SOMEBODY BEEN DOING IT FOR YOU ALL THIS TIME?
... ...
PEOPLE LIKE HER REALLY PISS ME OFF...
I ENVY YOU, BEING IN AN ENVIRONMENT WHERE YOU CAN GET AWAY WITH IT.
BUT YOU SHOULD TRY A LITTLE HARDER. OR DO YOU HAVE NO INTENTION OF EVER USING YOUR HEAD?

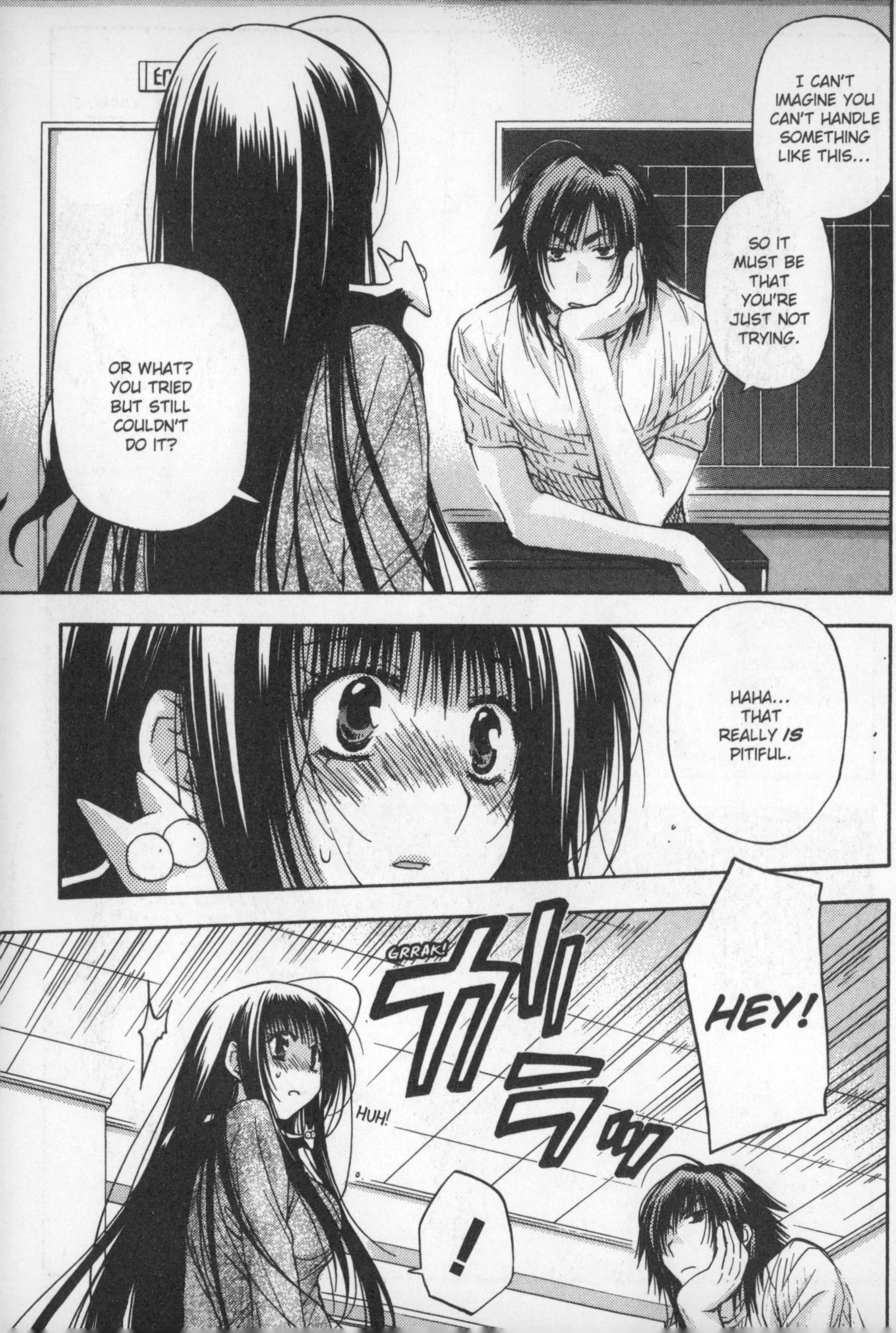
I CAN'T IMAGINE YOU CAN'T HANDLE SOMETHING LIKE THIS...
SO IT MUST BE THAT YOU'RE JUST NOT TRYING.
OR WHAT? YOU TRIED BUT STILL COULDN'T DO IT?
HAHA... THAT REALLY *IS* PITIFUL.
HEY!
GRRAK!
HUH!
!

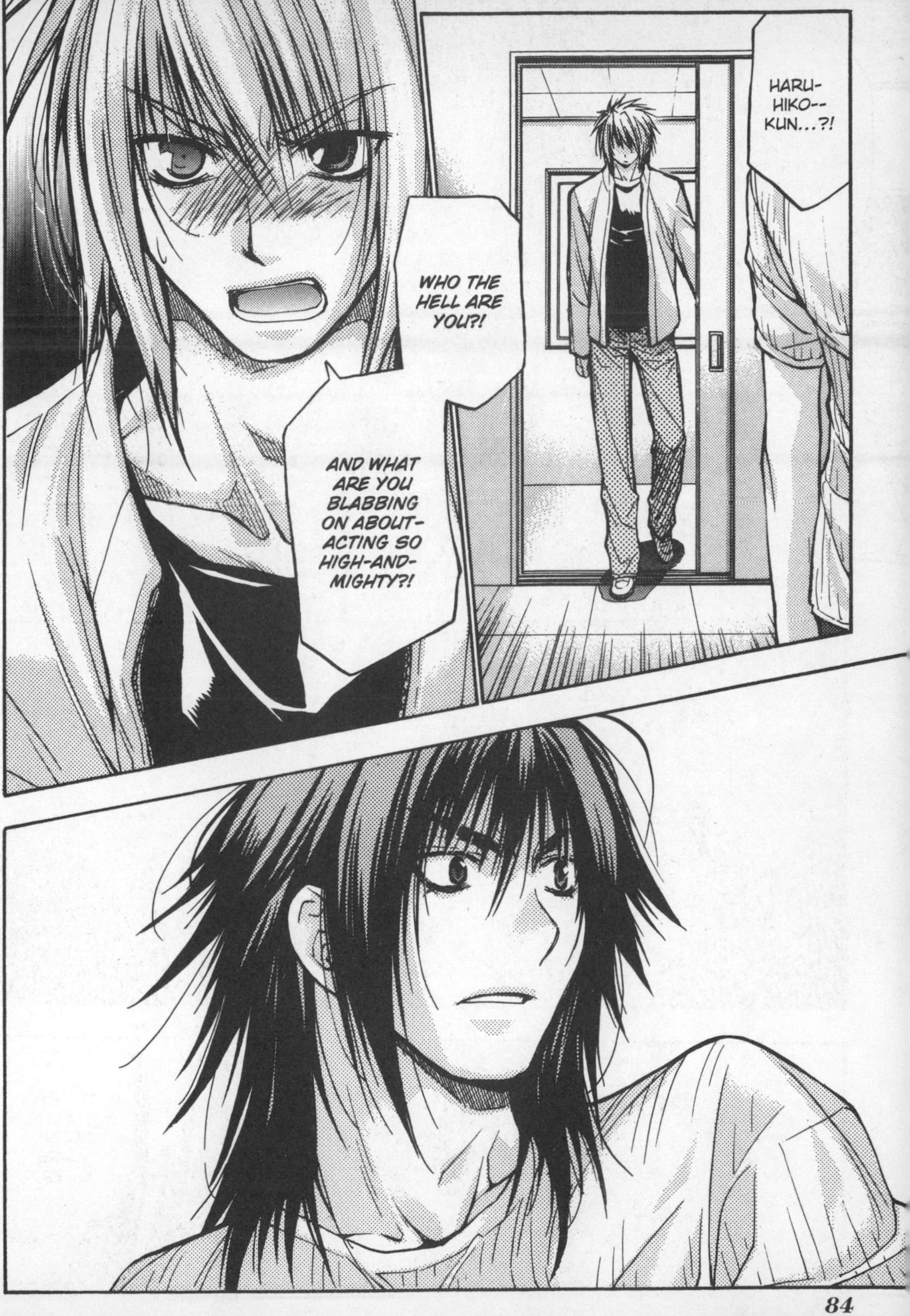
HARU-HIKO--KUN...?!
WHO THE HELL ARE YOU?!
AND WHAT ARE YOU BLABBING ON ABOUT-ACTING SO HIGH-AND-MIGHTY?!

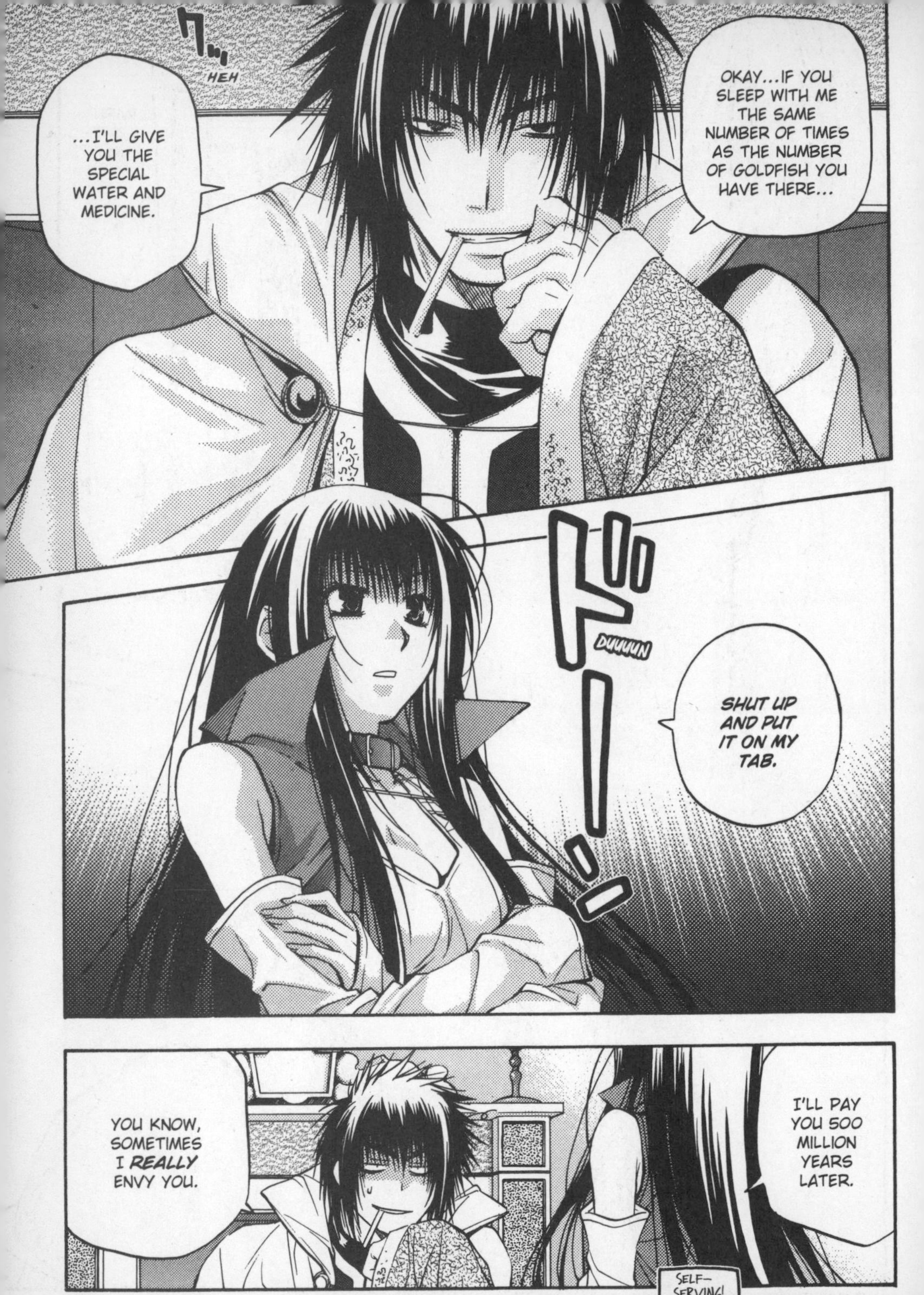
OKAY...IF YOU SLEEP WITH ME THE SAME NUMBER OF TIMES AS THE NUMBER OF GOLDFISH YOU HAVE THERE...
HEH
...I'LL GIVE YOU THE SPECIAL WATER AND MEDICINE.
DUUUUN
SHUT UP AND PUT IT ON MY TAB.
I'LL PAY YOU 500 MILLION YEARS LATER.
YOU KNOW, SOMETIMES I REALLY ENVY YOU.
SELF-SERVING!

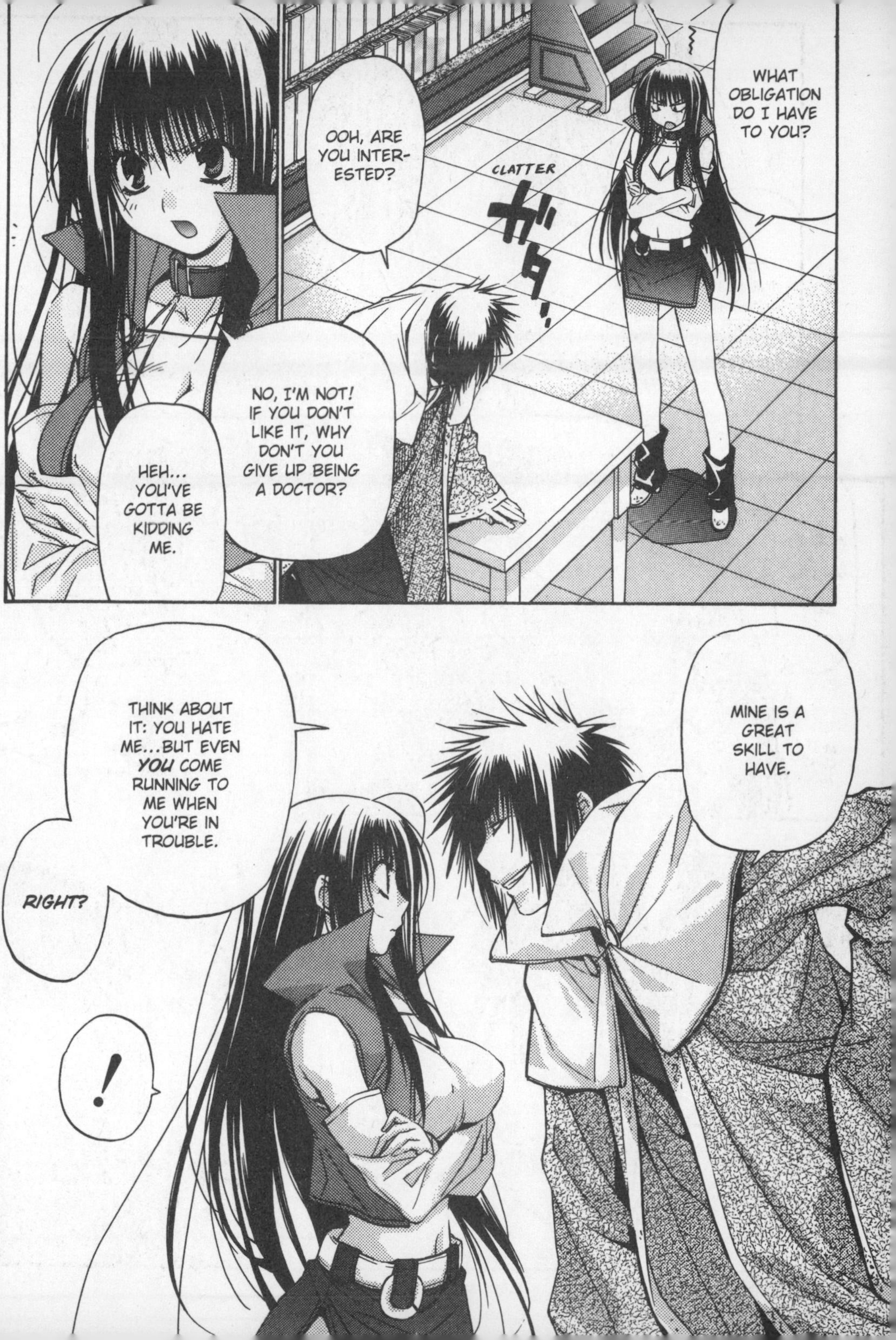
WHAT OBLIGATION DO I HAVE TO YOU?
OOH, ARE YOU INTERESTED?
CLATTER
ガタ
NO, I'M NOT! IF YOU DON'T LIKE IT, WHY DON'T YOU GIVE UP BEING A DOCTOR?
HEH... YOU'VE GOTTA BE KIDDING ME.
MINE IS A GREAT SKILL TO HAVE.
THINK ABOUT IT: YOU HATE ME...BUT EVEN *YOU* COME RUNNING TO ME WHEN YOU'RE IN TROUBLE.
RIGHT?
!

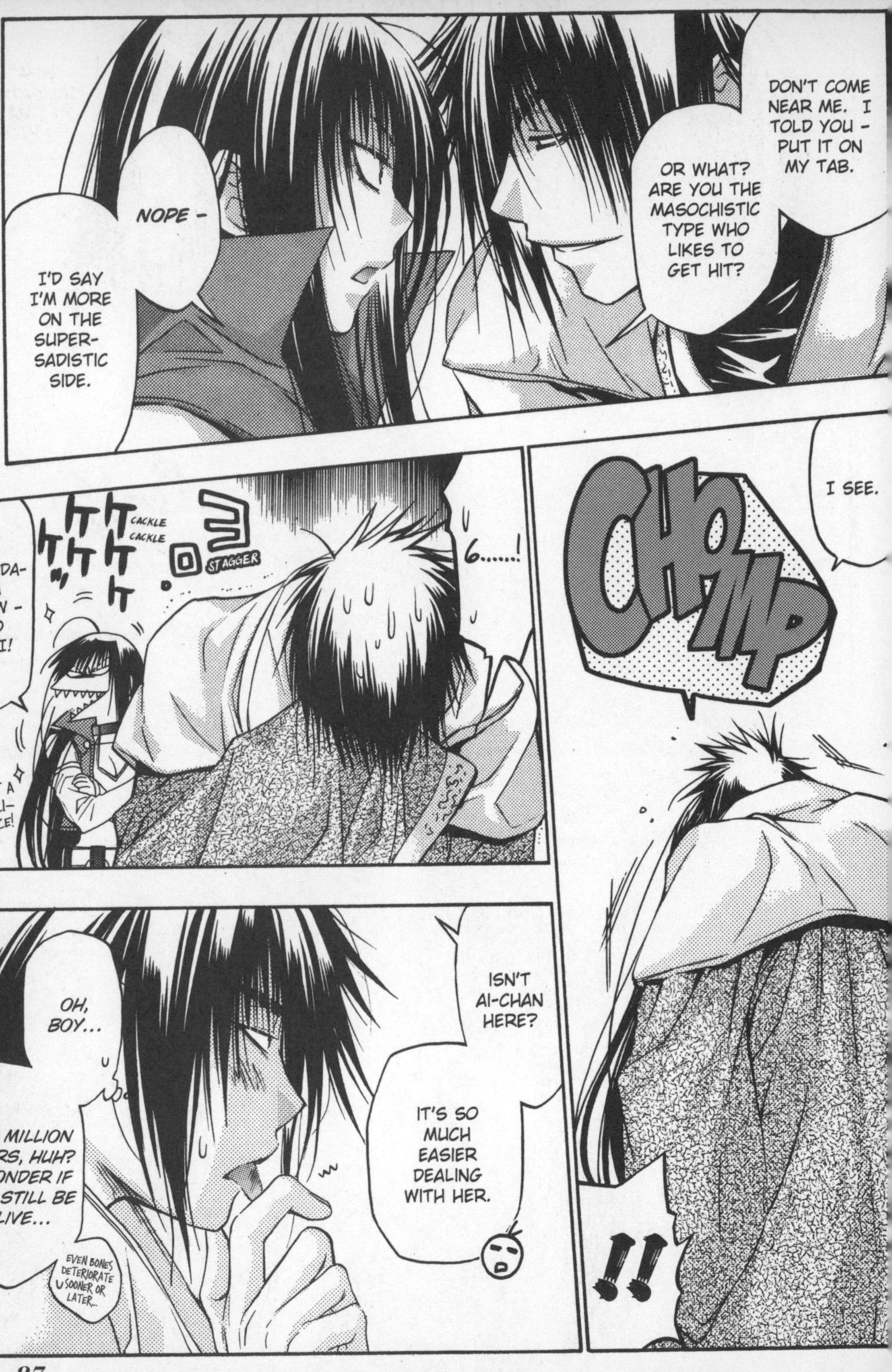
DON'T COME NEAR ME. I TOLD YOU - PUT IT ON MY TAB.
OR WHAT? ARE YOU THE MASOCHISTIC TYPE WHO LIKES TO GET HIT?
NOPE -
I'D SAY I'M MORE ON THE SUPER-SADISTIC SIDE.
I SEE.
CHOMP
!!
6......!
STAGGER
CACKLE CACKLE
WHADDA-YA KNOW - SO AM I!
WHAT A COINCI-DENCE!
ISN'T AI-CHAN HERE?
IT'S SO MUCH EASIER DEALING WITH HER.
OH, BOY...
500 MILLION YEARS, HUH? I WONDER IF I'LL STILL BE ALIVE...
EVEN BONES DETERIORATE SOONER OR LATER...

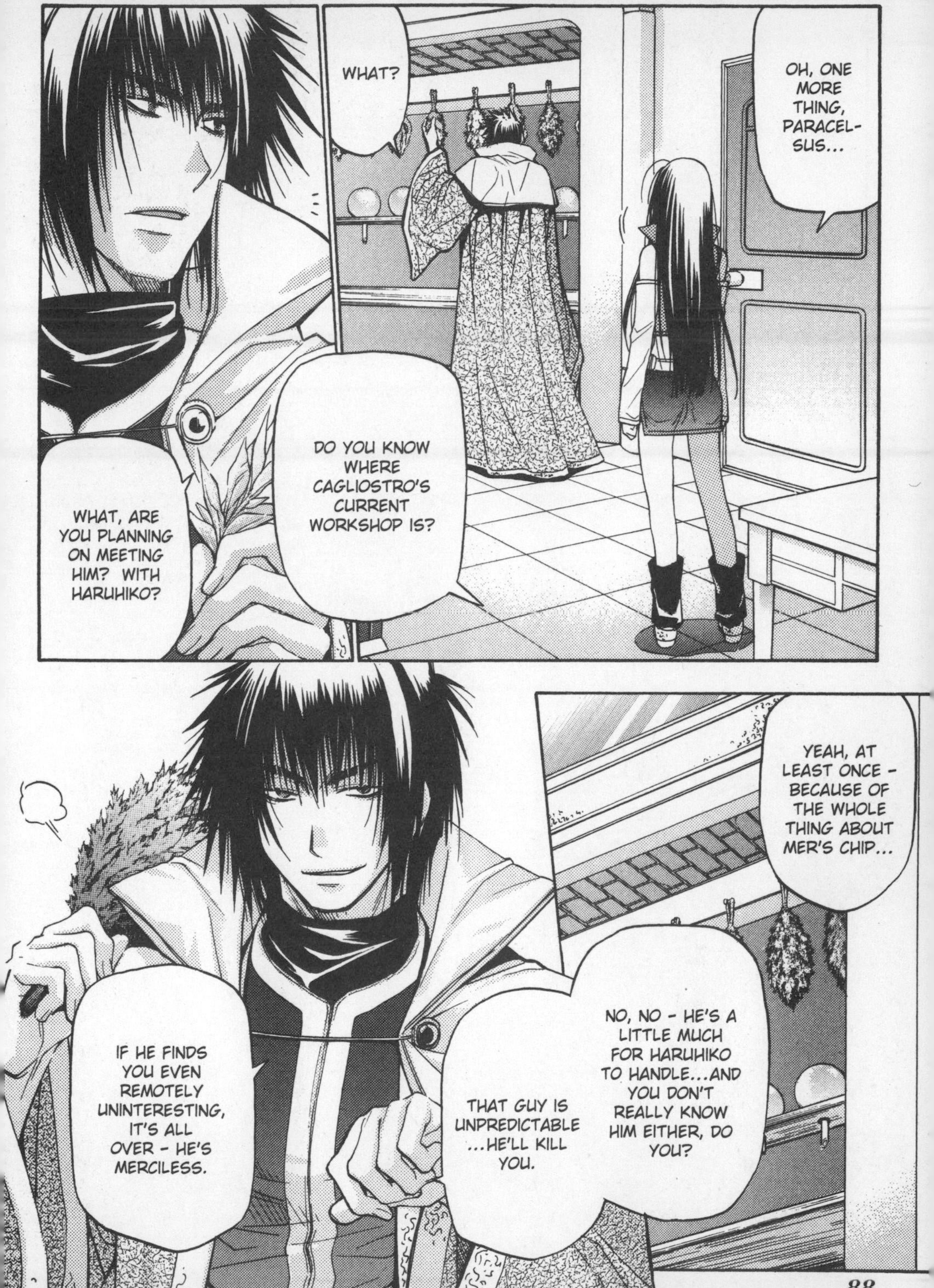
OH, ONE MORE THING, PARACEL-SUS...
WHAT?
DO YOU KNOW WHERE CAGLIOSTRO'S CURRENT WORKSHOP IS?
WHAT, ARE YOU PLANNING ON MEETING HIM? WITH HARUHIKO?
YEAH, AT LEAST ONCE - BECAUSE OF THE WHOLE THING ABOUT MER'S CHIP...
NO, NO - HE'S A LITTLE MUCH FOR HARUHIKO TO HANDLE...AND YOU DON'T REALLY KNOW HIM EITHER, DO YOU?
THAT GUY IS UNPREDICTABLE ...HE'LL KILL YOU.
IF HE FINDS YOU EVEN REMOTELY UNINTERESTING, IT'S ALL OVER - HE'S MERCILESS.

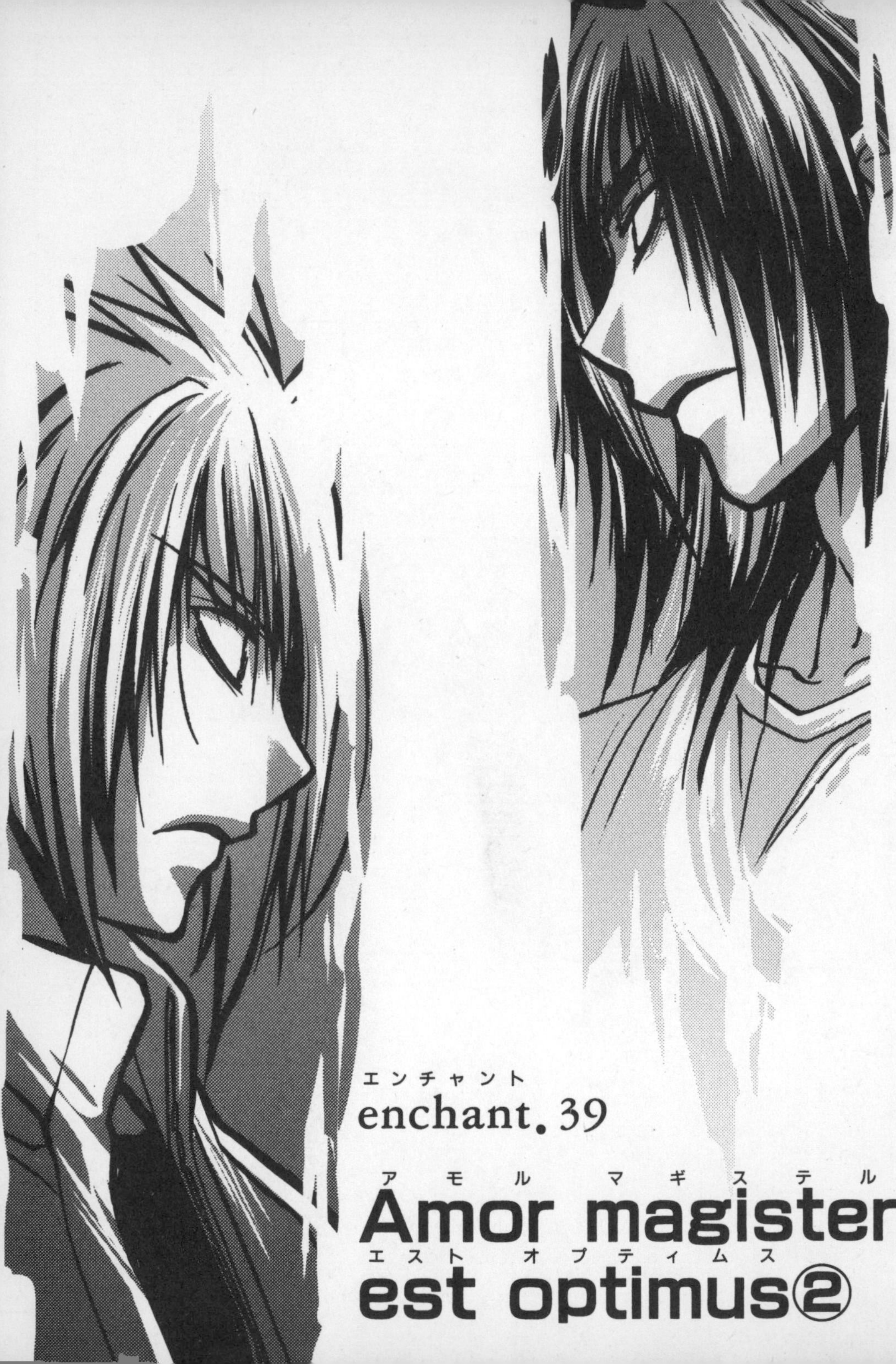

エンチャント
enchant. 39

アモル マギステル エスト オプティムス
Amor magister est optimus②

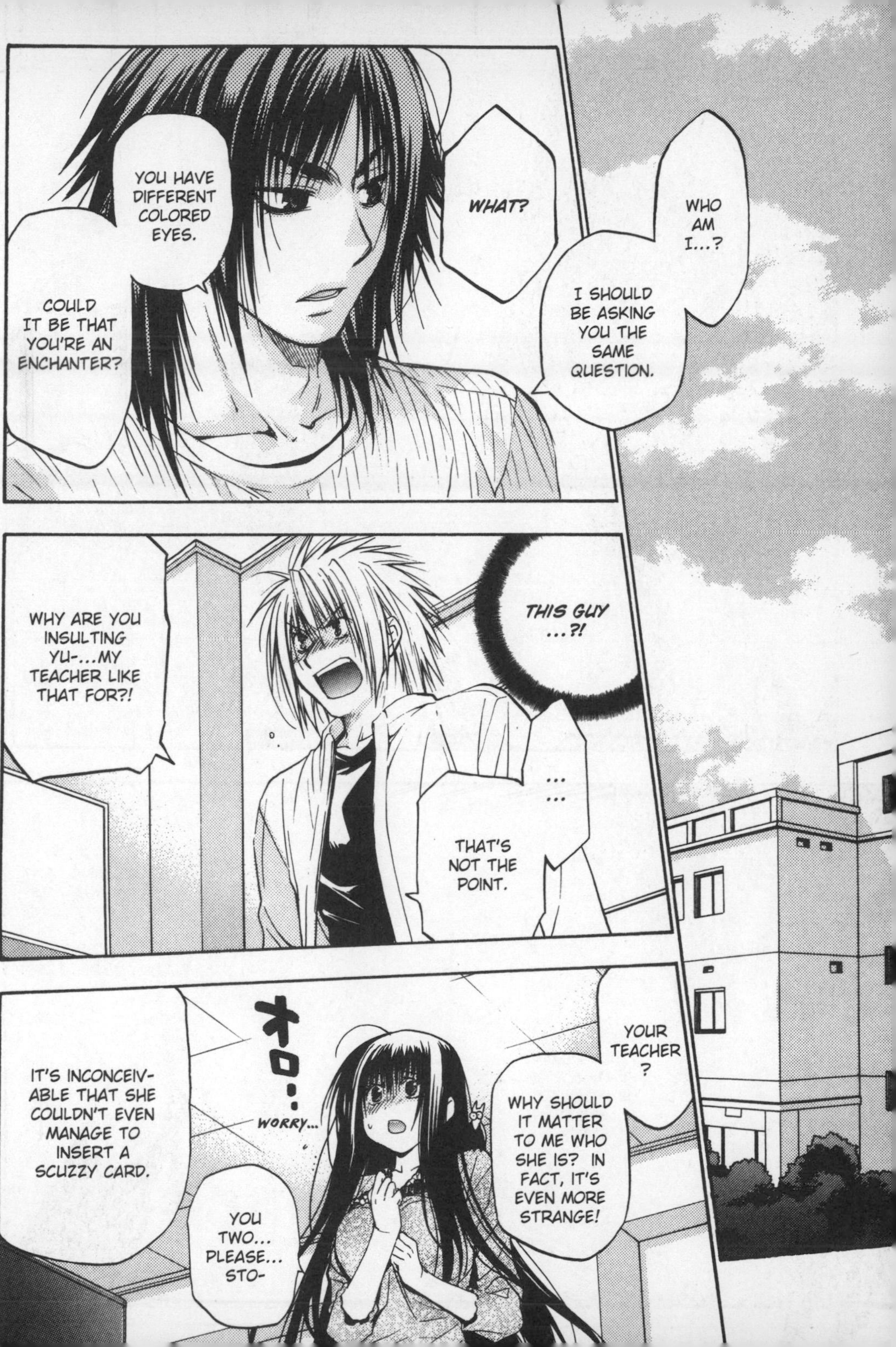
WHO AM I...?
I SHOULD BE ASKING YOU THE SAME QUESTION.
WHAT?
YOU HAVE DIFFERENT COLORED EYES.
COULD IT BE THAT YOU'RE AN ENCHANTER?
THIS GUY ...?!
... ...
THAT'S NOT THE POINT.
WHY ARE YOU INSULTING YU-...MY TEACHER LIKE THAT FOR?!
YOUR TEACHER ?
WHY SHOULD IT MATTER TO ME WHO SHE IS? IN FACT, IT'S EVEN MORE STRANGE!
オロ‥
WORRY...
IT'S INCONCEIV-ABLE THAT SHE COULDN'T EVEN MANAGE TO INSERT A SCUZZY CARD.
YOU TWO... PLEASE... STO-

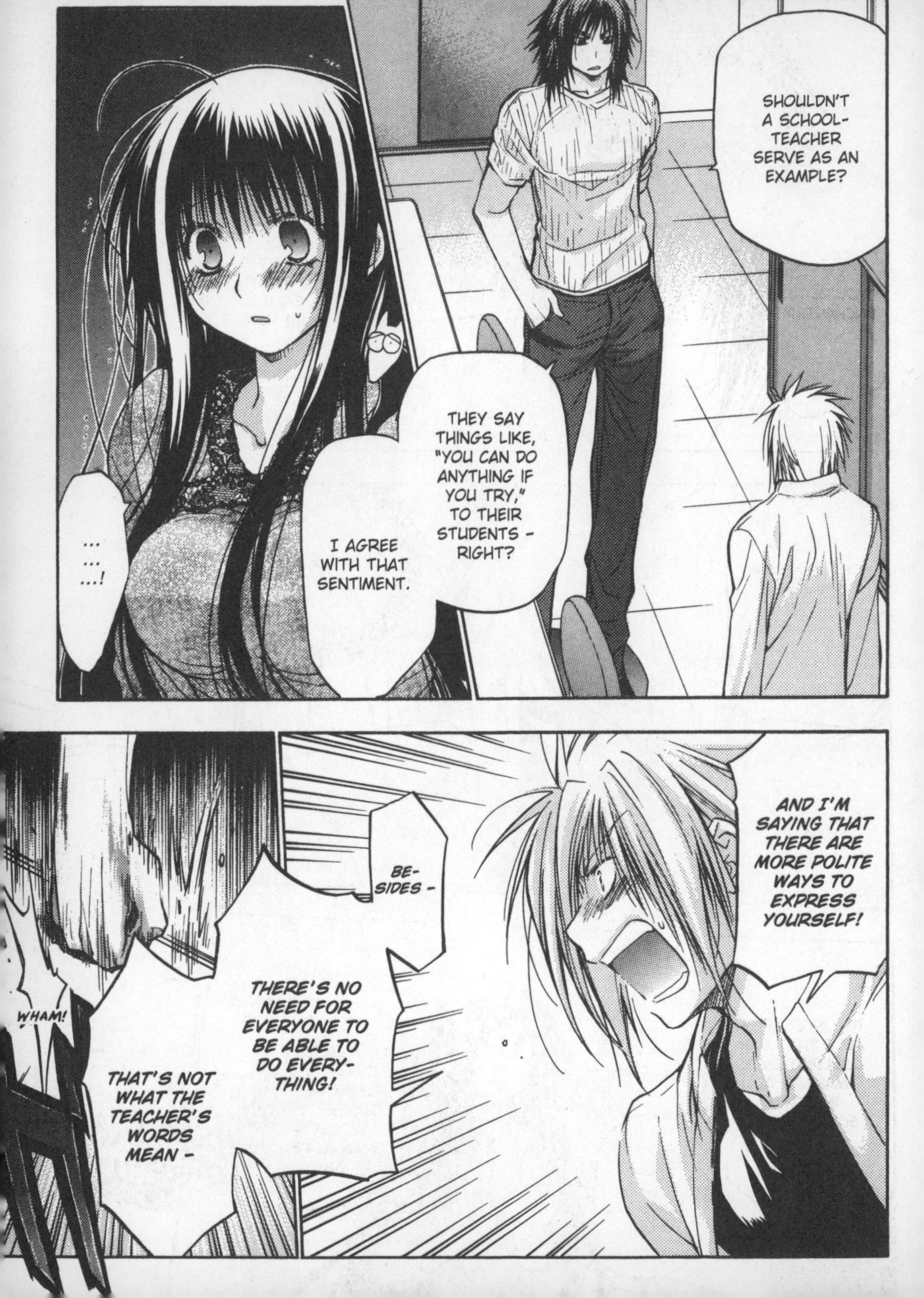
SHOULDN'T A SCHOOL-TEACHER SERVE AS AN EXAMPLE?
THEY SAY THINGS LIKE, "YOU CAN DO ANYTHING IF YOU TRY," TO THEIR STUDENTS - RIGHT?
I AGREE WITH THAT SENTIMENT.
... ...!
AND I'M SAYING THAT THERE ARE MORE POLITE WAYS TO EXPRESS YOURSELF!
BE-SIDES -
THERE'S NO NEED FOR EVERYONE TO BE ABLE TO DO EVERY-THING!
THAT'S NOT WHAT THE TEACHER'S WORDS MEAN -
WHAM!

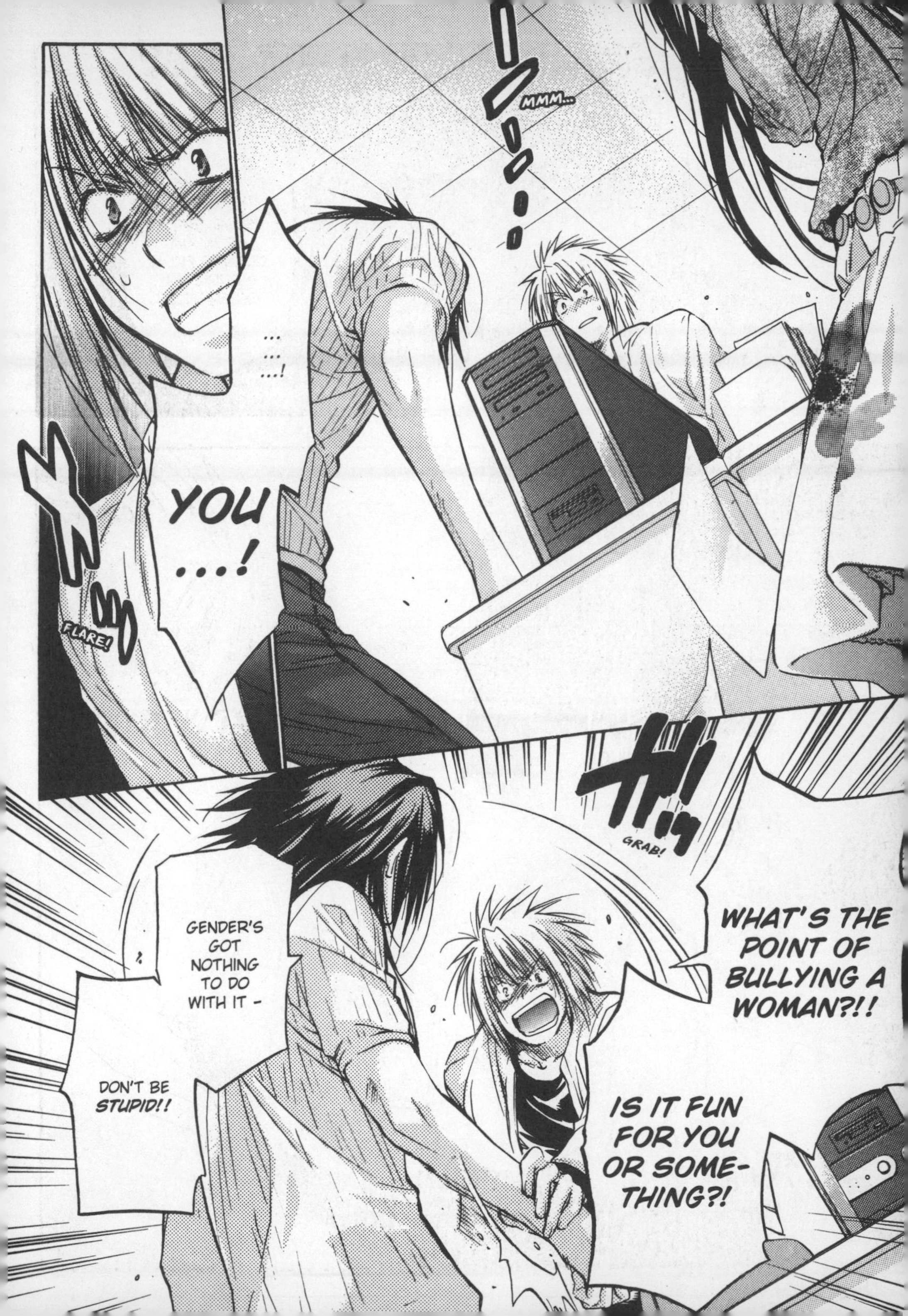
MMM...
...
...
...!
YOU ...!
FLARE!
GRAB!
WHAT'S THE POINT OF BULLYING A WOMAN?!!
IS IT FUN FOR YOU OR SOME-THING?!
GENDER'S GOT NOTHING TO DO WITH IT -
DON'T BE STUPID!!

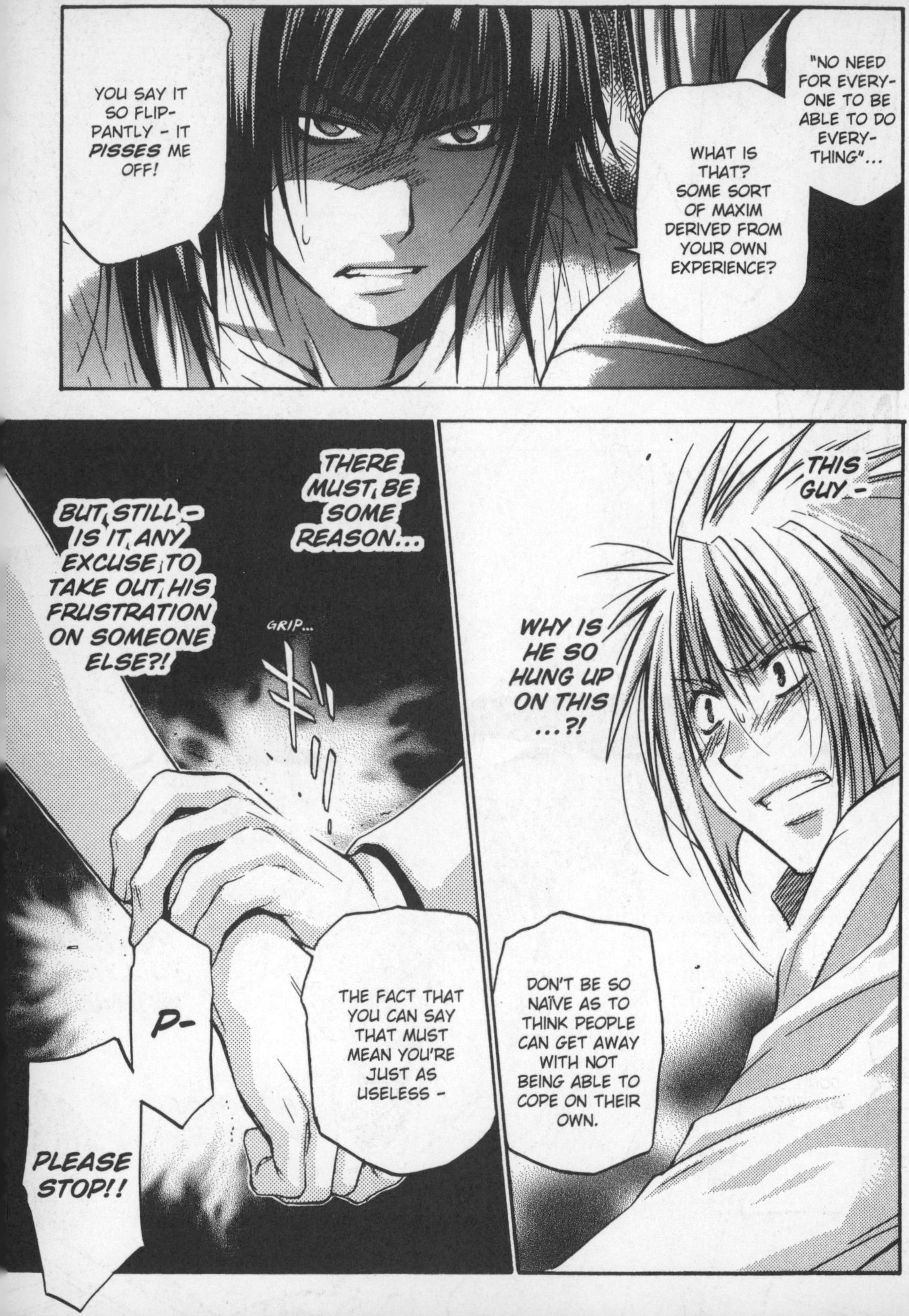
"NO NEED FOR EVERYONE TO BE ABLE TO DO EVERYTHING"...
WHAT IS THAT? SOME SORT OF MAXIM DERIVED FROM YOUR OWN EXPERIENCE?
YOU SAY IT SO FLIPPANTLY - IT *PISSES* ME OFF!
THIS GUY -
WHY IS HE SO HUNG UP ON THIS ...?!
DON'T BE SO NAÏVE AS TO THINK PEOPLE CAN GET AWAY WITH NOT BEING ABLE TO COPE ON THEIR OWN.
THERE MUST BE SOME REASON...
BUT STILL - IS IT ANY EXCUSE TO TAKE OUT HIS FRUSTRATION ON SOMEONE ELSE?!
GRIP...
THE FACT THAT YOU CAN SAY THAT MUST MEAN YOU'RE JUST AS USELESS -
P-
PLEASE STOP!!

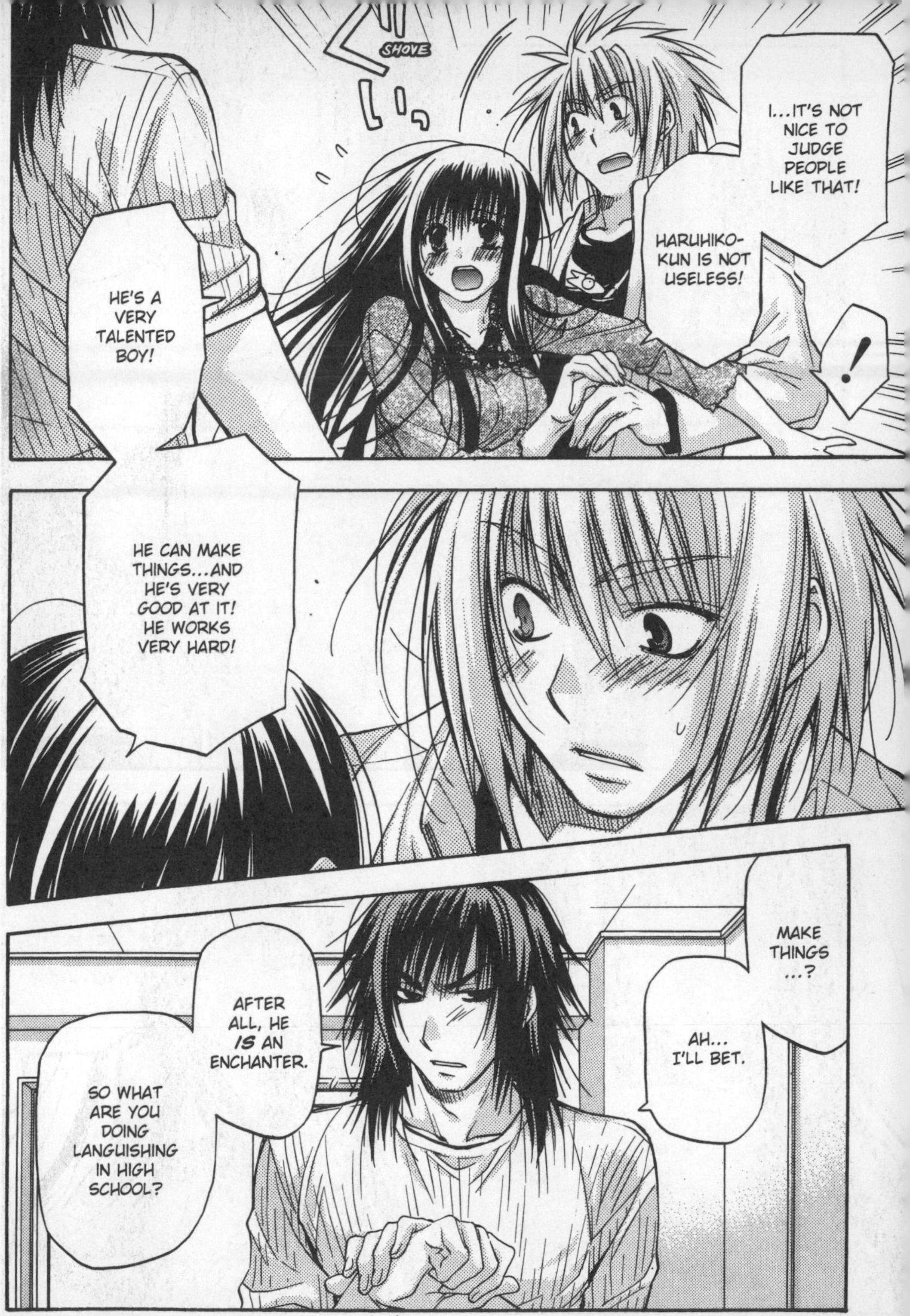
SHOVE
I...IT'S NOT NICE TO JUDGE PEOPLE LIKE THAT!
HARUHIKO-KUN IS NOT USELESS!
!
HE'S A VERY TALENTED BOY!
HE CAN MAKE THINGS...AND HE'S VERY GOOD AT IT! HE WORKS VERY HARD!
MAKE THINGS ...?
AH... I'LL BET.
AFTER ALL, HE *IS* AN ENCHANTER.
SO WHAT ARE YOU DOING LANGUISHING IN HIGH SCHOOL?

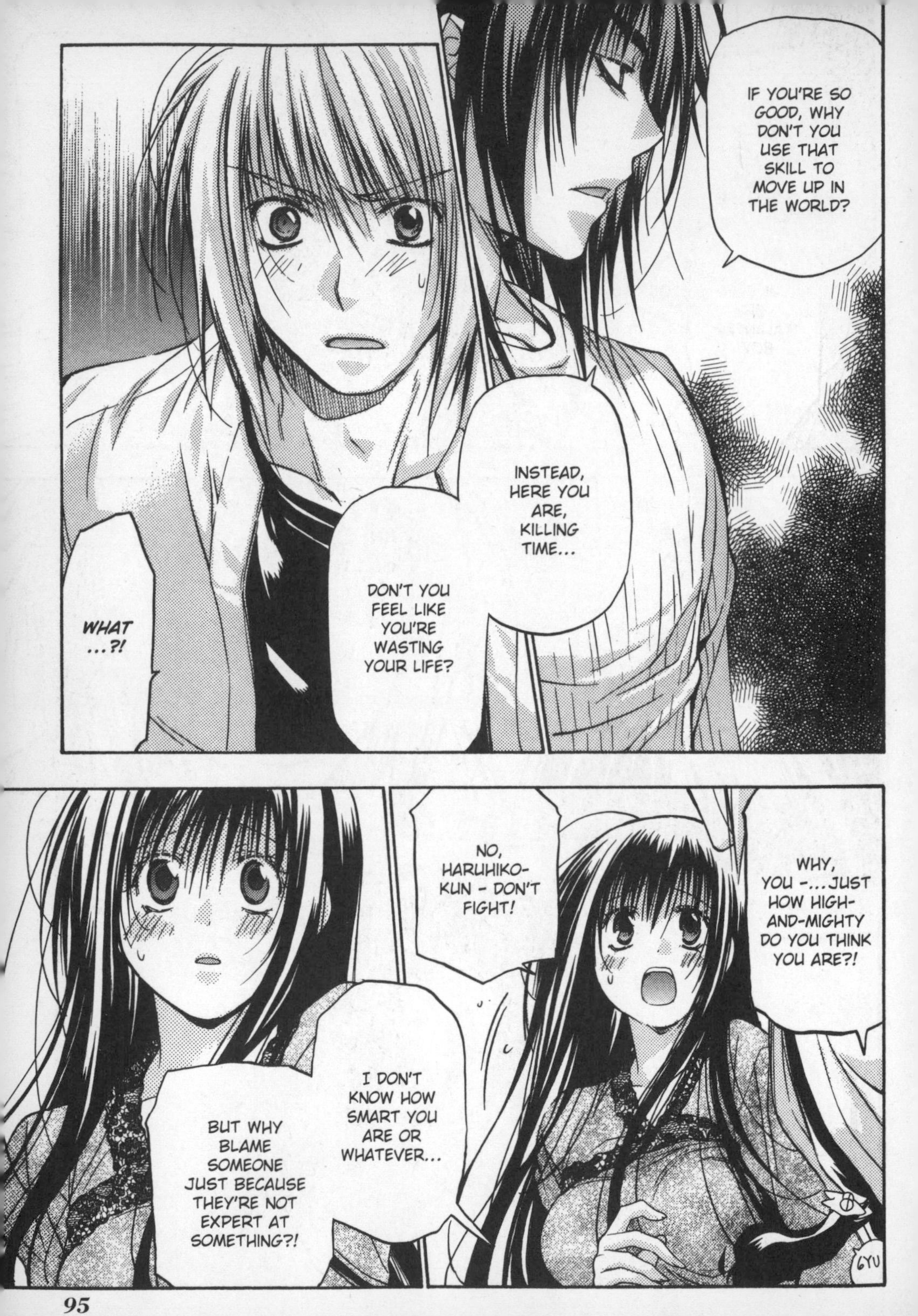
IF YOU'RE SO GOOD, WHY DON'T YOU USE THAT SKILL TO MOVE UP IN THE WORLD?
INSTEAD, HERE YOU ARE, KILLING TIME...
DON'T YOU FEEL LIKE YOU'RE WASTING YOUR LIFE?
WHAT ...?!
WHY, YOU -...JUST HOW HIGH-AND-MIGHTY DO YOU THINK YOU ARE?!
NO, HARUHIKO-KUN - DON'T FIGHT!
GYU
I DON'T KNOW HOW SMART YOU ARE OR WHATEVER...
BUT WHY BLAME SOMEONE JUST BECAUSE THEY'RE NOT EXPERT AT SOMETHING?!

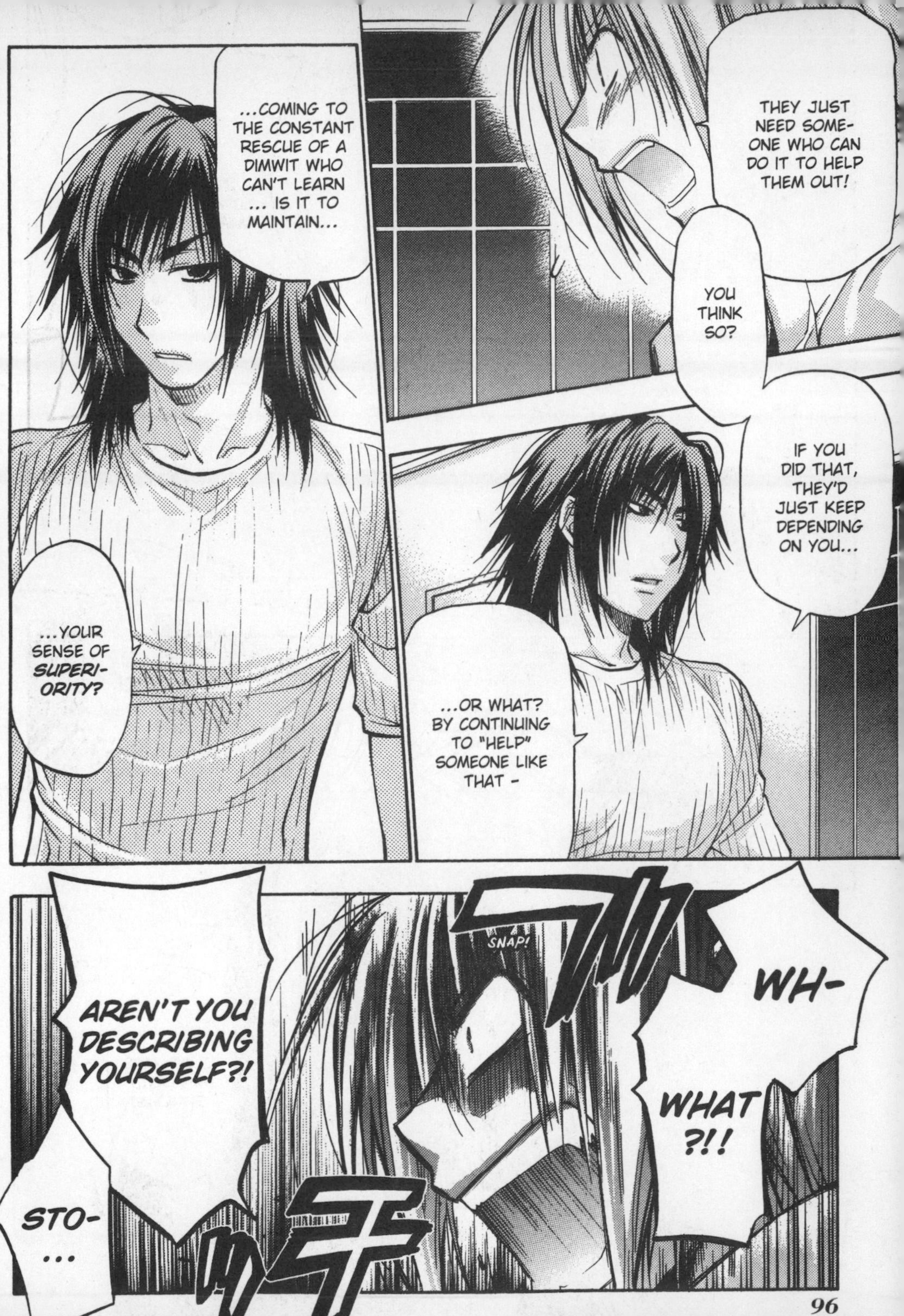
THEY JUST NEED SOME-ONE WHO CAN DO IT TO HELP THEM OUT!
YOU THINK SO?
IF YOU DID THAT, THEY'D JUST KEEP DEPENDING ON YOU...
...OR WHAT? BY CONTINUING TO "HELP" SOMEONE LIKE THAT -
...COMING TO THE CONSTANT RESCUE OF A DIMWIT WHO CAN'T LEARN ... IS IT TO MAINTAIN...
...YOUR SENSE OF *SUPERI-ORITY?*
WH-
SNAP!
WHAT ?!!
AREN'T YOU DESCRIBING YOURSELF?!
STO- ...

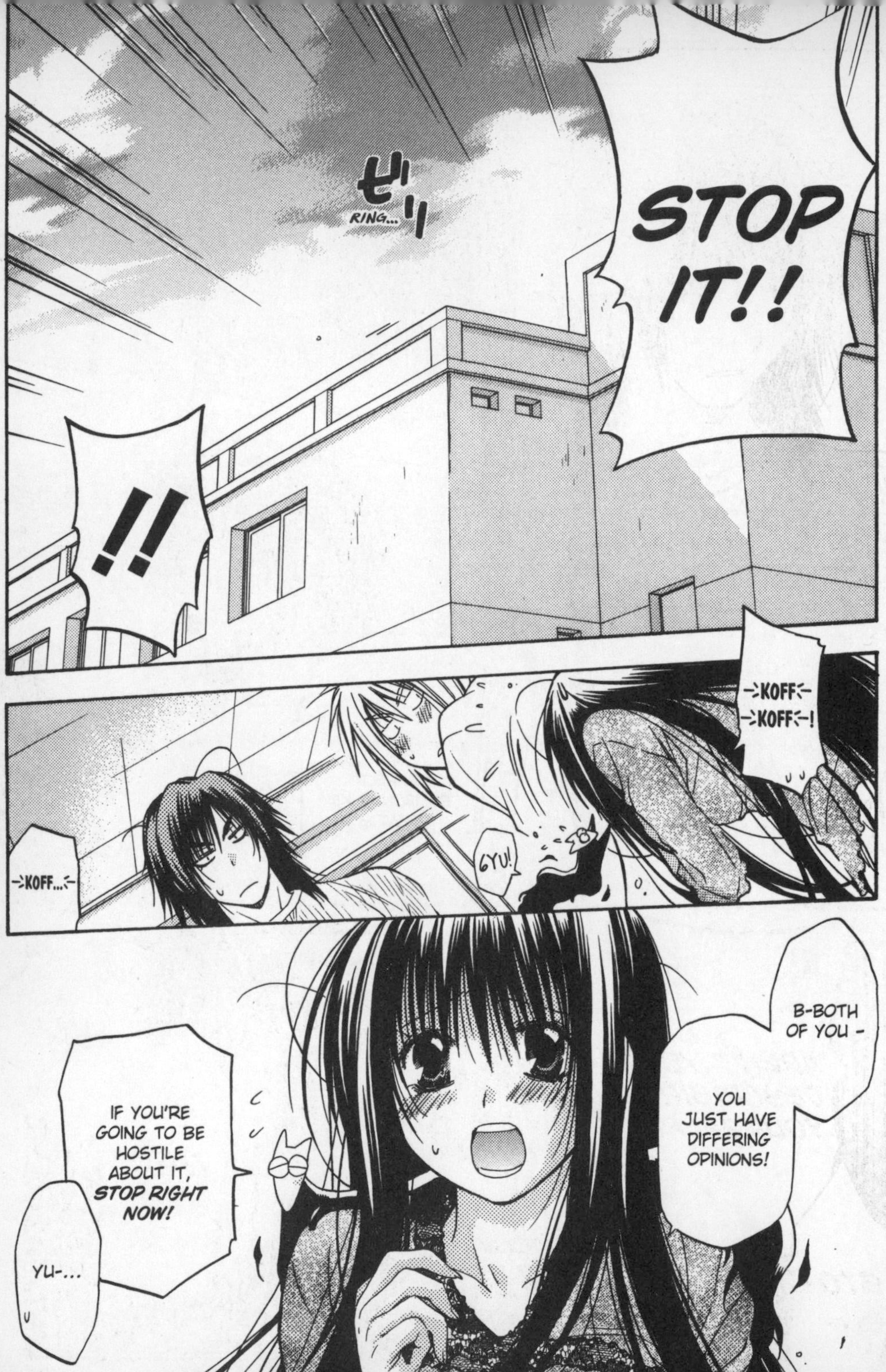
STOP IT!!
RING...
!!
-KOFF-
-KOFF-!
6YU!
-KOFF...-
B-BOTH OF YOU -
YOU JUST HAVE DIFFERING OPINIONS!
IF YOU'RE GOING TO BE HOSTILE ABOUT IT, **STOP RIGHT NOW!**
YU-...

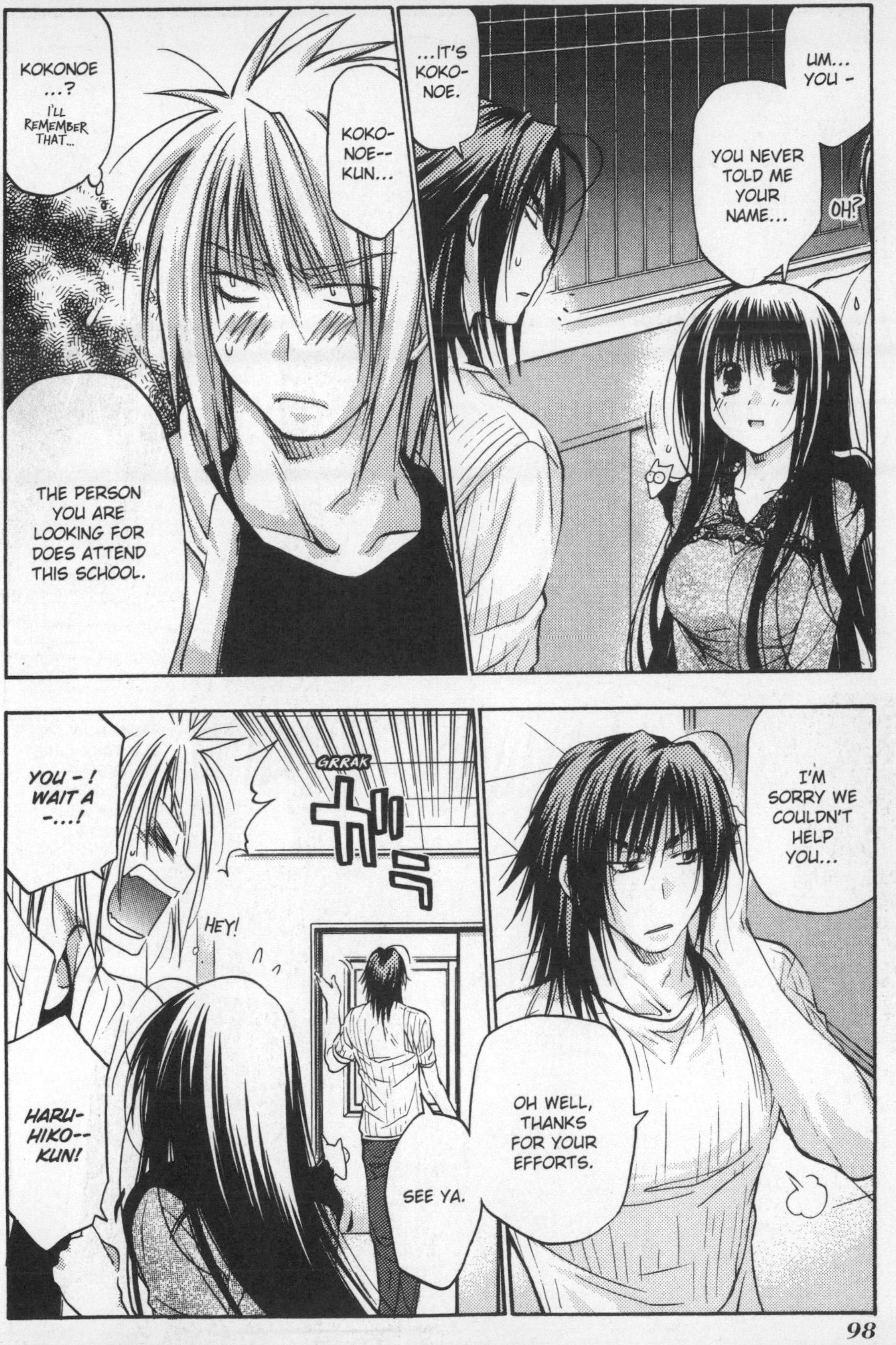
UM... YOU -
YOU NEVER TOLD ME YOUR NAME...
OH?
...IT'S KOKO-NOE.
KOKO-NOE--KUN...
KOKONOE ...?
I'LL REMEMBER THAT...
THE PERSON YOU ARE LOOKING FOR DOES ATTEND THIS SCHOOL.
I'M SORRY WE COULDN'T HELP YOU...
OH WELL, THANKS FOR YOUR EFFORTS.
SEE YA.
GRRAK
ガラ
YOU - ! WAIT A -...!
HEY!
HARU-HIKO--KUN!

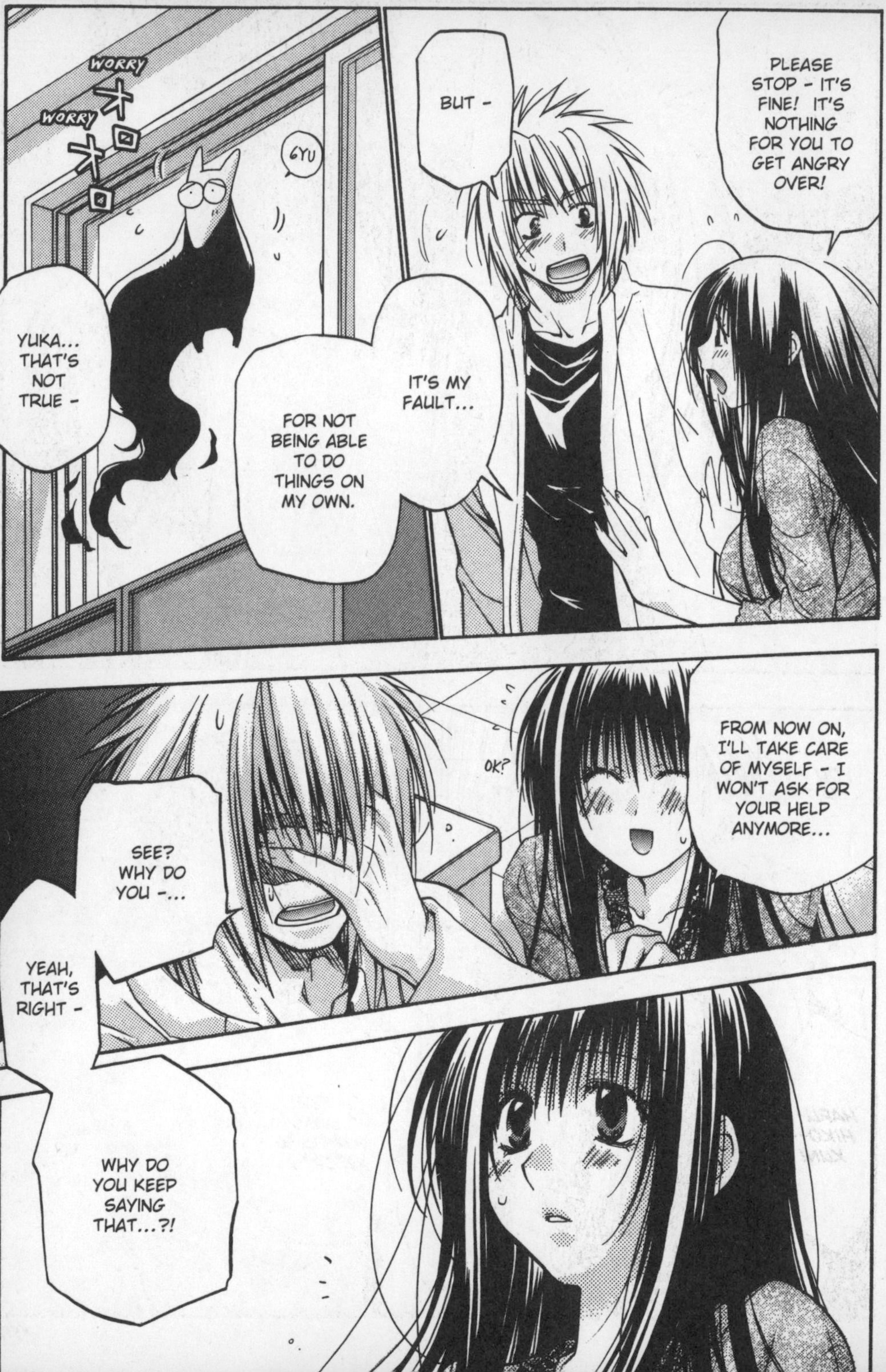
PLEASE STOP - IT'S FINE! IT'S NOTHING FOR YOU TO GET ANGRY OVER!
BUT -
IT'S MY FAULT...
FOR NOT BEING ABLE TO DO THINGS ON MY OWN.
6YU
WORRY
WORRY
YUKA... THAT'S NOT TRUE -
FROM NOW ON, I'LL TAKE CARE OF MYSELF - I WON'T ASK FOR YOUR HELP ANYMORE...
OK?
SEE? WHY DO YOU -...
YEAH, THAT'S RIGHT -
WHY DO YOU KEEP SAYING THAT...?!

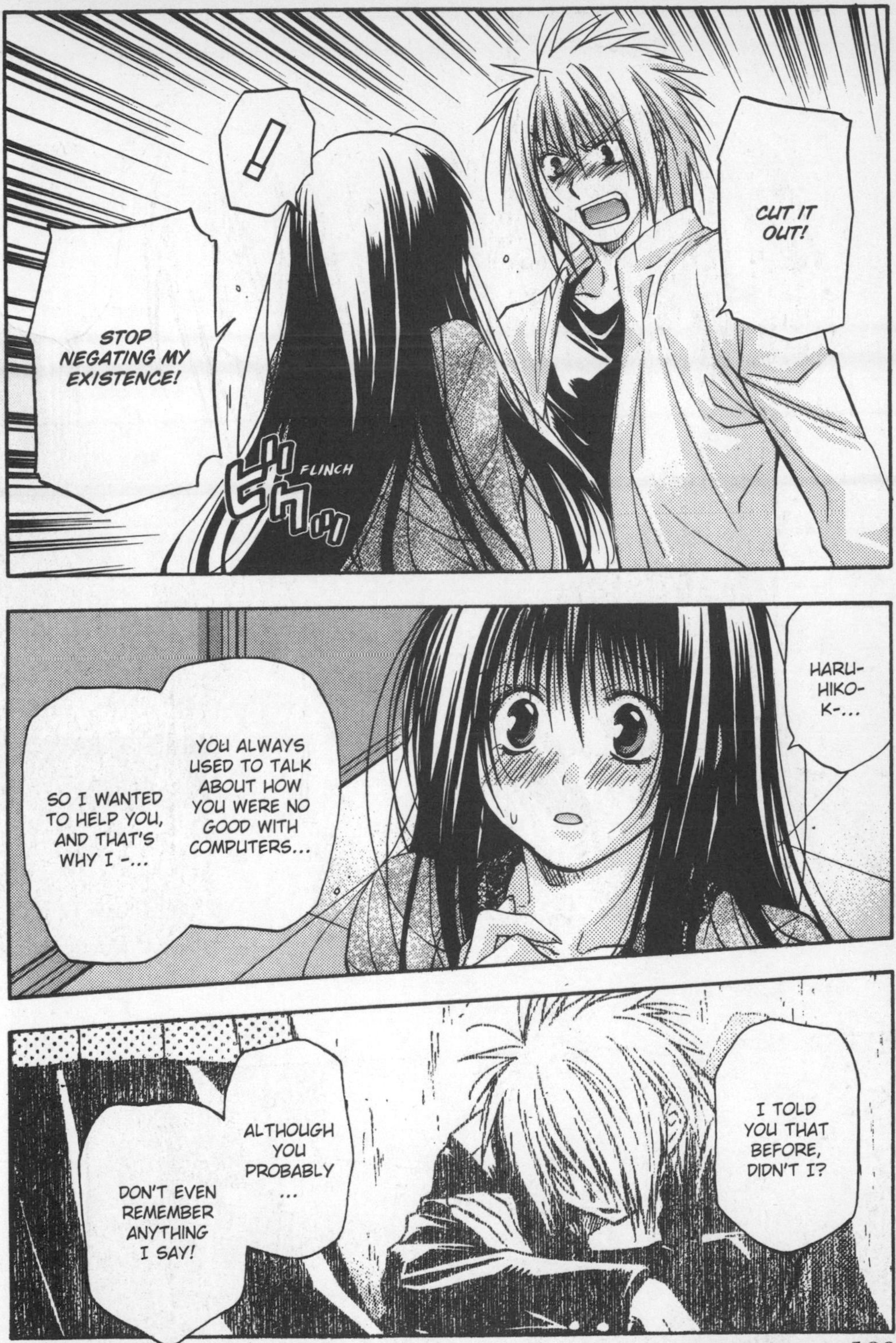
CUT IT OUT!
!
STOP NEGATING MY EXISTENCE!
FLINCH
HARU-HIKO-K-...
YOU ALWAYS USED TO TALK ABOUT HOW YOU WERE NO GOOD WITH COMPUTERS...
SO I WANTED TO HELP YOU, AND THAT'S WHY I -...
I TOLD YOU THAT BEFORE, DIDN'T I?
ALTHOUGH YOU PROBABLY ...
DON'T EVEN REMEMBER ANYTHING I SAY!

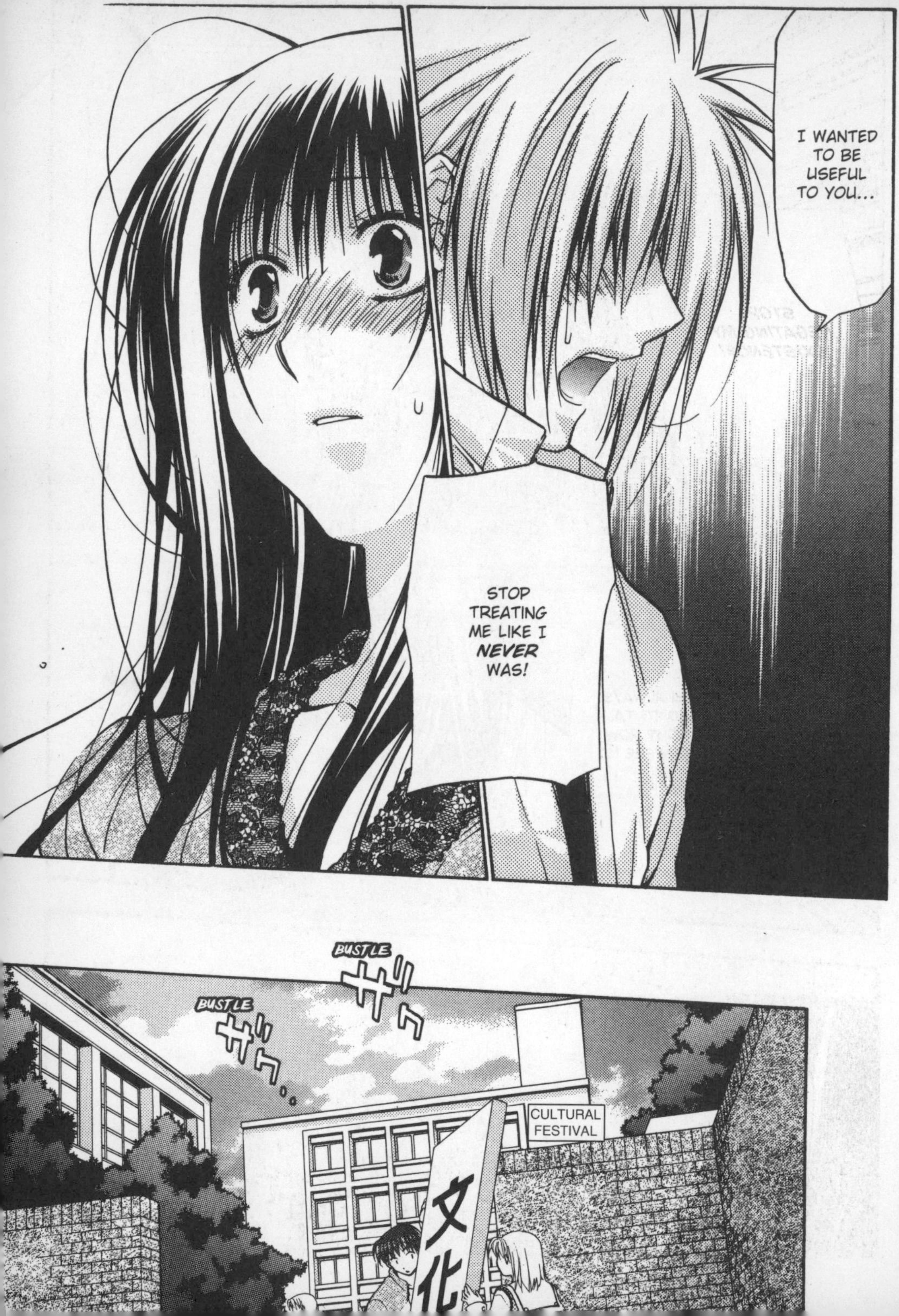
I WANTED TO BE USEFUL TO YOU...
STOP TREATING ME LIKE I *NEVER* WAS!
BUSTLE
BUSTLE
CULTURAL FESTIVAL
文化

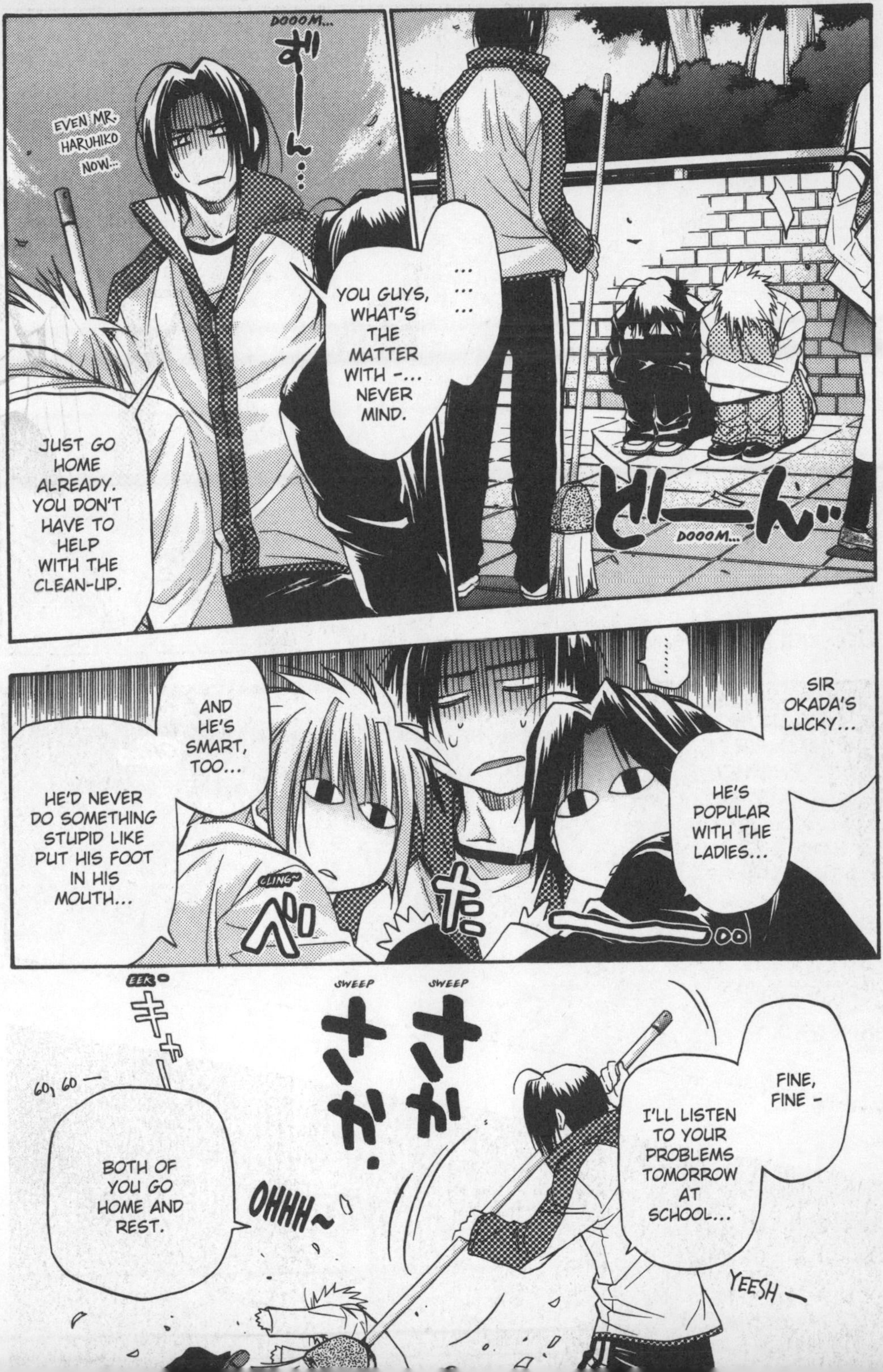

DOOOM...
...
...
...
YOU GUYS, WHAT'S THE MATTER WITH -... NEVER MIND.
DOOOM...
ずーん…
EVEN MR. HARUHIKO NOW...
JUST GO HOME ALREADY. YOU DON'T HAVE TO HELP WITH THE CLEAN-UP.
......
SIR OKADA'S LUCKY...
HE'S POPULAR WITH THE LADIES...
AND HE'S SMART, TOO...
HE'D NEVER DO SOMETHING STUPID LIKE PUT HIS FOOT IN HIS MOUTH...
CLING~
FINE, FINE - I'LL LISTEN TO YOUR PROBLEMS TOMORROW AT SCHOOL...
YEESH -
SWEEP
SWEEP
OHHH~
EEK
GO, GO -
BOTH OF YOU GO HOME AND REST.

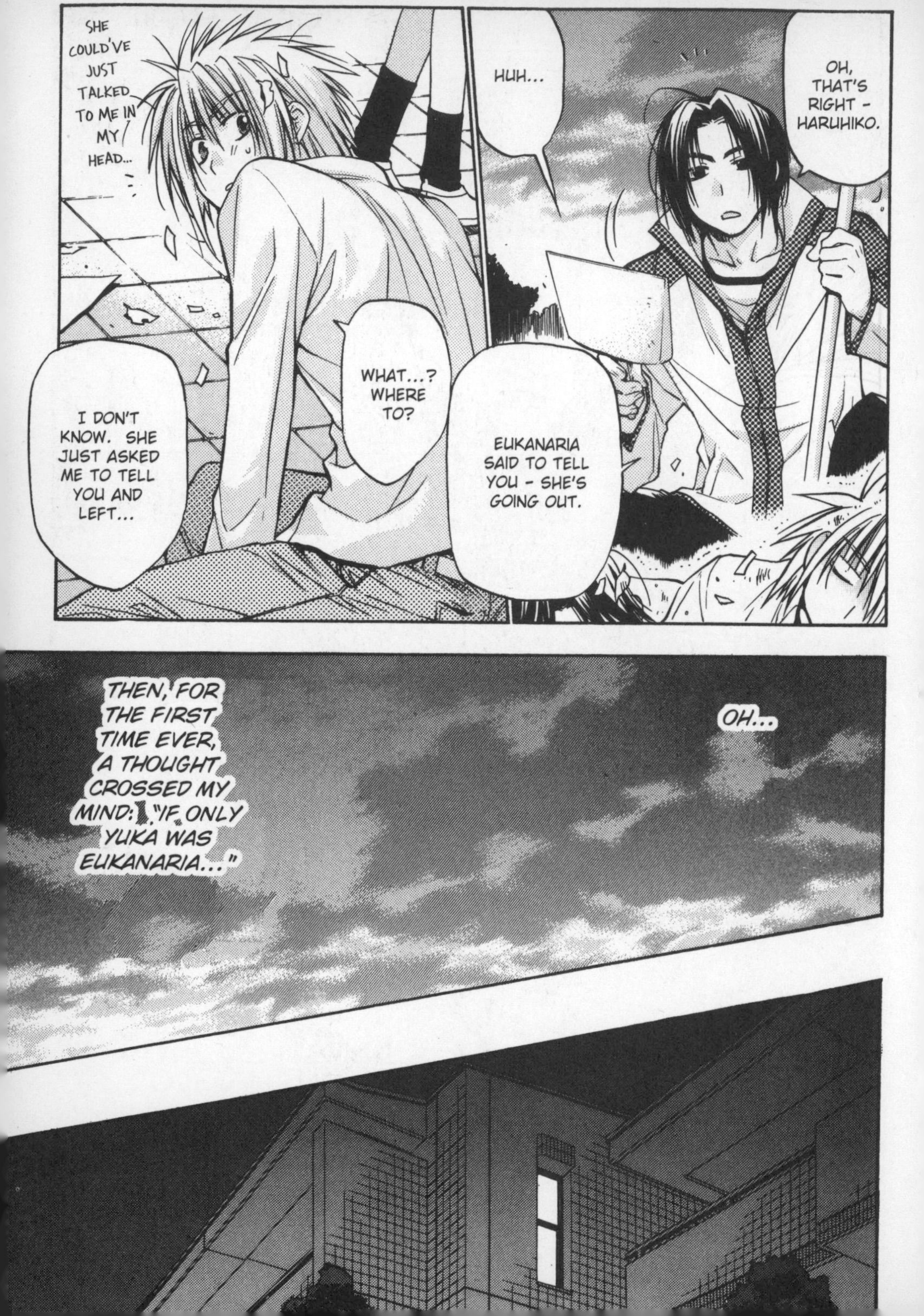
OH, THAT'S RIGHT - HARUHIKO.
HUH...
EUKANARIA SAID TO TELL YOU - SHE'S GOING OUT.
WHAT...? WHERE TO?
I DON'T KNOW. SHE JUST ASKED ME TO TELL YOU AND LEFT...
SHE COULD'VE JUST TALKED TO ME IN MY HEAD...
OH...
THEN, FOR THE FIRST TIME EVER, A THOUGHT CROSSED MY MIND: "IF ONLY YUKA WAS EUKANARIA..."

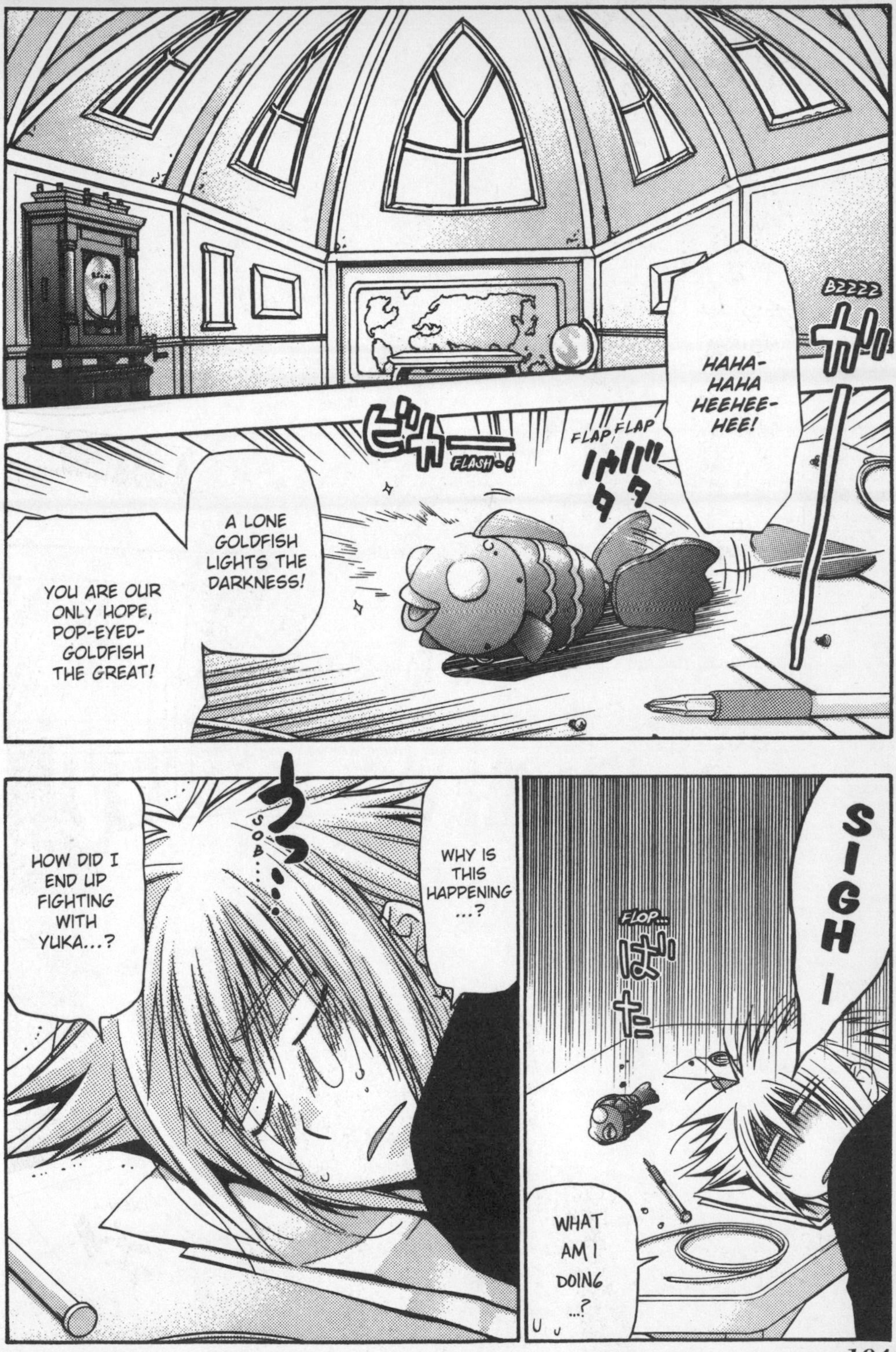
BZZZZ
HAHA-HAHA HEEHEE-HEE!
FLAP, FLAP
FLASH-!
A LONE GOLDFISH LIGHTS THE DARKNESS!
YOU ARE OUR ONLY HOPE, POP-EYED-GOLDFISH THE GREAT!
SIGH!
FLOP...
WHAT AM I DOING...?
SOB...
WHY IS THIS HAPPENING...?
HOW DID I END UP FIGHTING WITH YUKA...?

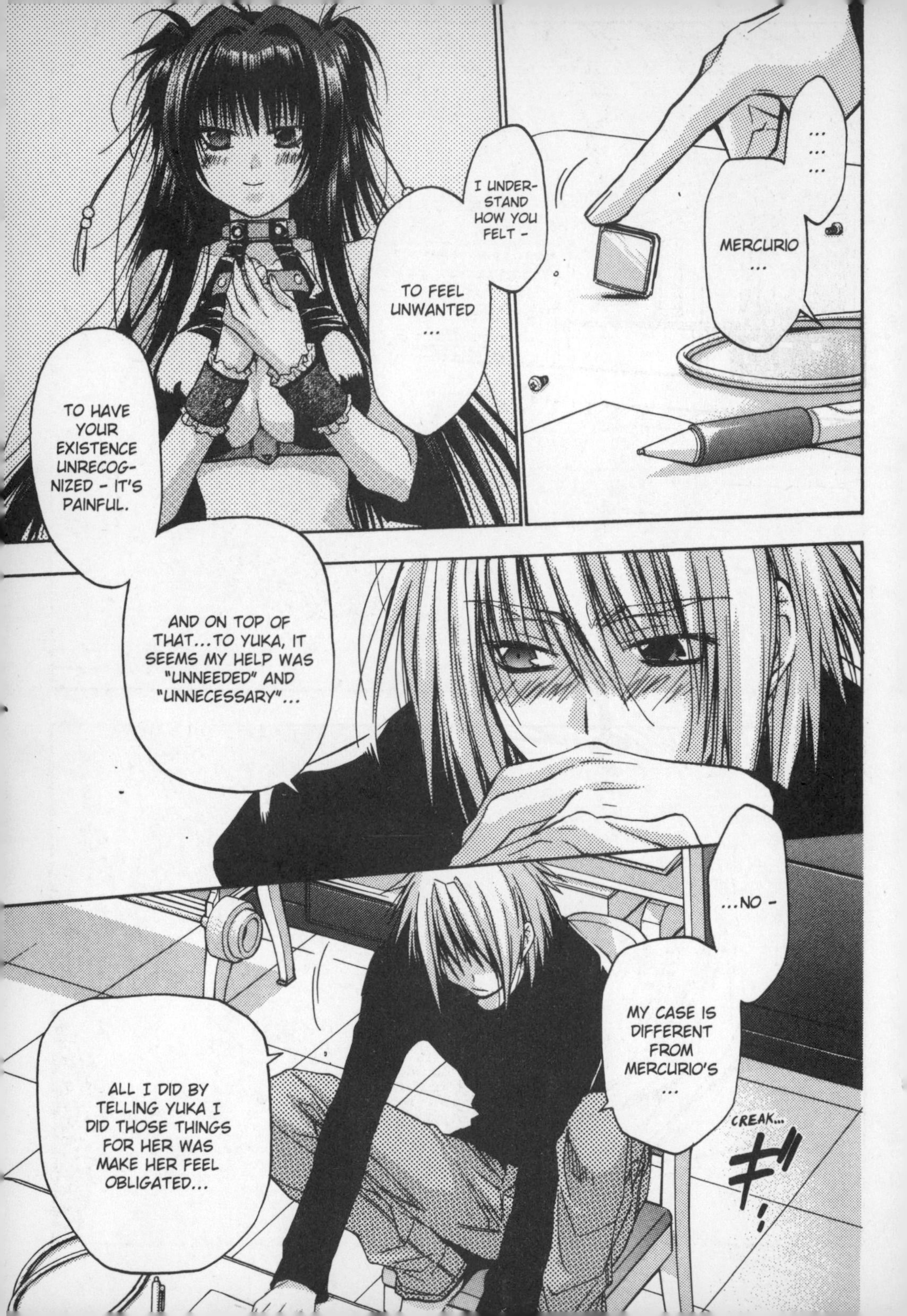
... ...
MERCURIO ...
I UNDER-STAND HOW YOU FELT -
TO FEEL UNWANTED ...
TO HAVE YOUR EXISTENCE UNRECOG-NIZED - IT'S PAINFUL.
AND ON TOP OF THAT... TO YUKA, IT SEEMS MY HELP WAS "UNNEEDED" AND "UNNECESSARY"...
...NO -
MY CASE IS DIFFERENT FROM MERCURIO'S ...
CREAK...
ALL I DID BY TELLING YUKA I DID THOSE THINGS FOR HER WAS MAKE HER FEEL OBLIGATED...

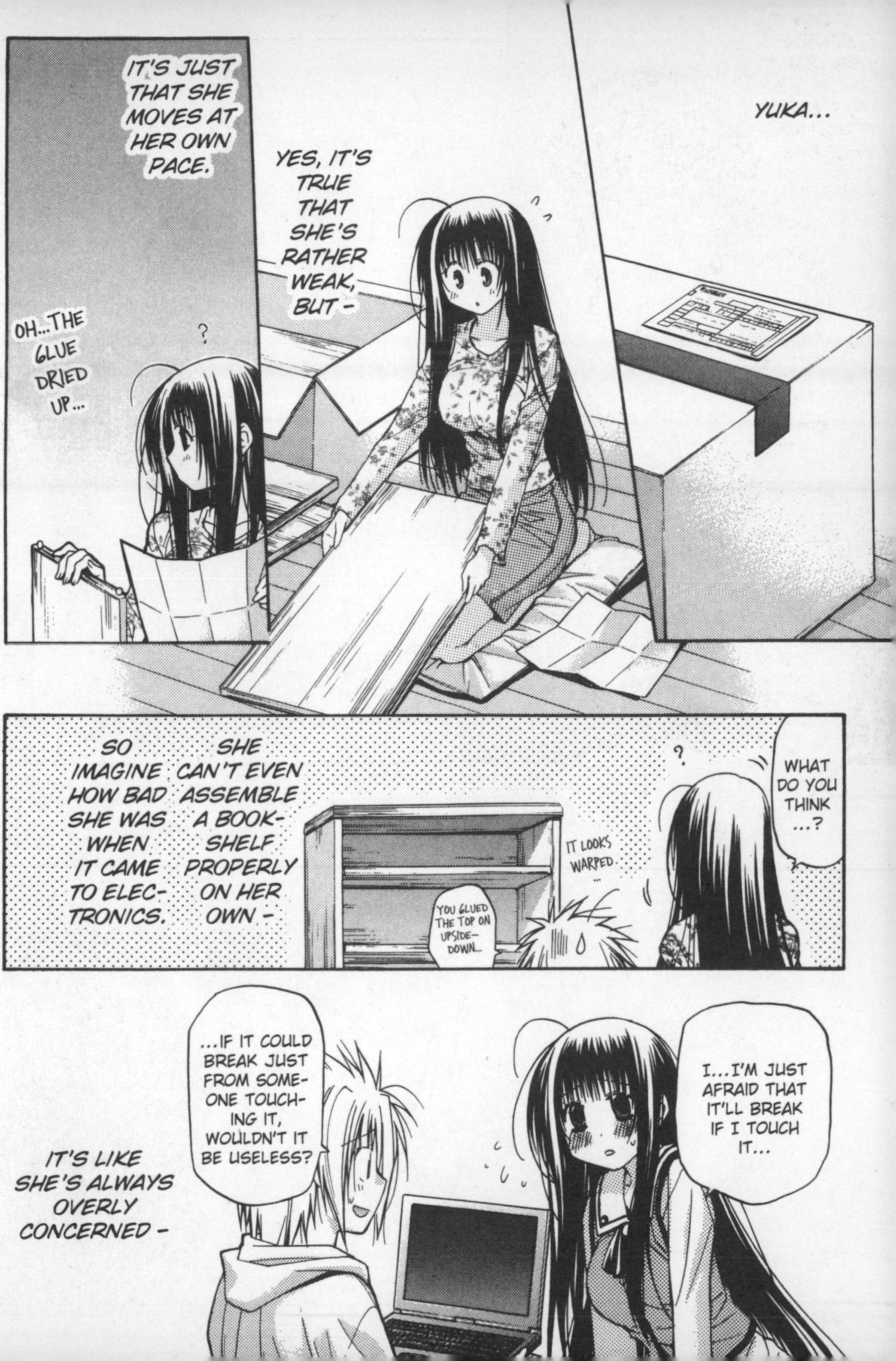
YUKA...
YES, IT'S TRUE THAT SHE'S RATHER WEAK, BUT -
IT'S JUST THAT SHE MOVES AT HER OWN PACE.
OH...THE GLUE DRIED UP...
WHAT DO YOU THINK ...?
IT LOOKS WARPED ...
YOU GLUED THE TOP ON UPSIDE-DOWN...
SHE CAN'T EVEN ASSEMBLE A BOOK-SHELF PROPERLY ON HER OWN -
SO IMAGINE HOW BAD SHE WAS WHEN IT CAME TO ELEC-TRONICS.
I...I'M JUST AFRAID THAT IT'LL BREAK IF I TOUCH IT...
...IF IT COULD BREAK JUST FROM SOME-ONE TOUCH-ING IT, WOULDN'T IT BE USELESS?
IT'S LIKE SHE'S ALWAYS OVERLY CONCERNED -

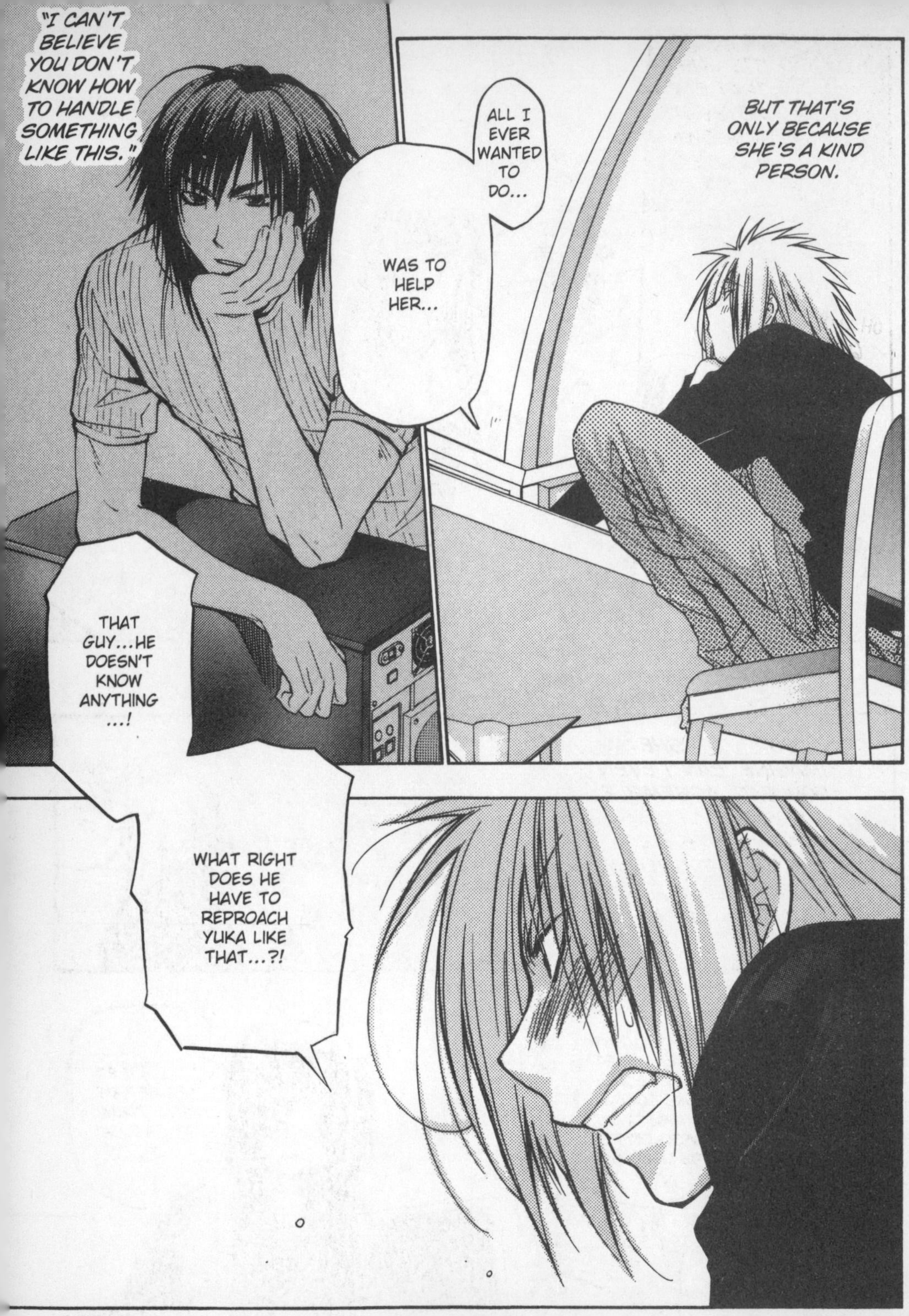
BUT THAT'S ONLY BECAUSE SHE'S A KIND PERSON.
ALL I EVER WANTED TO DO...
WAS TO HELP HER...
"I CAN'T BELIEVE YOU DON'T KNOW HOW TO HANDLE SOMETHING LIKE THIS."
THAT GUY...HE DOESN'T KNOW ANYTHING...!
WHAT RIGHT DOES HE HAVE TO REPROACH YUKA LIKE THAT...?!

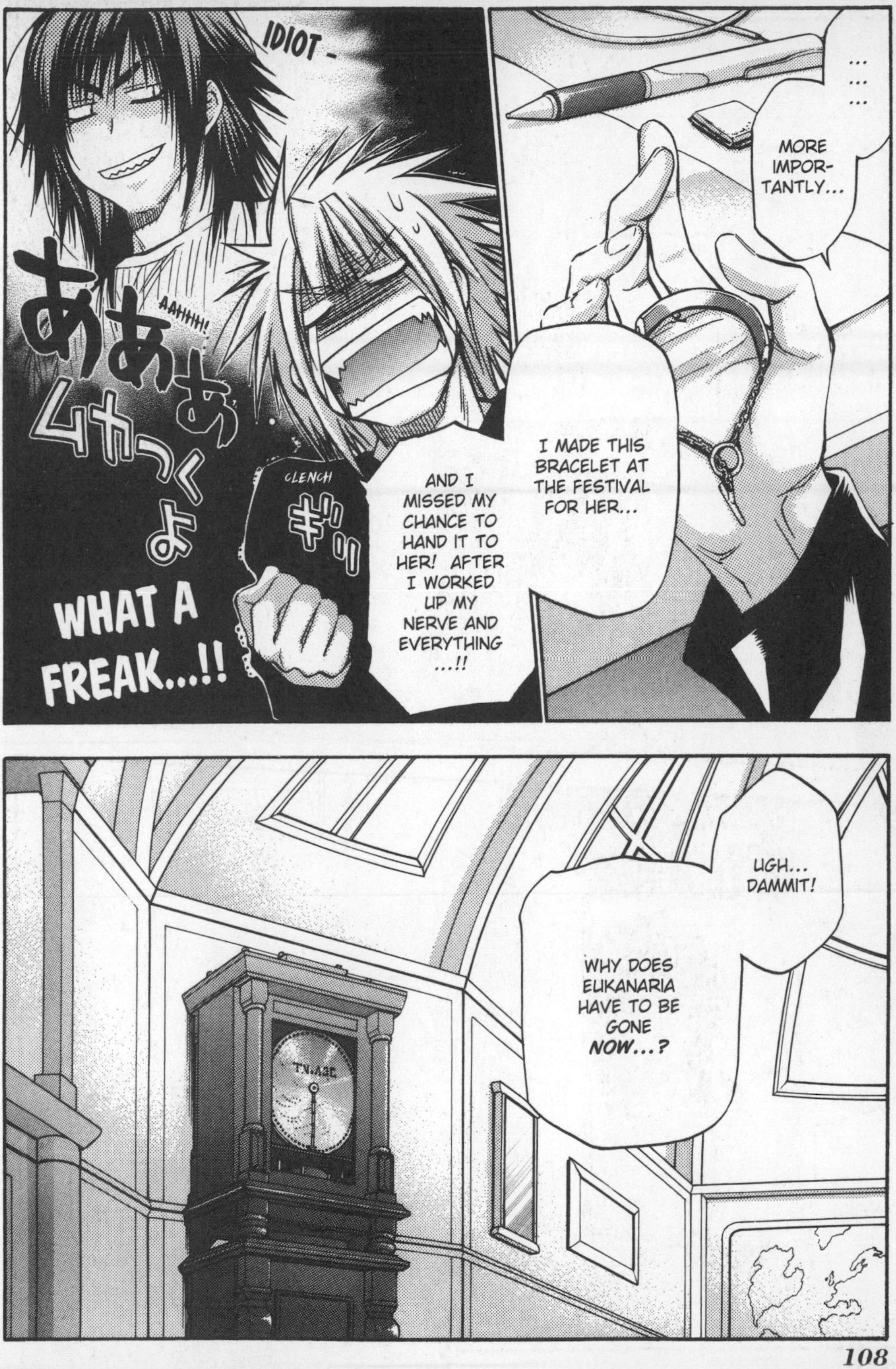
... ...
MORE IMPORTANTLY...
I MADE THIS BRACELET AT THE FESTIVAL FOR HER...
AND I MISSED MY CHANCE TO HAND IT TO HER! AFTER I WORKED UP MY NERVE AND EVERYTHING ...!!
IDIOT –
AAHHHH!
ああああムかつくよ
WHAT A FREAK...!!
CLENCH
ぎゅ
UGH... DAMMIT!
WHY DOES EUKANARIA HAVE TO BE GONE *NOW...?*

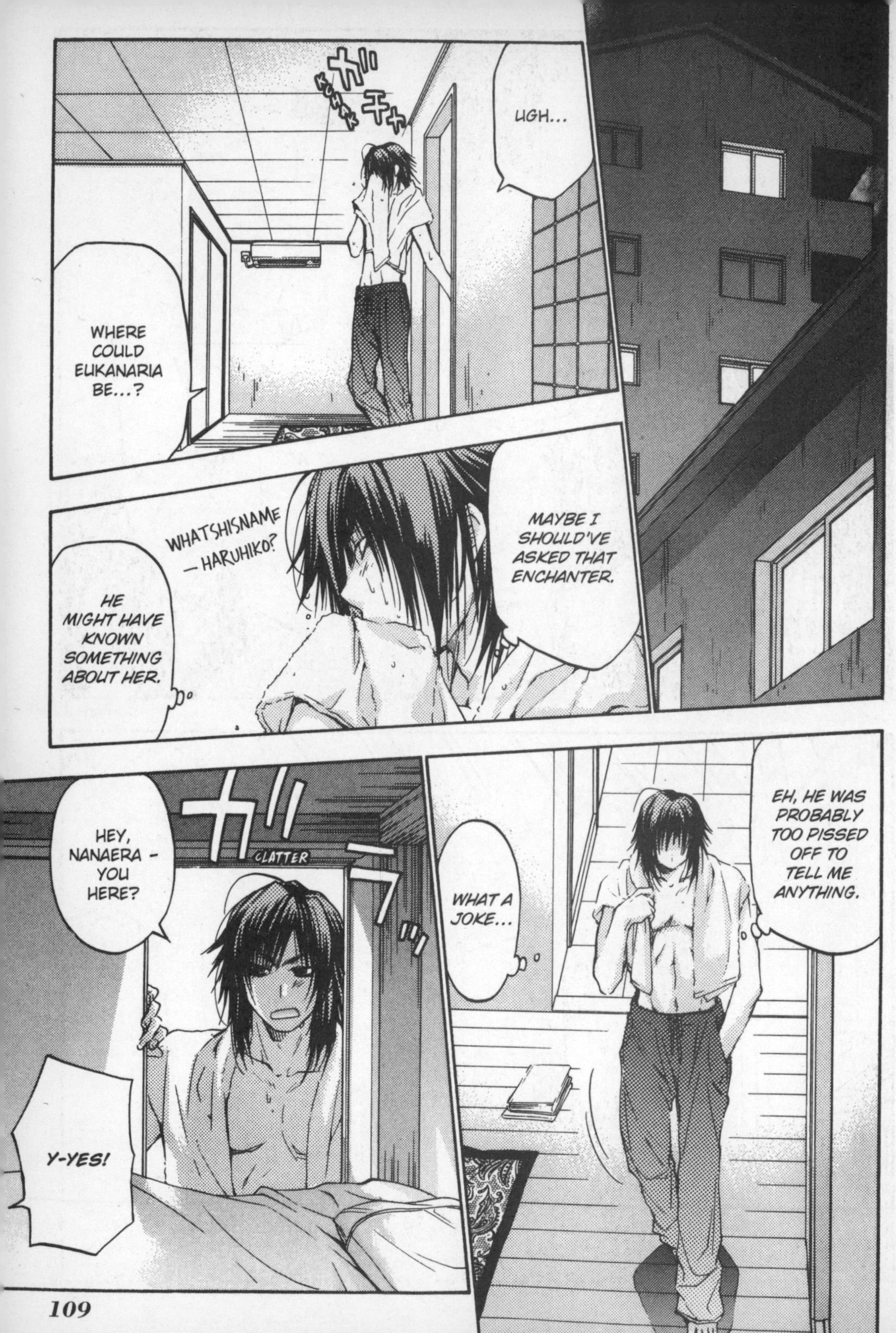
KUHAK
UGH...
WHERE COULD EUKANARIA BE...?
MAYBE I SHOULD'VE ASKED THAT ENCHANTER.
WHATSHISNAME — HARUHIKO?
HE MIGHT HAVE KNOWN SOMETHING ABOUT HER.
EH, HE WAS PROBABLY TOO PISSED OFF TO TELL ME ANYTHING.
WHAT A JOKE...
CLATTER
HEY, NANAERA - YOU HERE?
Y-YES!

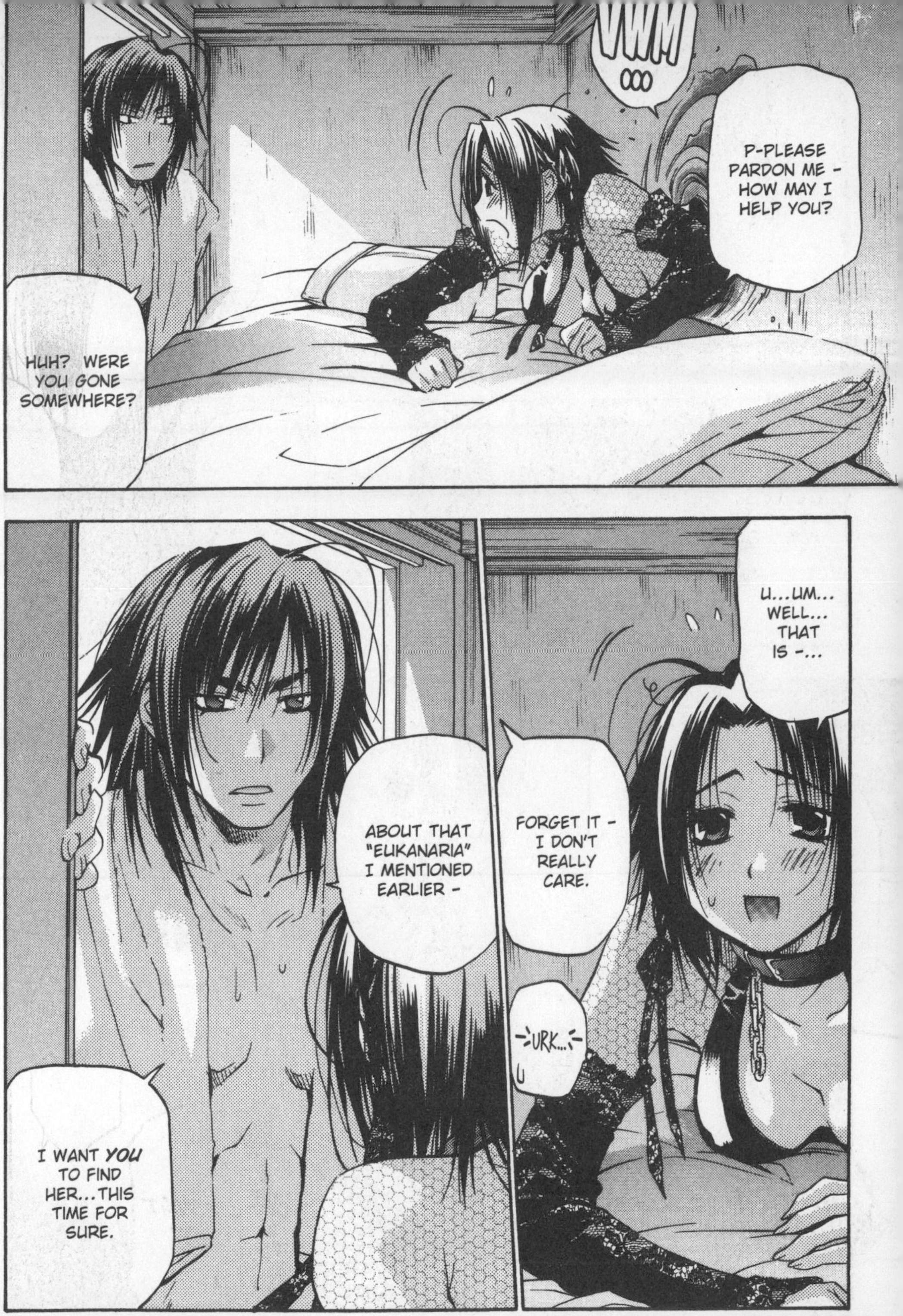
VWM
OOO
P-PLEASE PARDON ME - HOW MAY I HELP YOU?
HUH? WERE YOU GONE SOMEWHERE?
U...UM... WELL... THAT IS -...
FORGET IT - I DON'T REALLY CARE.
URK...
ABOUT THAT "EUKANARIA" I MENTIONED EARLIER -
I WANT *YOU* TO FIND HER...THIS TIME FOR SURE.

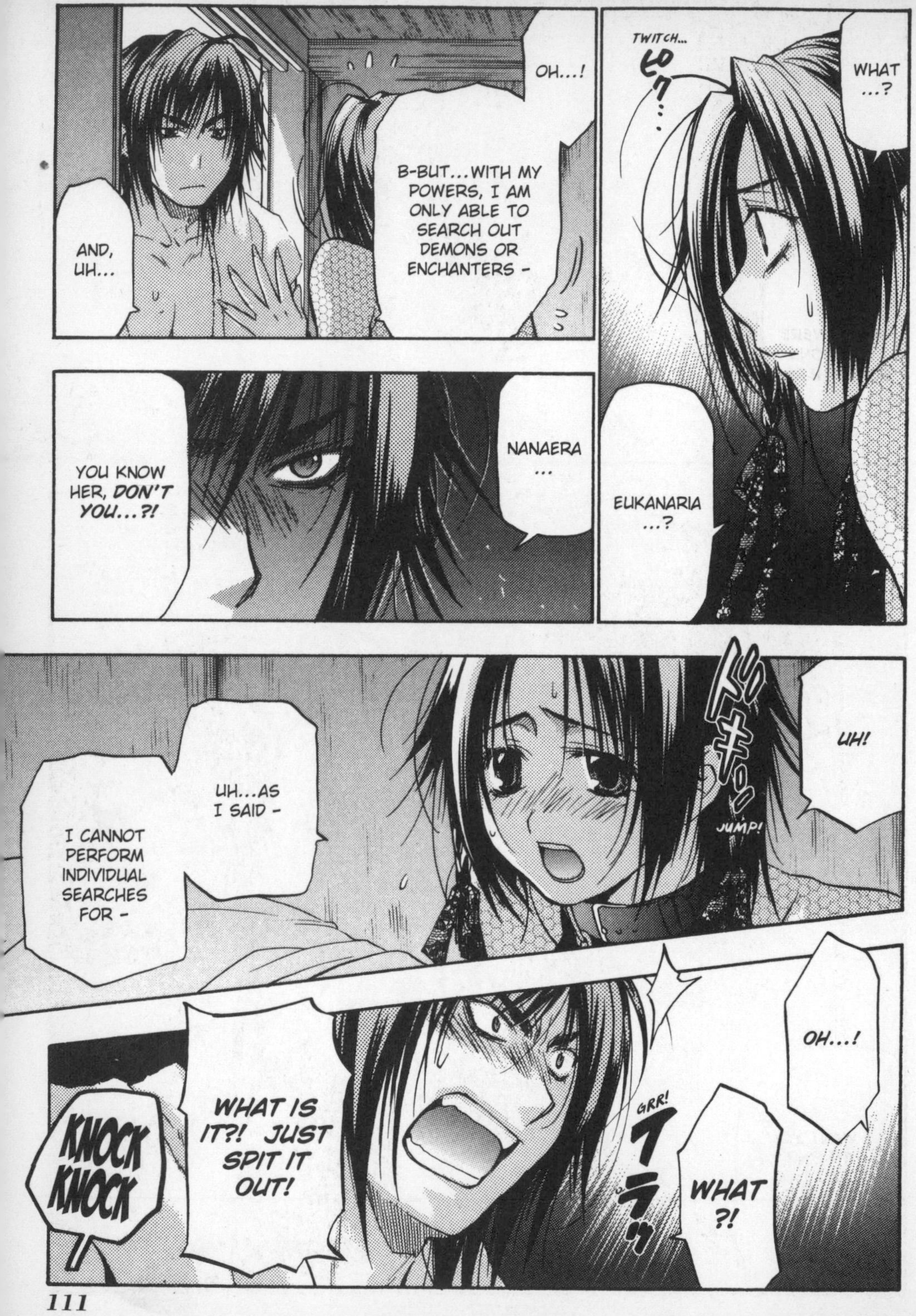
TWITCH...
WHAT ...?
EUKANARIA ...?
OH...!
B-BUT...WITH MY POWERS, I AM ONLY ABLE TO SEARCH OUT DEMONS OR ENCHANTERS -
AND, UH...
NANAERA ...
YOU KNOW HER, *DON'T YOU...?!*
JUMP!
UH!
UH...AS I SAID -
I CANNOT PERFORM INDIVIDUAL SEARCHES FOR -
OH...!
GRR!
WHAT ?!
WHAT IS IT?! JUST SPIT IT OUT!
KNOCK KNOCK

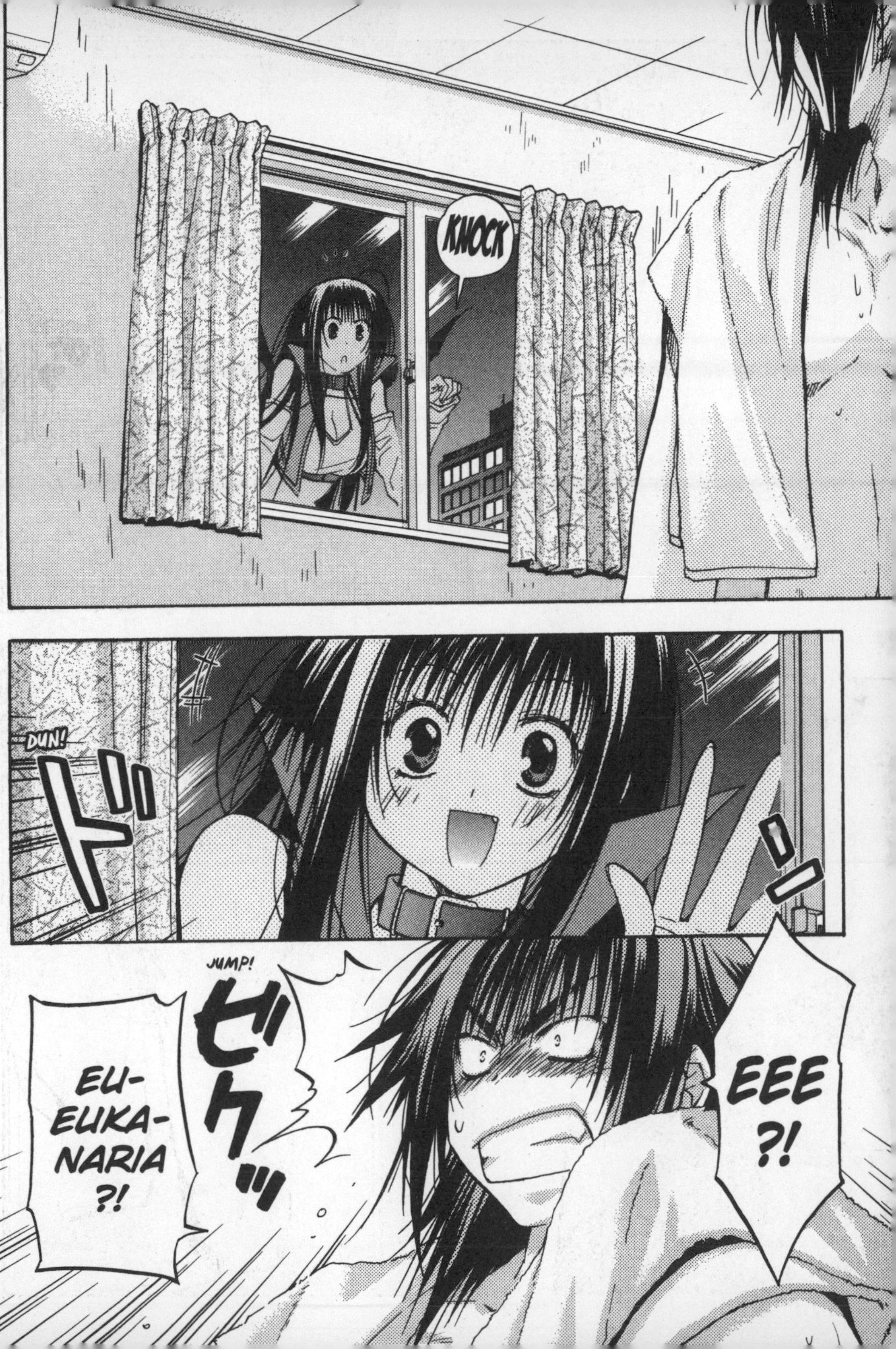
KNOCK
DUN!
EEE ?!
JUMP!
EU-EUKA-NARIA ?!

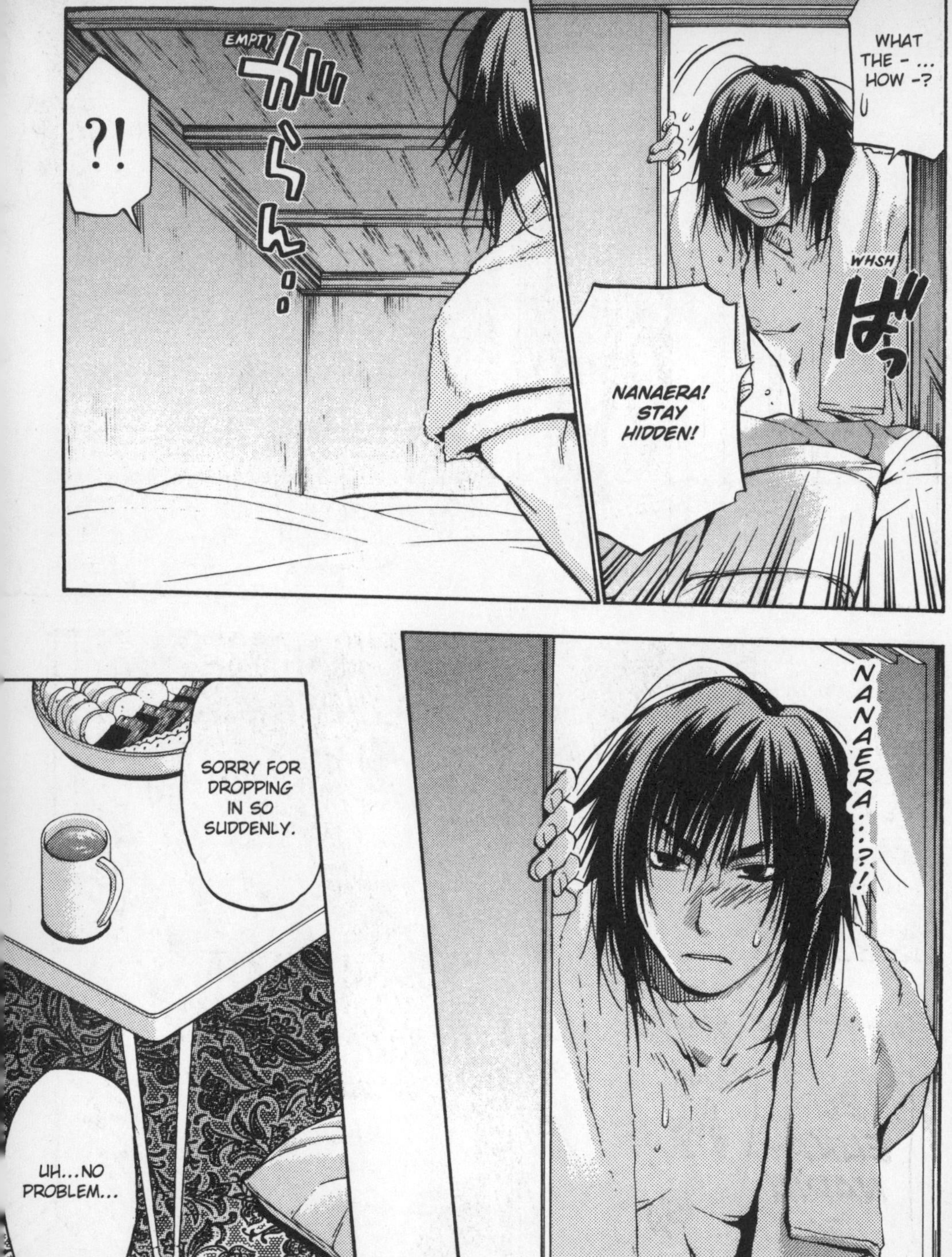
WHAT THE -... HOW -?
WHSH
ばっ
NANAERA! STAY HIDDEN!
EMPTY
がらん
?!
NANAERA...?!
SORRY FOR DROPPING IN SO SUDDENLY.
UH...NO PROBLEM...

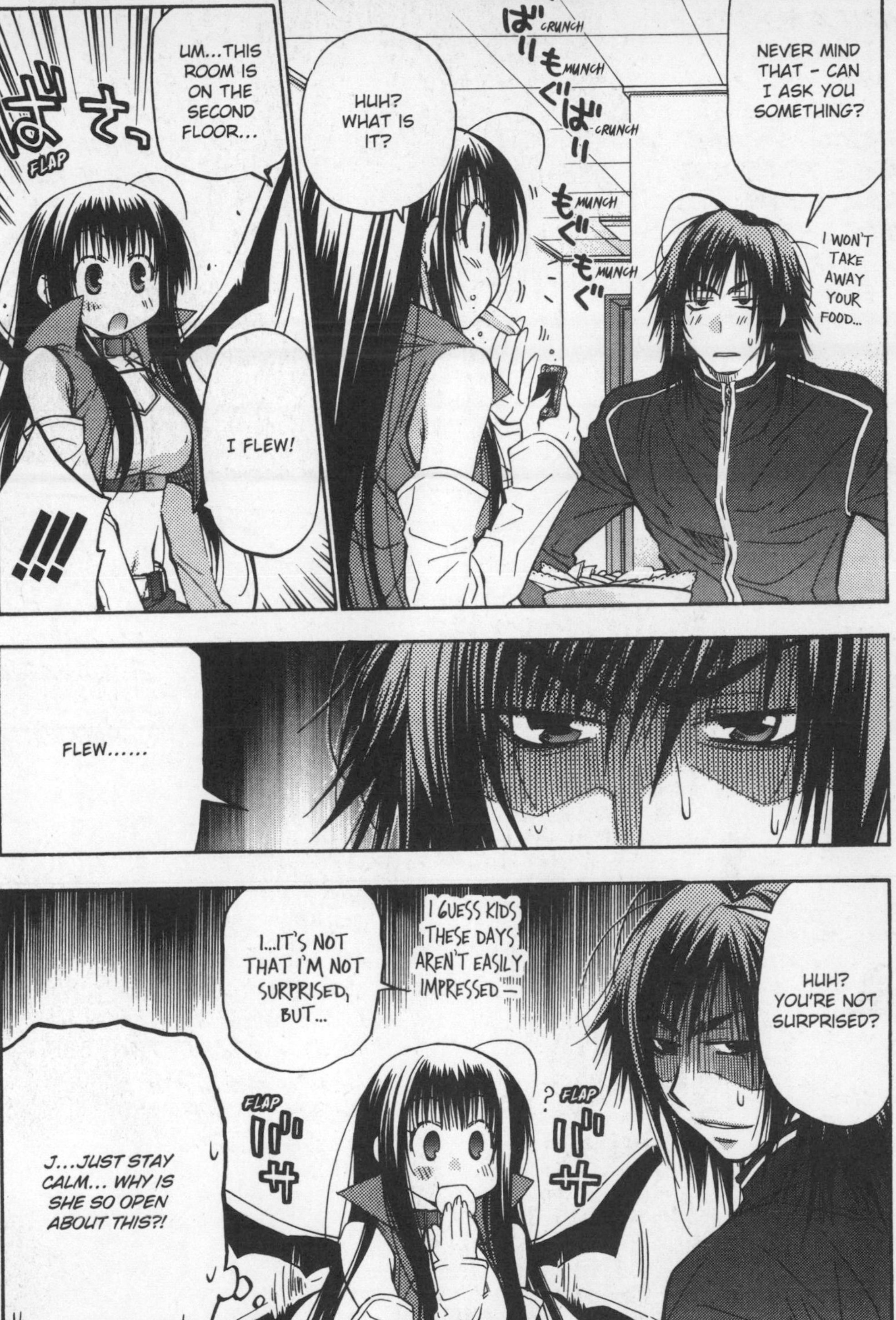
MUNCH CRUNCH MUNCH CRUNCH
NEVER MIND THAT - CAN I ASK YOU SOMETHING?
HUH? WHAT IS IT?
MUNCH MUNCH
I WON'T TAKE AWAY YOUR FOOD...
UM...THIS ROOM IS ON THE SECOND FLOOR...
FLAP
I FLEW!
!!!
FLEW......
HUH? YOU'RE NOT SURPRISED?
I GUESS KIDS THESE DAYS AREN'T EASILY IMPRESSED—
I...IT'S NOT THAT I'M NOT SURPRISED, BUT...
FLAP
FLAP
J...JUST STAY CALM... WHY IS SHE SO OPEN ABOUT THIS?!

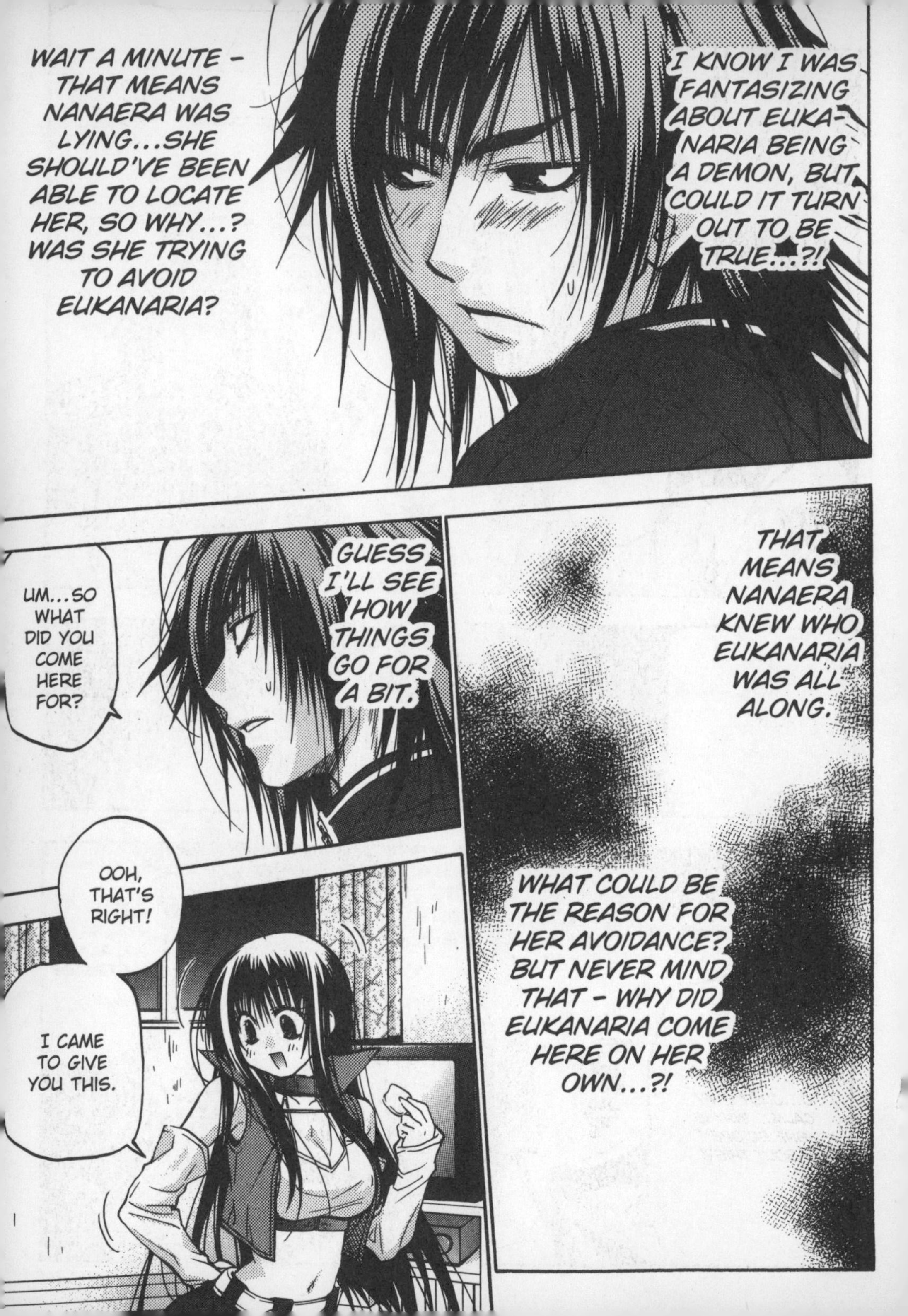
I KNOW I WAS FANTASIZING ABOUT EUKA-NARIA BEING A DEMON, BUT COULD IT TURN OUT TO BE TRUE...?!
WAIT A MINUTE - THAT MEANS NANAERA WAS LYING...SHE SHOULD'VE BEEN ABLE TO LOCATE HER, SO WHY...? WAS SHE TRYING TO AVOID EUKANARIA?
THAT MEANS NANAERA KNEW WHO EUKANARIA WAS ALL ALONG.
WHAT COULD BE THE REASON FOR HER AVOIDANCE? BUT NEVER MIND THAT - WHY DID EUKANARIA COME HERE ON HER OWN...?!
GUESS I'LL SEE HOW THINGS GO FOR A BIT.
UM...SO WHAT DID YOU COME HERE FOR?
OOH, THAT'S RIGHT!
I CAME TO GIVE YOU THIS.

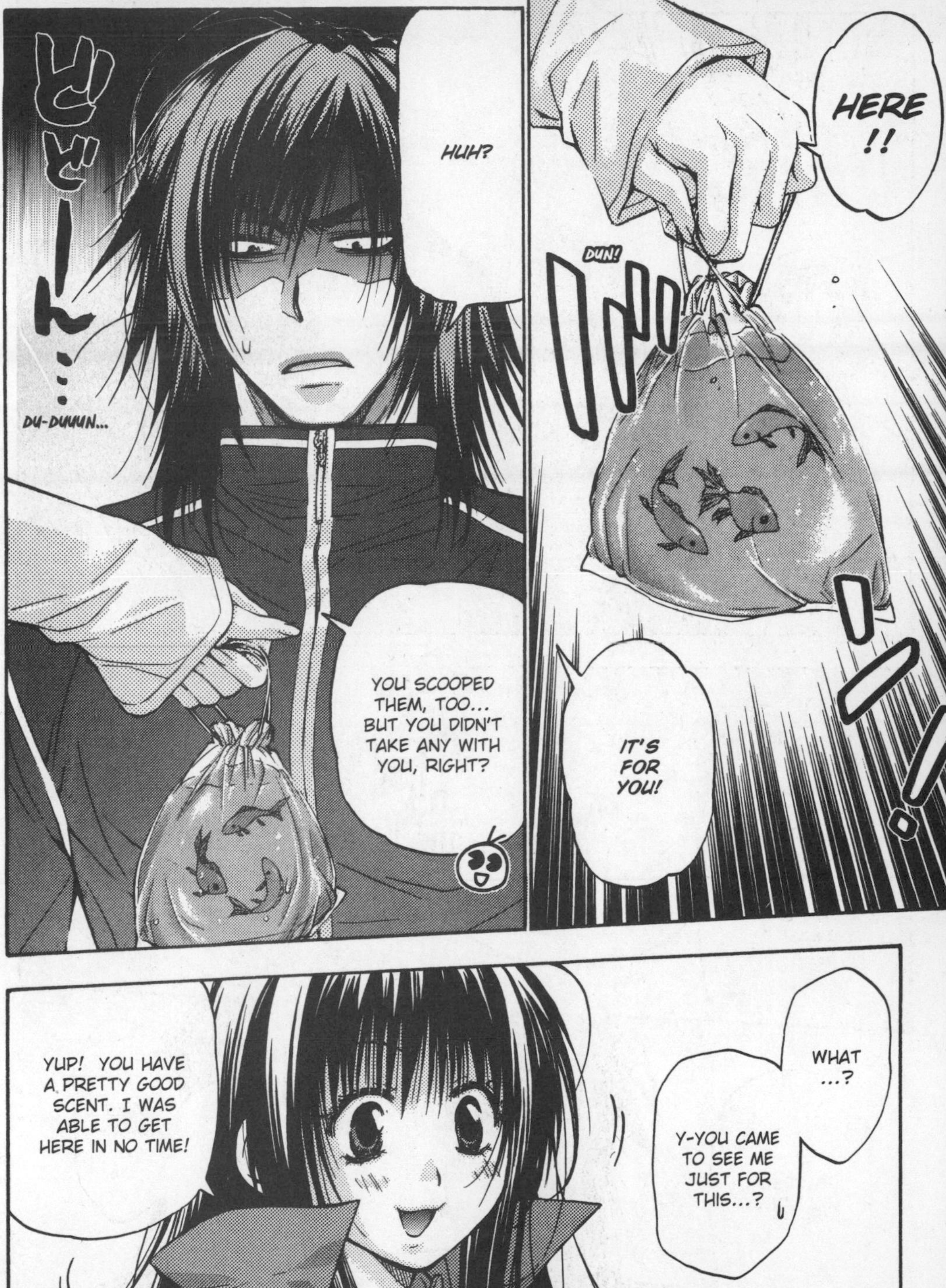
HERE!!
DUN!
IT'S FOR YOU!
HUH?
どどーん…
DU-DUUUN...
YOU SCOOPED THEM, TOO... BUT YOU DIDN'T TAKE ANY WITH YOU, RIGHT?
WHAT ...?
Y-YOU CAME TO SEE ME JUST FOR THIS...?
YUP! YOU HAVE A PRETTY GOOD SCENT. I WAS ABLE TO GET HERE IN NO TIME!

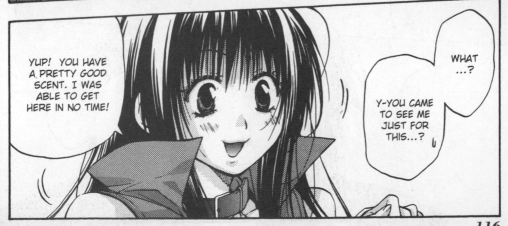

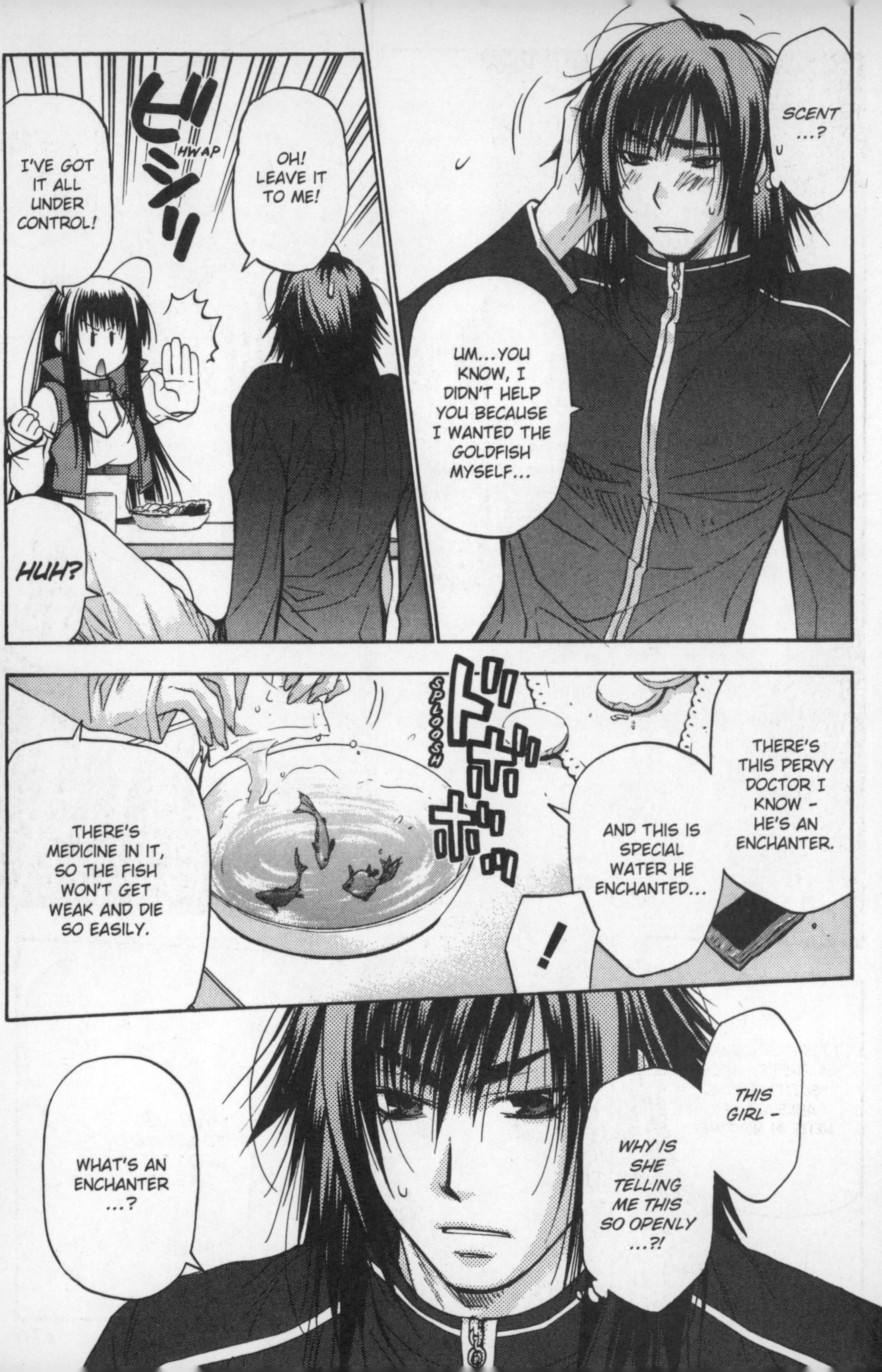
SCENT ...?
UM...YOU KNOW, I DIDN'T HELP YOU BECAUSE I WANTED THE GOLDFISH MYSELF...
HWAP
OH! LEAVE IT TO ME!
I'VE GOT IT ALL UNDER CONTROL!
HUH?
THERE'S THIS PERVY DOCTOR I KNOW - HE'S AN ENCHANTER.
AND THIS IS SPECIAL WATER HE ENCHANTED...
SPLOOSH
THERE'S MEDICINE IN IT, SO THE FISH WON'T GET WEAK AND DIE SO EASILY.
!
THIS GIRL -
WHY IS SHE TELLING ME THIS SO OPENLY ...?!
WHAT'S AN ENCHANTER ...?

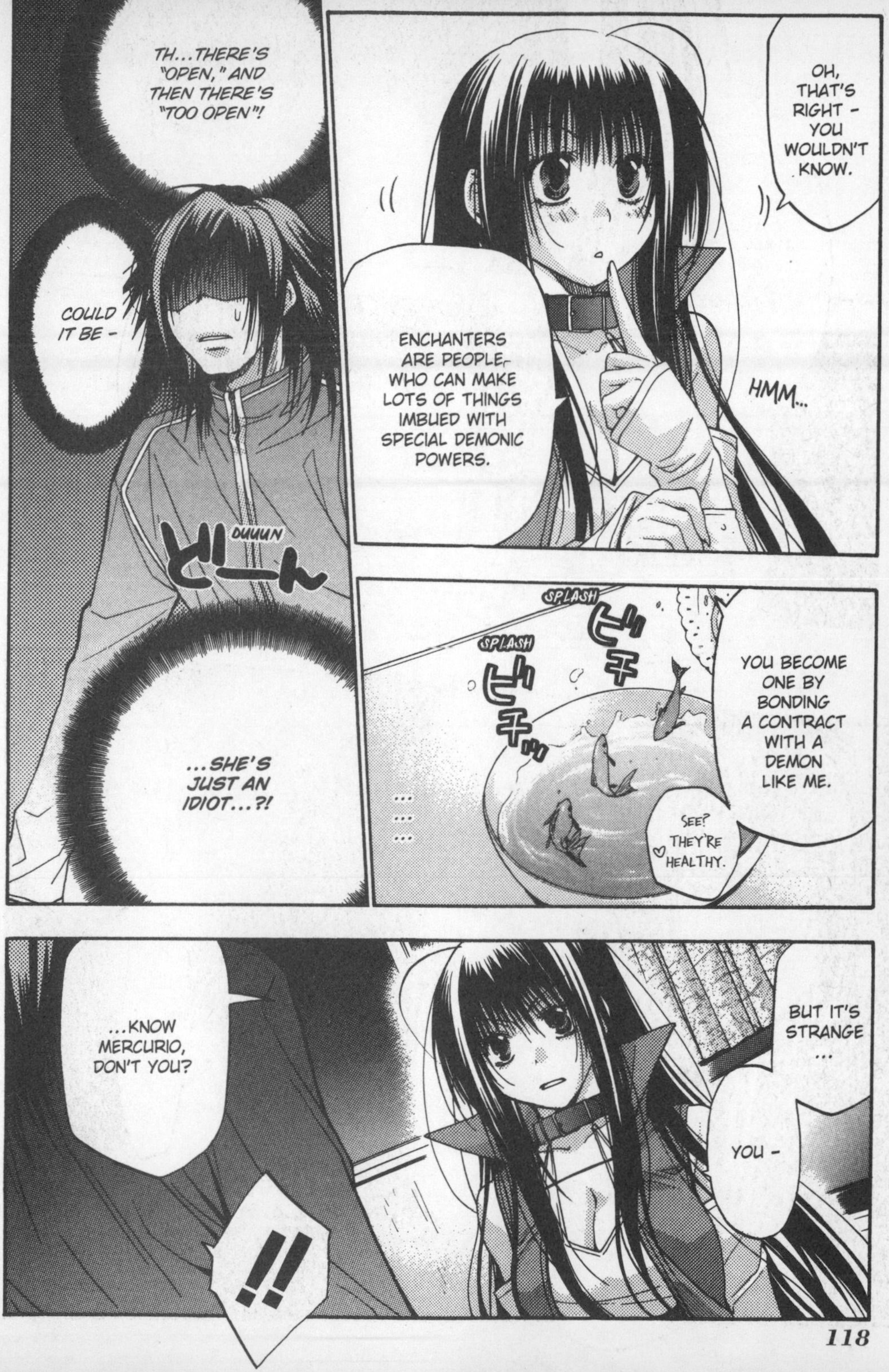
OH, THAT'S RIGHT - YOU WOULDN'T KNOW.
HMM...
ENCHANTERS ARE PEOPLE WHO CAN MAKE LOTS OF THINGS IMBUED WITH SPECIAL DEMONIC POWERS.
SPLASH
ビチ
SPLASH
ビチッ
YOU BECOME ONE BY BONDING A CONTRACT WITH A DEMON LIKE ME.
SEE? THEY'RE HEALTHY.
......
TH...THERE'S "OPEN," AND THEN THERE'S "TOO OPEN"!
COULD IT BE -
DUUUN
どーん
...SHE'S JUST AN IDIOT...?!
BUT IT'S STRANGE ...
YOU -
...KNOW MERCURIO, DON'T YOU?
!!

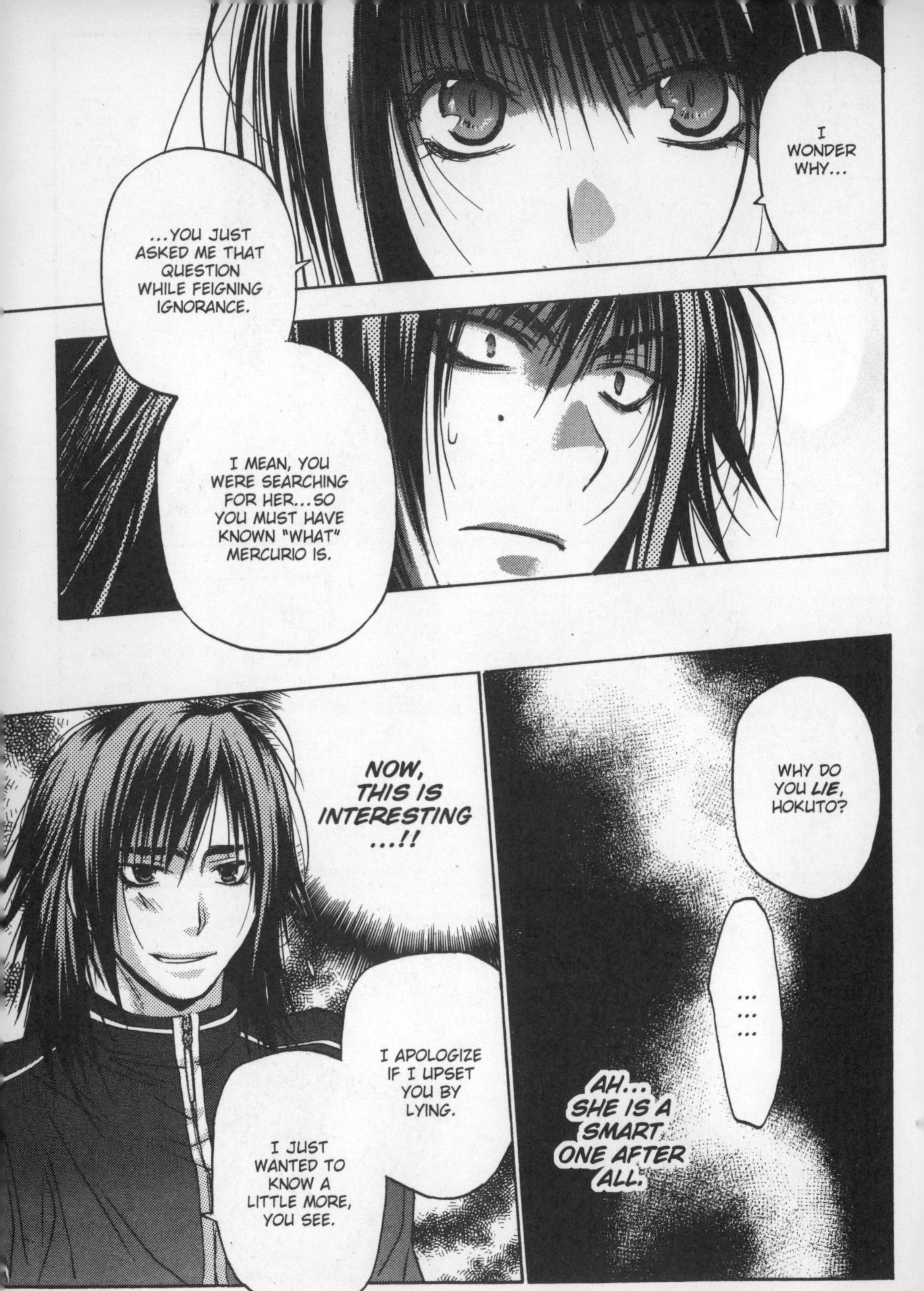
I WONDER WHY...
...YOU JUST ASKED ME THAT QUESTION WHILE FEIGNING IGNORANCE.
I MEAN, YOU WERE SEARCHING FOR HER...SO YOU MUST HAVE KNOWN "WHAT" MERCURIO IS.
WHY DO YOU *LIE*, HOKUTO?
....
AH... SHE IS A SMART ONE AFTER ALL.
NOW, THIS IS INTERESTING ...!!
I APOLOGIZE IF I UPSET YOU BY LYING.
I JUST WANTED TO KNOW A LITTLE MORE, YOU SEE.

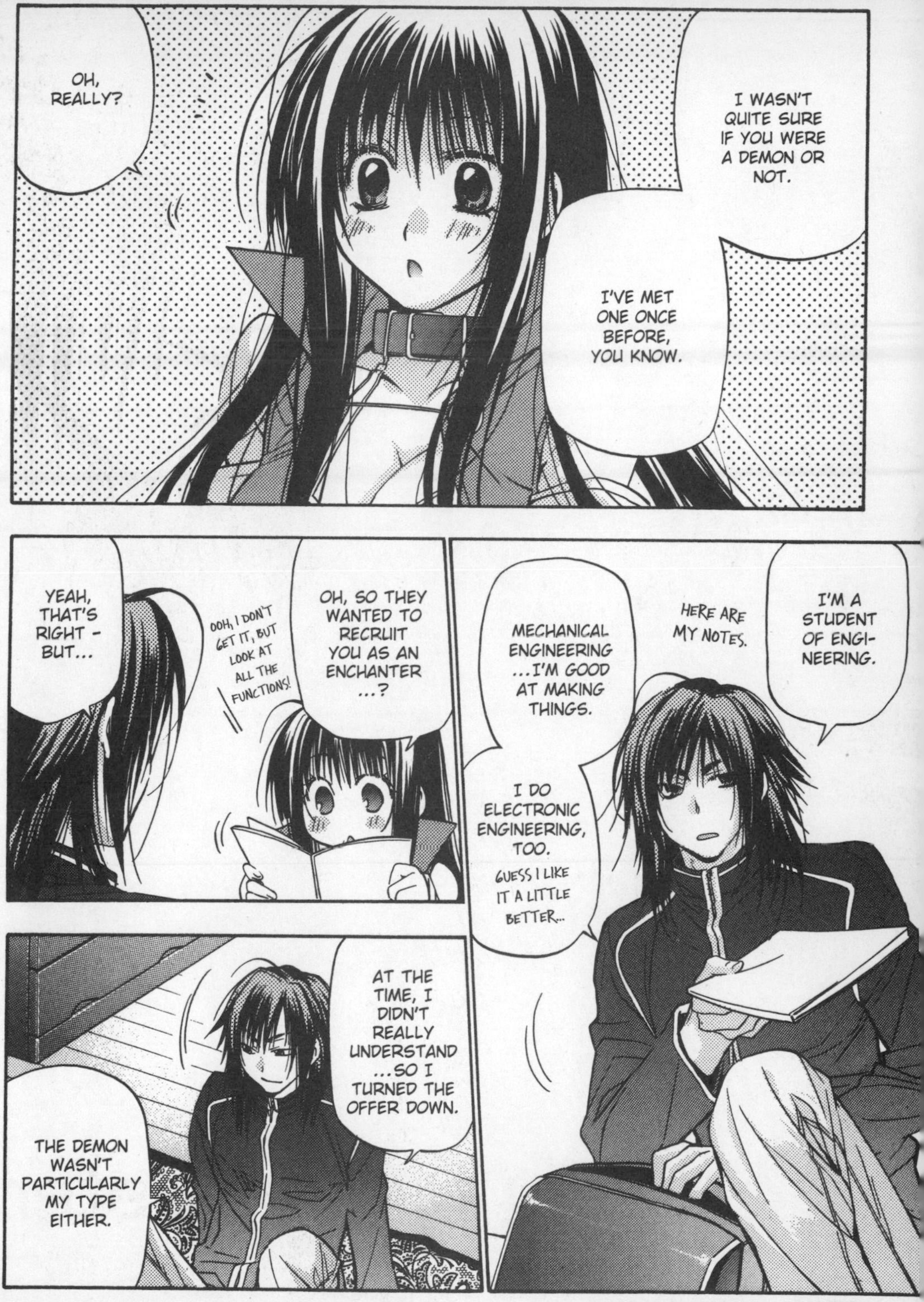
I WASN'T QUITE SURE IF YOU WERE A DEMON OR NOT.
I'VE MET ONE ONCE BEFORE, YOU KNOW.
OH, REALLY?
I'M A STUDENT OF ENGI-NEERING.
HERE ARE MY NOTES.
MECHANICAL ENGINEERING ...I'M GOOD AT MAKING THINGS.
I DO ELECTRONIC ENGINEERING, TOO.
GUESS I LIKE IT A LITTLE BETTER...
OH, SO THEY WANTED TO RECRUIT YOU AS AN ENCHANTER ...?
OOH, I DON'T GET IT, BUT LOOK AT ALL THE FUNCTIONS!
YEAH, THAT'S RIGHT - BUT...
AT THE TIME, I DIDN'T REALLY UNDERSTAND ...SO I TURNED THE OFFER DOWN.
THE DEMON WASN'T PARTICULARLY MY TYPE EITHER.

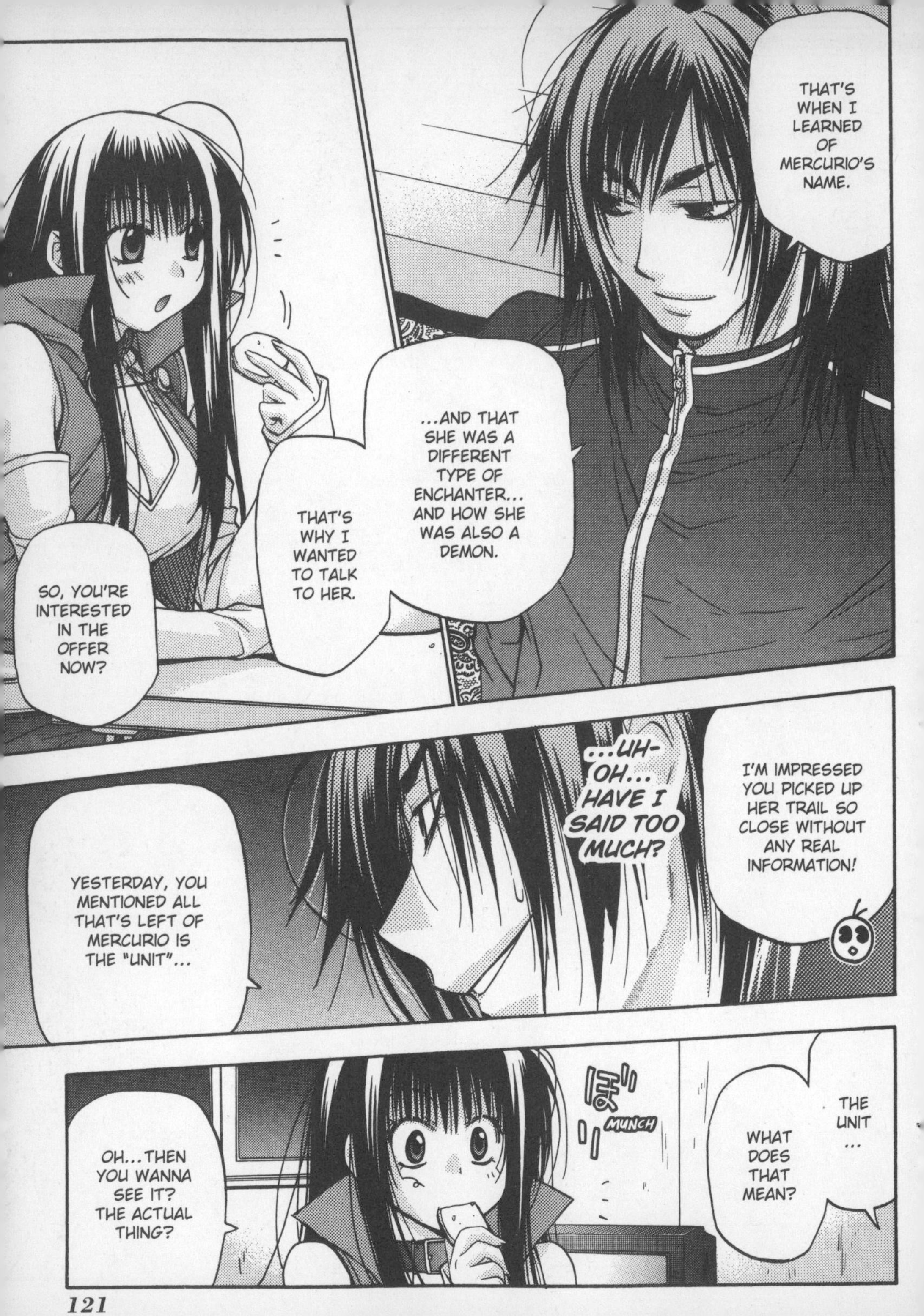
THAT'S WHEN I LEARNED OF MERCURIO'S NAME.
...AND THAT SHE WAS A DIFFERENT TYPE OF ENCHANTER... AND HOW SHE WAS ALSO A DEMON.
THAT'S WHY I WANTED TO TALK TO HER.
SO, YOU'RE INTERESTED IN THE OFFER NOW?
I'M IMPRESSED YOU PICKED UP HER TRAIL SO CLOSE WITHOUT ANY REAL INFORMATION!
...UH-OH... HAVE I SAID TOO MUCH?
YESTERDAY, YOU MENTIONED ALL THAT'S LEFT OF MERCURIO IS THE "UNIT"...
THE UNIT...
WHAT DOES THAT MEAN?
MUNCH
OH...THEN YOU WANNA SEE IT? THE ACTUAL THING?

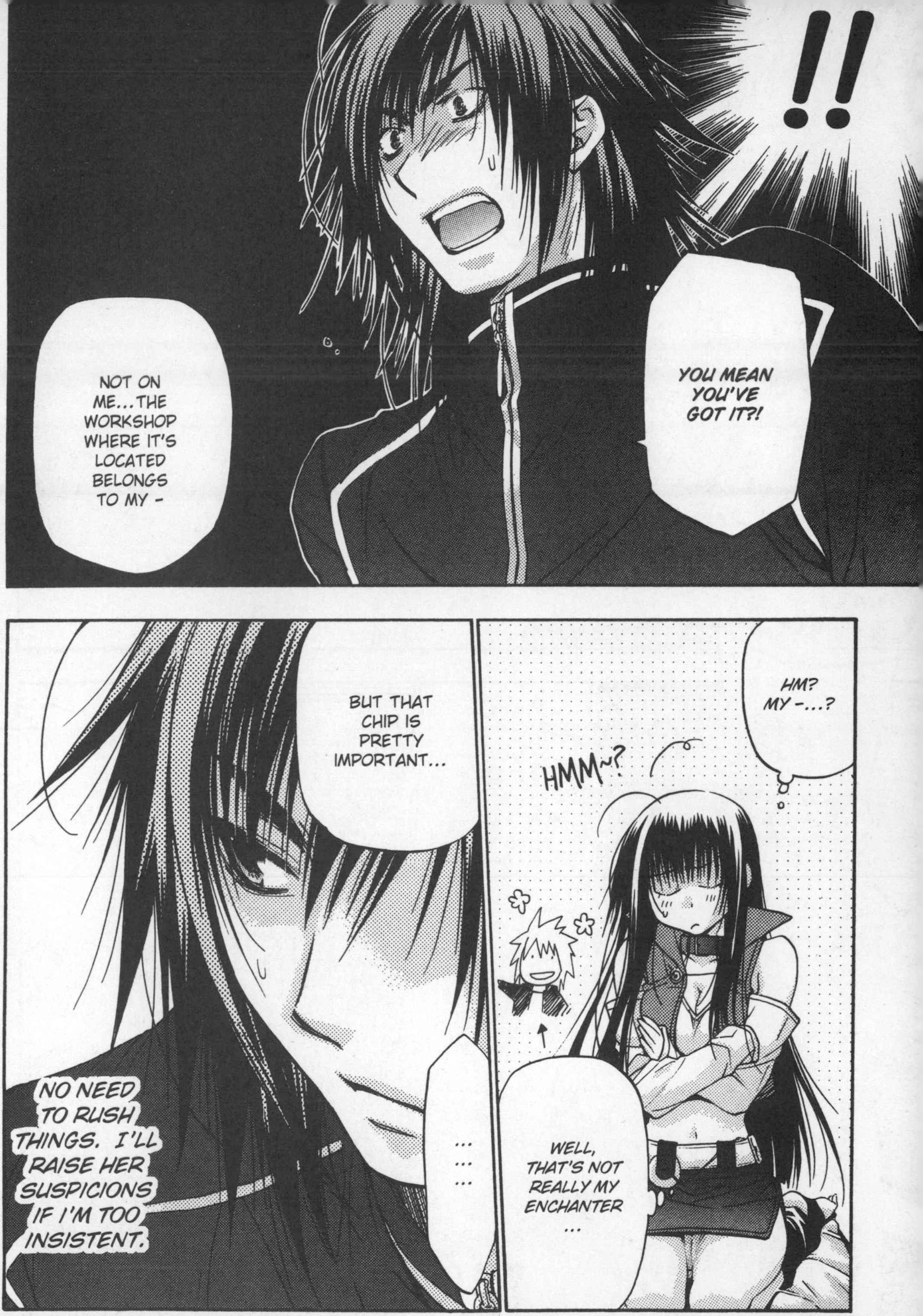
!!
YOU MEAN YOU'VE GOT IT?!
NOT ON ME...THE WORKSHOP WHERE IT'S LOCATED BELONGS TO MY -
HM? MY -...?
HMM~?
WELL, THAT'S NOT REALLY MY ENCHANTER ...
BUT THAT CHIP IS PRETTY IMPORTANT...
... ...
NO NEED TO RUSH THINGS. I'LL RAISE HER SUSPICIONS IF I'M TOO INSISTENT.

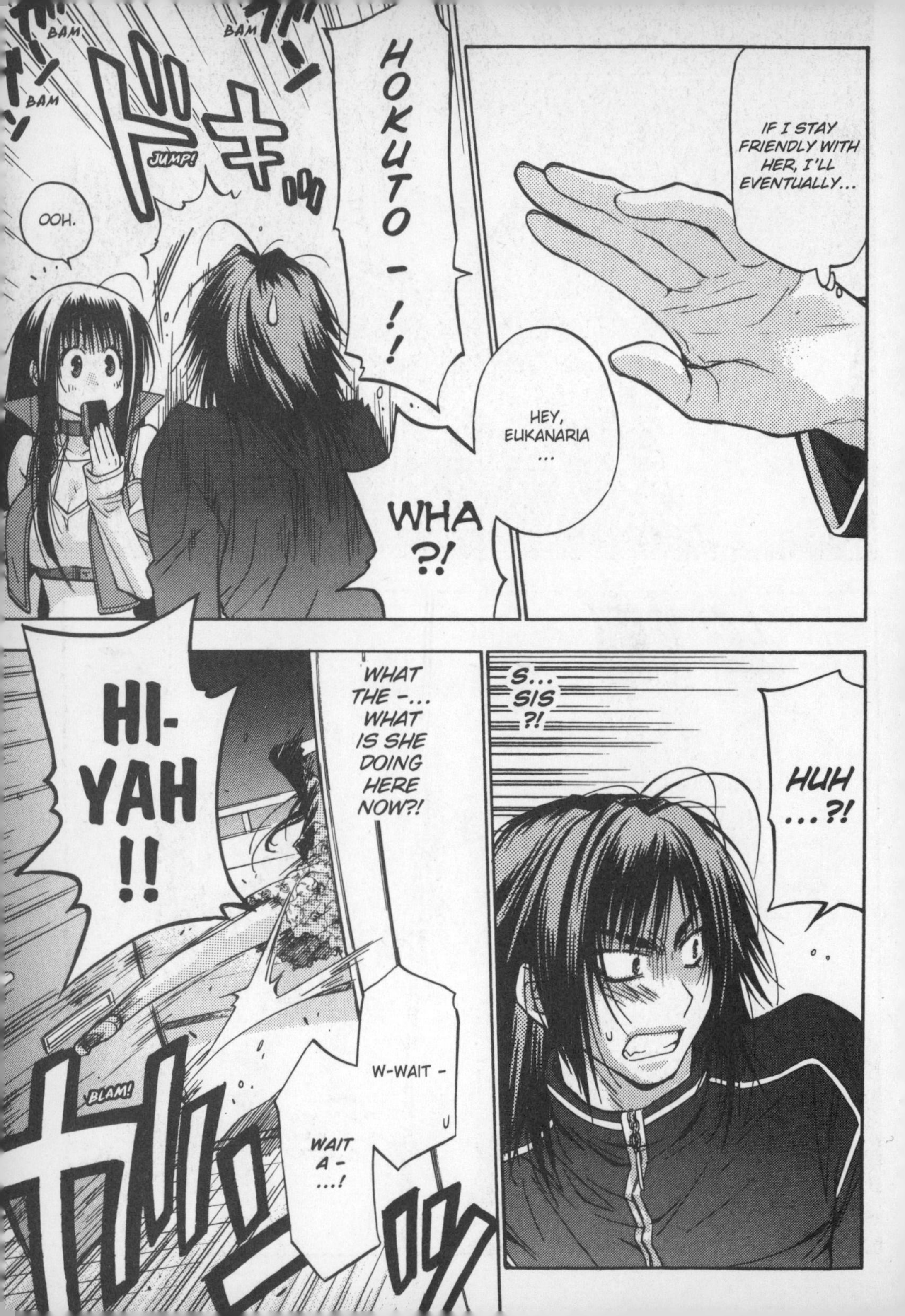
IF I STAY FRIENDLY WITH HER, I'LL EVENTUALLY...
HEY, EUKANARIA ...
HOKUTO -!!
BAM
BAM
BAM
JUMP!
WHA ?!
OOH.
HUH ...?!
S... SIS ?!
WHAT THE -... WHAT IS SHE DOING HERE NOW?!
W-WAIT -
WAIT A - ...!
HI-YAH !!
BLAM!

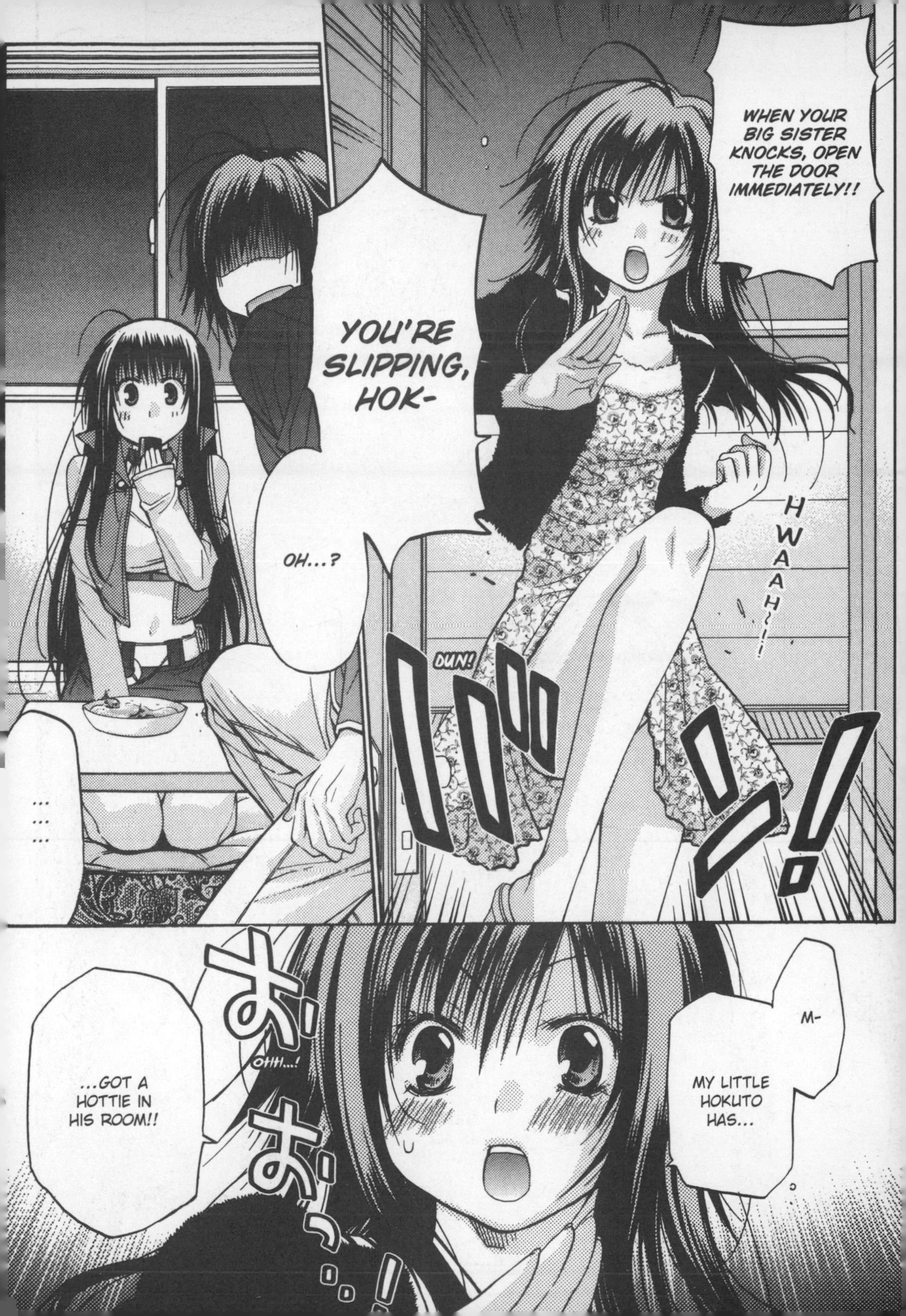
WHEN YOUR BIG SISTER KNOCKS, OPEN THE DOOR IMMEDIATELY!!
HWAAH~!!
YOU'RE SLIPPING, HOK-
DUN!
OH...?
...
...
...
M-
MY LITTLE HOKUTO HAS...
...GOT A HOTTIE IN HIS ROOM!!
おおおっ…!
OHH...!

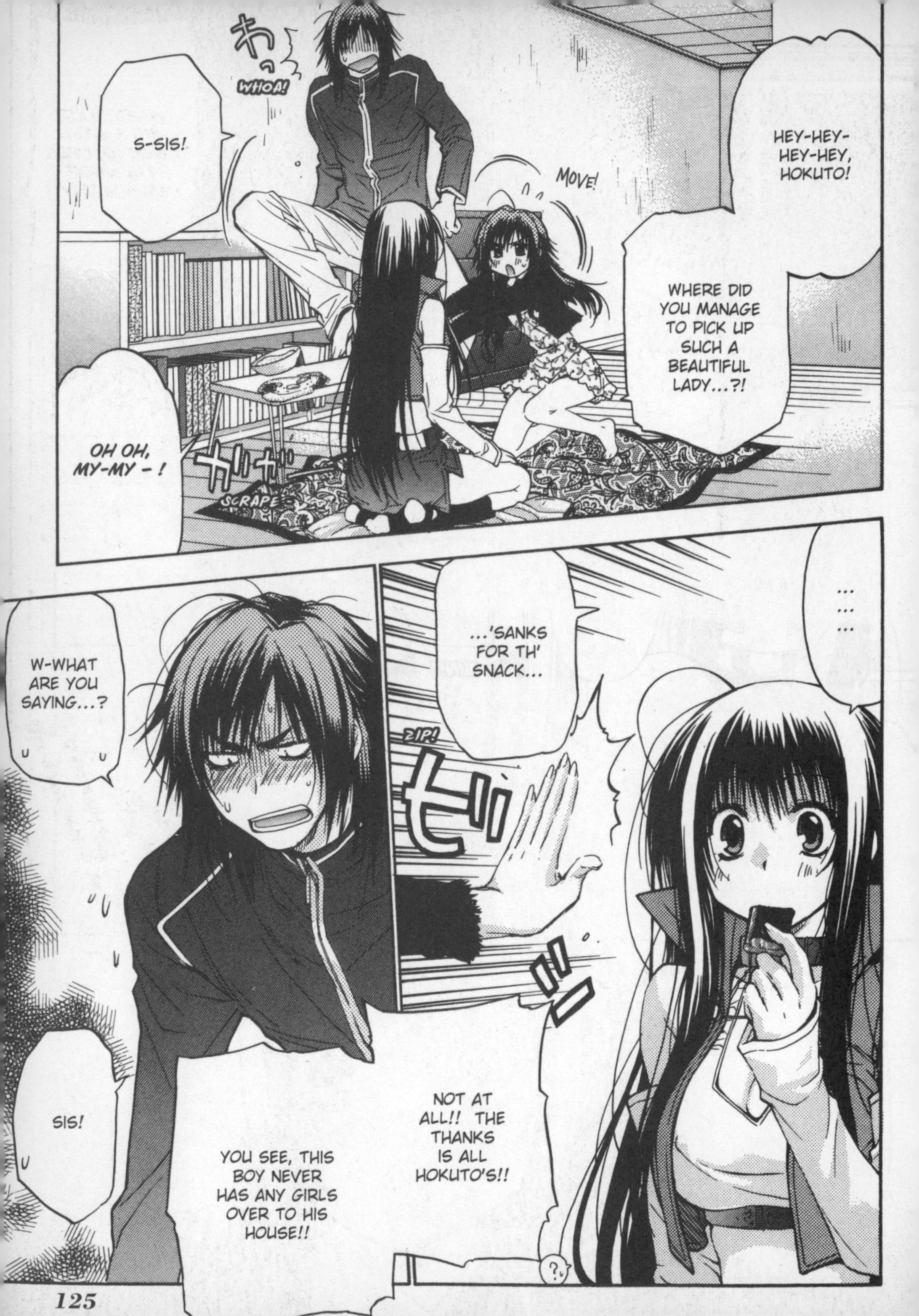
HEY-HEY-HEY-HEY, HOKUTO!
WHERE DID YOU MANAGE TO PICK UP SUCH A BEAUTIFUL LADY...?!
MOVE!
わっ
WHOA!
S-SIS!
OH OH, MY-MY -!
SCRAPE
... ...
...'SANKS FOR TH' SNACK...
ZIP!
NOT AT ALL!! THE THANKS IS ALL HOKUTO'S!!
YOU SEE, THIS BOY NEVER HAS ANY GIRLS OVER TO HIS HOUSE!!
?
W-WHAT ARE YOU SAYING...?
SIS!

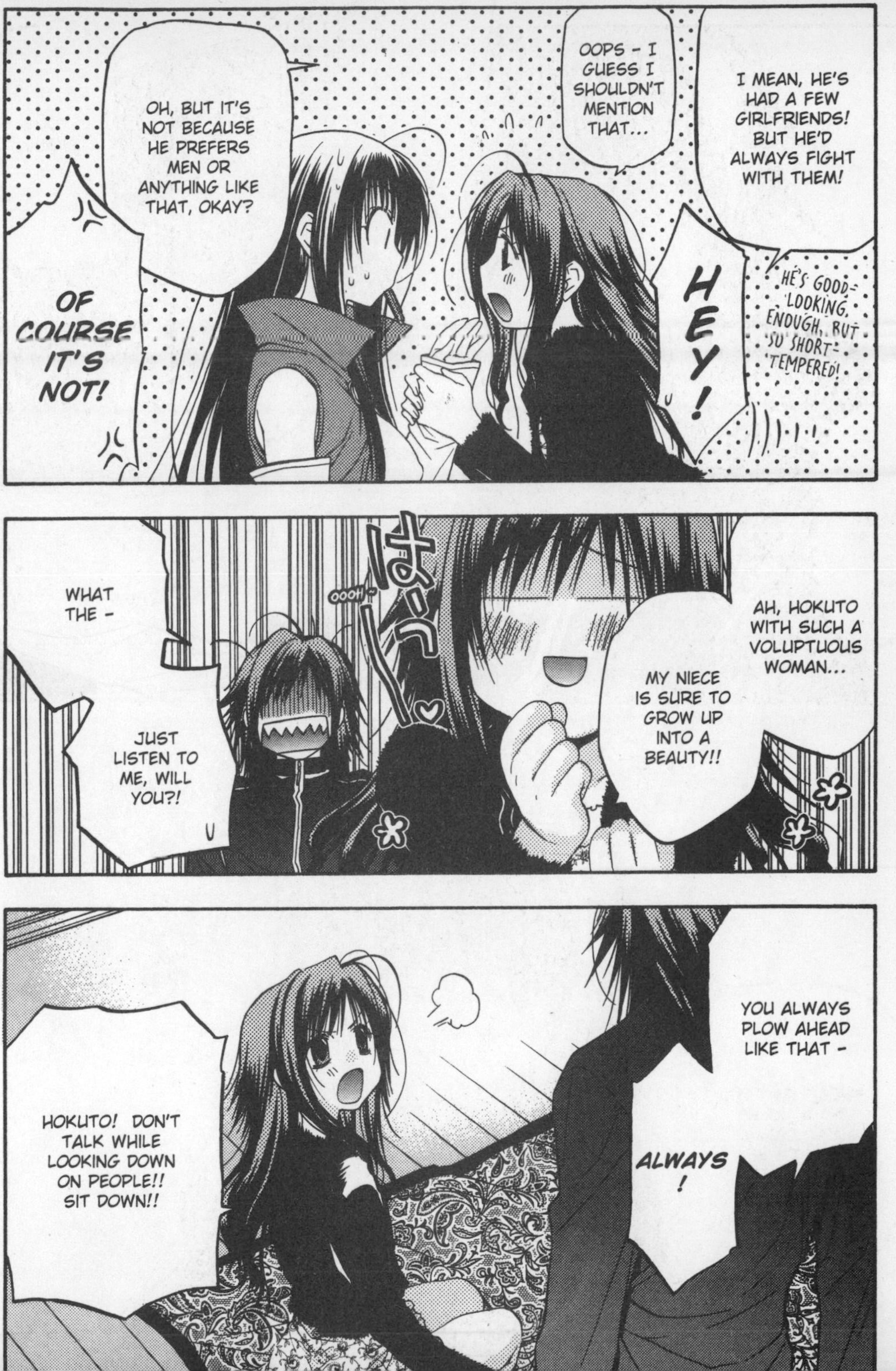
I MEAN, HE'S HAD A FEW GIRLFRIENDS! BUT HE'D ALWAYS FIGHT WITH THEM!
HE'S GOOD-LOOKING ENOUGH, BUT SO SHORT-TEMPERED!
HEY!
OOPS - I GUESS I SHOULDN'T MENTION THAT...
OH, BUT IT'S NOT BECAUSE HE PREFERS MEN OR ANYTHING LIKE THAT, OKAY?
OF COURSE IT'S NOT!
AH, HOKUTO WITH SUCH A VOLUPTUOUS WOMAN...
MY NIECE IS SURE TO GROW UP INTO A BEAUTY!!
OOOH
WHAT THE -
JUST LISTEN TO ME, WILL YOU?!
YOU ALWAYS PLOW AHEAD LIKE THAT -
ALWAYS!
HOKUTO! DON'T TALK WHILE LOOKING DOWN ON PEOPLE!! SIT DOWN!!

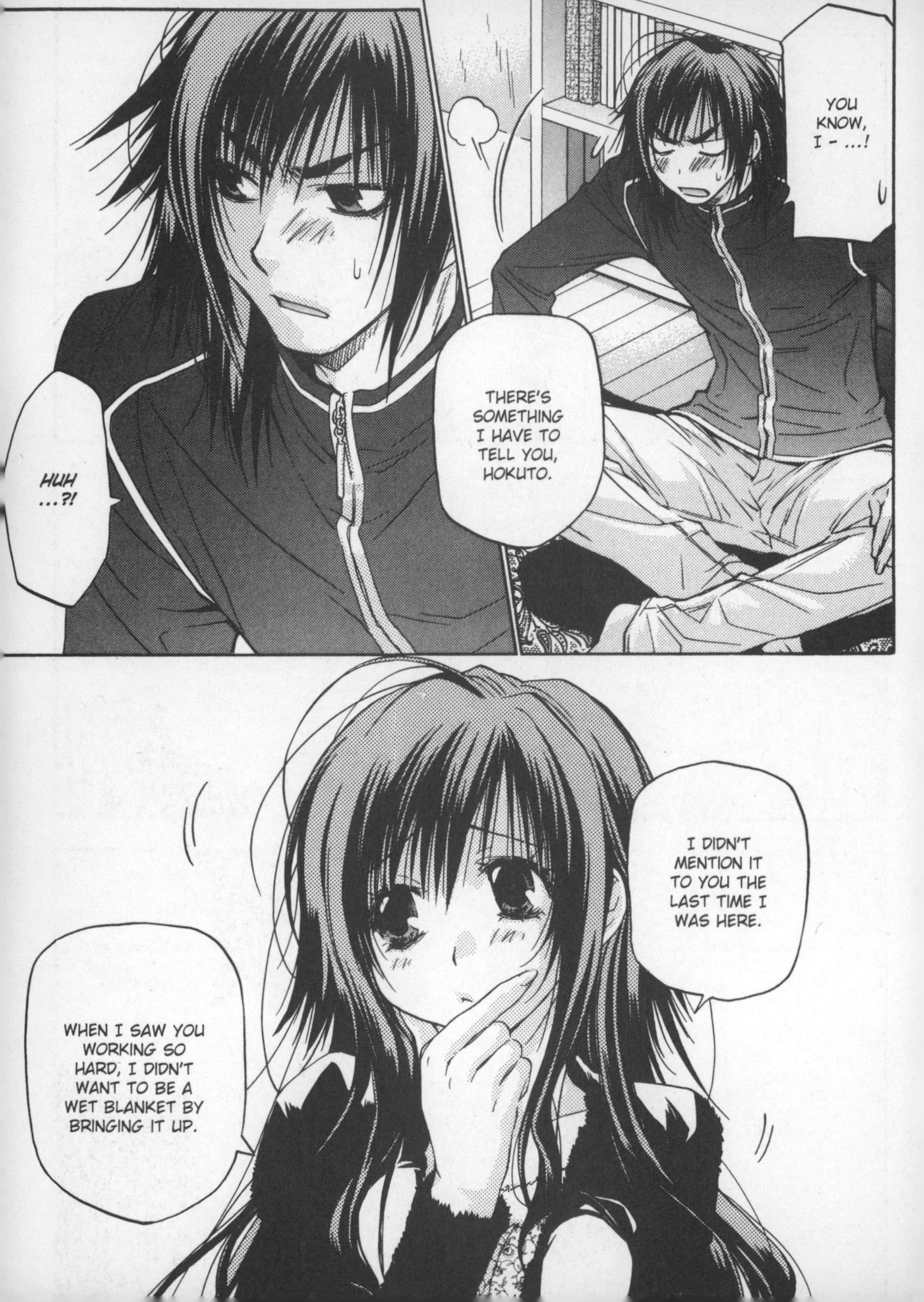
YOU KNOW, I - ...!
THERE'S SOMETHING I HAVE TO TELL YOU, HOKUTO.
HUH ...?!
I DIDN'T MENTION IT TO YOU THE LAST TIME I WAS HERE.
WHEN I SAW YOU WORKING SO HARD, I DIDN'T WANT TO BE A WET BLANKET BY BRINGING IT UP.

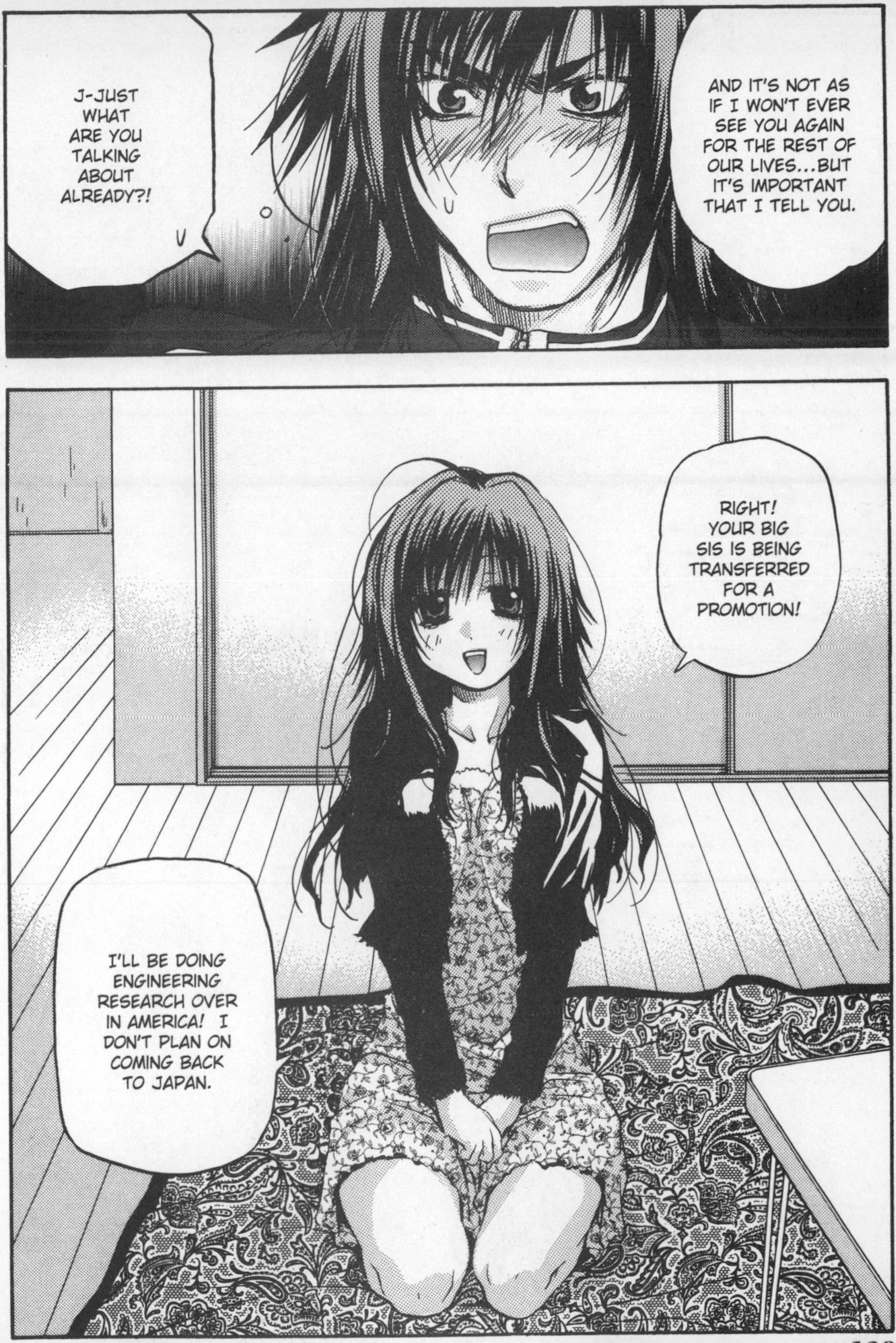
AND IT'S NOT AS IF I WON'T EVER SEE YOU AGAIN FOR THE REST OF OUR LIVES...BUT IT'S IMPORTANT THAT I TELL YOU.
J-JUST WHAT ARE YOU TALKING ABOUT ALREADY?!
RIGHT! YOUR BIG SIS IS BEING TRANSFERRED FOR A PROMOTION!
I'LL BE DOING ENGINEERING RESEARCH OVER IN AMERICA! I DON'T PLAN ON COMING BACK TO JAPAN.

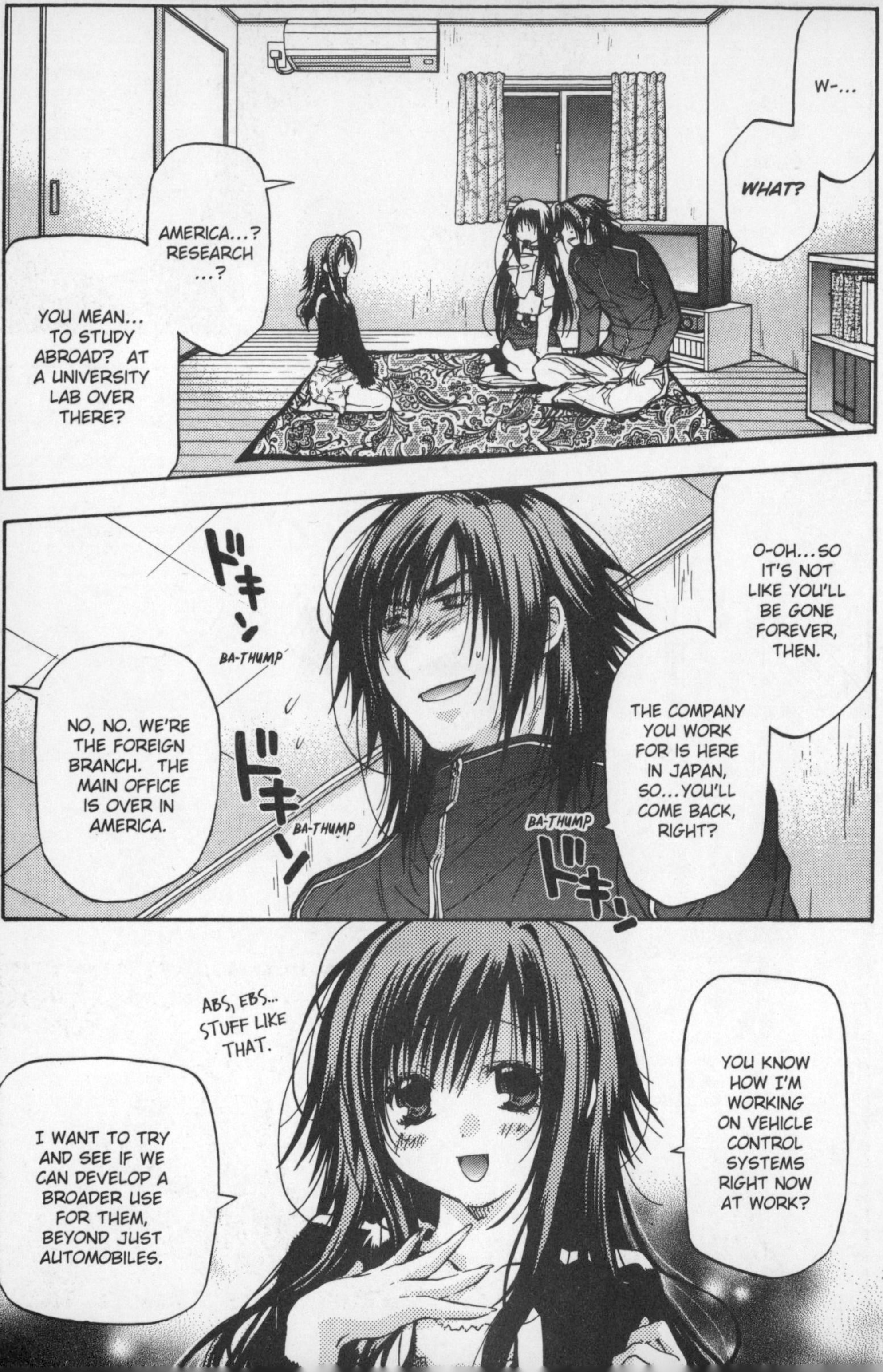
W-...
WHAT?
AMERICA...? RESEARCH ...?
YOU MEAN... TO STUDY ABROAD? AT A UNIVERSITY LAB OVER THERE?
O-OH...SO IT'S NOT LIKE YOU'LL BE GONE FOREVER, THEN.
THE COMPANY YOU WORK FOR IS HERE IN JAPAN, SO...YOU'LL COME BACK, RIGHT?
ドキン
BA-THUMP
ドキン
BA-THUMP
ドキン
BA-THUMP
NO, NO. WE'RE THE FOREIGN BRANCH. THE MAIN OFFICE IS OVER IN AMERICA.
YOU KNOW HOW I'M WORKING ON VEHICLE CONTROL SYSTEMS RIGHT NOW AT WORK?
ABS, EBS... STUFF LIKE THAT.
I WANT TO TRY AND SEE IF WE CAN DEVELOP A BROADER USE FOR THEM, BEYOND JUST AUTOMOBILES.

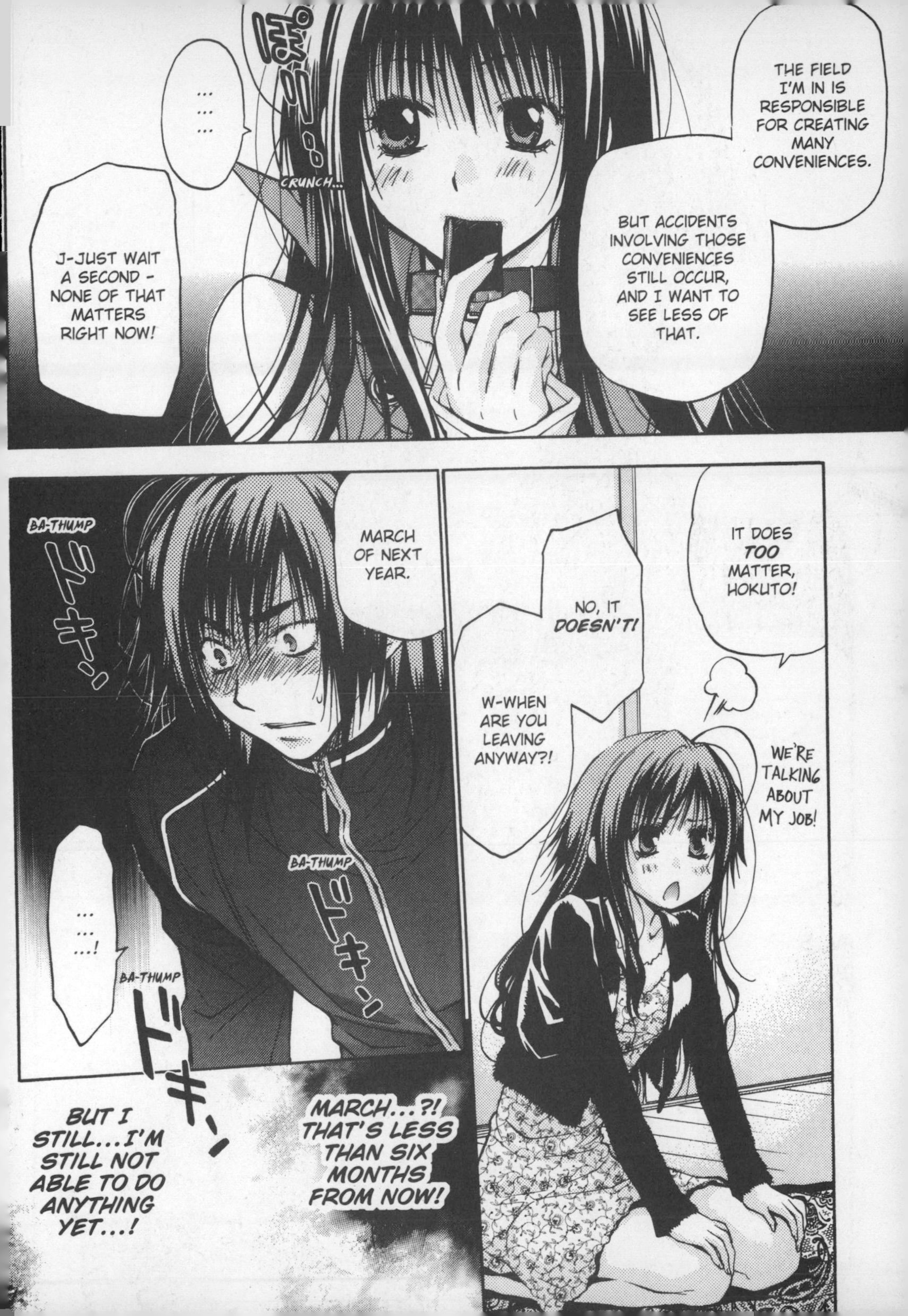
THE FIELD I'M IN IS RESPONSIBLE FOR CREATING MANY CONVENIENCES.
BUT ACCIDENTS INVOLVING THOSE CONVENIENCES STILL OCCUR, AND I WANT TO SEE LESS OF THAT.
CRUNCH...
... ...
J-JUST WAIT A SECOND - NONE OF THAT MATTERS RIGHT NOW!
IT DOES TOO MATTER, HOKUTO!
NO, IT DOESN'T!
WE'RE TALKING ABOUT MY JOB!
W-WHEN ARE YOU LEAVING ANYWAY?!
MARCH OF NEXT YEAR.
BA-THUMP
BA-THUMP
... ...!
BA-THUMP
MARCH...?! THAT'S LESS THAN SIX MONTHS FROM NOW!
BUT I STILL...I'M STILL NOT ABLE TO DO ANYTHING YET...!

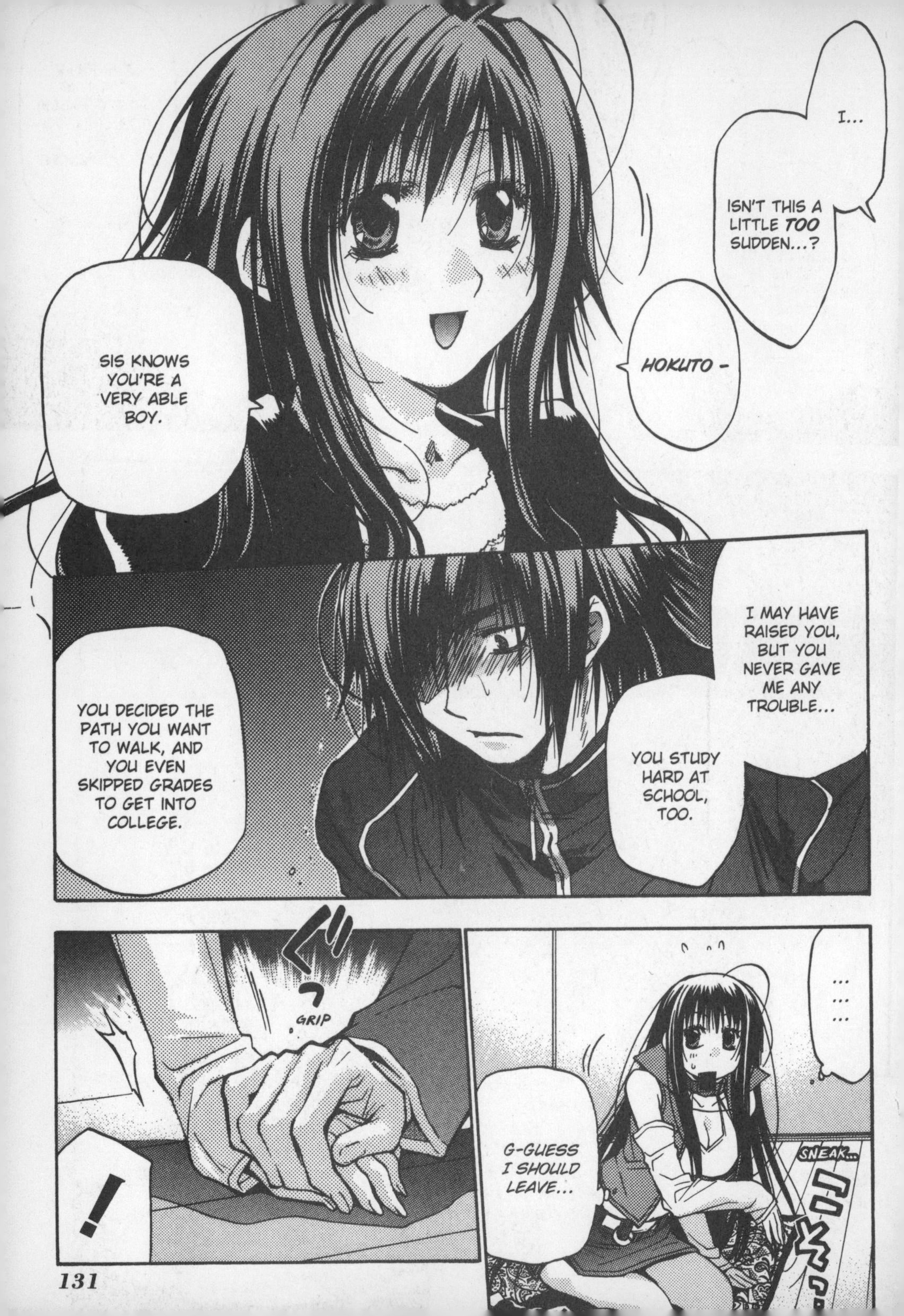
I...
ISN'T THIS A LITTLE *TOO* SUDDEN...?
HOKUTO -
SIS KNOWS YOU'RE A VERY ABLE BOY.
I MAY HAVE RAISED YOU, BUT YOU NEVER GAVE ME ANY TROUBLE...
YOU STUDY HARD AT SCHOOL, TOO.
YOU DECIDED THE PATH YOU WANT TO WALK, AND YOU EVEN SKIPPED GRADES TO GET INTO COLLEGE.
... ...
SNEAK...
G-GUESS I SHOULD LEAVE...
GRIP
!

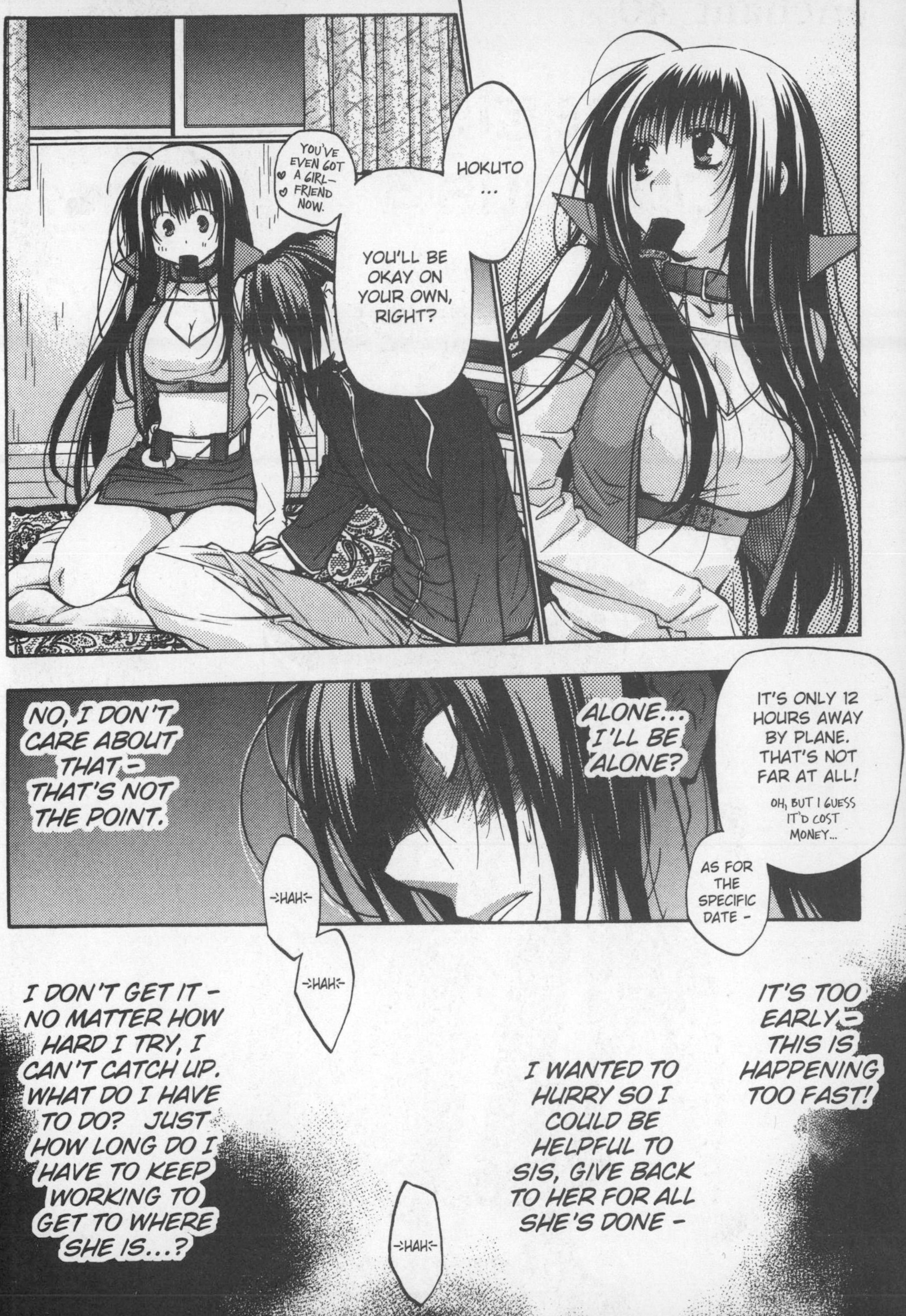
HOKUTO ...
YOU'LL BE OKAY ON YOUR OWN, RIGHT?
YOU'VE EVEN GOT A GIRL-FRIEND NOW.
IT'S ONLY 12 HOURS AWAY BY PLANE. THAT'S NOT FAR AT ALL!
OH, BUT I GUESS IT'D COST MONEY...
AS FOR THE SPECIFIC DATE -
ALONE... I'LL BE ALONE?
NO, I DON'T CARE ABOUT THAT - THAT'S NOT THE POINT.
-HAH-
-HAH-
IT'S TOO EARLY - THIS IS HAPPENING TOO FAST!
I WANTED TO HURRY SO I COULD BE HELPFUL TO SIS, GIVE BACK TO HER FOR ALL SHE'S DONE -
-HAH-
I DON'T GET IT - NO MATTER HOW HARD I TRY, I CAN'T CATCH UP. WHAT DO I HAVE TO DO? JUST HOW LONG DO I HAVE TO KEEP WORKING TO GET TO WHERE SHE IS...?

エンチャント
enchant. 40

アモル　マギステル
Amor magister
エスト　オプティムス
est optimus③

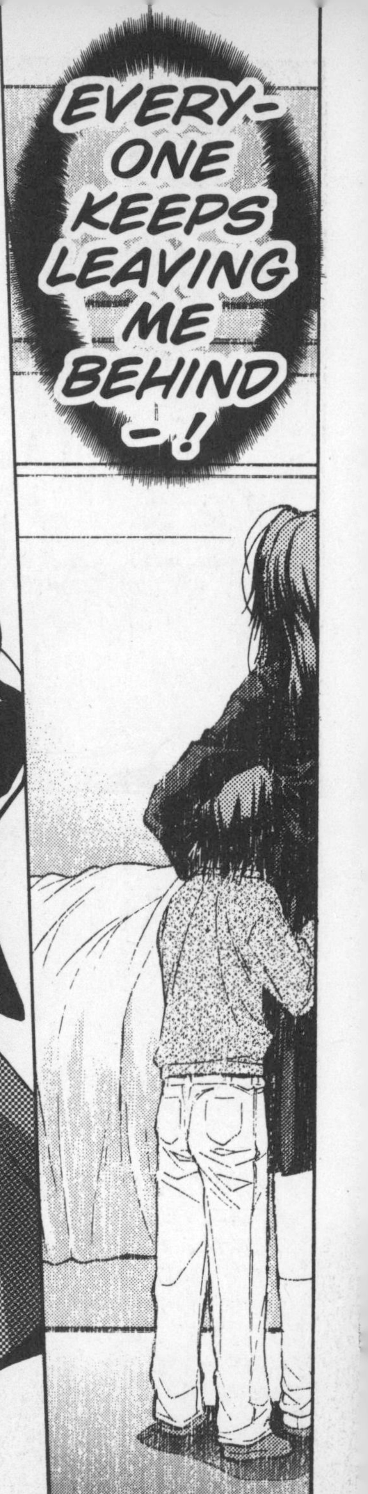
EVERY-ONE KEEPS LEAVING ME BEHIND --!

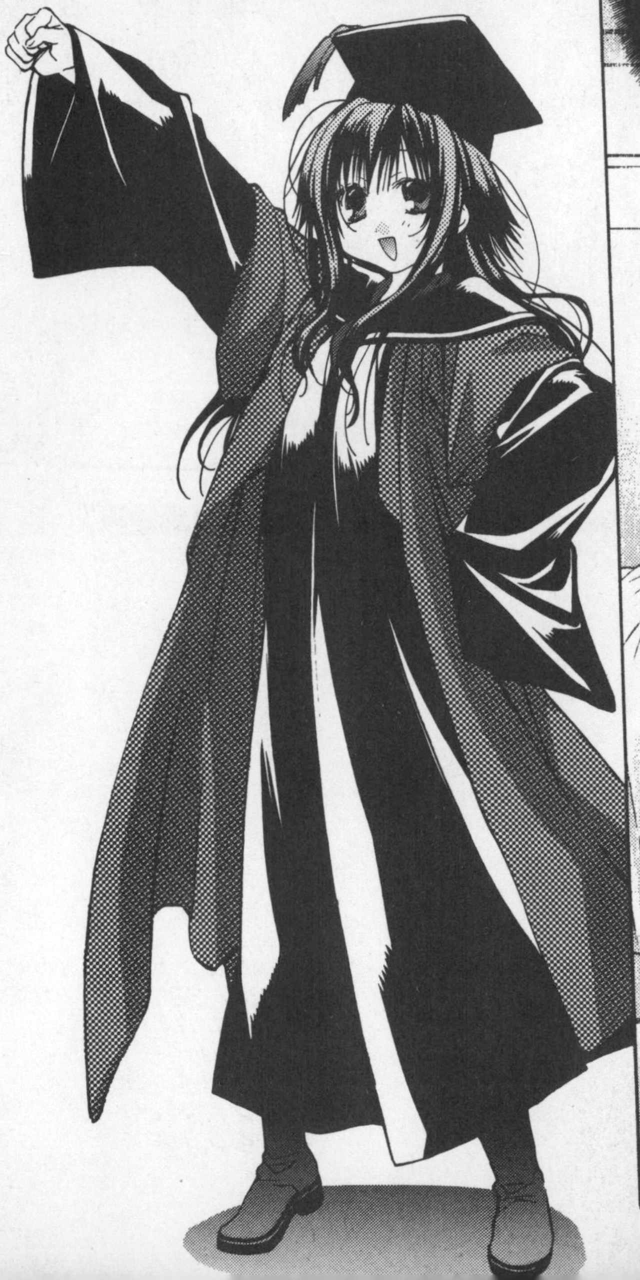

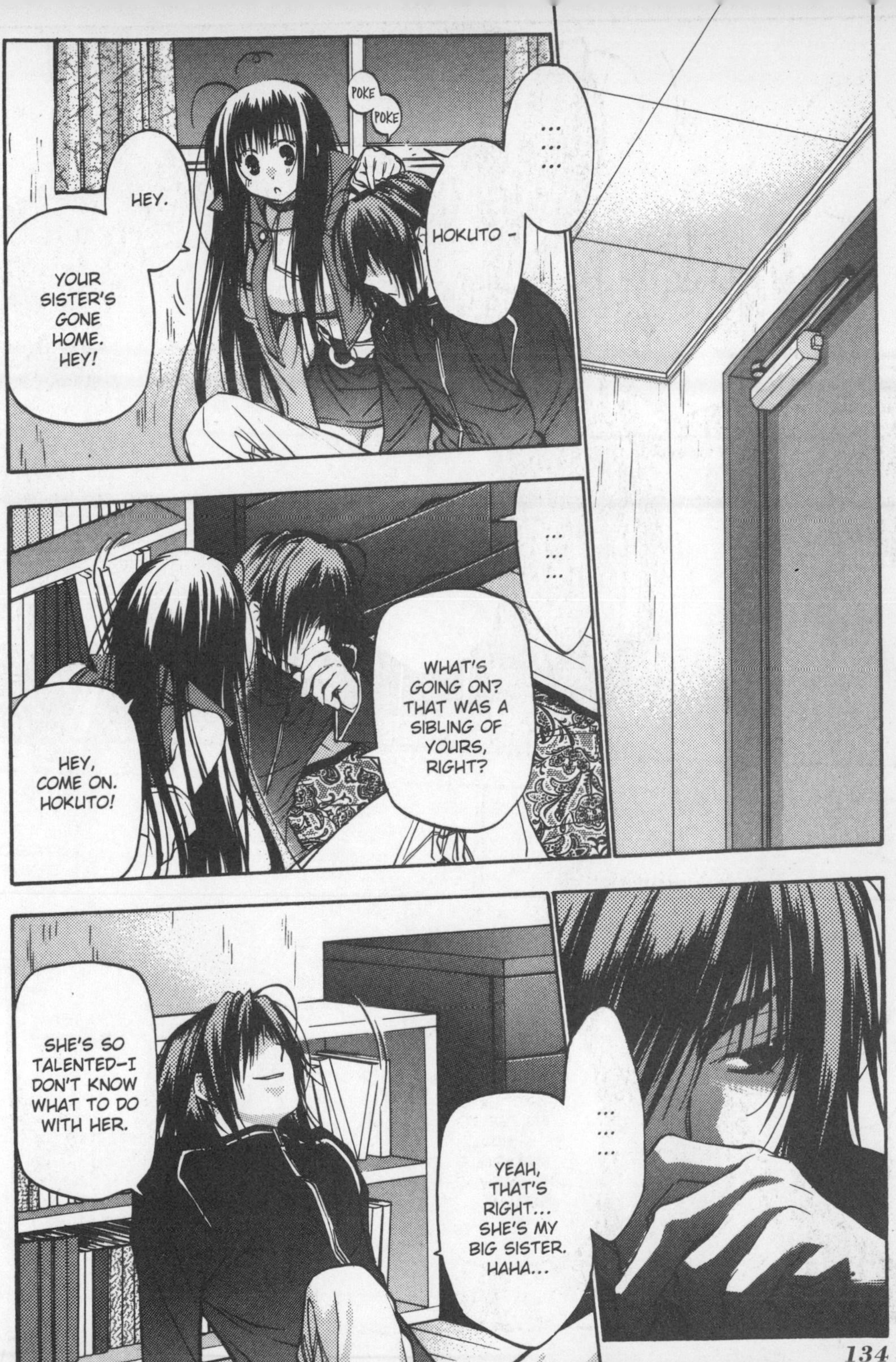
POKE
POKE
....
HEY.
HOKUTO -
YOUR SISTER'S GONE HOME. HEY!
....
WHAT'S GOING ON? THAT WAS A SIBLING OF YOURS, RIGHT?
HEY, COME ON. HOKUTO!
....
YEAH, THAT'S RIGHT... SHE'S MY BIG SISTER. HAHA...
SHE'S SO TALENTED—I DON'T KNOW WHAT TO DO WITH HER.

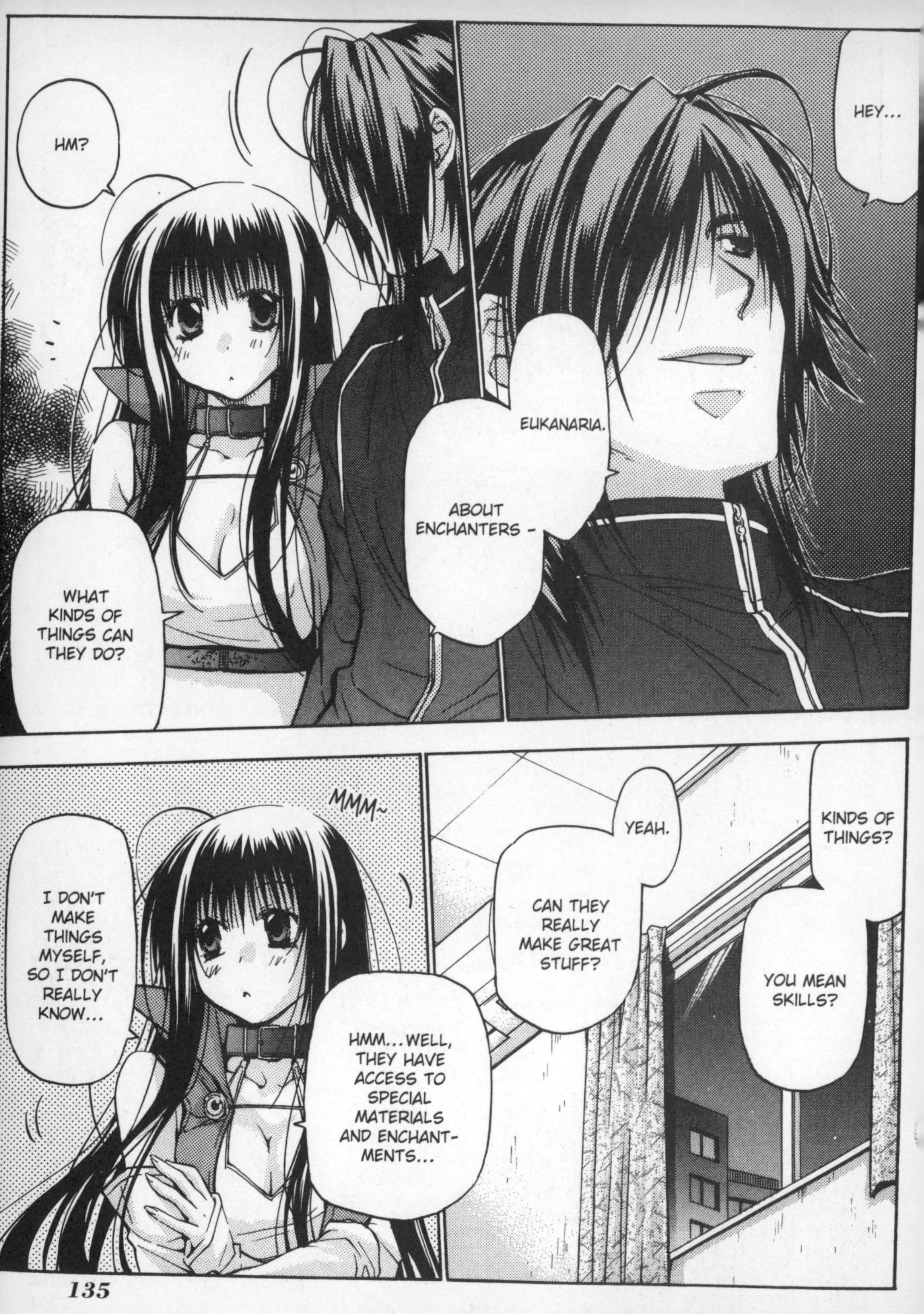
HEY...
EUKANARIA.
ABOUT ENCHANTERS –
HM?
WHAT KINDS OF THINGS CAN THEY DO?
KINDS OF THINGS?
YOU MEAN SKILLS?
YEAH.
CAN THEY REALLY MAKE GREAT STUFF?
MMM~
I DON'T MAKE THINGS MYSELF, SO I DON'T REALLY KNOW...
HMM...WELL, THEY HAVE ACCESS TO SPECIAL MATERIALS AND ENCHANT-MENTS...

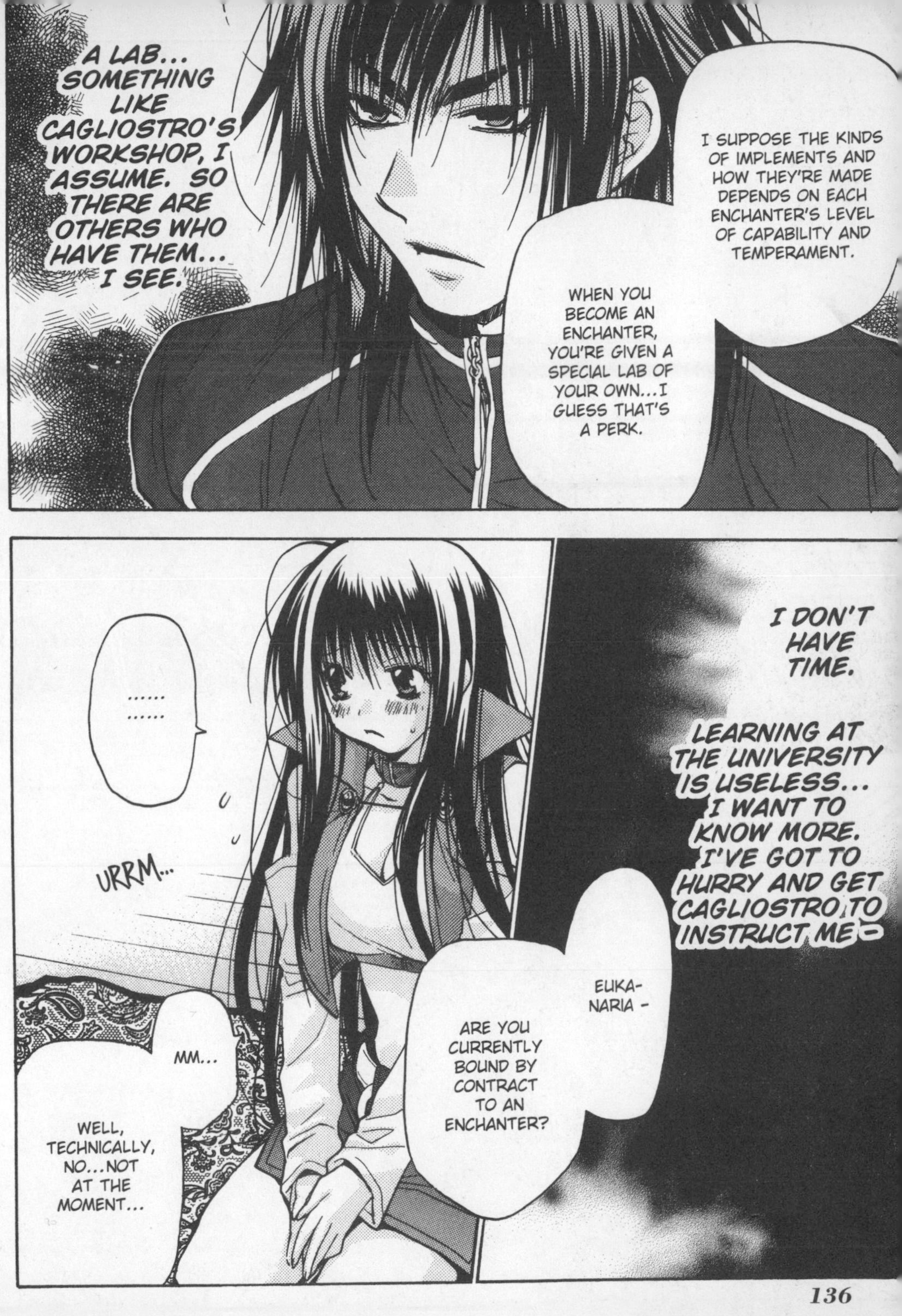
I SUPPOSE THE KINDS OF IMPLEMENTS AND HOW THEY'RE MADE DEPENDS ON EACH ENCHANTER'S LEVEL OF CAPABILITY AND TEMPERAMENT.
WHEN YOU BECOME AN ENCHANTER, YOU'RE GIVEN A SPECIAL LAB OF YOUR OWN...I GUESS THAT'S A PERK.
A LAB... SOMETHING LIKE CAGLIOSTRO'S WORKSHOP, I ASSUME. SO THERE ARE OTHERS WHO HAVE THEM... I SEE.
I DON'T HAVE TIME.
LEARNING AT THE UNIVERSITY IS USELESS... I WANT TO KNOW MORE. I'VE GOT TO HURRY AND GET CAGLIOSTRO TO INSTRUCT ME —
EUKA-NARIA –
ARE YOU CURRENTLY BOUND BY CONTRACT TO AN ENCHANTER?
....
URRM...
MM...
WELL, TECHNICALLY, NO...NOT AT THE MOMENT...

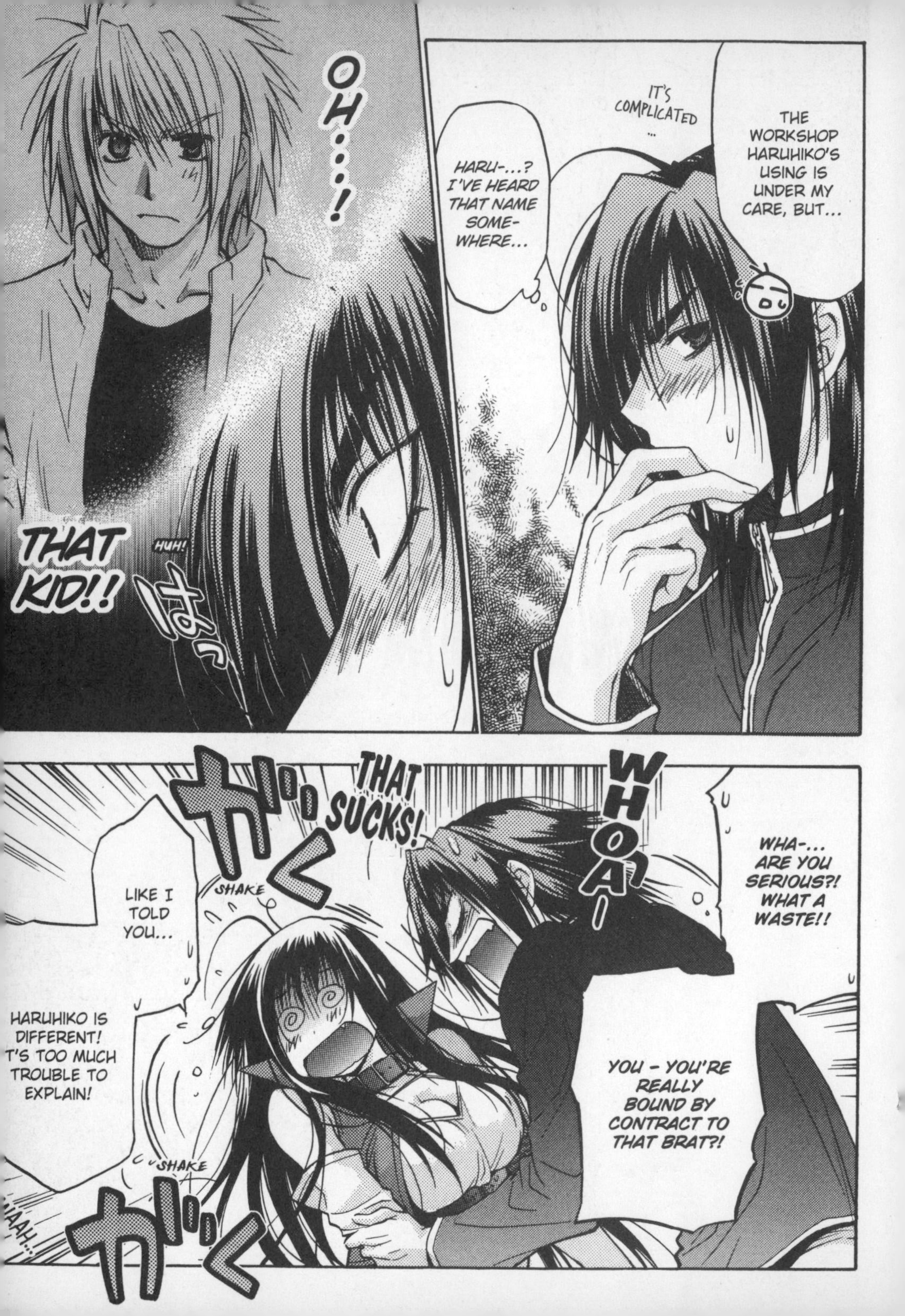
THE WORKSHOP HARUHIKO'S USING IS UNDER MY CARE, BUT...
IT'S COMPLICATED ...
HARU-...? I'VE HEARD THAT NAME SOME-WHERE...
OH...!
THAT KID!!
HUH!
はっ
WHOA-
WHA-... ARE YOU SERIOUS?! WHAT A WASTE!!
YOU - YOU'RE REALLY BOUND BY CONTRACT TO THAT BRAT?!
THAT SUCKS!
がく
SHAKE
LIKE I TOLD YOU...
HARUHIKO IS DIFFERENT! T'S TOO MUCH TROUBLE TO EXPLAIN!
SHAKE
がく
HAAH...

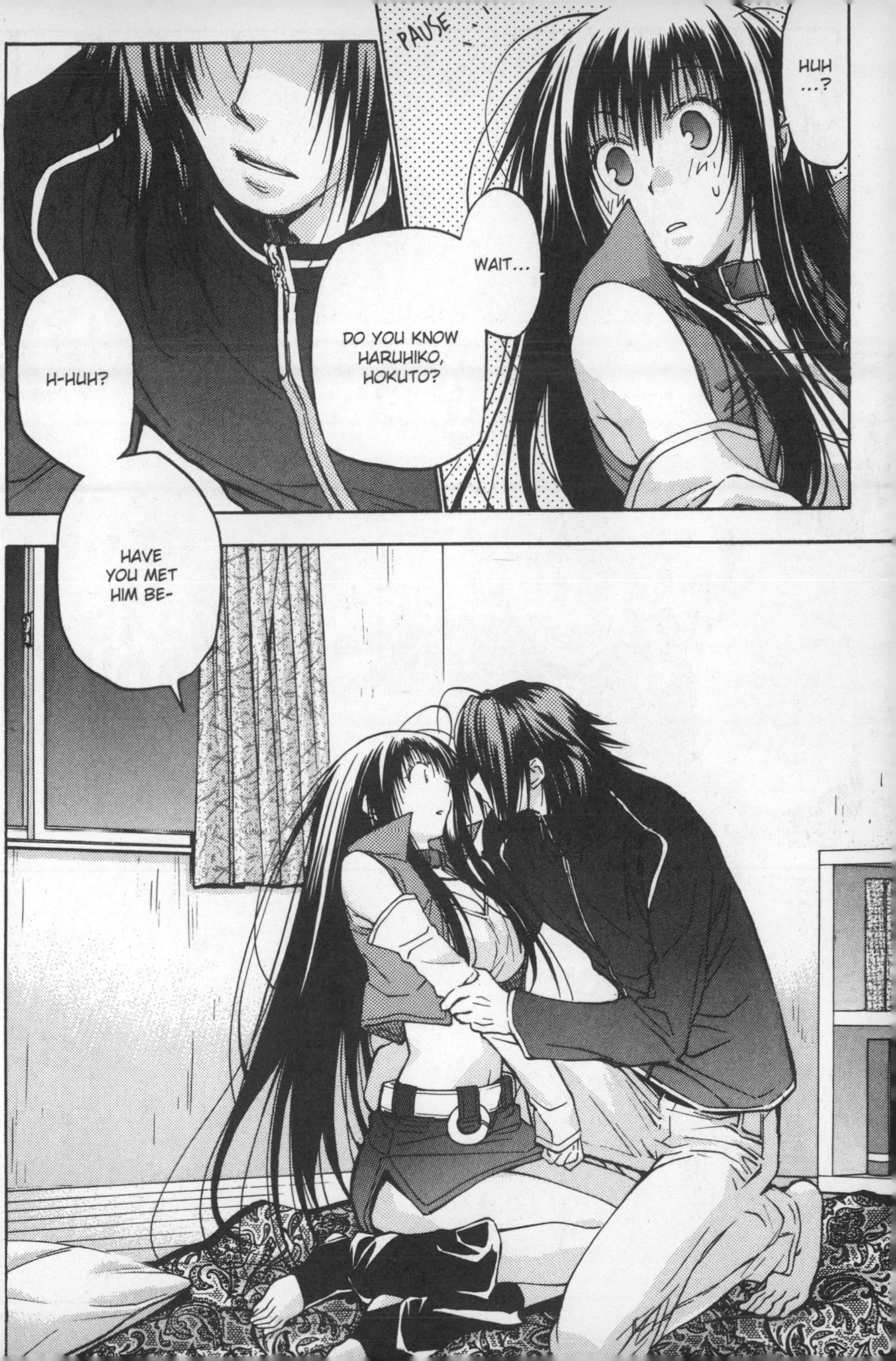
PAUSE
HUH ...?
WAIT...
DO YOU KNOW HARUHIKO, HOKUTO?
H-HUH?
HAVE YOU MET HIM BE-

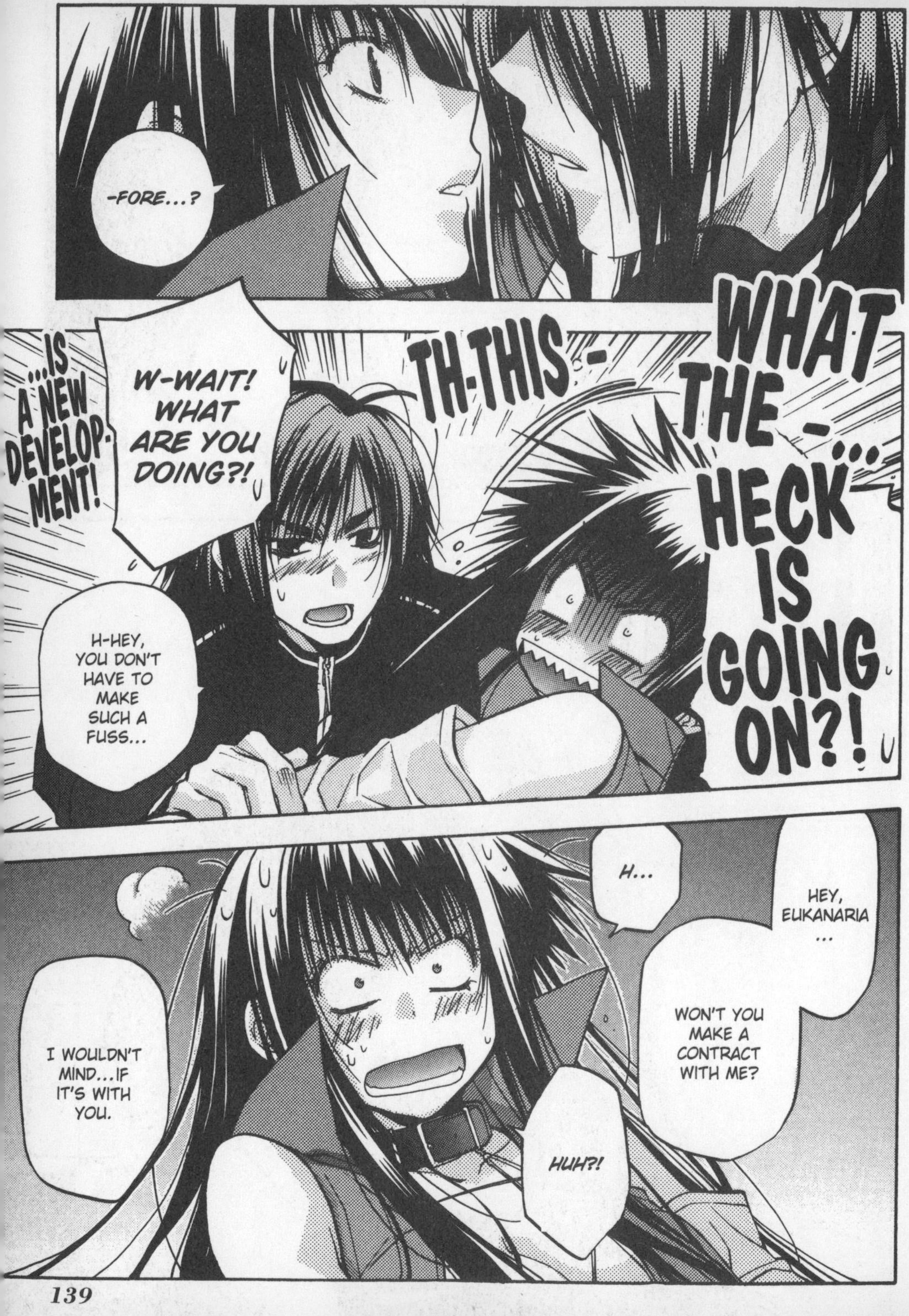

-FORE...?
WHAT THE... HECK IS GOING ON?!
TH-THIS-
W-WAIT! WHAT ARE YOU DOING?!
...IS A NEW DEVELOPMENT!
H-HEY, YOU DON'T HAVE TO MAKE SUCH A FUSS...
HEY, EUKANARIA ...
WON'T YOU MAKE A CONTRACT WITH ME?
H...
HUH?!
I WOULDN'T MIND...IF IT'S WITH YOU.

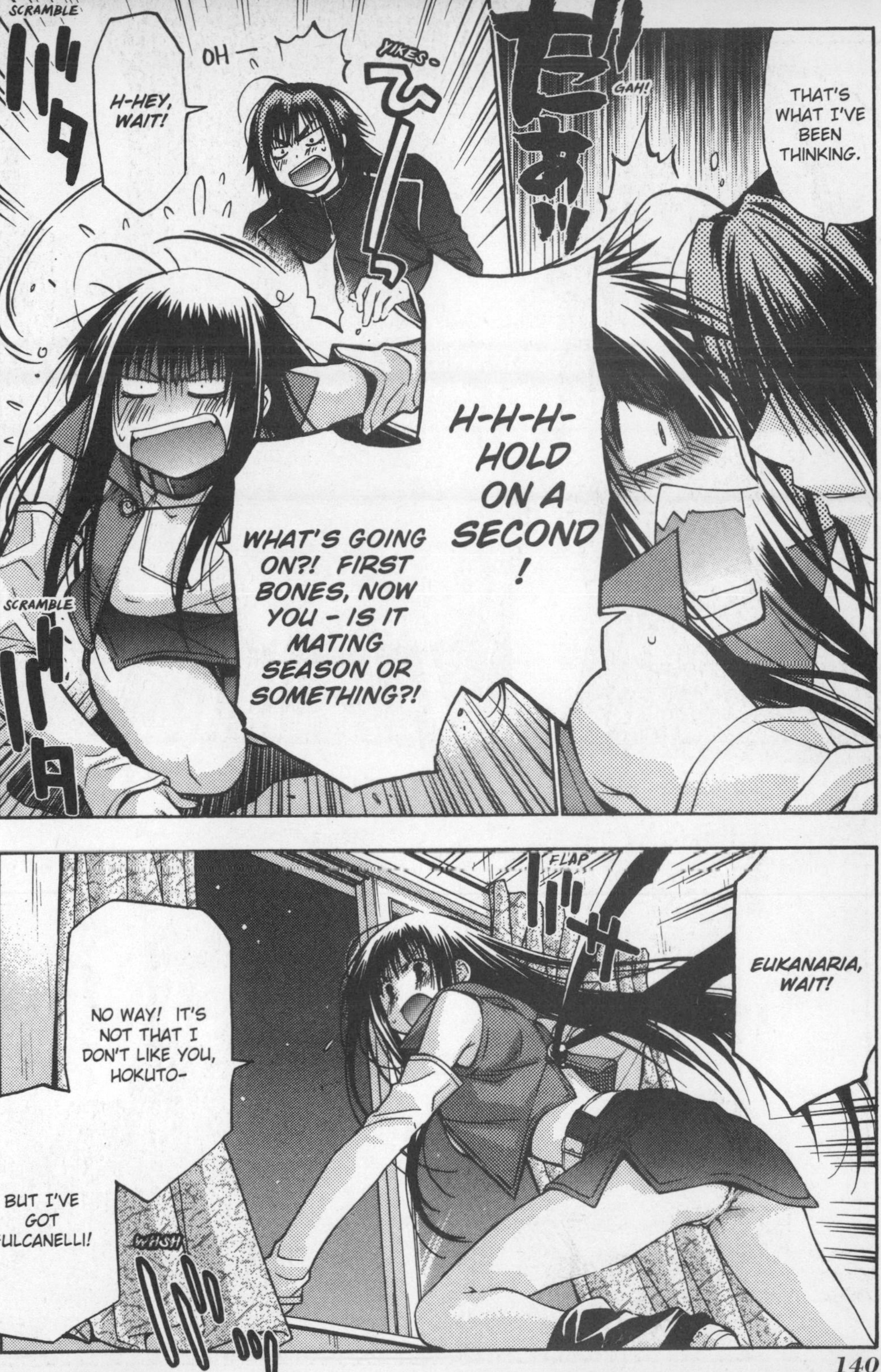
THAT'S WHAT I'VE BEEN THINKING.
GAH!
H-H-H-HOLD ON A SECOND!
WHAT'S GOING ON?! FIRST BONES, NOW YOU - IS IT MATING SEASON OR SOMETHING?!
YIKES
OH—
H-HEY, WAIT!
SCRAMBLE
SCRAMBLE
EUKANARIA, WAIT!
FLAP
NO WAY! IT'S NOT THAT I DON'T LIKE YOU, HOKUTO-
BUT I'VE GOT FULCANELLI!
WHSH

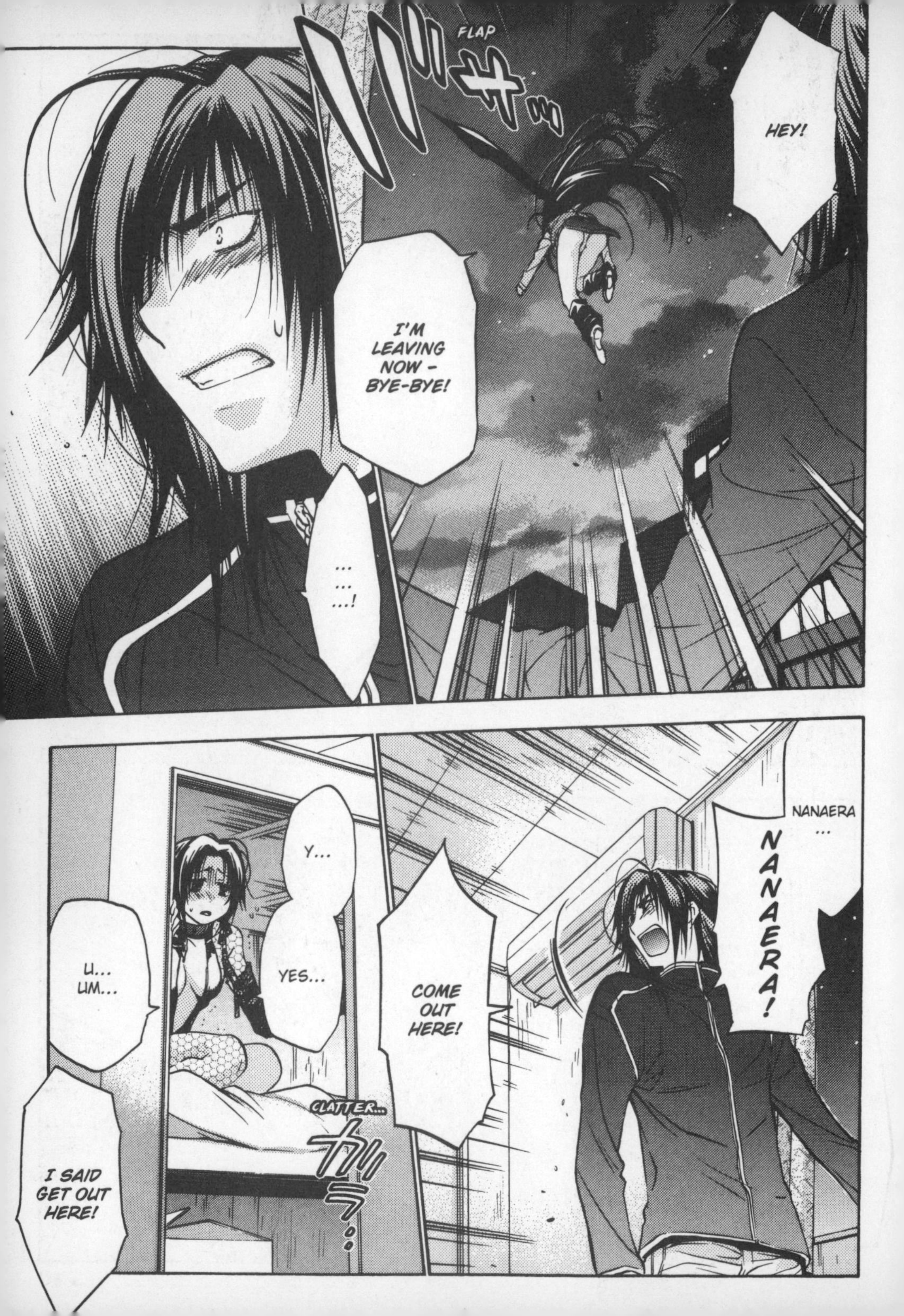
FLAP
HEY!
I'M LEAVING NOW - BYE-BYE!
... ...!
NANAERA ...
NANAERA!
COME OUT HERE!
Y...
YES...
CLATTER...
U... UM...
I SAID GET OUT HERE!

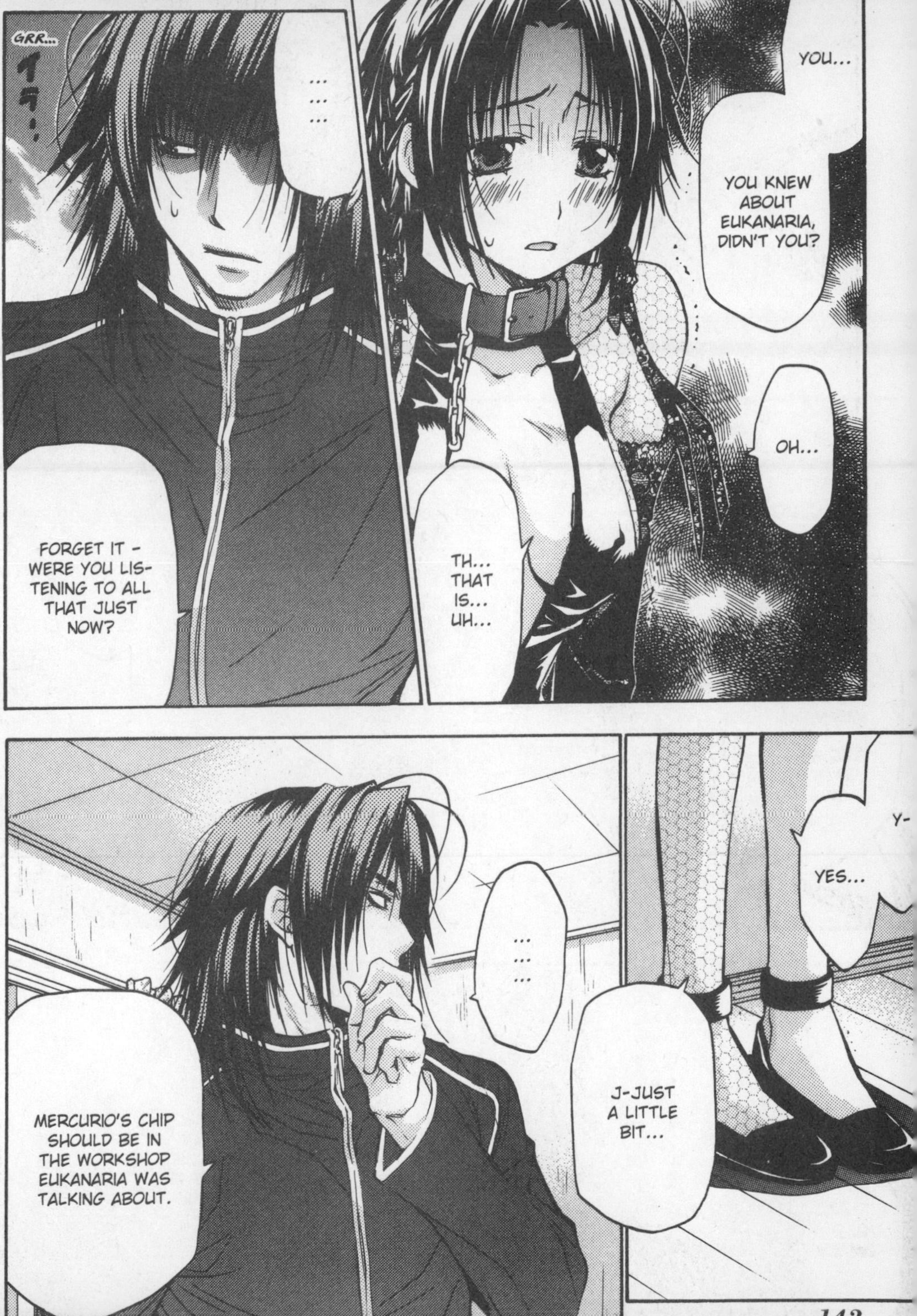
YOU...
YOU KNEW ABOUT EUKANARIA, DIDN'T YOU?
OH...
TH... THAT IS... UH...
GRR...
イラ・・
... ...
FORGET IT - WERE YOU LISTENING TO ALL THAT JUST NOW?
Y- YES...
... ...
J-JUST A LITTLE BIT...
MERCURIO'S CHIP SHOULD BE IN THE WORKSHOP EUKANARIA WAS TALKING ABOUT.

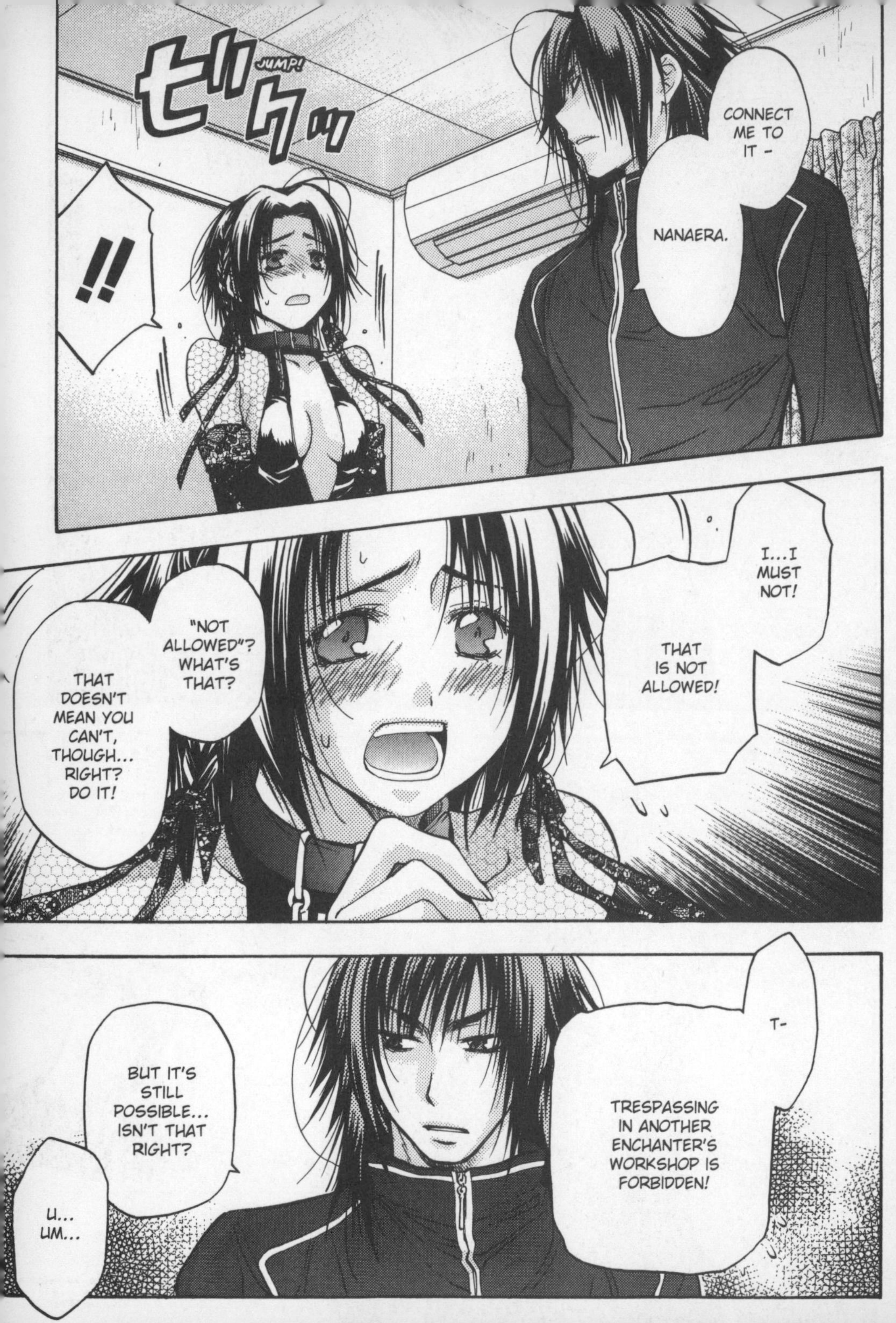
CONNECT ME TO IT –
NANAERA.
JUMP!
!!
I...I MUST NOT!
THAT IS NOT ALLOWED!
"NOT ALLOWED"? WHAT'S THAT?
THAT DOESN'T MEAN YOU CAN'T, THOUGH... RIGHT? DO IT!
T-
TRESPASSING IN ANOTHER ENCHANTER'S WORKSHOP IS FORBIDDEN!
BUT IT'S STILL POSSIBLE... ISN'T THAT RIGHT?
U... UM...

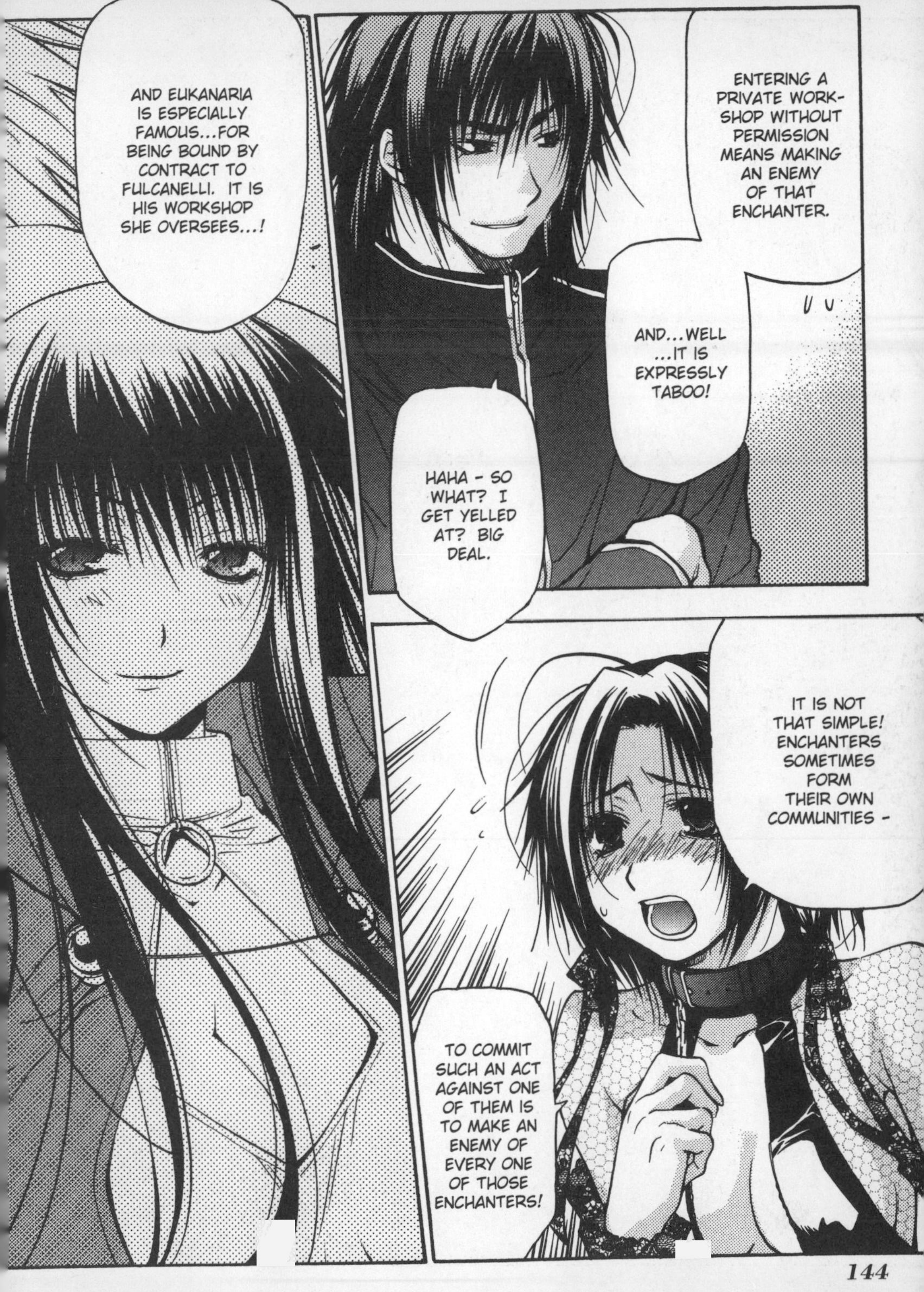
ENTERING A PRIVATE WORK-SHOP WITHOUT PERMISSION MEANS MAKING AN ENEMY OF THAT ENCHANTER.
AND...WELL ...IT IS EXPRESSLY TABOO!
HAHA - SO WHAT? I GET YELLED AT? BIG DEAL.
IT IS NOT THAT SIMPLE! ENCHANTERS SOMETIMES FORM THEIR OWN COMMUNITIES -
TO COMMIT SUCH AN ACT AGAINST ONE OF THEM IS TO MAKE AN ENEMY OF EVERY ONE OF THOSE ENCHANTERS!
AND EUKANARIA IS ESPECIALLY FAMOUS...FOR BEING BOUND BY CONTRACT TO FULCANELLI. IT IS HIS WORKSHOP SHE OVERSEES...!

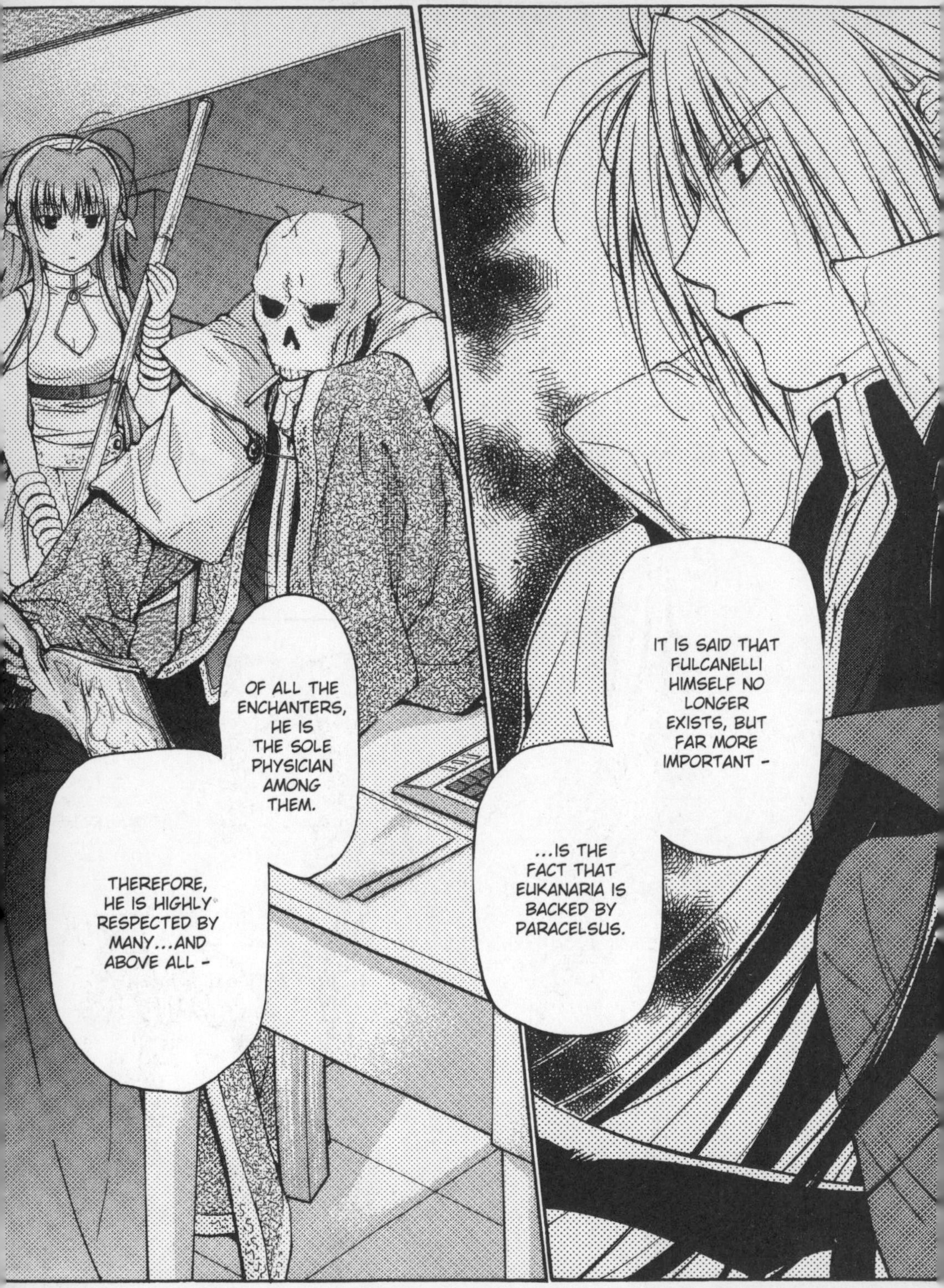
IT IS SAID THAT FULCANELLI HIMSELF NO LONGER EXISTS, BUT FAR MORE IMPORTANT -
...IS THE FACT THAT EUKANARIA IS BACKED BY PARACELSUS.
OF ALL THE ENCHANTERS, HE IS THE SOLE PHYSICIAN AMONG THEM.
THEREFORE, HE IS HIGHLY RESPECTED BY MANY...AND ABOVE ALL -

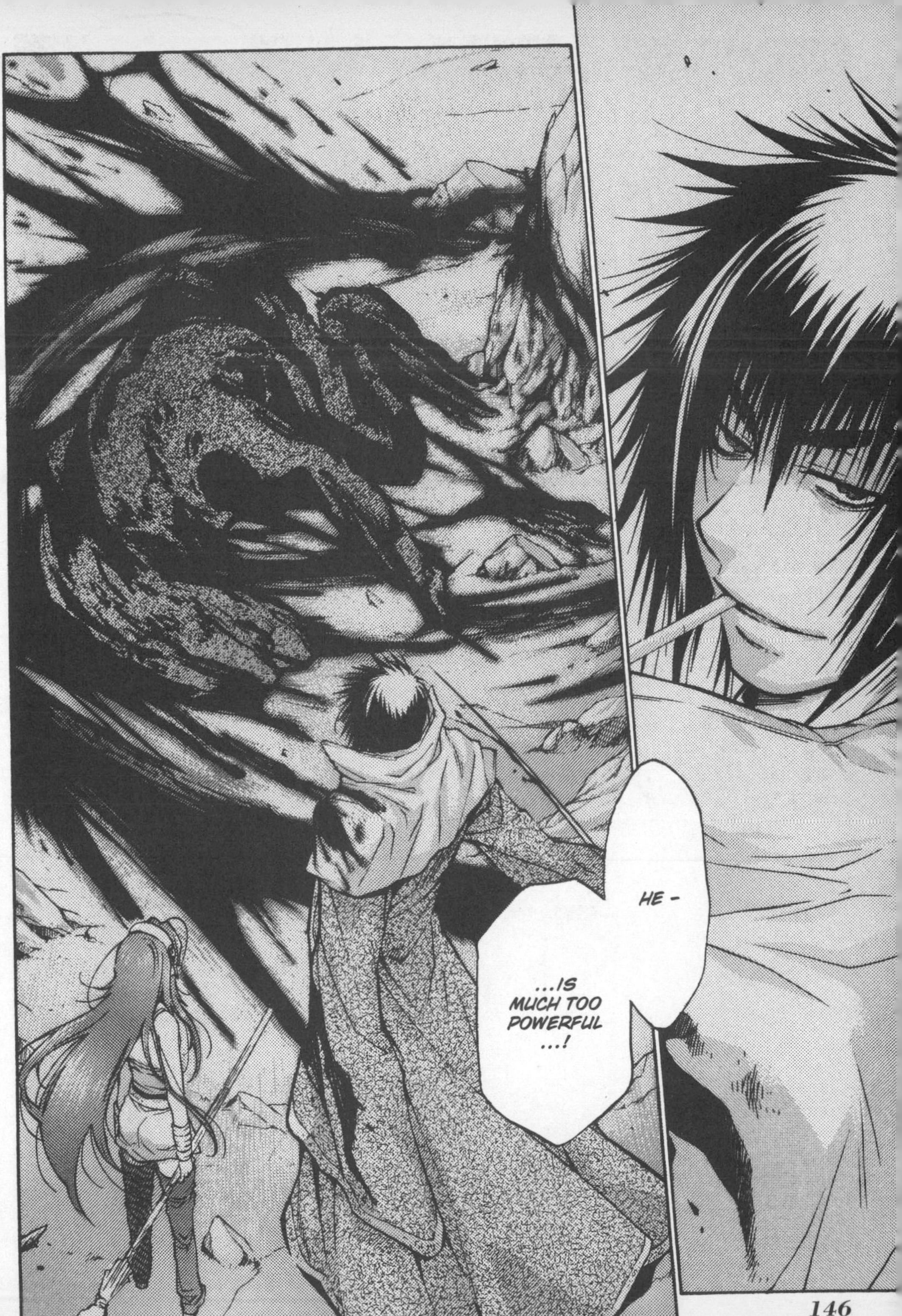
HE -
...IS MUCH TOO POWERFUL ...!

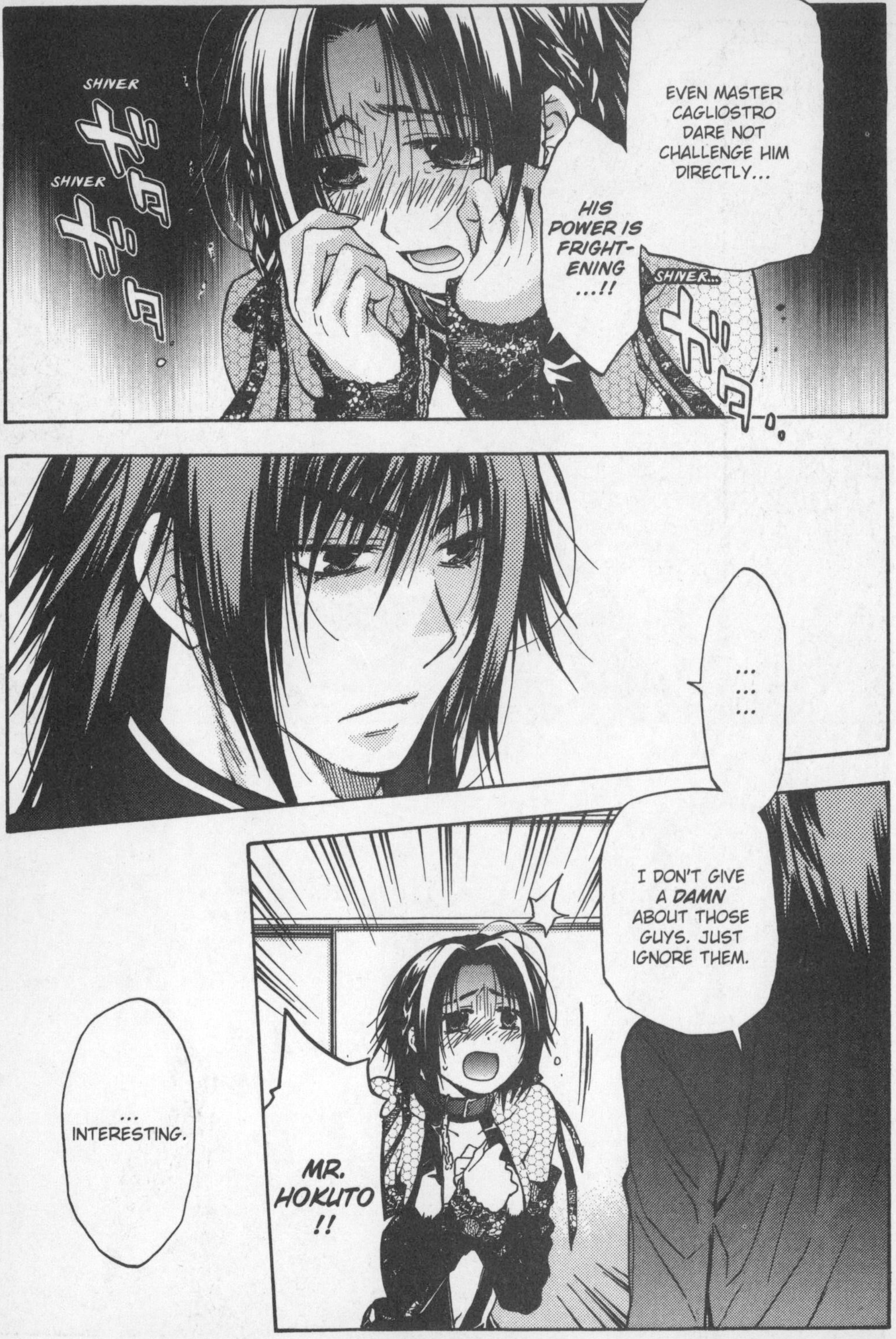
EVEN MASTER CAGLIOSTRO DARE NOT CHALLENGE HIM DIRECTLY...
SHIVER...
HIS POWER IS FRIGHT-ENING ...!!
SHIVER
SHIVER
... ...
I DON'T GIVE A DAMN ABOUT THOSE GUYS. JUST IGNORE THEM.
MR. HOKUTO !!
... INTERESTING.

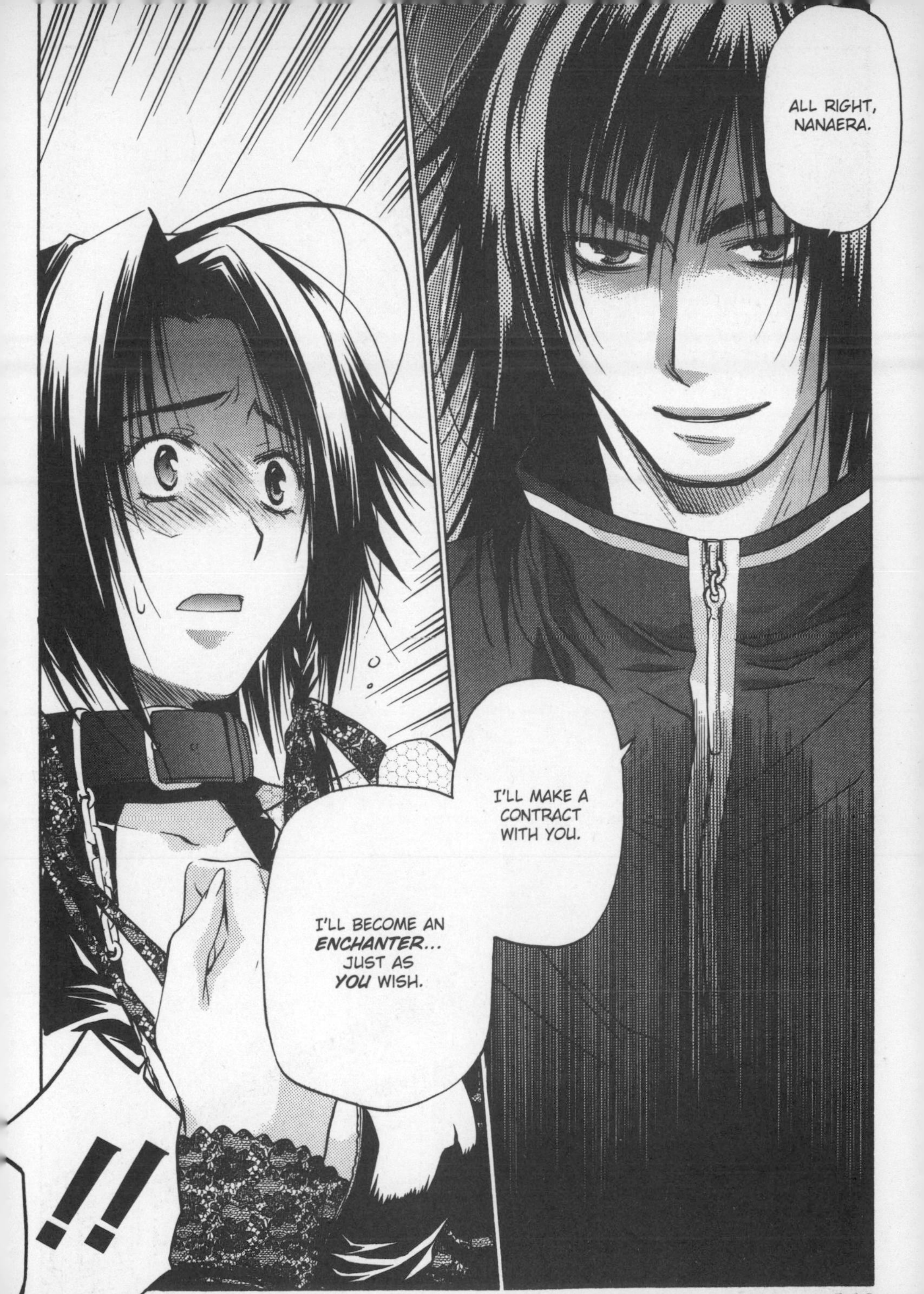
ALL RIGHT, NANAERA.
I'LL MAKE A CONTRACT WITH YOU.
I'LL BECOME AN ENCHANTER... JUST AS YOU WISH.
!!

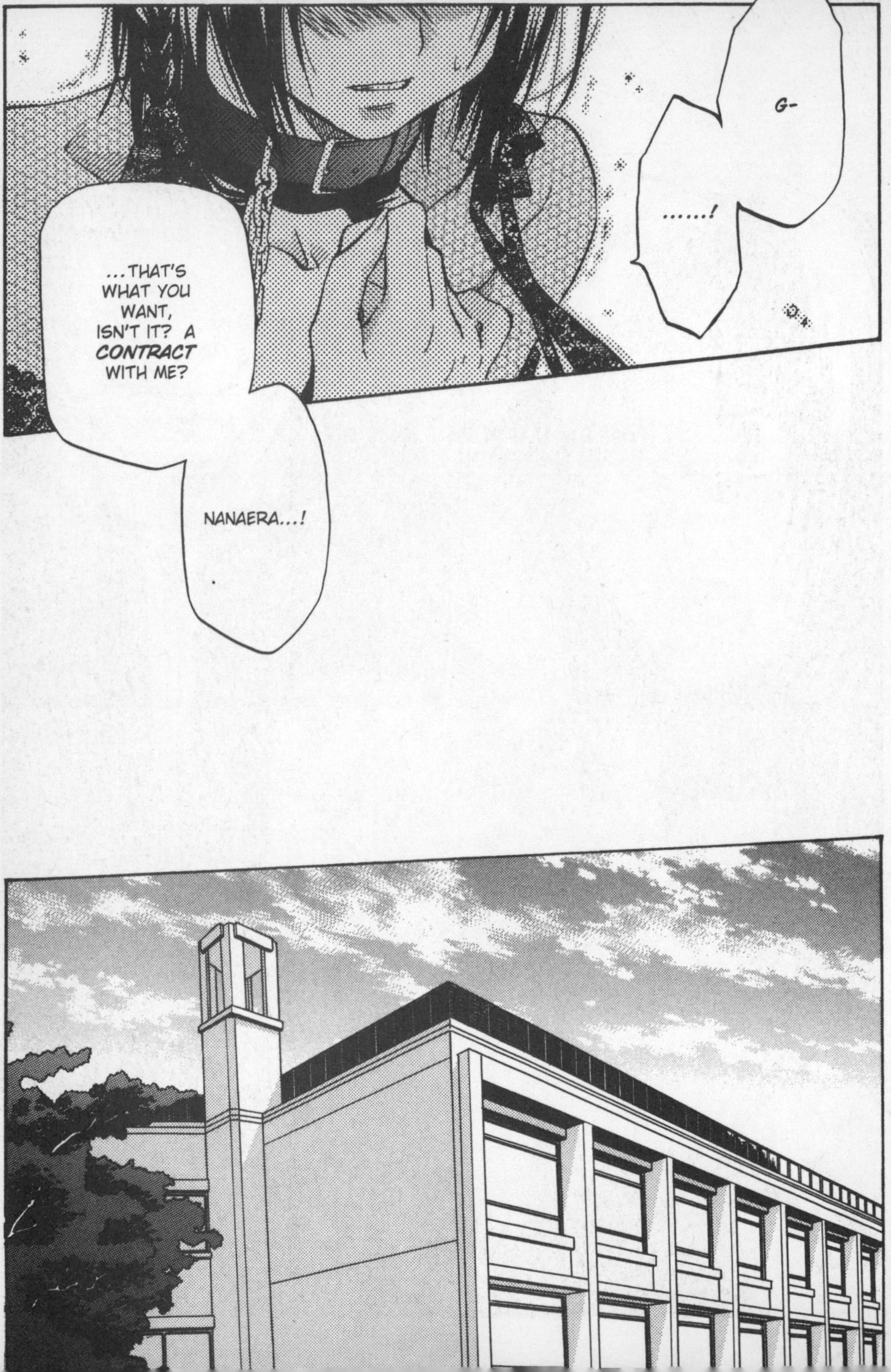
G-
......!
...THAT'S WHAT YOU WANT, ISN'T IT? A CONTRACT WITH ME?
NANAERA...!

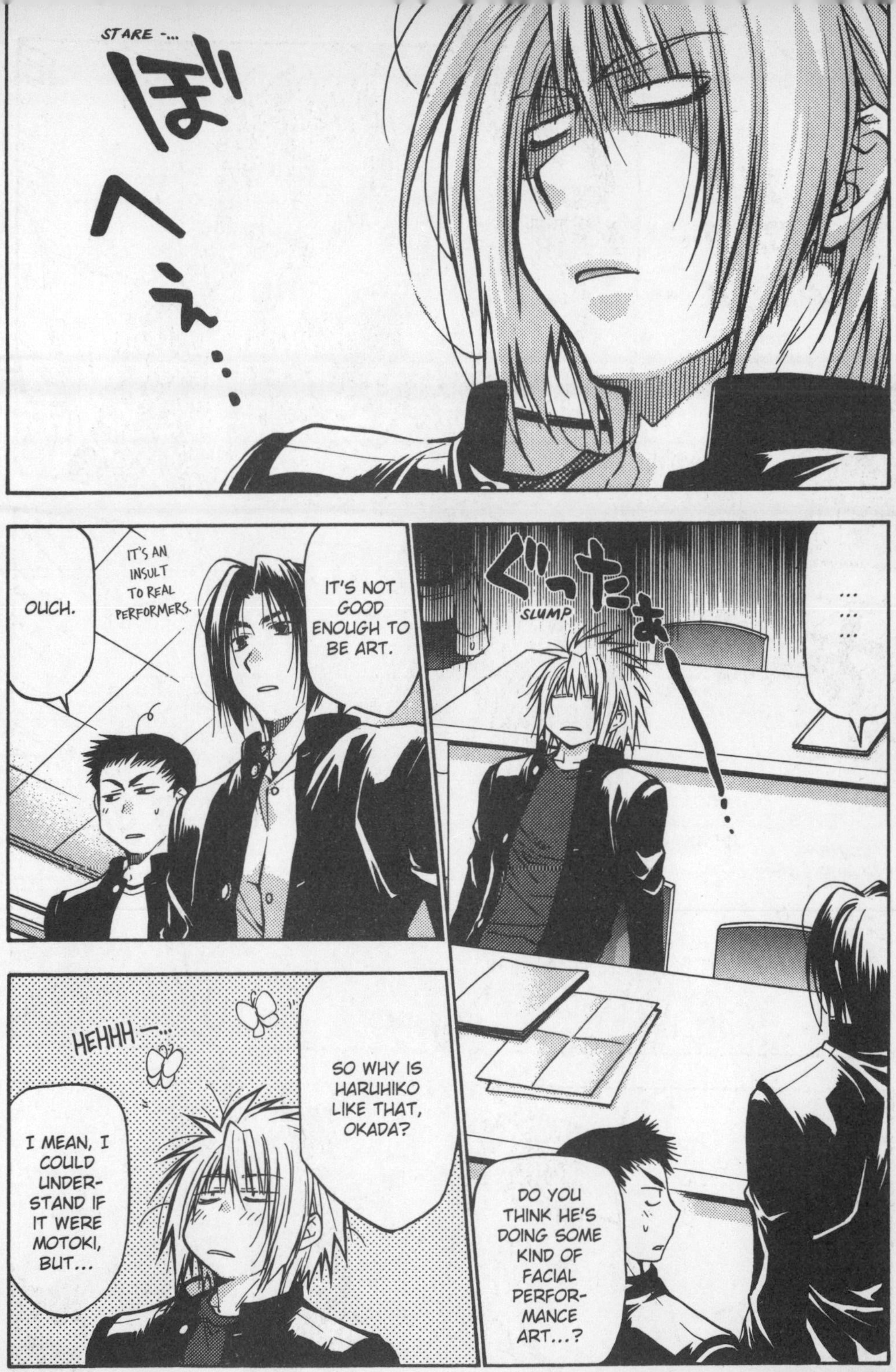
STARE -...
ぼへぇ…
……
ぐったぁ
SLUMP
DO YOU THINK HE'S DOING SOME KIND OF FACIAL PERFORMANCE ART...?
IT'S NOT GOOD ENOUGH TO BE ART.
IT'S AN INSULT TO REAL PERFORMERS.
OUCH.
SO WHY IS HARUHIKO LIKE THAT, OKADA?
HEHHH—...
I MEAN, I COULD UNDERSTAND IF IT WERE MOTOKI, BUT...

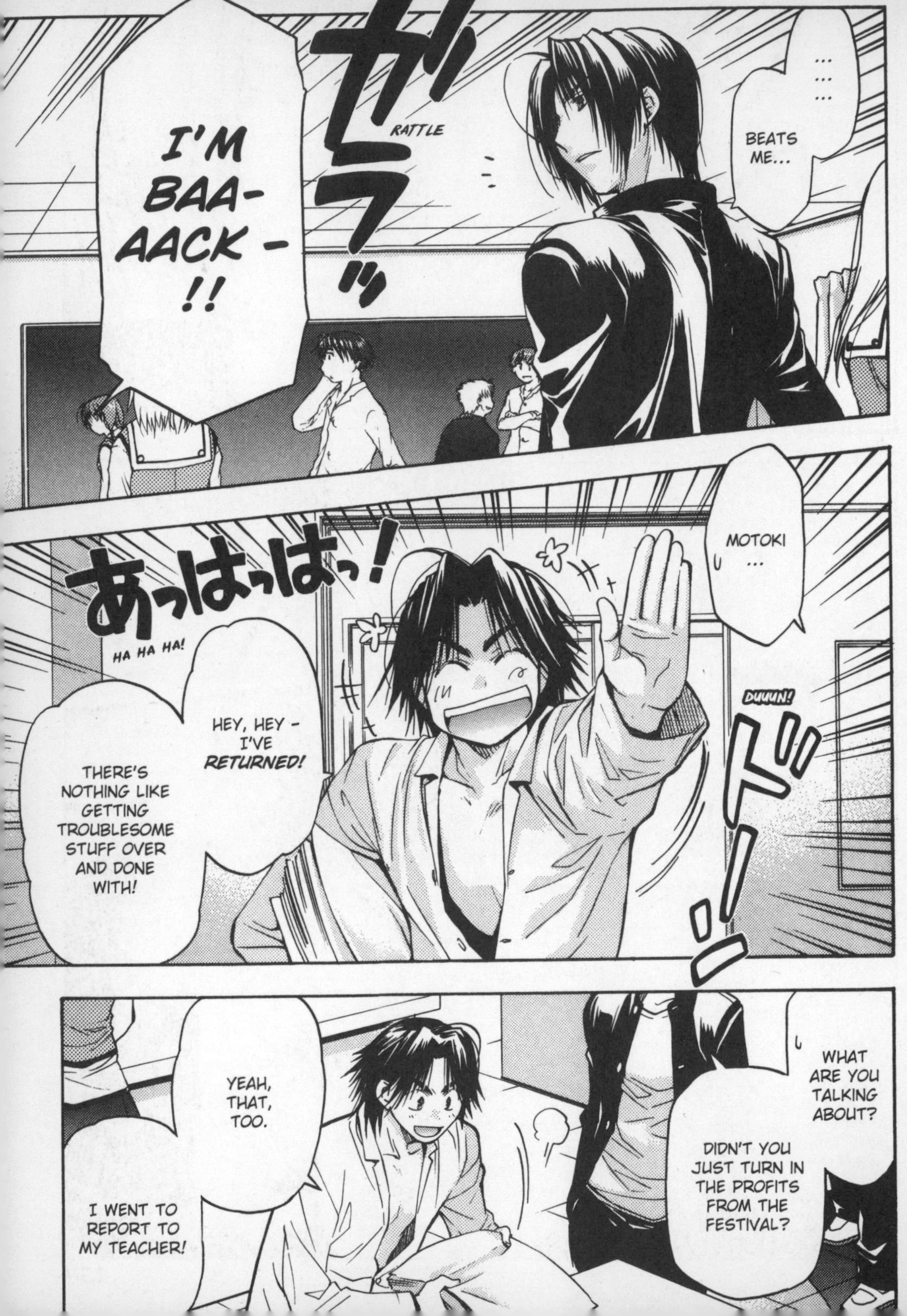

… … … BEATS ME…
RATTLE
I'M BAAA-AACK-!!
MOTOKI …
DUUUN!
HEY, HEY - I'VE RETURNED!
あっはっはっ!
HA HA HA!
THERE'S NOTHING LIKE GETTING TROUBLESOME STUFF OVER AND DONE WITH!
WHAT ARE YOU TALKING ABOUT?
DIDN'T YOU JUST TURN IN THE PROFITS FROM THE FESTIVAL?
YEAH, THAT, TOO.
I WENT TO REPORT TO MY TEACHER!

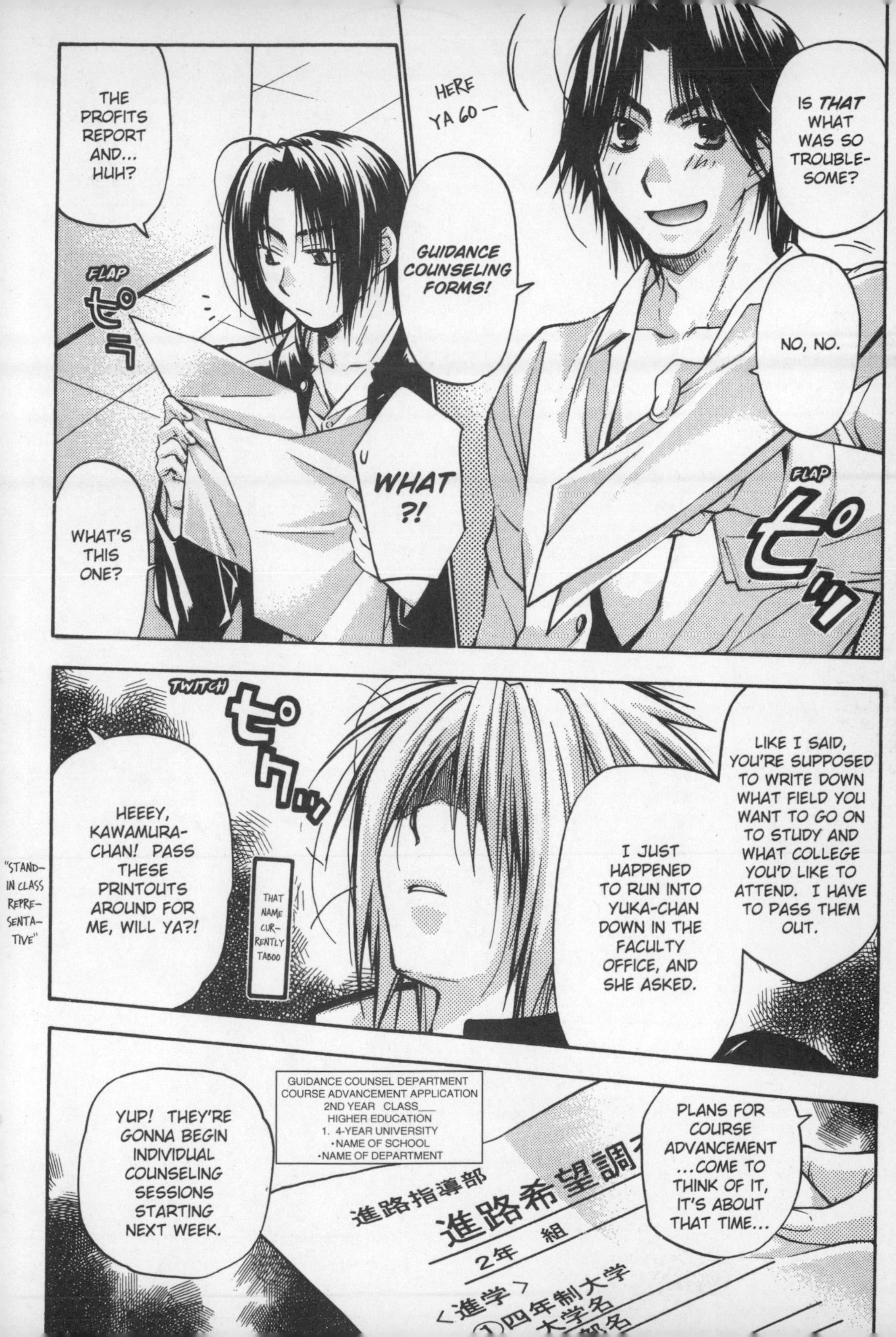
IS *THAT* WHAT WAS SO TROUBLE-SOME?
HERE YA GO—
GUIDANCE COUNSELING FORMS!
THE PROFITS REPORT AND... HUH?
FLAP
ピラ
NO, NO.
FLAP
ピッ
WHAT ?!
WHAT'S THIS ONE?
LIKE I SAID, YOU'RE SUPPOSED TO WRITE DOWN WHAT FIELD YOU WANT TO GO ON TO STUDY AND WHAT COLLEGE YOU'D LIKE TO ATTEND. I HAVE TO PASS THEM OUT.
I JUST HAPPENED TO RUN INTO YUKA-CHAN DOWN IN THE FACULTY OFFICE, AND SHE ASKED.
TWITCH
ピクッ
HEEEY, KAWAMURA-CHAN! PASS THESE PRINTOUTS AROUND FOR ME, WILL YA?!
THAT NAME CUR-RENTLY TABOO
"STAND-IN CLASS REPRE-SENTA-TIVE"
PLANS FOR COURSE ADVANCEMENT ...COME TO THINK OF IT, IT'S ABOUT THAT TIME...
GUIDANCE COUNSEL DEPARTMENT
COURSE ADVANCEMENT APPLICATION
2ND YEAR CLASS___
HIGHER EDUCATION
1. 4-YEAR UNIVERSITY
•NAME OF SCHOOL
•NAME OF DEPARTMENT
進路指導部
進路希望調
2年 組
〈進学〉
①四年制大学
大学名
YUP! THEY'RE GONNA BEGIN INDIVIDUAL COUNSELING SESSIONS STARTING NEXT WEEK.

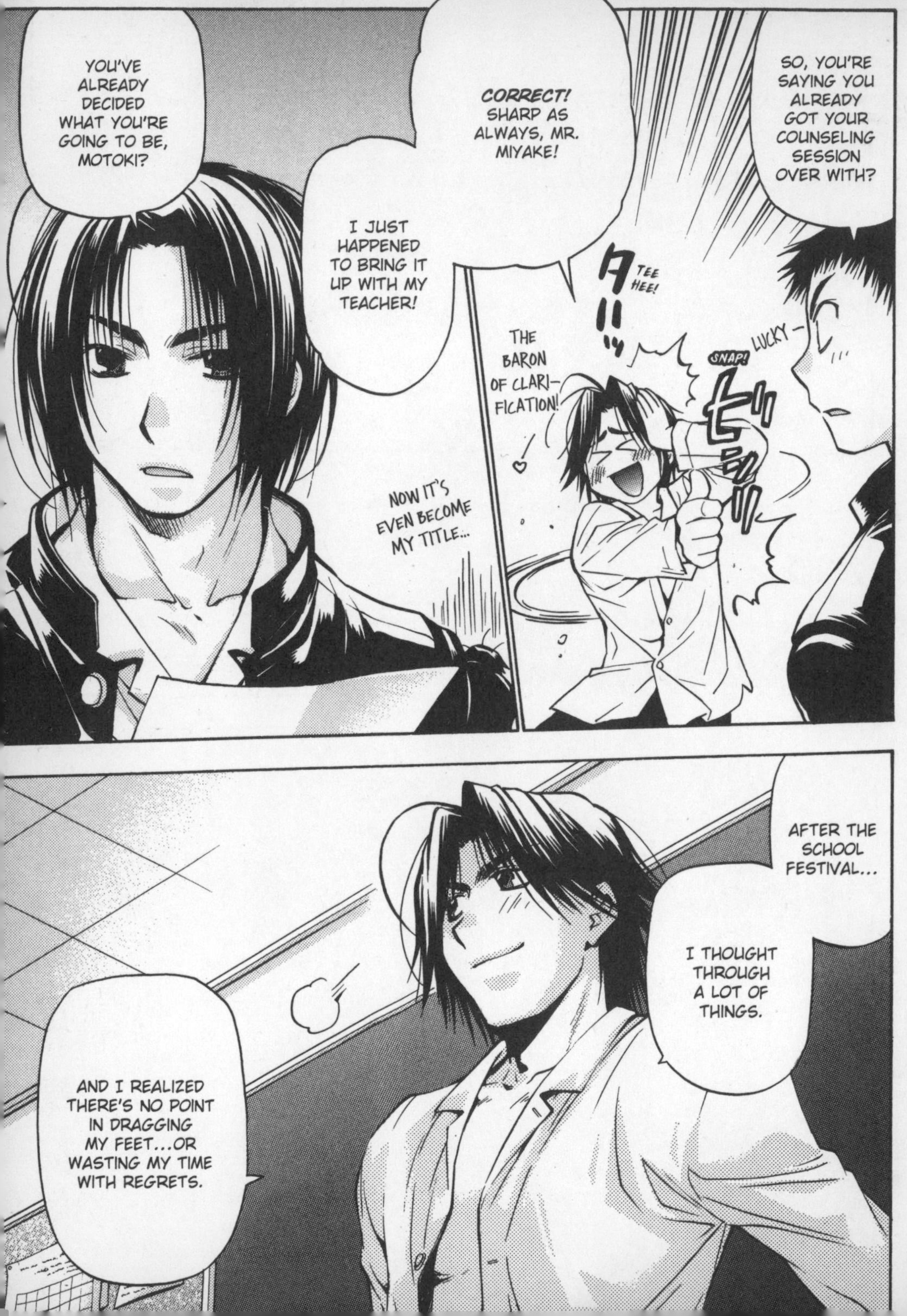
SO, YOU'RE SAYING YOU ALREADY GOT YOUR COUNSELING SESSION OVER WITH?
CORRECT! SHARP AS ALWAYS, MR. MIYAKE!
I JUST HAPPENED TO BRING IT UP WITH MY TEACHER!
TEE HEE!
LUCKY—
SNAP!
THE BARON OF CLARI-FICATION!
NOW IT'S EVEN BECOME MY TITLE...
YOU'VE ALREADY DECIDED WHAT YOU'RE GOING TO BE, MOTOKI?
AFTER THE SCHOOL FESTIVAL...
I THOUGHT THROUGH A LOT OF THINGS.
AND I REALIZED THERE'S NO POINT IN DRAGGING MY FEET...OR WASTING MY TIME WITH REGRETS.

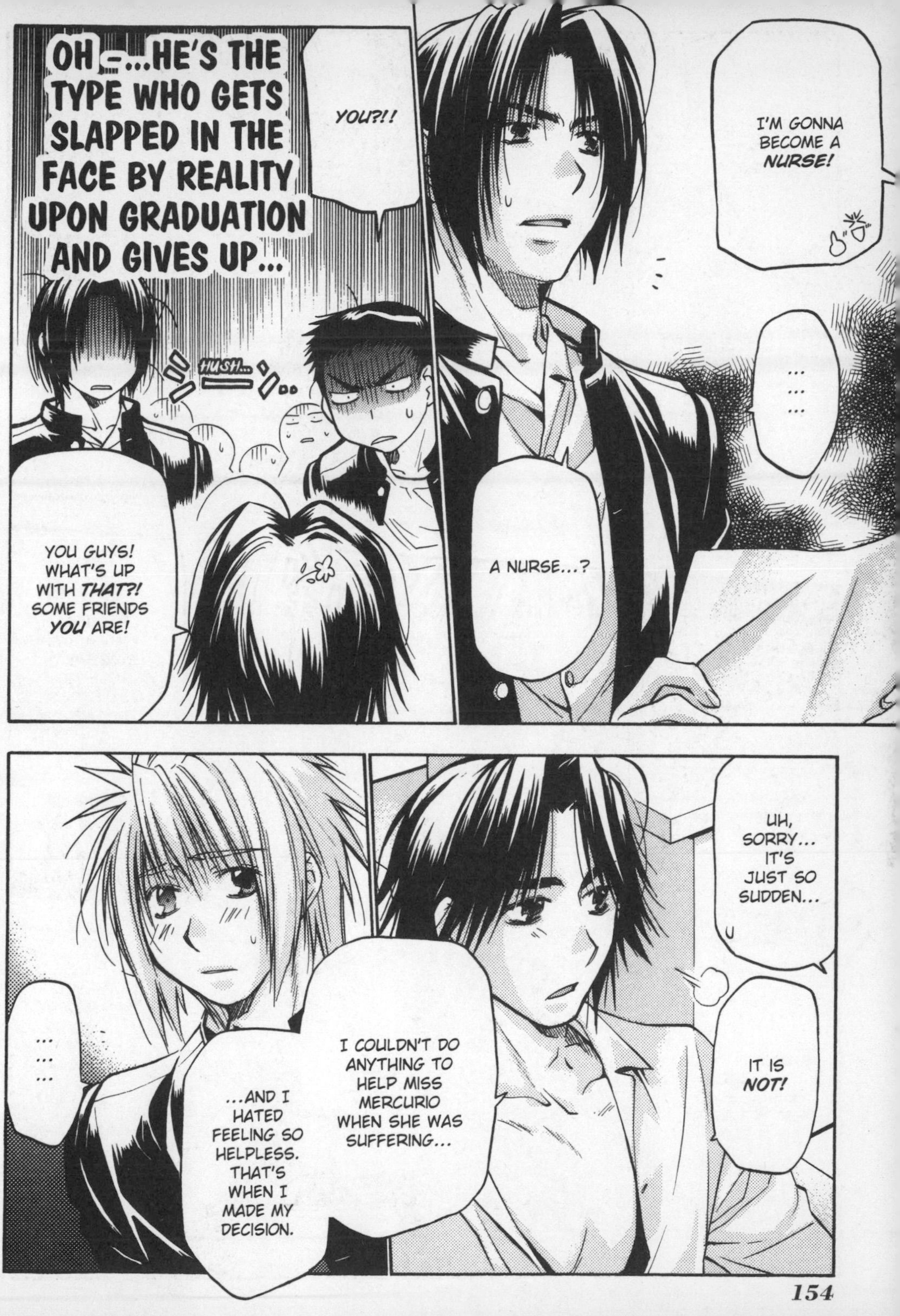

I'M GONNA BECOME A NURSE!
... ...
A NURSE...?
YOU?!!
OH -...HE'S THE TYPE WHO GETS SLAPPED IN THE FACE BY REALITY UPON GRADUATION AND GIVES UP...
HUSH...
YOU GUYS! WHAT'S UP WITH THAT?! SOME FRIENDS YOU ARE!
UH, SORRY... IT'S JUST SO SUDDEN...
IT IS NOT!
I COULDN'T DO ANYTHING TO HELP MISS MERCURIO WHEN SHE WAS SUFFERING...
...AND I HATED FEELING SO HELPLESS. THAT'S WHEN I MADE MY DECISION.
... ...

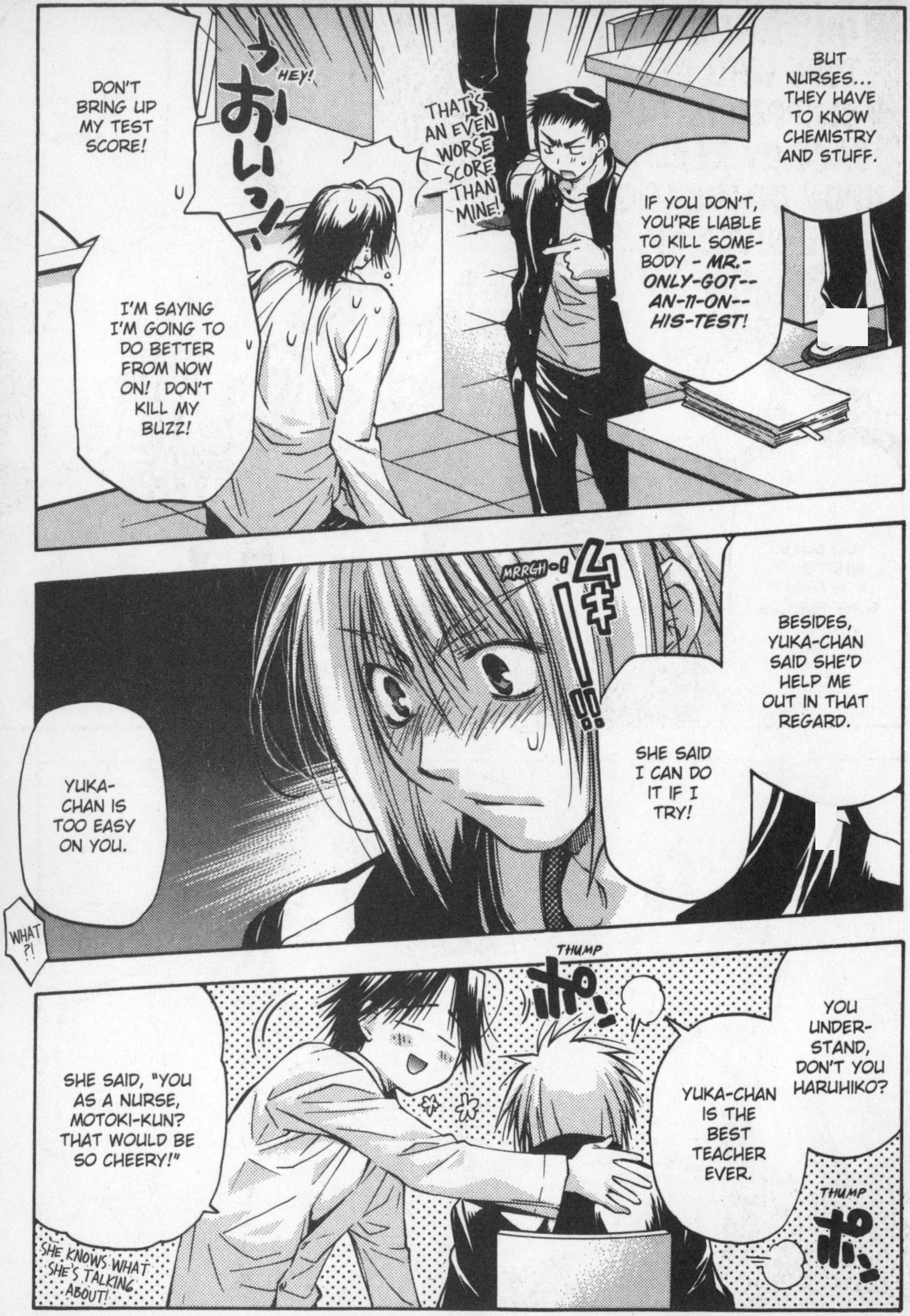
BUT NURSES... THEY HAVE TO KNOW CHEMISTRY AND STUFF.
IF YOU DON'T, YOU'RE LIABLE TO KILL SOMEBODY - MR.-ONLY-GOT--AN-11-ON--HIS-TEST!
THAT'S AN EVEN WORSE SCORE THAN MINE!
HEY!
DON'T BRING UP MY TEST SCORE!
I'M SAYING I'M GOING TO DO BETTER FROM NOW ON! DON'T KILL MY BUZZ!
BESIDES, YUKA-CHAN SAID SHE'D HELP ME OUT IN THAT REGARD.
SHE SAID I CAN DO IT IF I TRY!
MRRGH-!
YUKA-CHAN IS TOO EASY ON YOU.
WHAT?!
YOU UNDERSTAND, DON'T YOU HARUHIKO?
THUMP
YUKA-CHAN IS THE BEST TEACHER EVER.
THUMP
SHE SAID, "YOU AS A NURSE, MOTOKI-KUN? THAT WOULD BE SO CHEERY!"
SHE KNOWS WHAT SHE'S TALKING ABOUT!

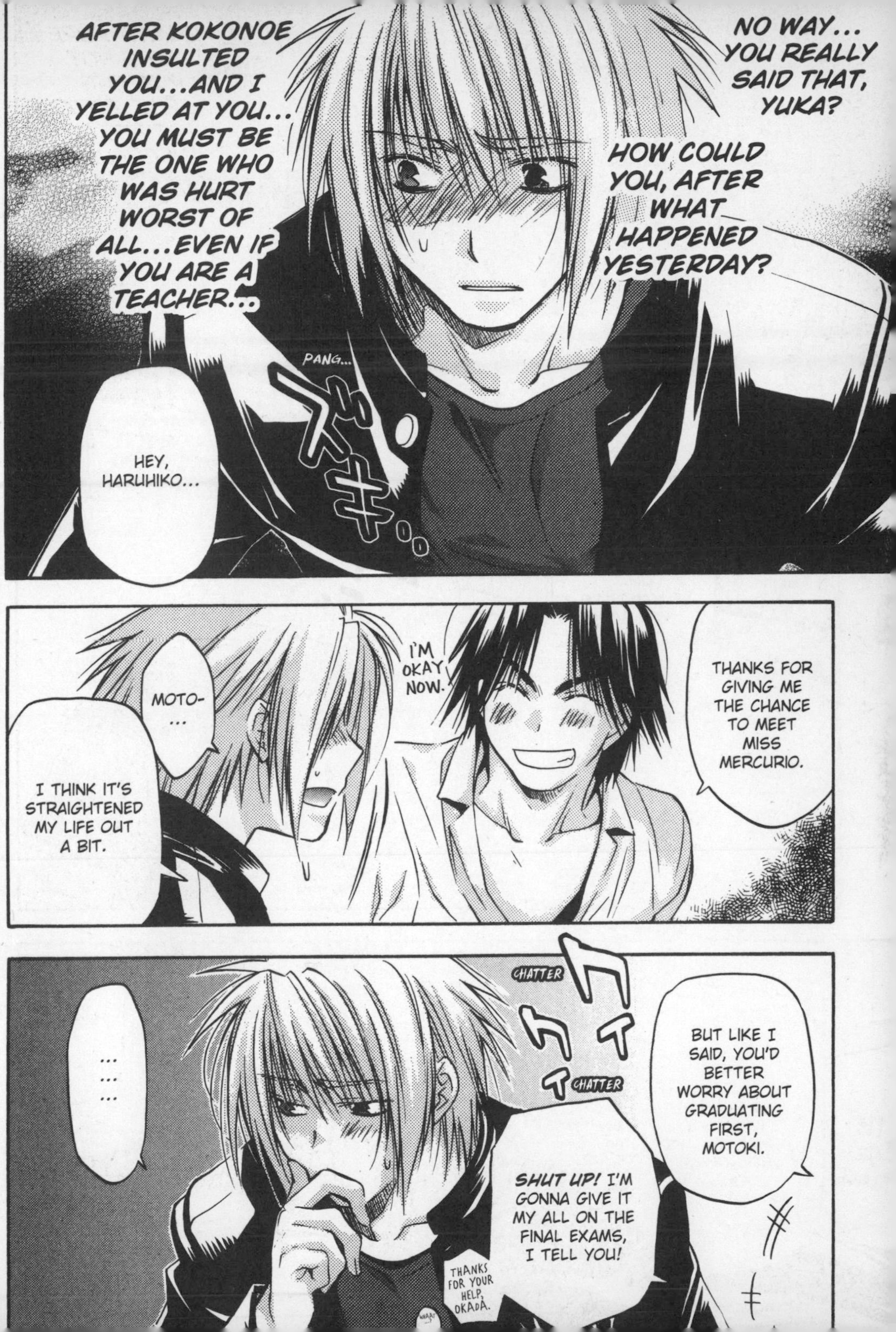
NO WAY... YOU REALLY SAID THAT, YUKA?
HOW COULD YOU, AFTER WHAT HAPPENED YESTERDAY?
AFTER KOKONOE INSULTED YOU... AND I YELLED AT YOU... YOU MUST BE THE ONE WHO WAS HURT WORST OF ALL... EVEN IF YOU ARE A TEACHER...
PANG...
HEY, HARUHIKO...
THANKS FOR GIVING ME THE CHANCE TO MEET MISS MERCURIO.
I'M OKAY NOW.
MOTO-...
I THINK IT'S STRAIGHTENED MY LIFE OUT A BIT.
BUT LIKE I SAID, YOU'D BETTER WORRY ABOUT GRADUATING FIRST, MOTOKI.
CHATTER
CHATTER
SHUT UP! I'M GONNA GIVE IT MY ALL ON THE FINAL EXAMS, I TELL YOU!
THANKS FOR YOUR HELP, OKADA.
......
......
......

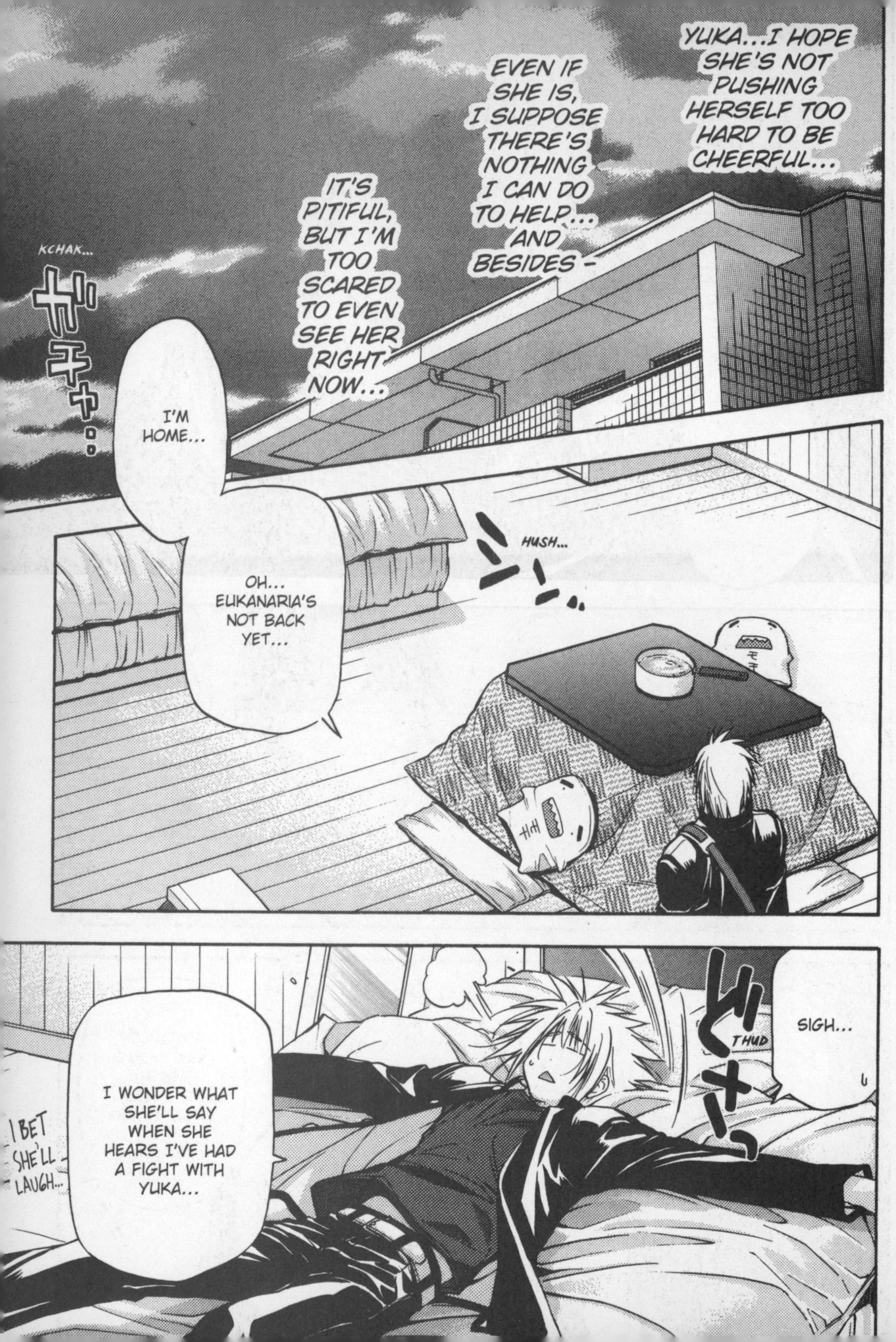
YUKA...I HOPE SHE'S NOT PUSHING HERSELF TOO HARD TO BE CHEERFUL...
EVEN IF SHE IS, I SUPPOSE THERE'S NOTHING I CAN DO TO HELP... AND BESIDES -
IT'S PITIFUL, BUT I'M TOO SCARED TO EVEN SEE HER RIGHT NOW...
KCHAK...
ガチャ..
I'M HOME...
HUSH...
OH... EUKANARIA'S NOT BACK YET...
SIGH...
THUD
どさっ
I WONDER WHAT SHE'LL SAY WHEN SHE HEARS I'VE HAD A FIGHT WITH YUKA...
I BET SHE'LL LAUGH...

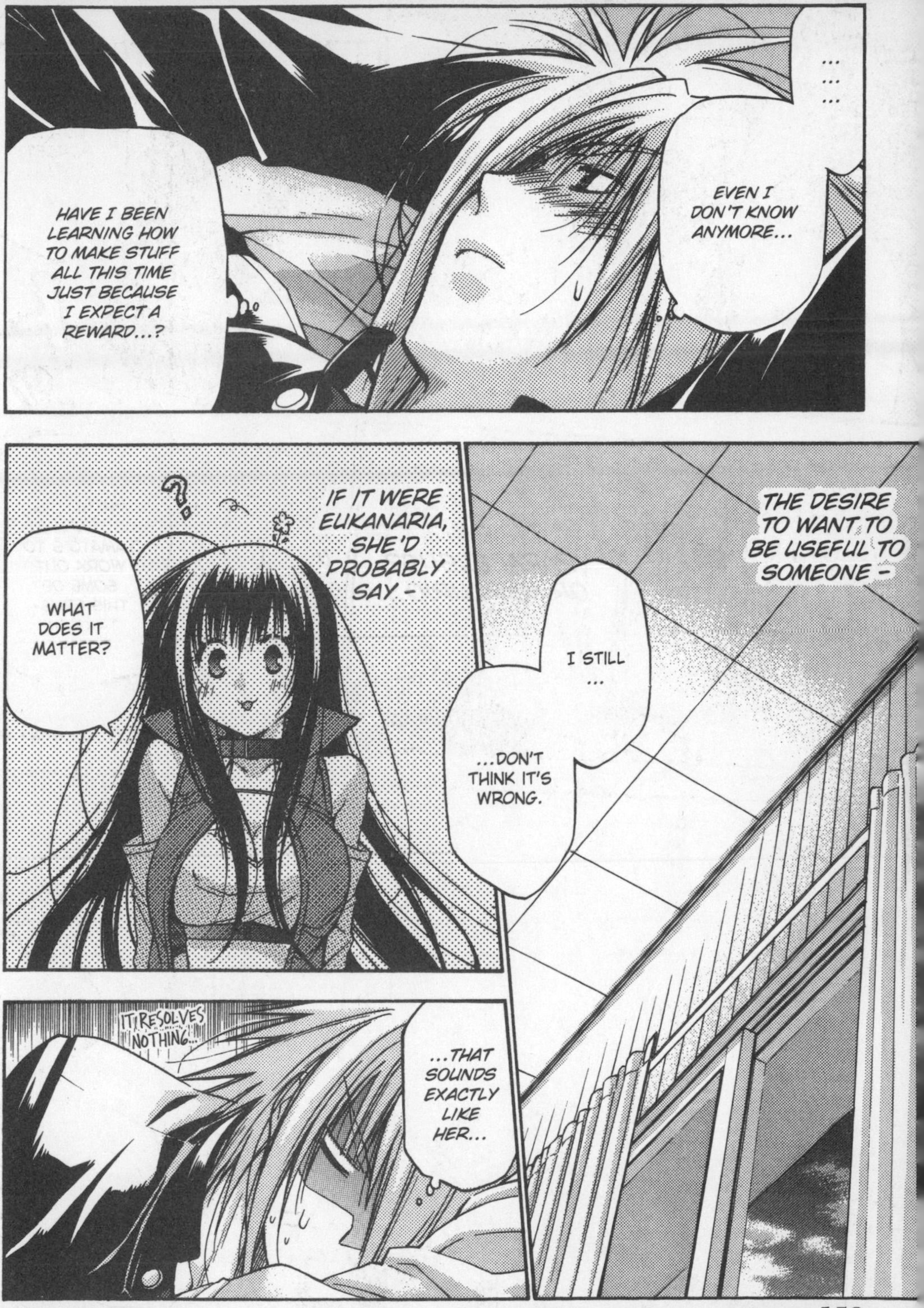
...
...
...
EVEN I DON'T KNOW ANYMORE...
HAVE I BEEN LEARNING HOW TO MAKE STUFF ALL THIS TIME JUST BECAUSE I EXPECT A REWARD...?
THE DESIRE TO WANT TO BE USEFUL TO SOMEONE -
I STILL ...
...DON'T THINK IT'S WRONG.
IF IT WERE EUKANARIA, SHE'D PROBABLY SAY -
WHAT DOES IT MATTER?
...THAT SOUNDS EXACTLY LIKE HER...
IT RESOLVES NOTHING...

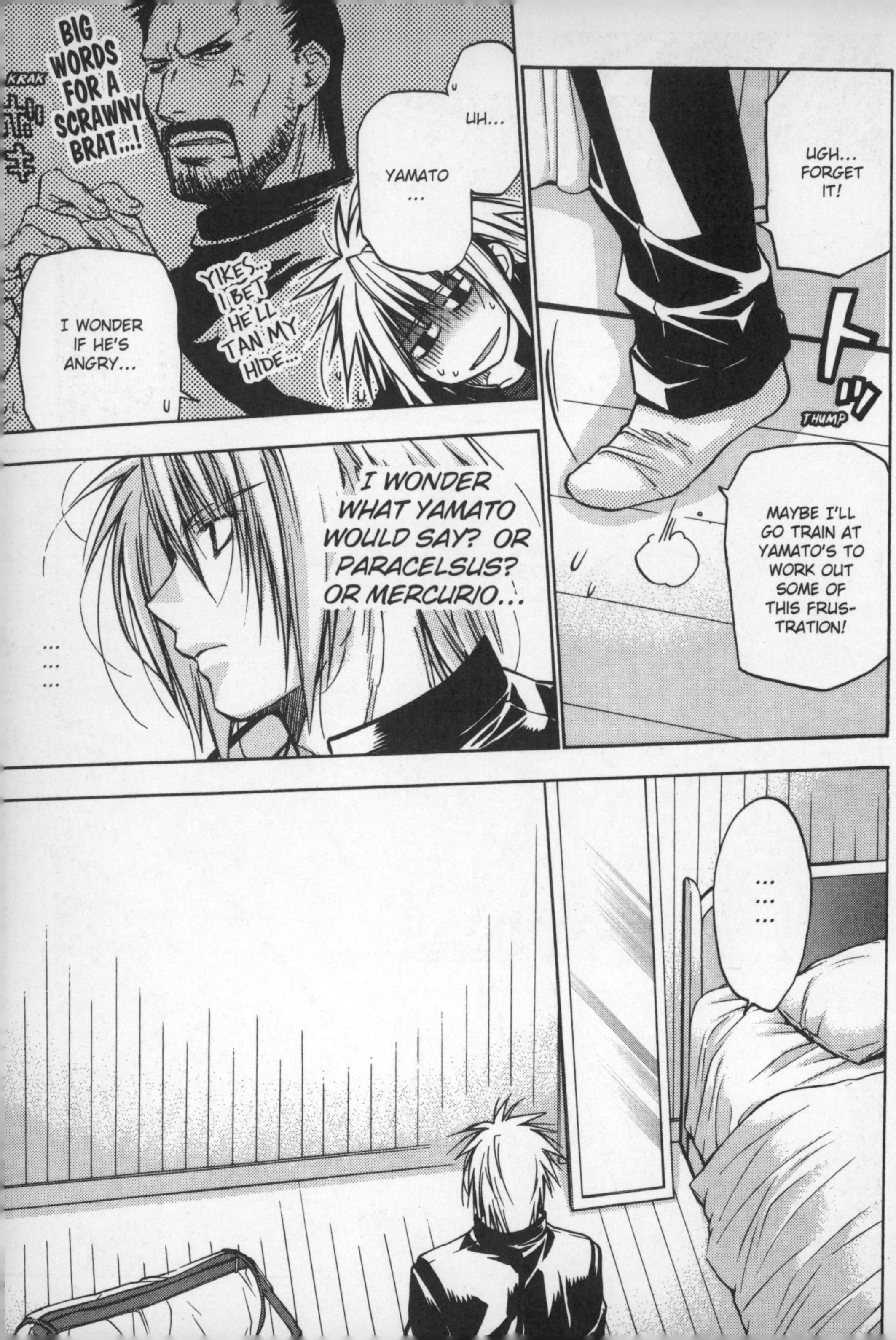
UGH... FORGET IT!
THUMP
MAYBE I'LL GO TRAIN AT YAMATO'S TO WORK OUT SOME OF THIS FRUS-TRATION!
UH...
YAMATO ...
BIG WORDS FOR A SCRAWNY BRAT...!
KRAK
YIKES... I BET HE'LL TAN MY HIDE...
I WONDER IF HE'S ANGRY...
I WONDER WHAT YAMATO WOULD SAY? OR PARACELSUS? OR MERCURIO...
... ...
... ...

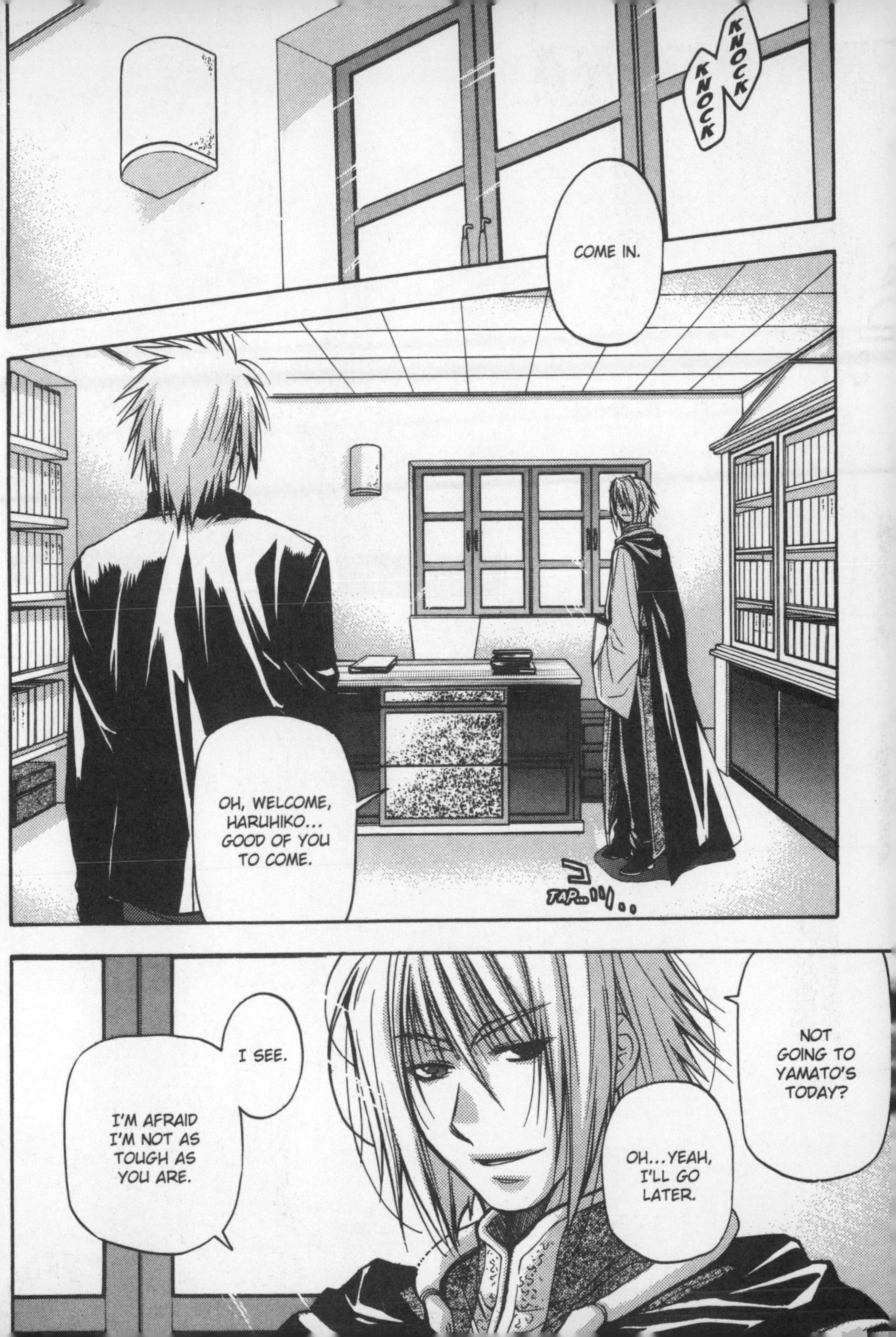
KNOCK KNOCK
COME IN.
OH, WELCOME, HARUHIKO... GOOD OF YOU TO COME.
TAP...
NOT GOING TO YAMATO'S TODAY?
OH...YEAH, I'LL GO LATER.
I SEE.
I'M AFRAID I'M NOT AS TOUGH AS YOU ARE.

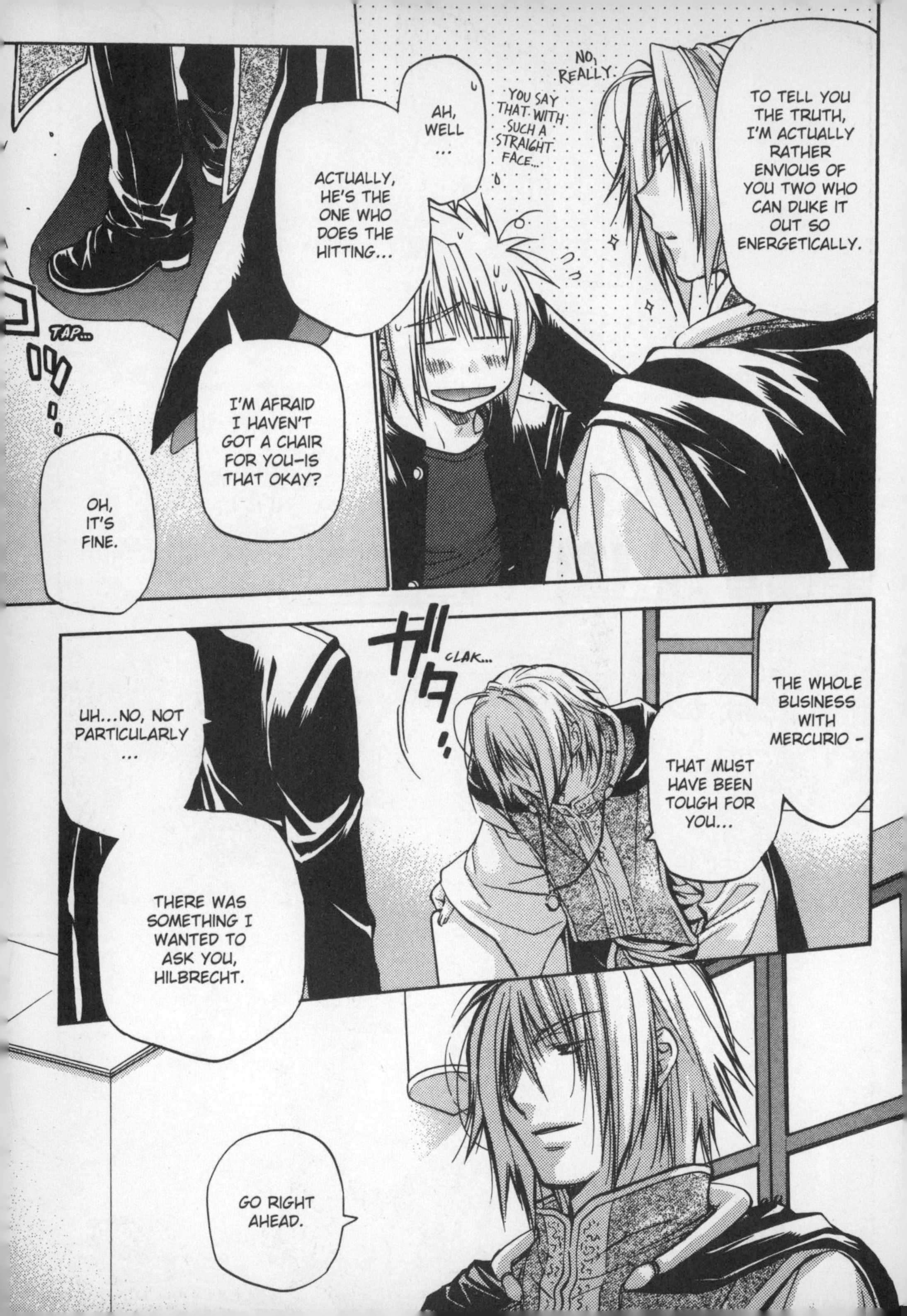
TO TELL YOU THE TRUTH, I'M ACTUALLY RATHER ENVIOUS OF YOU TWO WHO CAN DUKE IT OUT SO ENERGETICALLY.
NO, REALLY.
YOU SAY THAT WITH SUCH A STRAIGHT FACE...
AH, WELL...
ACTUALLY, HE'S THE ONE WHO DOES THE HITTING...
TAP...
I'M AFRAID I HAVEN'T GOT A CHAIR FOR YOU–IS THAT OKAY?
OH, IT'S FINE.
THE WHOLE BUSINESS WITH MERCURIO -
THAT MUST HAVE BEEN TOUGH FOR YOU...
CLAK...
UH...NO, NOT PARTICULARLY...
THERE WAS SOMETHING I WANTED TO ASK YOU, HILBRECHT.
GO RIGHT AHEAD.

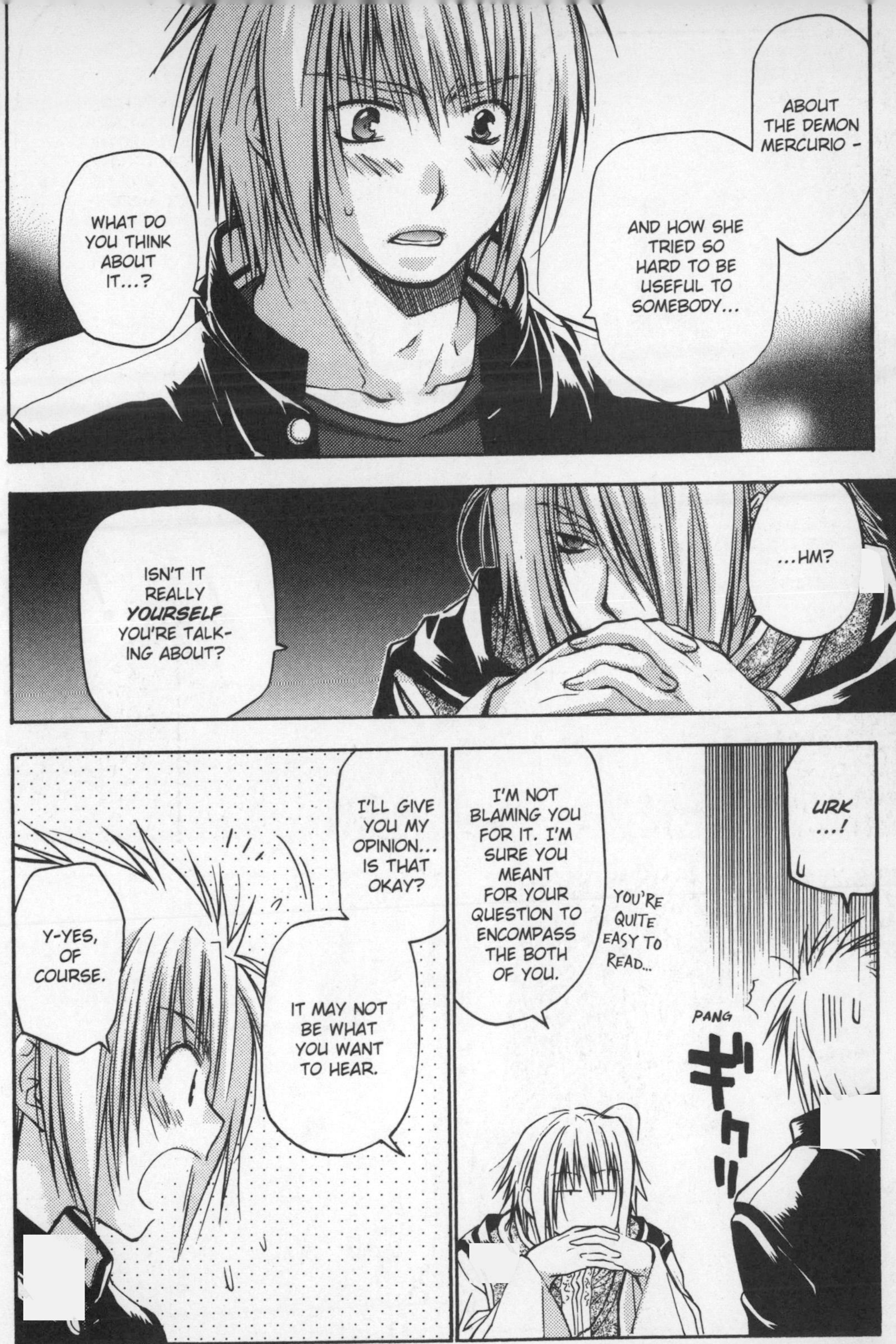
ABOUT THE DEMON MERCURIO -
AND HOW SHE TRIED SO HARD TO BE USEFUL TO SOMEBODY...
WHAT DO YOU THINK ABOUT IT...?
...HM?
ISN'T IT REALLY *YOURSELF* YOU'RE TALKING ABOUT?
URK ...!
PANG
YOU'RE QUITE EASY TO READ...
I'M NOT BLAMING YOU FOR IT. I'M SURE YOU MEANT FOR YOUR QUESTION TO ENCOMPASS THE BOTH OF YOU.
I'LL GIVE YOU MY OPINION... IS THAT OKAY?
IT MAY NOT BE WHAT YOU WANT TO HEAR.
Y-YES, OF COURSE.

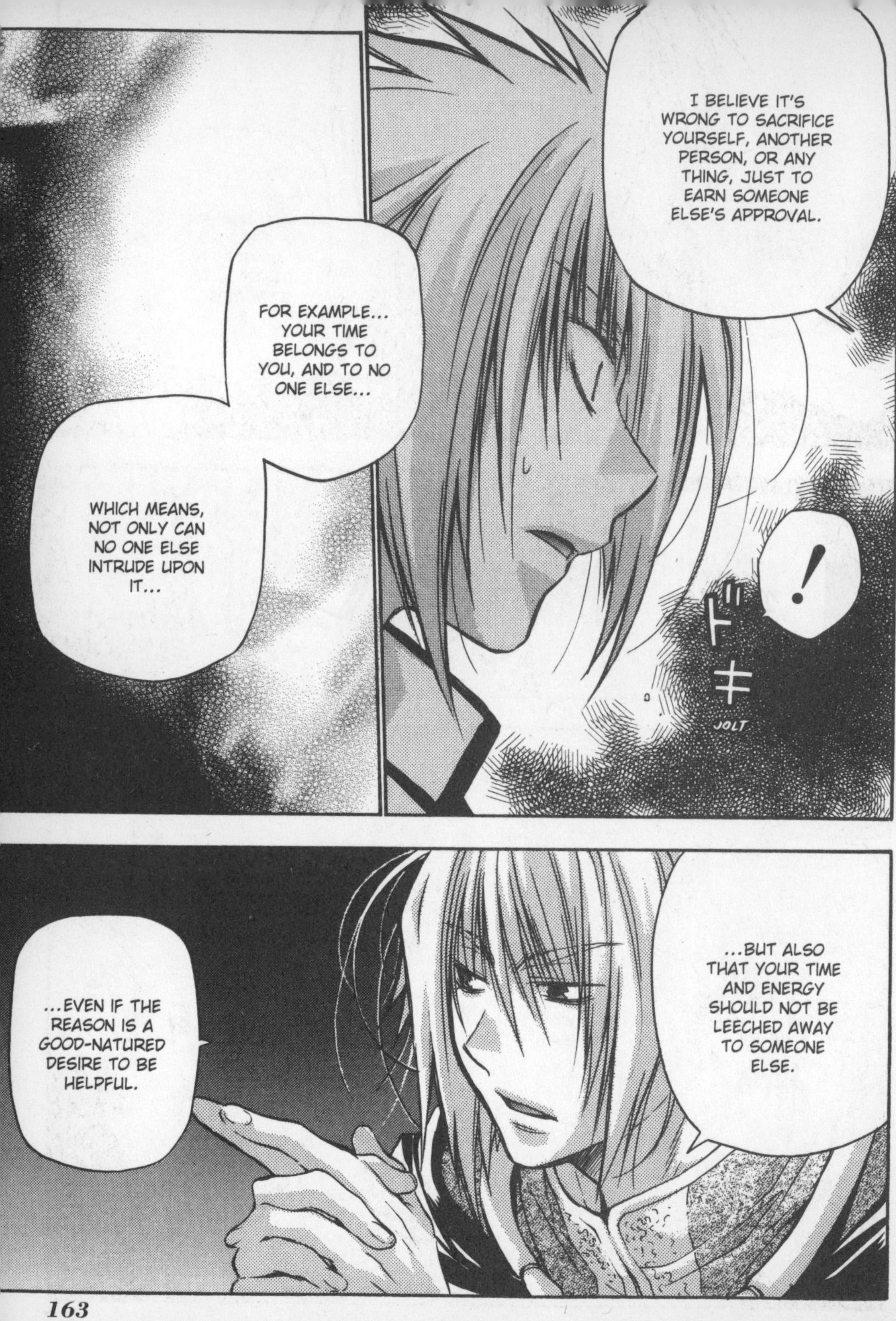
I BELIEVE IT'S WRONG TO SACRIFICE YOURSELF, ANOTHER PERSON, OR ANY THING, JUST TO EARN SOMEONE ELSE'S APPROVAL.
FOR EXAMPLE... YOUR TIME BELONGS TO YOU, AND TO NO ONE ELSE...
WHICH MEANS, NOT ONLY CAN NO ONE ELSE INTRUDE UPON IT...
!
ドキ
JOLT
...BUT ALSO THAT YOUR TIME AND ENERGY SHOULD NOT BE LEECHED AWAY TO SOMEONE ELSE.
...EVEN IF THE REASON IS A GOOD-NATURED DESIRE TO BE HELPFUL.

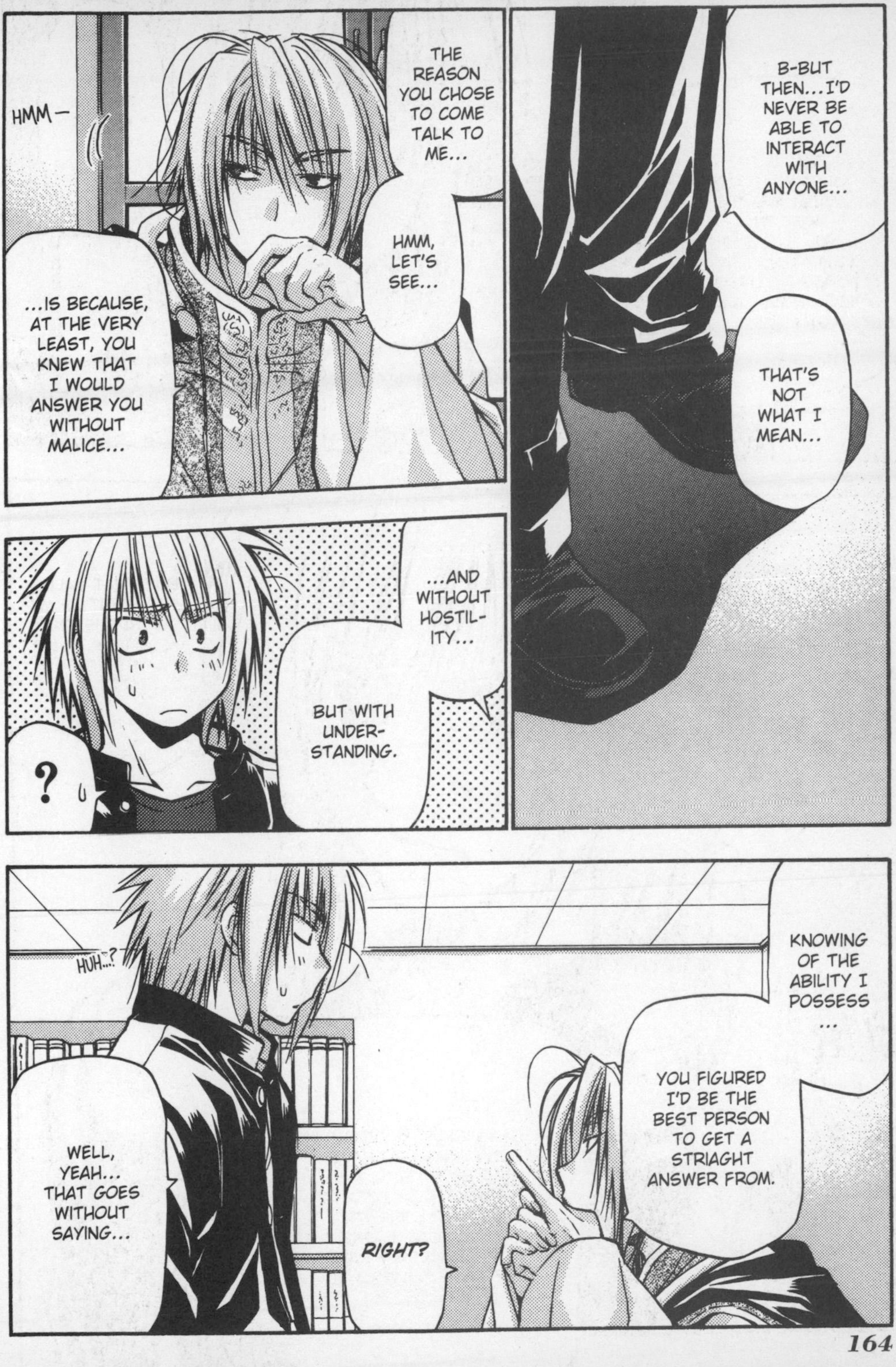
B-BUT THEN...I'D NEVER BE ABLE TO INTERACT WITH ANYONE...
THAT'S NOT WHAT I MEAN...
THE REASON YOU CHOSE TO COME TALK TO ME...
HMM —
HMM, LET'S SEE...
...IS BECAUSE, AT THE VERY LEAST, YOU KNEW THAT I WOULD ANSWER YOU WITHOUT MALICE...
...AND WITHOUT HOSTIL-ITY...
BUT WITH UNDER-STANDING.
?
KNOWING OF THE ABILITY I POSSESS ...
YOU FIGURED I'D BE THE BEST PERSON TO GET A STRIAGHT ANSWER FROM.
HUH...?
RIGHT?
WELL, YEAH... THAT GOES WITHOUT SAYING...

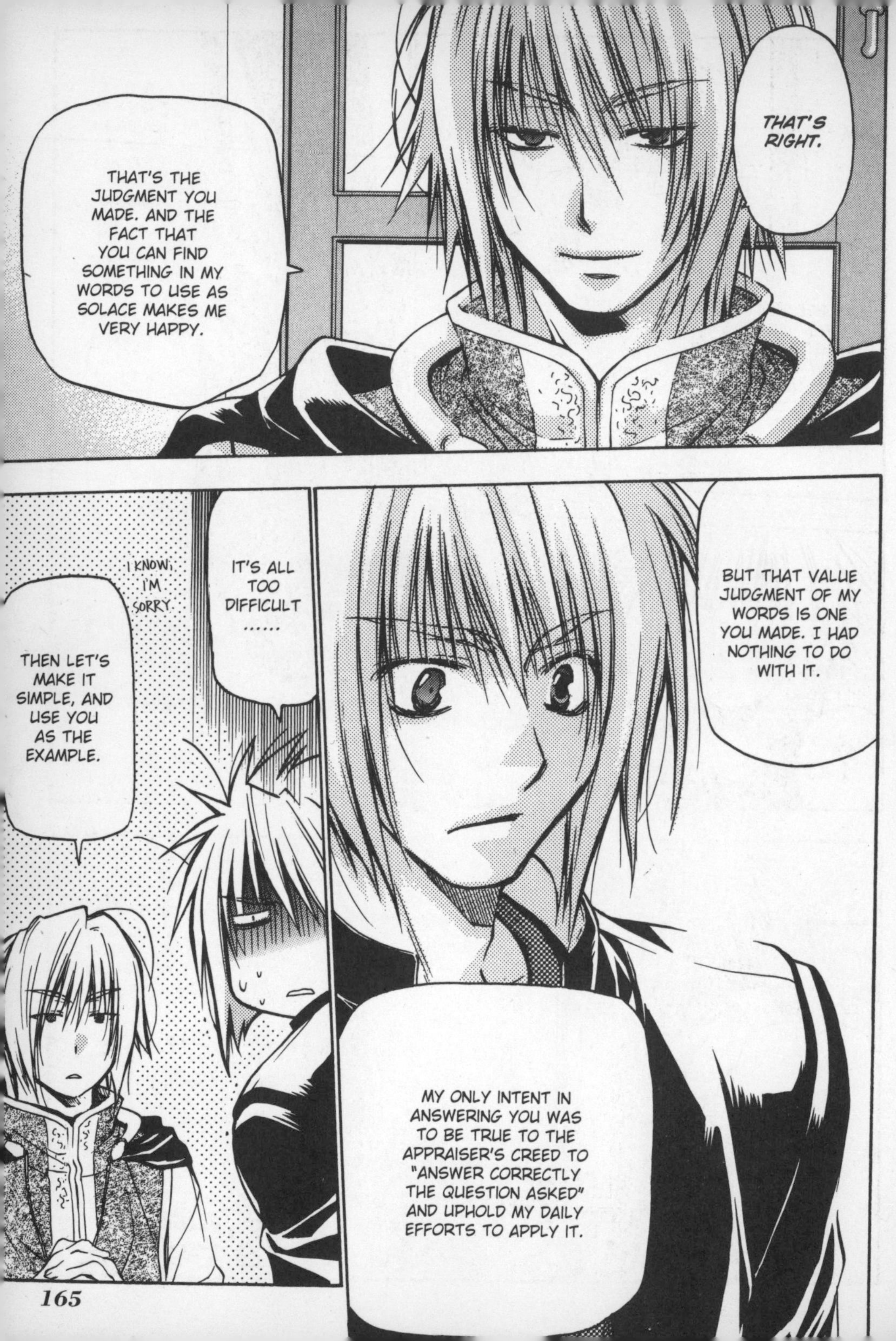
THAT'S RIGHT.
THAT'S THE JUDGMENT YOU MADE. AND THE FACT THAT YOU CAN FIND SOMETHING IN MY WORDS TO USE AS SOLACE MAKES ME VERY HAPPY.
BUT THAT VALUE JUDGMENT OF MY WORDS IS ONE YOU MADE. I HAD NOTHING TO DO WITH IT.
MY ONLY INTENT IN ANSWERING YOU WAS TO BE TRUE TO THE APPRAISER'S CREED TO "ANSWER CORRECTLY THE QUESTION ASKED" AND UPHOLD MY DAILY EFFORTS TO APPLY IT.
IT'S ALL TOO DIFFICULT ......
I KNOW, I'M SORRY.
THEN LET'S MAKE IT SIMPLE, AND USE YOU AS THE EXAMPLE.

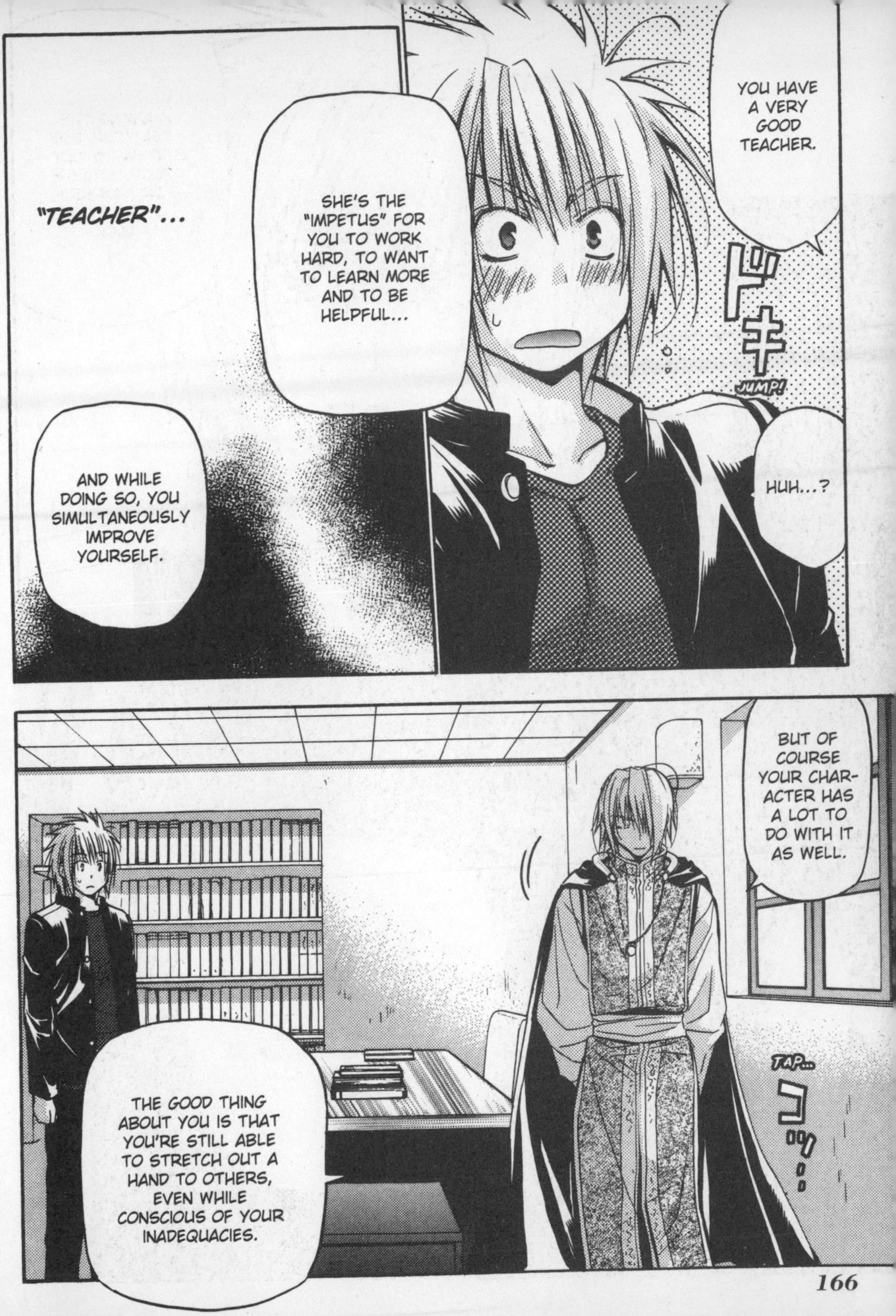
YOU HAVE A VERY GOOD TEACHER.
JUMP!
HUH...?
SHE'S THE "IMPETUS" FOR YOU TO WORK HARD, TO WANT TO LEARN MORE AND TO BE HELPFUL...
"TEACHER"...
AND WHILE DOING SO, YOU SIMULTANEOUSLY IMPROVE YOURSELF.
BUT OF COURSE YOUR CHAR-ACTER HAS A LOT TO DO WITH IT AS WELL.
TAP...
THE GOOD THING ABOUT YOU IS THAT YOU'RE STILL ABLE TO STRETCH OUT A HAND TO OTHERS, EVEN WHILE CONSCIOUS OF YOUR INADEQUACIES.

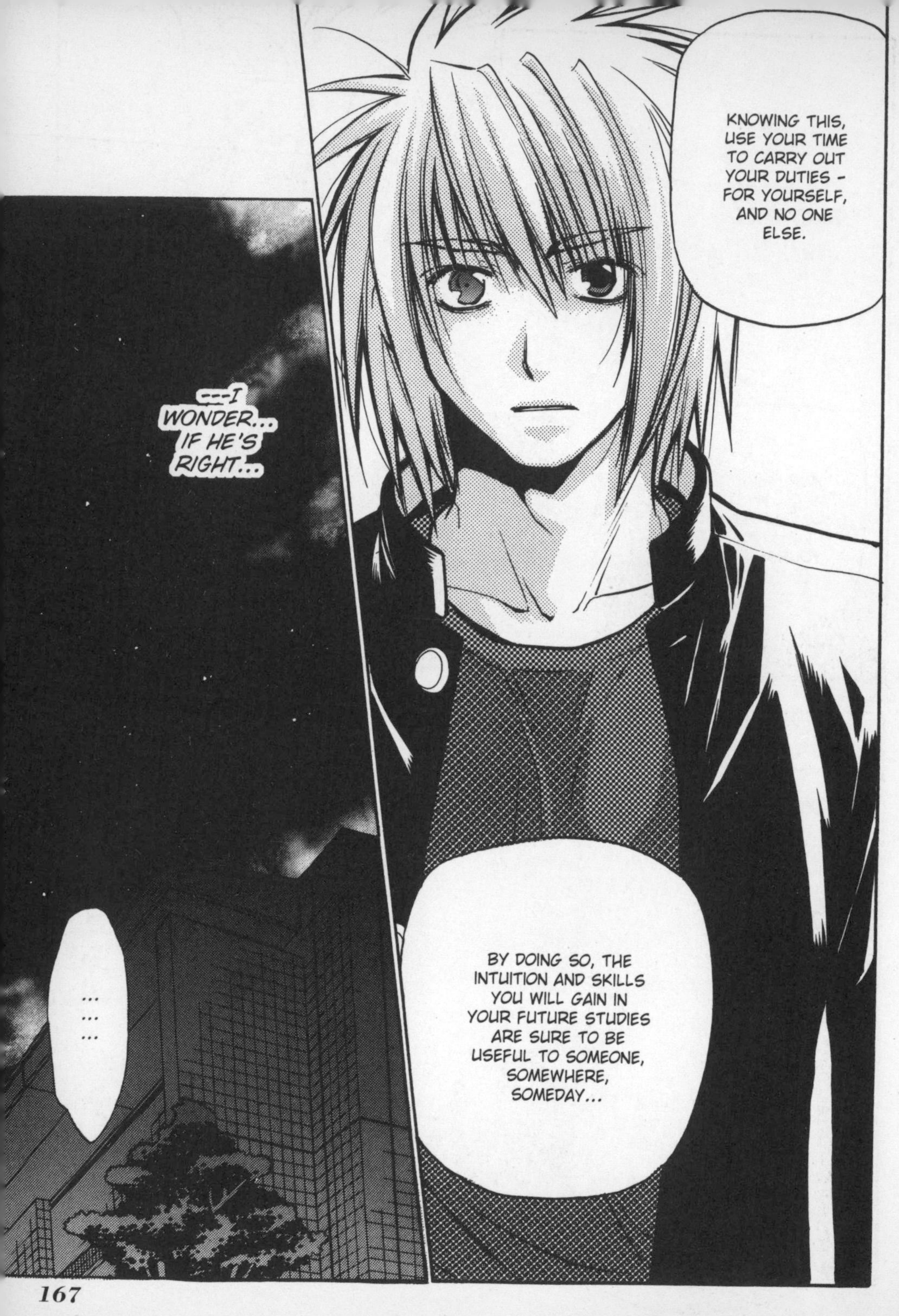
KNOWING THIS, USE YOUR TIME TO CARRY OUT YOUR DUTIES - FOR YOURSELF, AND NO ONE ELSE.
BY DOING SO, THE INTUITION AND SKILLS YOU WILL GAIN IN YOUR FUTURE STUDIES ARE SURE TO BE USEFUL TO SOMEONE, SOMEWHERE, SOMEDAY...
---I WONDER... IF HE'S RIGHT...
... ...

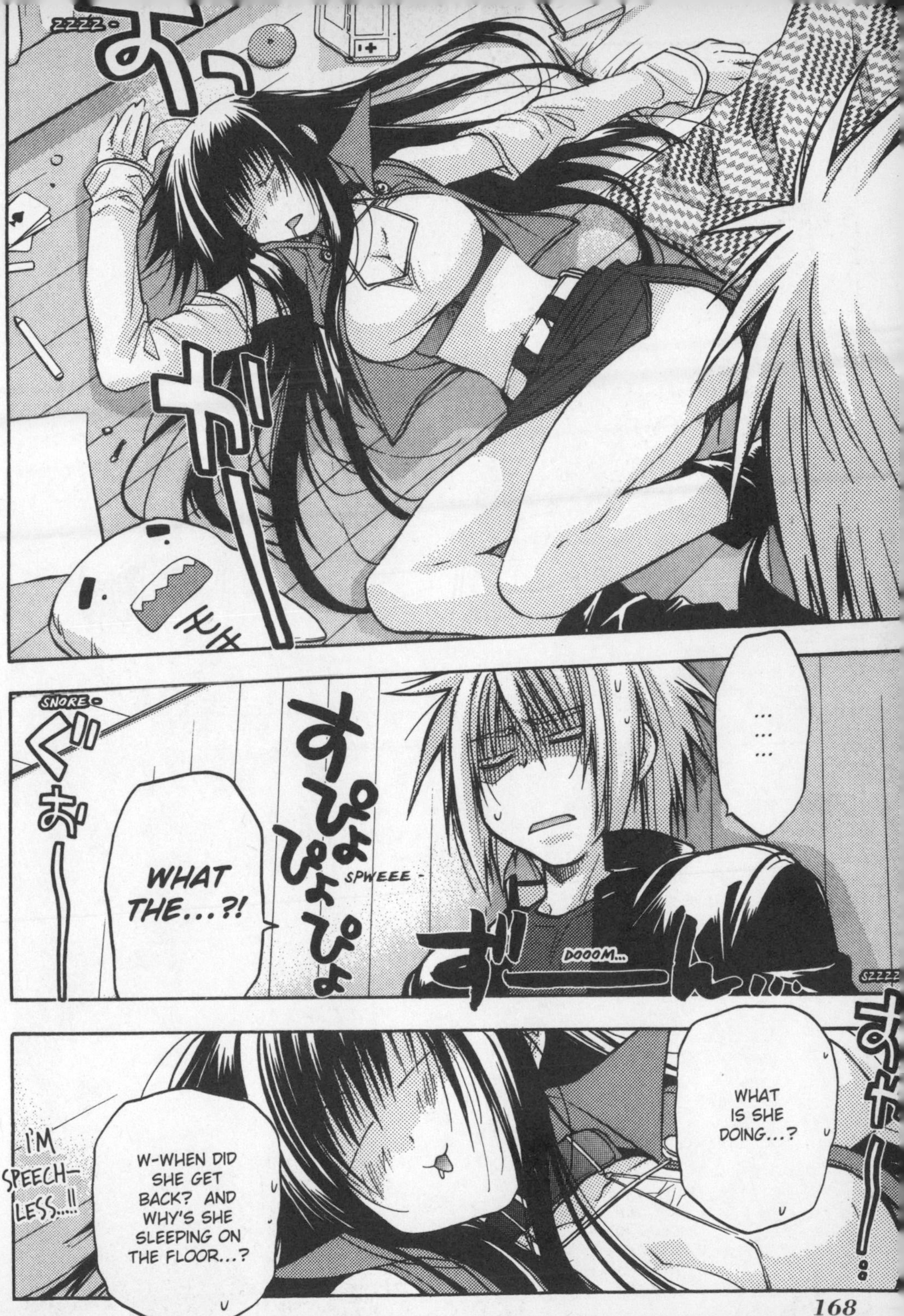
ZZZZ-
あっ
ホー
SZZZZ
...
...
...
SPWEEE-
すぴょぴょぴょぴょ
DOOOM...
ずーん...
WHAT THE...?!
SNORE-
ぐおー
すやー
WHAT IS SHE DOING...?
W-WHEN DID SHE GET BACK? AND WHY'S SHE SLEEPING ON THE FLOOR...?
I'M SPEECH-LESS...!!

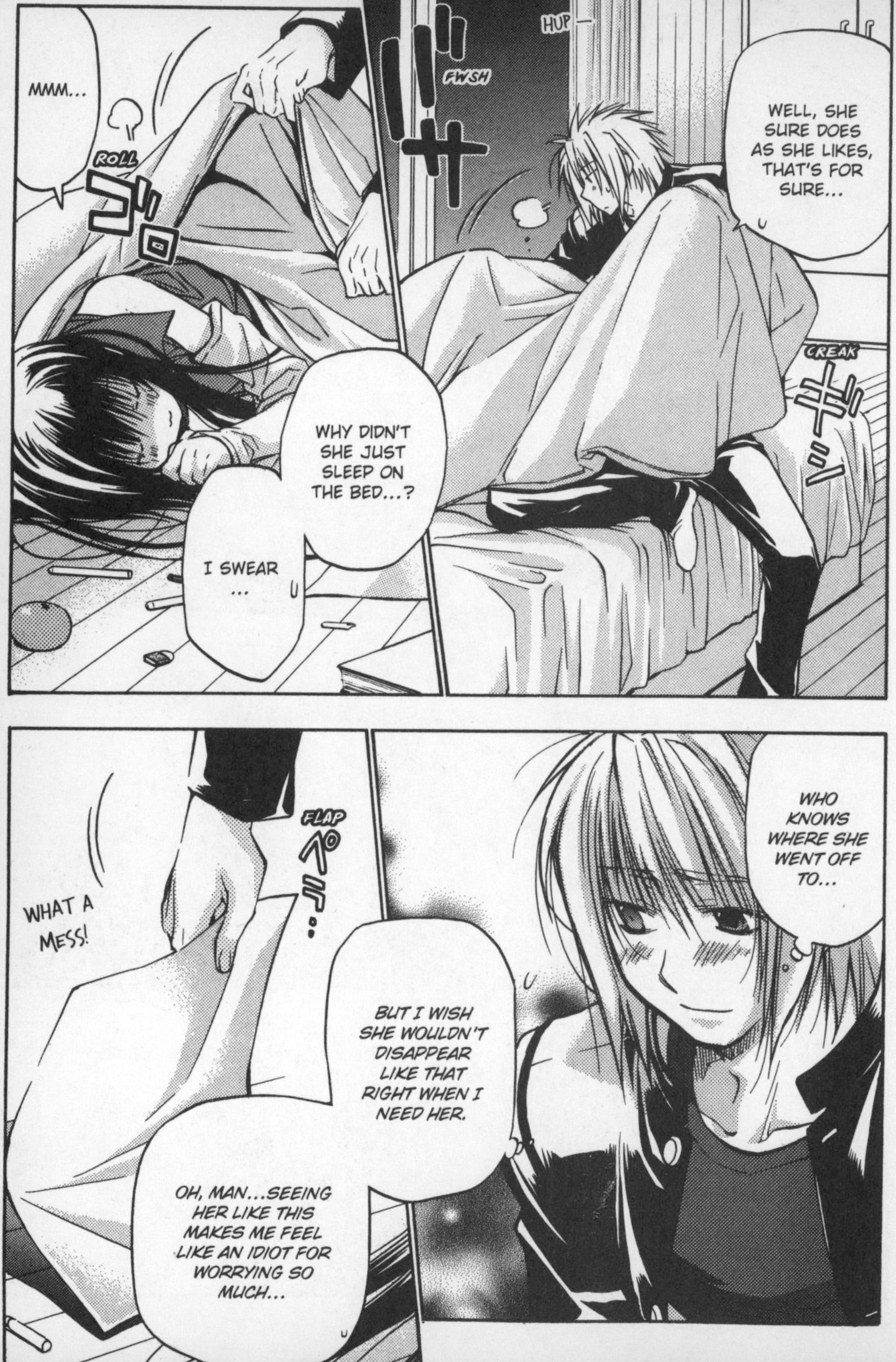
HUP—
FWSH
WELL, SHE SURE DOES AS SHE LIKES, THAT'S FOR SURE...
CREAK
ギシ
WHY DIDN'T SHE JUST SLEEP ON THE BED...?
I SWEAR...
MMM...
ROLL
ゴロ
WHO KNOWS WHERE SHE WENT OFF TO...
BUT I WISH SHE WOULDN'T DISAPPEAR LIKE THAT RIGHT WHEN I NEED HER.
OH, MAN...SEEING HER LIKE THIS MAKES ME FEEL LIKE AN IDIOT FOR WORRYING SO MUCH...
FLAP
ペラ..
WHAT A MESS!

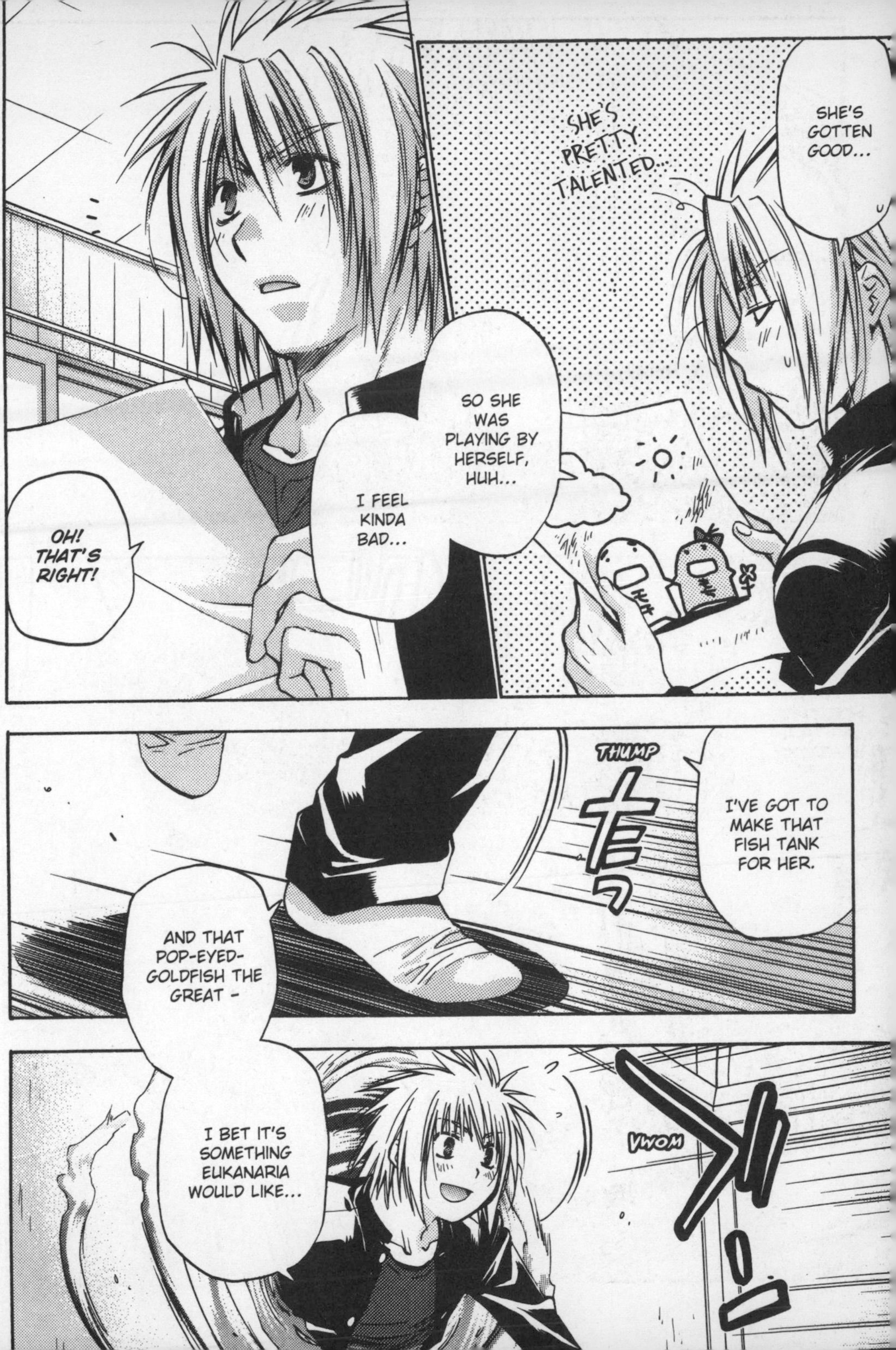
SHE'S GOTTEN GOOD...
SHE'S PRETTY TALENTED...
SO SHE WAS PLAYING BY HERSELF, HUH...
I FEEL KINDA BAD...
OH! THAT'S RIGHT!
THUMP
I'VE GOT TO MAKE THAT FISH TANK FOR HER.
AND THAT POP-EYED-GOLDFISH THE GREAT -
VWOM
I BET IT'S SOMETHING EUKANARIA WOULD LIKE...

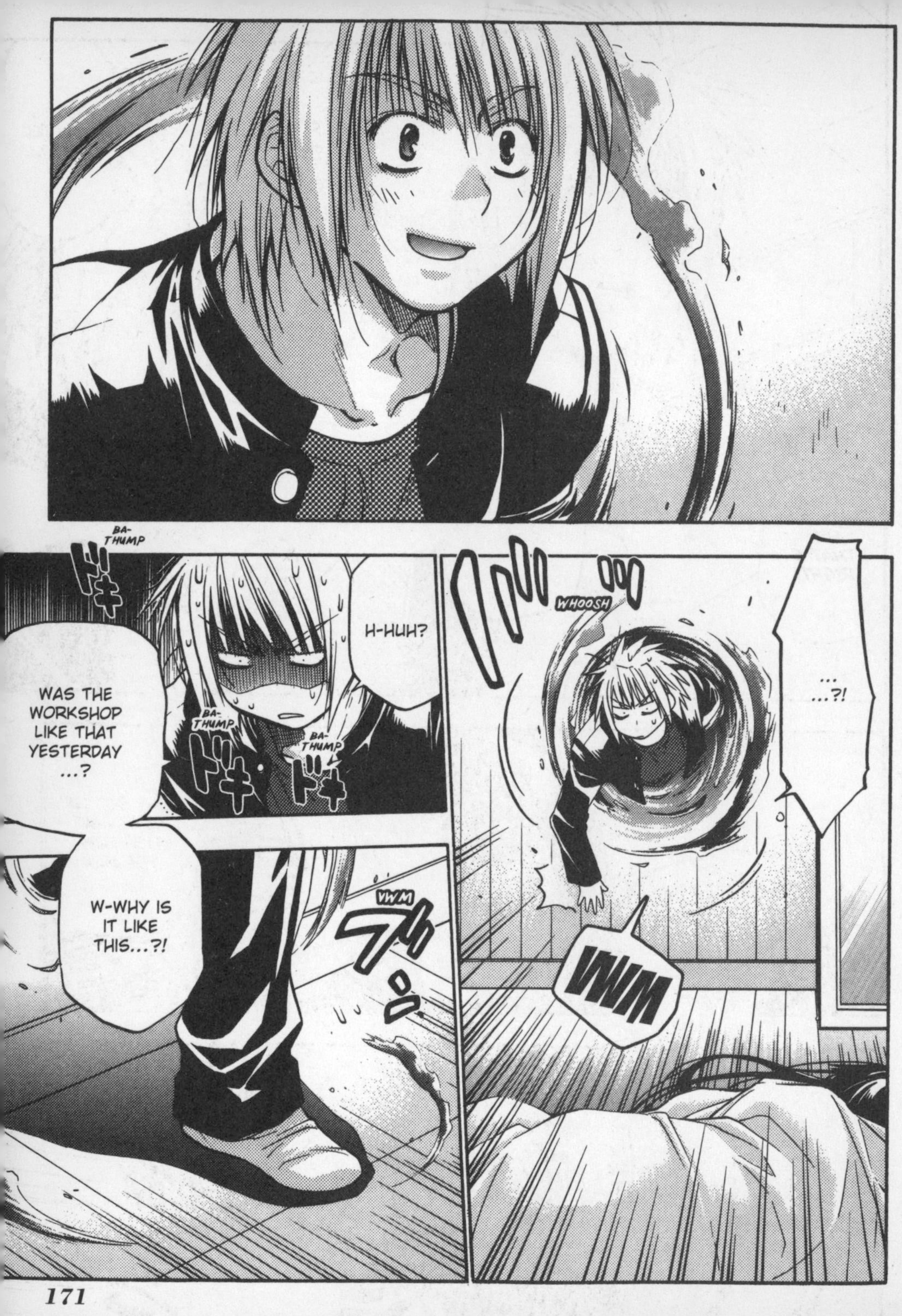
WHOOSH
...
...?!
VWM
BA-THUMP
H-HUH?
BA-THUMP
BA-THUMP
WAS THE WORKSHOP LIKE THAT YESTERDAY ...?
W-WHY IS IT LIKE THIS...?!
VWM

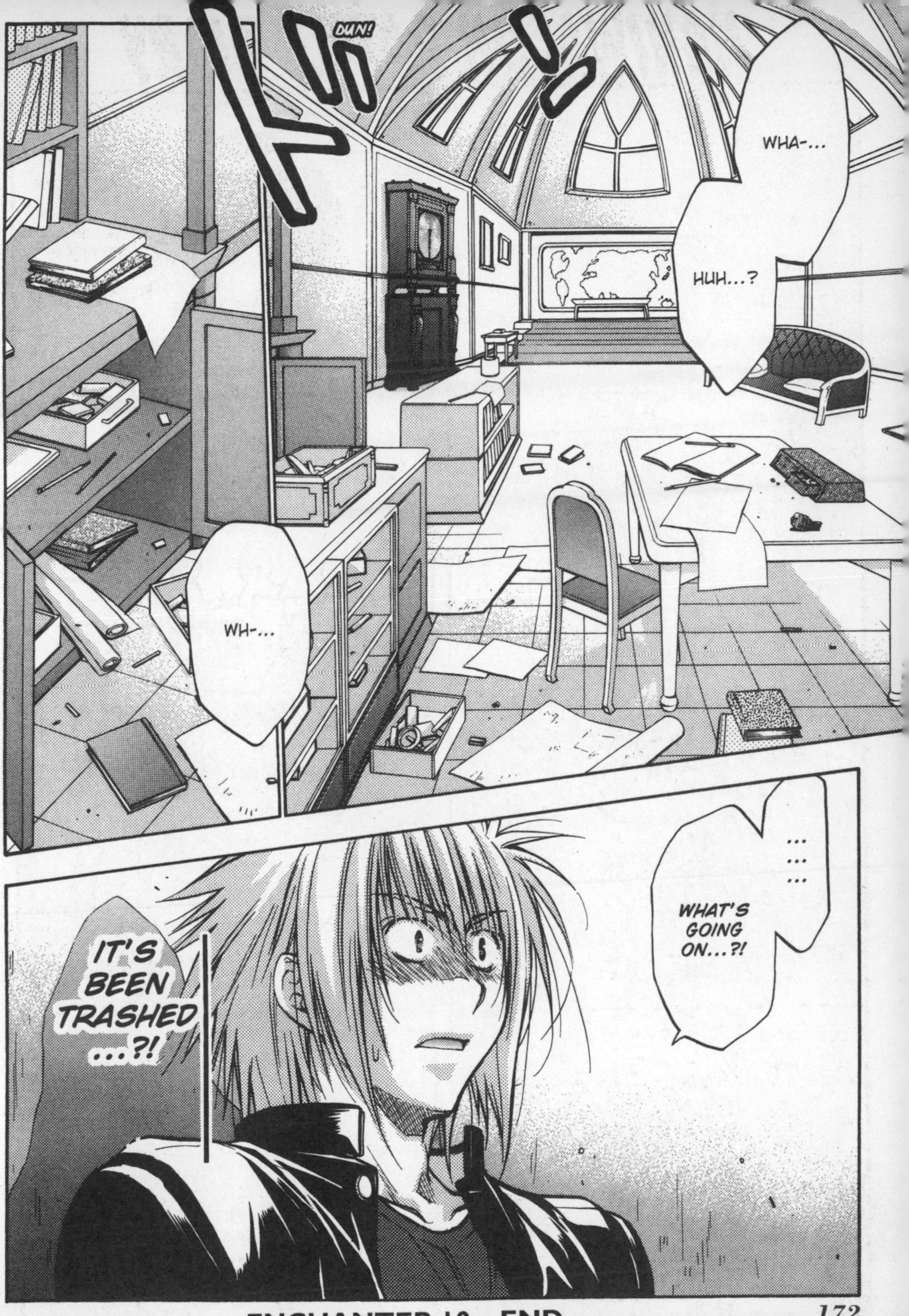
DUN!
WHA-...
HUH...?
WH-...
...
...
...
WHAT'S GOING ON...?!
IT'S BEEN TRASHED ...?!

ENCHANTER 10 – END

NANIWA-JIN BATTLE DIARY

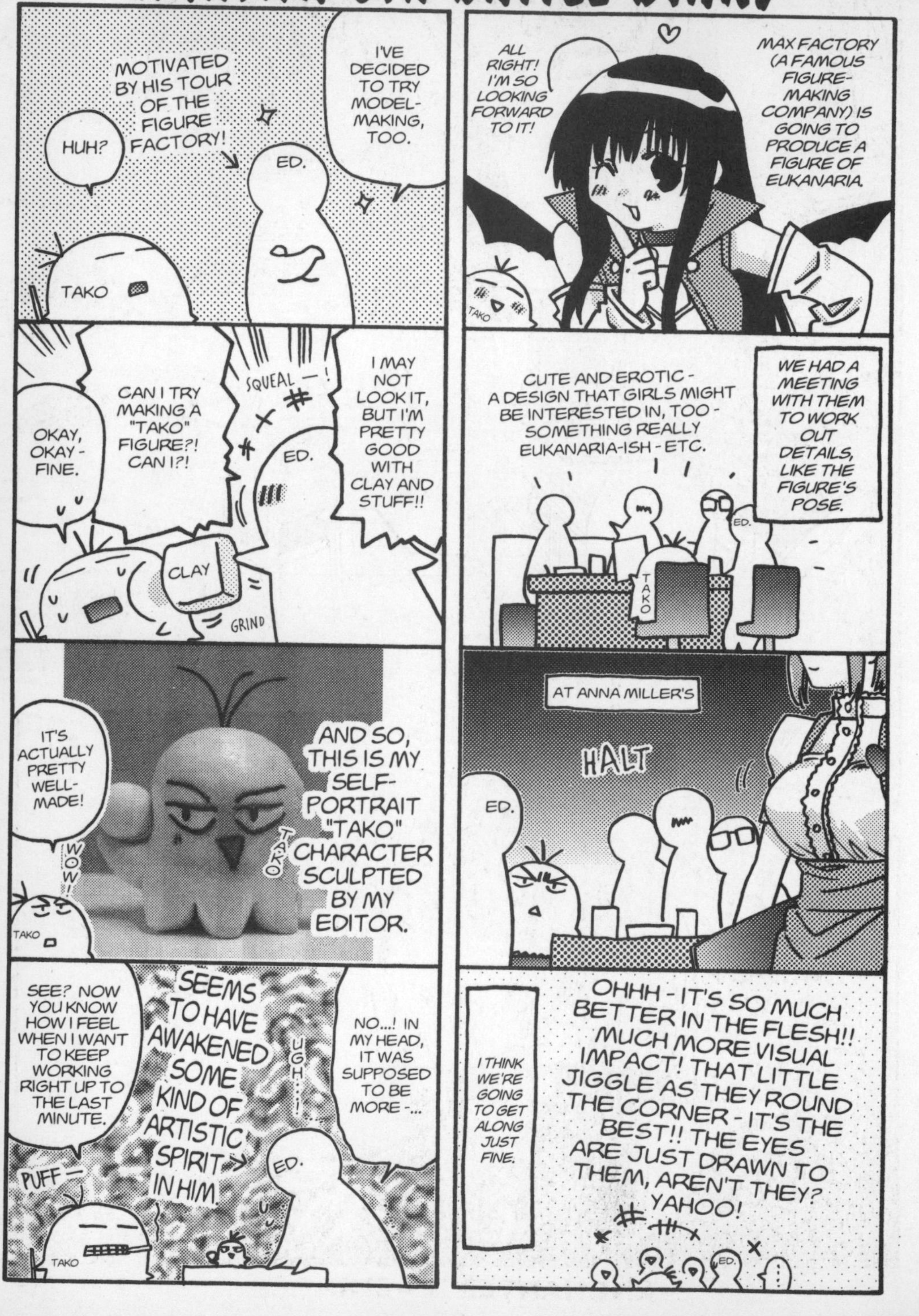

MAX FACTORY (A FAMOUS FIGURE-MAKING COMPANY) IS GOING TO PRODUCE A FIGURE OF EUKANARIA.
ALL RIGHT! I'M SO LOOKING FORWARD TO IT!
TAKO
WE HAD A MEETING WITH THEM TO WORK OUT DETAILS, LIKE THE FIGURE'S POSE.
CUTE AND EROTIC - A DESIGN THAT GIRLS MIGHT BE INTERESTED IN, TOO - SOMETHING REALLY EUKANARIA-ISH - ETC.
ED.
TAKO
AT ANNA MILLER'S
HALT
ED.
OHHH - IT'S SO MUCH BETTER IN THE FLESH!! MUCH MORE VISUAL IMPACT! THAT LITTLE JIGGLE AS THEY ROUND THE CORNER - IT'S THE BEST!! THE EYES ARE JUST DRAWN TO THEM, AREN'T THEY? YAHOO!
I THINK WE'RE GOING TO GET ALONG JUST FINE.
ED.
I'VE DECIDED TO TRY MODEL-MAKING, TOO.
MOTIVATED BY HIS TOUR OF THE FIGURE FACTORY!
ED.
HUH?
TAKO
I MAY NOT LOOK IT, BUT I'M PRETTY GOOD WITH CLAY AND STUFF!!
SQUEAL —!
ED.
CAN I TRY MAKING A "TAKO" FIGURE?! CAN I?!
OKAY, OKAY - FINE.
CLAY
GRIND
AND SO, THIS IS MY SELF-PORTRAIT "TAKO" CHARACTER SCULPTED BY MY EDITOR.
TAKO
IT'S ACTUALLY PRETTY WELL-MADE!
WOW!
TAKO
NO...! IN MY HEAD, IT WAS SUPPOSED TO BE MORE -...
UGH...!
SEEMS TO HAVE AWAKENED SOME KIND OF ARTISTIC SPIRIT IN HIM.
ED.
SEE? NOW YOU KNOW HOW I FEEL WHEN I WANT TO KEEP WORKING RIGHT UP TO THE LAST MINUTE.
PUFF —
TAKO

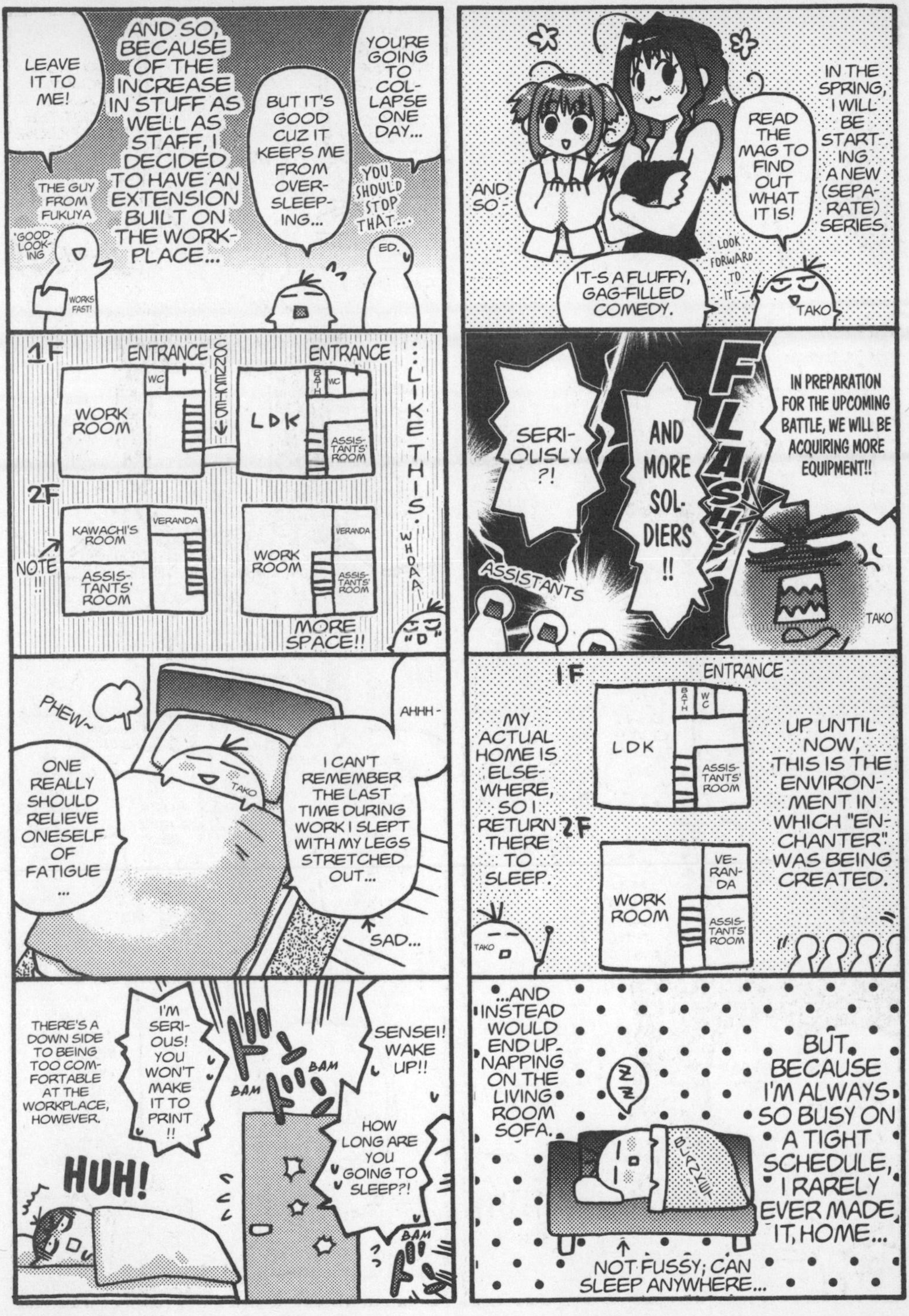
IN THE SPRING, I WILL BE STARTING A NEW (SEPARATE) SERIES.
READ THE MAG TO FIND OUT WHAT IT IS!
AND SO
LOOK FORWARD TO IT
IT-S A FLUFFY, GAG-FILLED COMEDY.
TAKO
IN PREPARATION FOR THE UPCOMING BATTLE, WE WILL BE ACQUIRING MORE EQUIPMENT!!
FLASH!
AND MORE SOLDIERS!!
SERIOUSLY ?!
ASSISTANTS
TAKO
UP UNTIL NOW, THIS IS THE ENVIRONMENT IN WHICH "ENCHANTER" WAS BEING CREATED.
1F
ENTRANCE
BATH
WC
LDK
ASSISTANTS' ROOM
2F
VERANDA
WORK ROOM
ASSISTANTS' ROOM
MY ACTUAL HOME IS ELSEWHERE, SO I RETURN THERE TO SLEEP.
TAKO
BUT BECAUSE I'M ALWAYS SO BUSY ON A TIGHT SCHEDULE, I RARELY EVER MADE IT HOME...
...AND INSTEAD WOULD END UP NAPPING ON THE LIVING ROOM SOFA.
ZZZ
BLANKET
NOT FUSSY; CAN SLEEP ANYWHERE...
YOU'RE GOING TO COLLAPSE ONE DAY...
BUT IT'S GOOD CUZ IT KEEPS ME FROM OVERSLEEPING...
AND SO, BECAUSE OF THE INCREASE IN STUFF AS WELL AS STAFF, I DECIDED TO HAVE AN EXTENSION BUILT ON THE WORKPLACE...
LEAVE IT TO ME!
YOU SHOULD STOP THAT...
ED.
THE GUY FROM FUKUYA
"GOOD-LOOKING
WORKS FAST!
...LIKE THIS.
WHOAA
ENTRANCE
BATH
WC
LDK
ASSISTANTS' ROOM
CONNECTED
ENTRANCE
1F
WC
WORK ROOM
2F
VERANDA
WORK ROOM
ASSISTANTS' ROOM
VERANDA
KAWACHI'S ROOM
ASSISTANTS' ROOM
NOTE!!
MORE SPACE!!
"D"
AHHH-
I CAN'T REMEMBER THE LAST TIME DURING WORK I SLEPT WITH MY LEGS STRETCHED OUT...
PHEW~
ONE REALLY SHOULD RELIEVE ONESELF OF FATIGUE...
TAKO
SAD...
SENSEI! WAKE UP!!
HOW LONG ARE YOU GOING TO SLEEP?!
BAM
BAM
BAM
I'M SERIOUS! YOU WON'T MAKE IT TO PRINT!!
BAM
THERE'S A DOWN SIDE TO BEING TOO COMFORTABLE AT THE WORKPLACE, HOWEVER.
HUH!

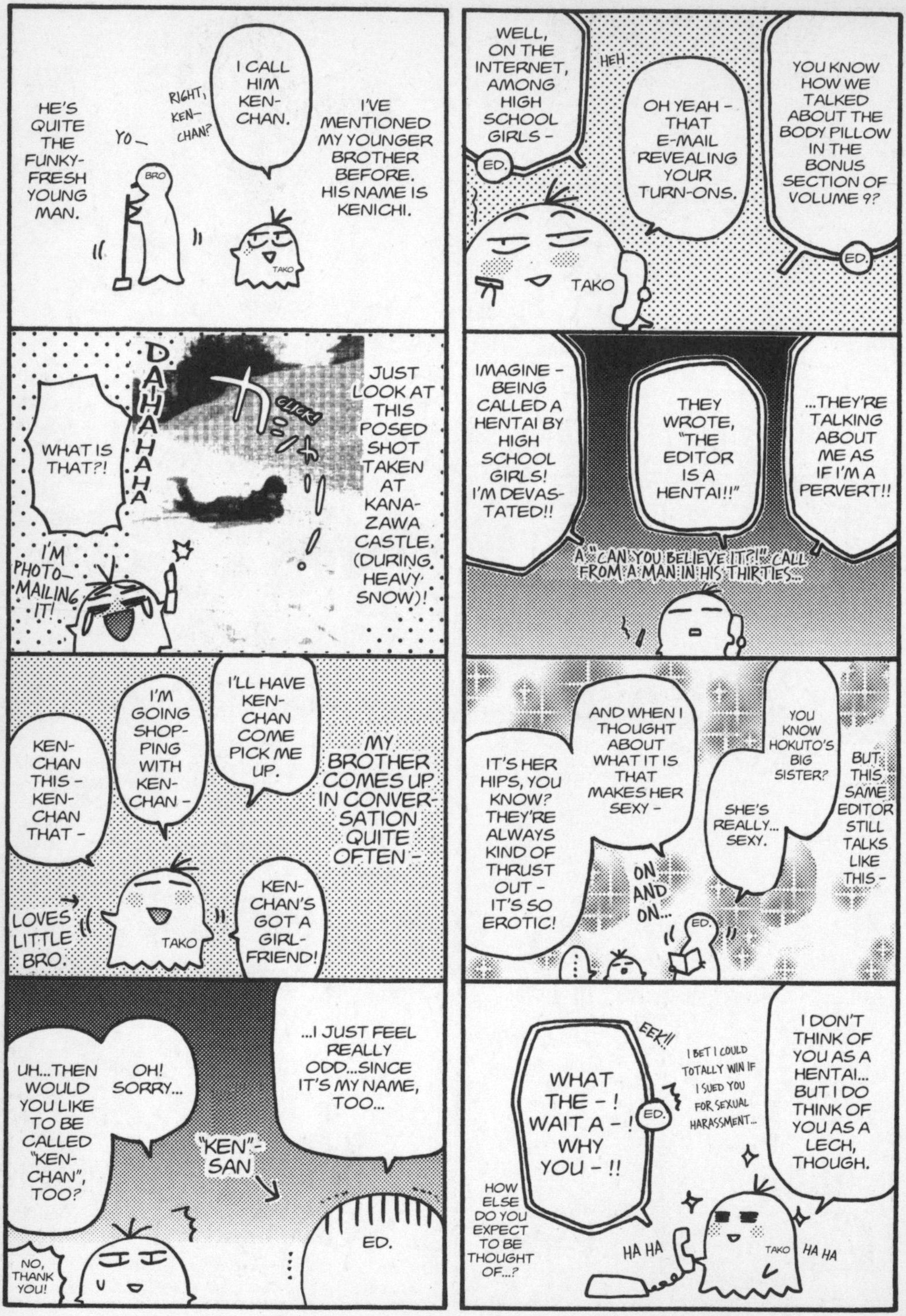
YOU KNOW HOW WE TALKED ABOUT THE BODY PILLOW IN THE BONUS SECTION OF VOLUME 9?
ED.
OH YEAH - THAT E-MAIL REVEALING YOUR TURN-ONS.
HEH
WELL, ON THE INTERNET, AMONG HIGH SCHOOL GIRLS -
ED.
TAKO
...THEY'RE TALKING ABOUT ME AS IF I'M A PERVERT!!
THEY WROTE, "THE EDITOR IS A HENTAI!!"
IMAGINE - BEING CALLED A HENTAI BY HIGH SCHOOL GIRLS! I'M DEVASTATED!!
A "CAN YOU BELIEVE IT?!" CALL FROM A MAN IN HIS THIRTIES...
BUT THIS SAME EDITOR STILL TALKS LIKE THIS -
YOU KNOW HOKUTO'S BIG SISTER?
SHE'S REALLY... SEXY.
AND WHEN I THOUGHT ABOUT WHAT IT IS THAT MAKES HER SEXY -
IT'S HER HIPS, YOU KNOW? THEY'RE ALWAYS KIND OF THRUST OUT - IT'S SO EROTIC!
ON AND ON...
ED.
I DON'T THINK OF YOU AS A HENTAI... BUT I DO THINK OF YOU AS A LECH, THOUGH.
EEK!!
I BET I COULD TOTALLY WIN IF I SUED YOU FOR SEXUAL HARASSMENT...
WHAT THE - ! WAIT A - ! WHY YOU - !!
ED.
HOW ELSE DO YOU EXPECT TO BE THOUGHT OF...?
HA HA
TAKO
HA HA
I'VE MENTIONED MY YOUNGER BROTHER BEFORE. HIS NAME IS KENICHI.
I CALL HIM KEN-CHAN.
RIGHT, KEN-CHAN?
YO—
HE'S QUITE THE FUNKY-FRESH YOUNG MAN.
BRO
TAKO
JUST LOOK AT THIS POSED SHOT TAKEN AT KANAZAWA CASTLE. (DURING HEAVY SNOW)!
CLICK!
DAHAHAHAHA
WHAT IS THAT?!
I'M PHOTO-MAILING IT!
MY BROTHER COMES UP IN CONVERSATION QUITE OFTEN -
I'LL HAVE KEN-CHAN COME PICK ME UP.
I'M GOING SHOPPING WITH KEN-CHAN -
KEN-CHAN THIS - KEN-CHAN THAT -
KEN-CHAN'S GOT A GIRLFRIEND!
TAKO
LOVES LITTLE BRO.
...I JUST FEEL REALLY ODD...SINCE IT'S MY NAME, TOO...
OH! SORRY...
UH...THEN WOULD YOU LIKE TO BE CALLED "KEN-CHAN", TOO?
"KEN"-SAN
ED.
NO, THANK YOU!

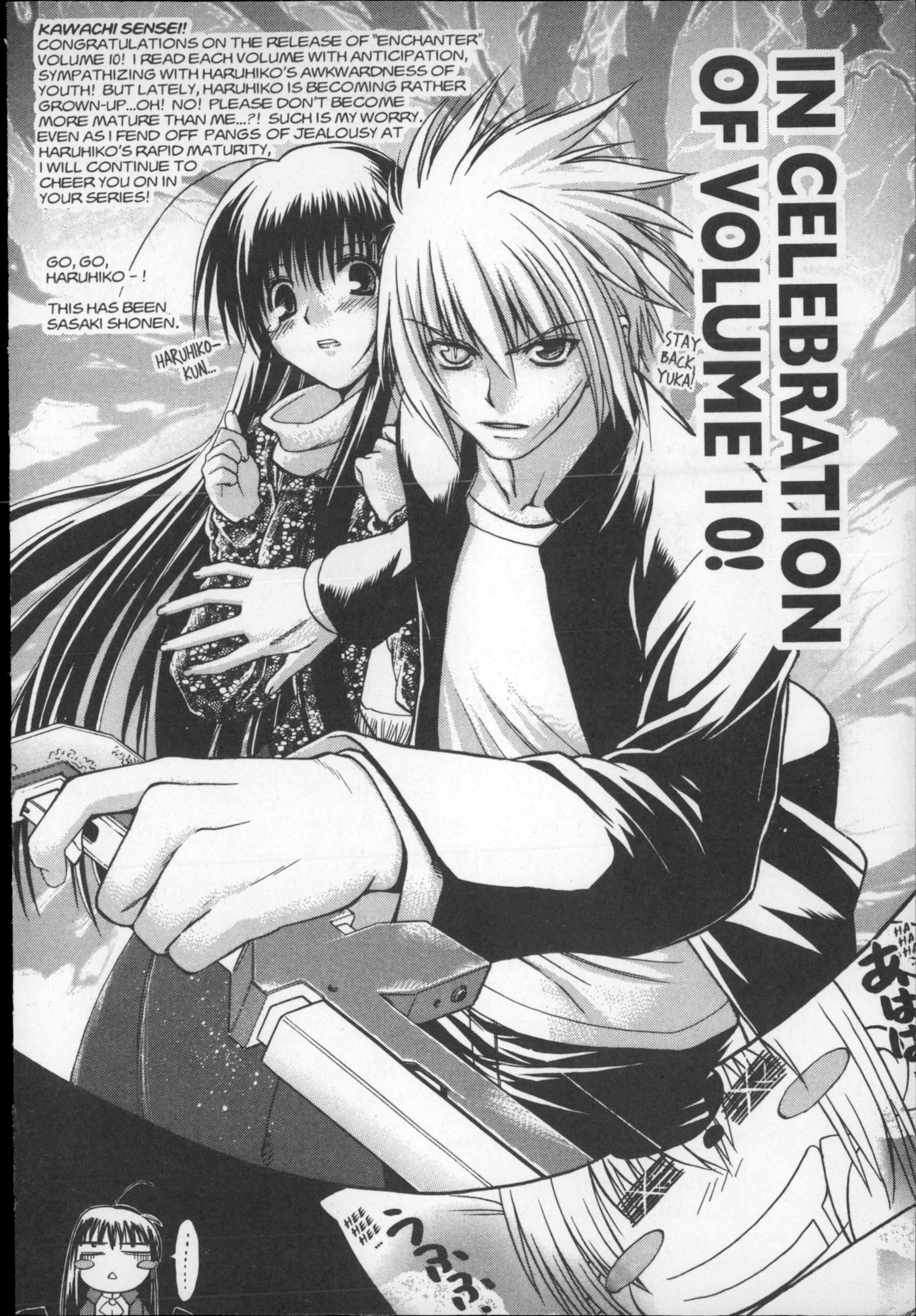
IN CELEBRATION OF VOLUME 10!
STAY BACK, YUKA!
HARUHIKO-KUN...
KAWACHI SENSEI!
CONGRATULATIONS ON THE RELEASE OF "ENCHANTER" VOLUME 10! I READ EACH VOLUME WITH ANTICIPATION, SYMPATHIZING WITH HARUHIKO'S AWKWARDNESS OF YOUTH! BUT LATELY, HARUHIKO IS BECOMING RATHER GROWN-UP...OH! NO! PLEASE DON'T BECOME MORE MATURE THAN ME...?! SUCH IS MY WORRY. EVEN AS I FEND OFF PANGS OF JEALOUSY AT HARUHIKO'S RAPID MATURITY, I WILL CONTINUE TO CHEER YOU ON IN YOUR SERIES!
GO, GO, HARUHIKO -!
THIS HAS BEEN SASAKI SHONEN.
HA HA HA
あはは
HEE HEE HEE...
うふふ
......

BONUS PAGE

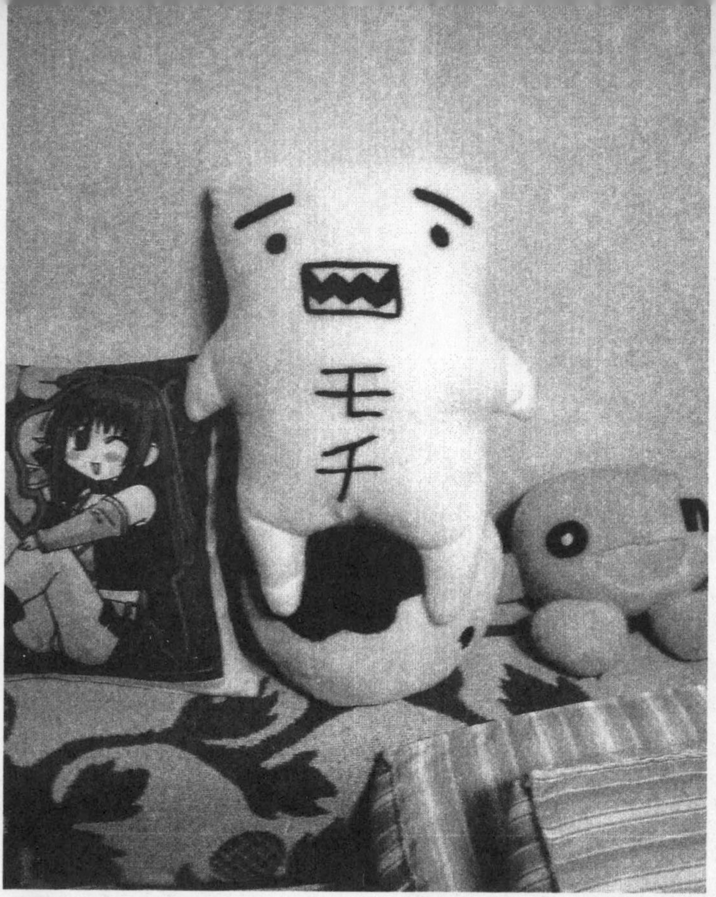
モチ

IT'S COLD AGAIN TODAY, DEAR, ISN'T IT...

NOW, THEN — THIS IS A PHOTO OF MOCHITTO-SAN (AND A FEW OTHER THINGS AS WELL), WHICH AN ACQUAINTANCE OF MINE MADE FOR ME. SO CUTE!! THANK YOU, INUSUKE-SAN!! IT FEELS REALLY SOFT, TOO! ALSO CONTRIBUTING ONE PAGE IS SASAKI SHONEN SENSEI, WHO IS CURRENTLY VERY ACTIVE OVER AT MEDIAWORKS! YAAAY!! I HAVE NOTHING TO ADD...I'M IMPRESSED!! (LAUGH) EVERYONE GAZE AND ENJOY AS WELL!! HARUHIKO MAY SEEM LIKE HE'S MATURING IN A LOT OF WAYS, BUT I THINK THIS IS HIS BASIC NATURE, YOU KNOW?! (LAUGH) AND MISS EUKANARIA IS VERY CUTE, TOO (LAUGH). THANK YOU VERY, VERY MUCH!!

ENCHANTER VOL:10 SPECIALTHANX
S.Miyazaki/N.Yabuta/M.Fujimoto/Y.Taniguchi/R.Takao
and
S.Sasaki/T.Inada/K.Nakagawa

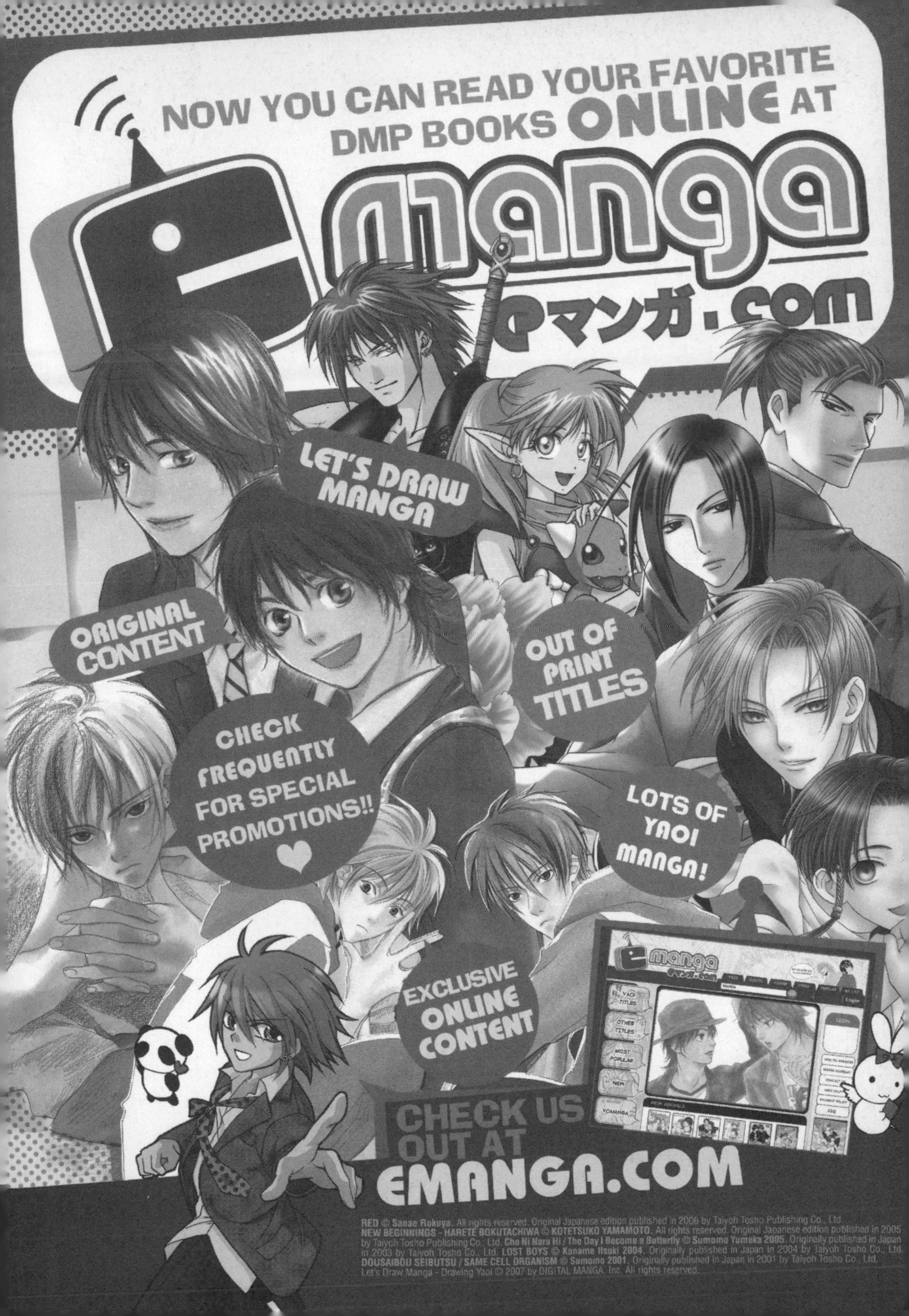
NOW YOU CAN READ YOUR FAVORITE DMP BOOKS ONLINE AT
emanga
eマンガ.com
LET'S DRAW MANGA
ORIGINAL CONTENT
OUT OF PRINT TITLES
CHECK FREQUENTLY FOR SPECIAL PROMOTIONS!!
LOTS OF YAOI MANGA!
EXCLUSIVE ONLINE CONTENT
CHECK US OUT AT
EMANGA.COM
RED © Sanae Rokuya. All rights reserved. Original Japanese edition published in 2006 by Taiyoh Tosho Publishing Co., Ltd.
NEW BEGINNINGS - HARETE BOKUTACHIWA © KOTETSUKO YAMAMOTO. All rights reserved. Original Japanese edition published in 2005 by Taiyoh Tosho Publishing Co., Ltd. Cho Ni Naru Hi / The Day I Become a Butterfly © Sumomo Yumeka 2005. Originally published in Japan in 2003 by Taiyoh Tosho Co., Ltd. LOST BOYS © Kaname Itsuki 2004. Originally published in Japan in 2004 by Taiyoh Tosho Co., Ltd. DOUSAIBOU SEIBUTSU / SAME CELL ORGANISM © Sumomo 2001. Originally published in Japan in 2001 by Taiyoh Tosho Co., Ltd.
Let's Draw Manga - Drawing Yaoi © 2007 by DIGITAL MANGA, Inc. All rights reserved.

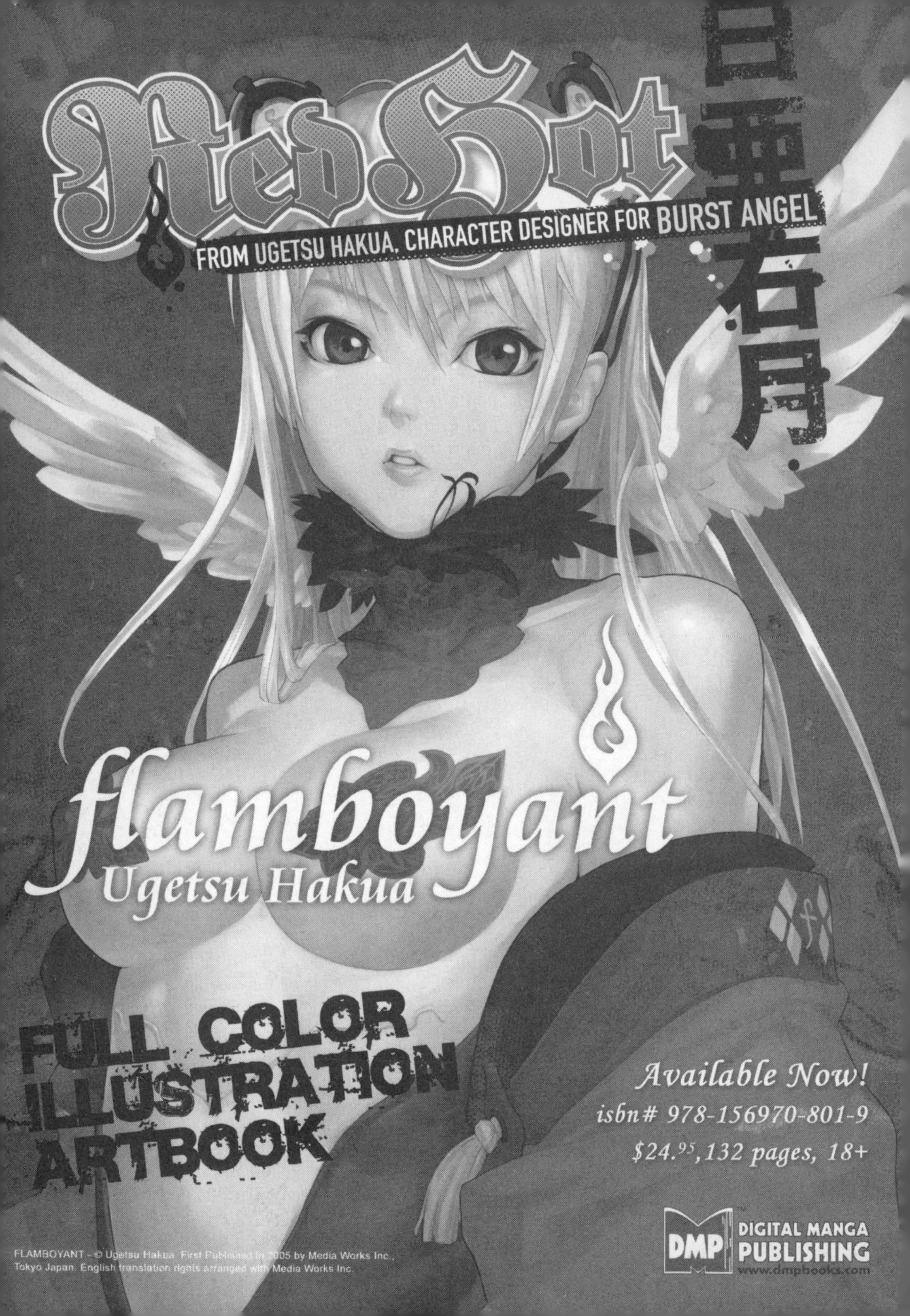
Red Hot
白亜右月
FROM UGETSU HAKUA, CHARACTER DESIGNER FOR BURST ANGEL
flamboyant
Ugetsu Hakua
FULL COLOR ILLUSTRATION ARTBOOK
Available Now!
isbn# 978-156970-801-9
$24.95, 132 pages, 18+
DMP DIGITAL MANGA PUBLISHING
www.dmpbooks.com
FLAMBOYANT - © Ugetsu Hakua. First Published in 2005 by Media Works Inc., Tokyo Japan. English translation rights arranged with Media Works Inc.

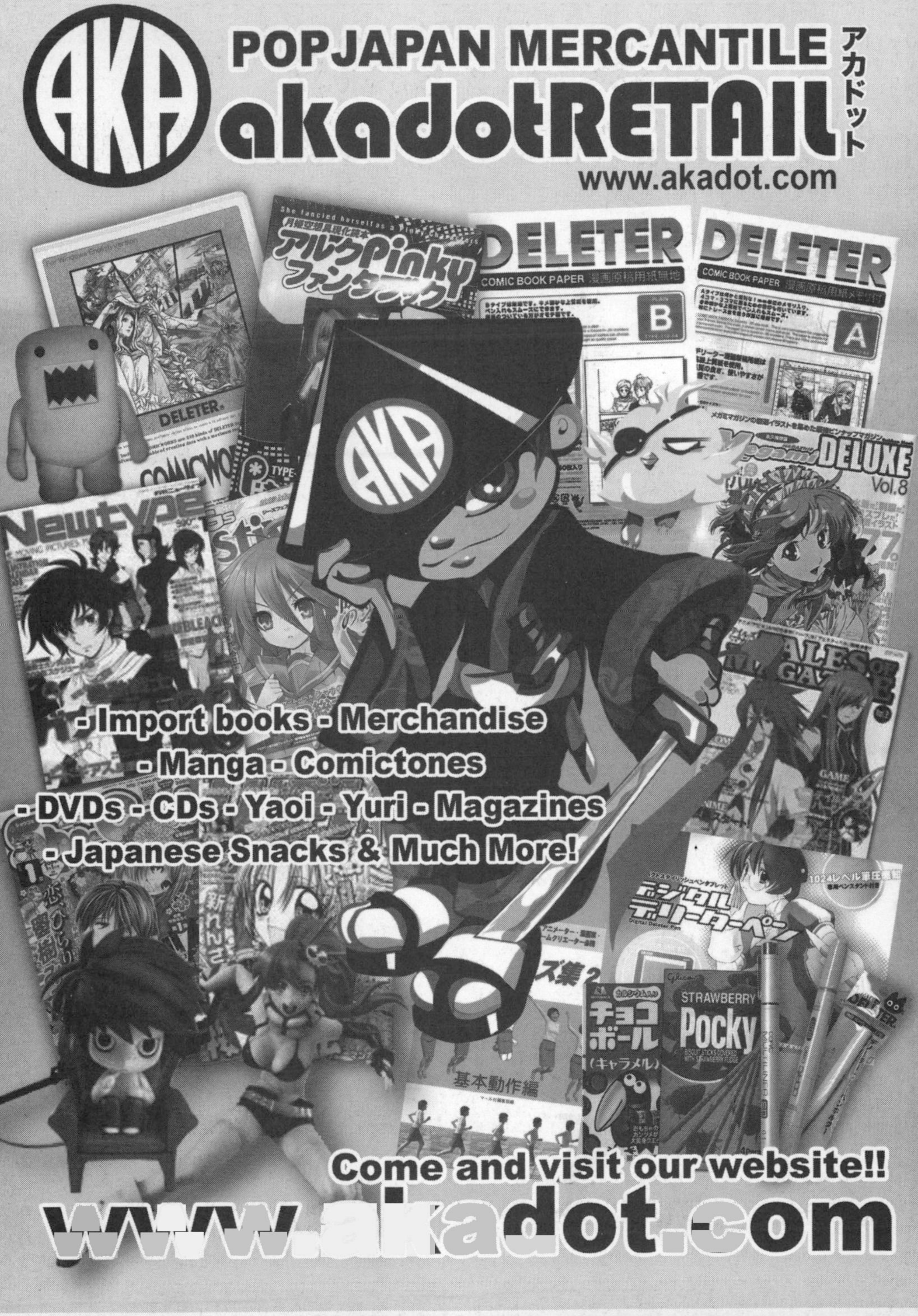
AKA
POPJAPAN MERCANTILE
akadotRETAIL
アカドット
www.akadot.com
- Import books - Merchandise
- Manga - Comictones
- DVDs - CDs - Yaoi - Yuri - Magazines
- Japanese Snacks & Much More!
Come and visit our website!!
www.akadot.com

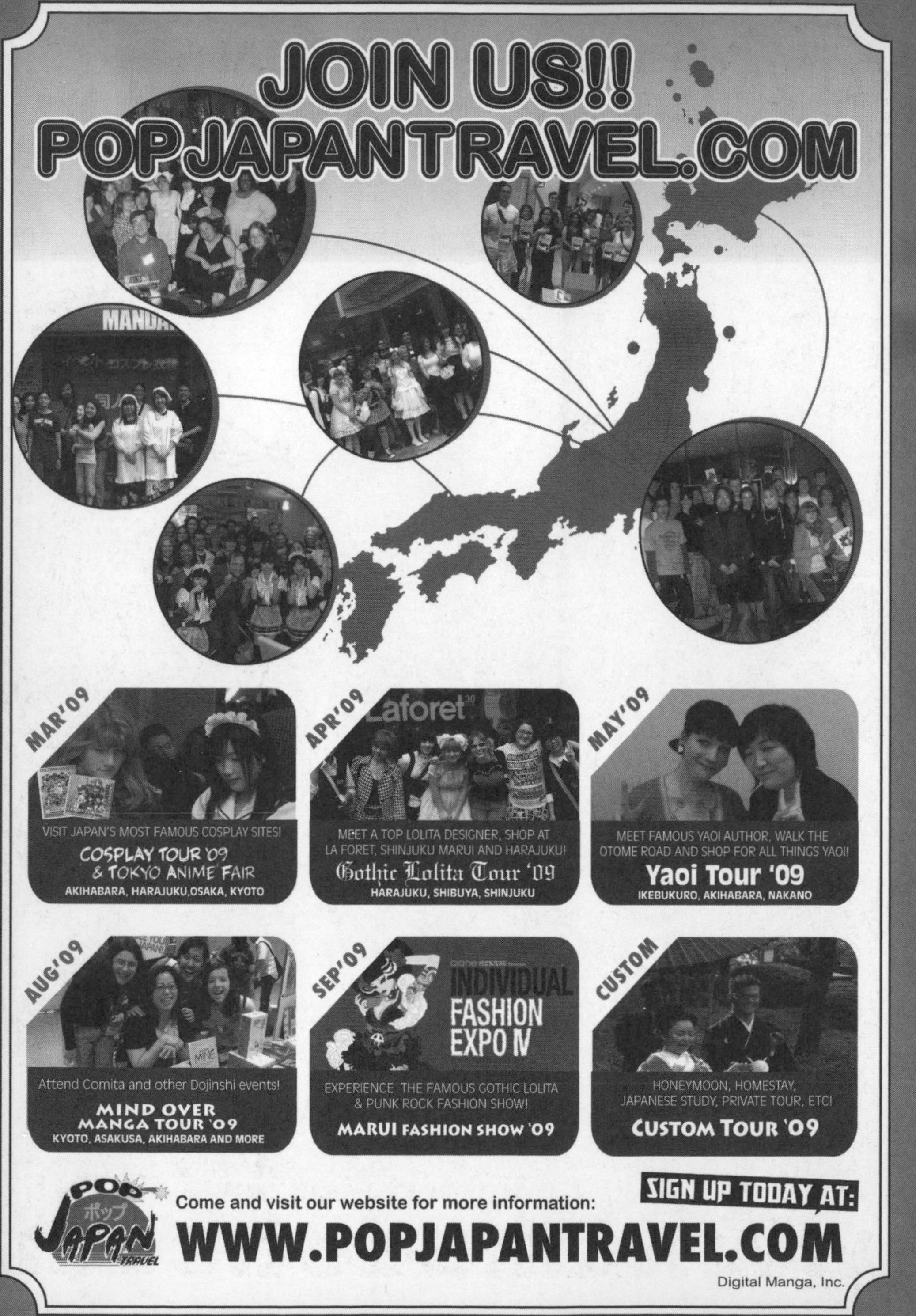
JOIN US!!
POPJAPANTRAVEL.COM
MAR'09
VISIT JAPAN'S MOST FAMOUS COSPLAY SITES!
COSPLAY TOUR '09
& TOKYO ANIME FAIR
AKIHABARA, HARAJUKU,OSAKA, KYOTO
APR'09
MEET A TOP LOLITA DESIGNER, SHOP AT
LA FORET, SHINJUKU MARUI AND HARAJUKU!
Gothic Lolita Tour '09
HARAJUKU, SHIBUYA, SHINJUKU
MAY'09
MEET FAMOUS YAOI AUTHOR, WALK THE
OTOME ROAD AND SHOP FOR ALL THINGS YAOI!
Yaoi Tour '09
IKEBUKURO, AKIHABARA, NAKANO
AUG'09
Attend Comita and other Dojinshi events!
MIND OVER
MANGA TOUR '09
KYOTO, ASAKUSA, AKIHABARA AND MORE
SEP'09
INDIVIDUAL
FASHION
EXPO IV
EXPERIENCE THE FAMOUS GOTHIC LOLITA
& PUNK ROCK FASHION SHOW!
MARUI FASHION SHOW '09
CUSTOM
HONEYMOON, HOMESTAY,
JAPANESE STUDY, PRIVATE TOUR, ETC!
CUSTOM TOUR '09
POP ポップ JAPAN TRAVEL
Come and visit our website for more information:
SIGN UP TODAY AT:
WWW.POPJAPANTRAVEL.COM
Digital Manga, Inc.

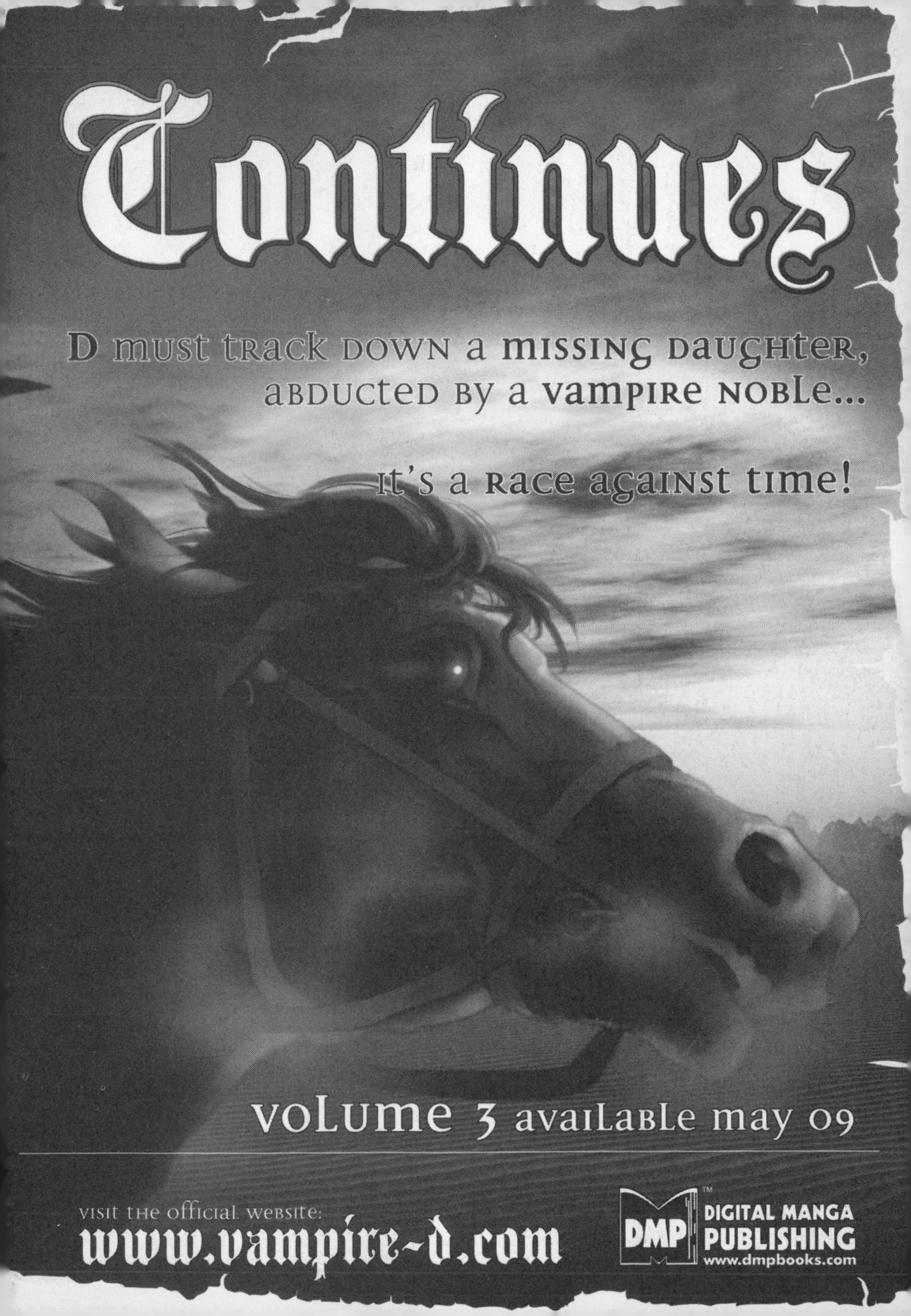
Continues
D must track down a missing daughter,
abducted by a vampire noble...
it's a race against time!
volume 3 available may 09
visit the official website:
www.vampire-d.com
DMP DIGITAL MANGA PUBLISHING
www.dmpbooks.com

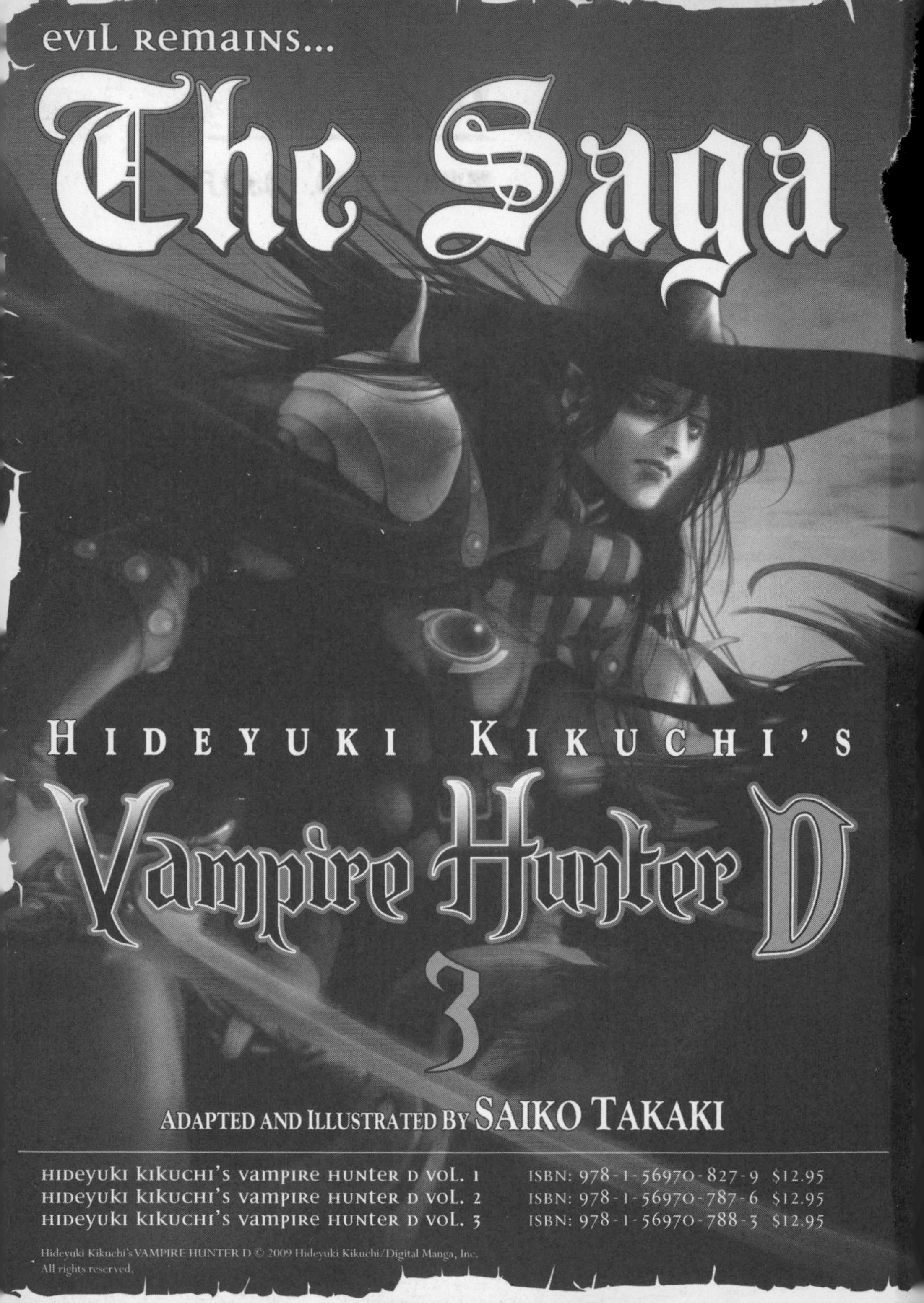

evil remains...
The Saga
Hideyuki Kikuchi's
Vampire Hunter D
3
Adapted and Illustrated by Saiko Takaki

This is the back of the book!
Start from the other side.

NATIVE MANGA
readers read manga from *right to left*.

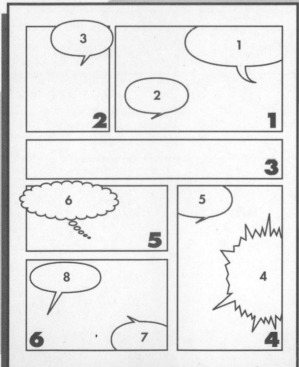

If you run into our **Native Manga** logo on any of our books... you'll know that this manga is published in it's true original native Japanese right to left reading format, as it was intended. Turn to the other side of the book and start reading from right to left, top to bottom.

Follow the diagram to see how its done. **Surf's Up!**

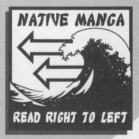

NATIVE MANGA
READ RIGHT TO LEFT